KENNETH GRAHAME

A Biography

KENNETH GRAHAME

A Biography

by

PETER GREEN

THE WORLD PUBLISHING COMPANY

CLEVELAND AND NEW YORK

Published by The World Publishing Company

2231 West 110th Street, Cleveland 2, Ohio

Library of Congress Catalog Card Number: 59-7751

FIRST EDITION

FOR MY SON TIMOTHY

CONTENTS

ILLUSTRATIONS

ILLUSTRATIONS

* *Photo. Leonard Smith, Sevenoaks.*

ACKNOWLEDGMENTS

This book could never have been written without the most generous co-operation given me by the Executors of the late Lord
Courtauld-Thomson. Elspeth Grahame, Kenneth's wife, was Lord
Courtauld-Thomson's sister. When she died, shortly after the end
of the last war, she left a vast mass of letters and documents, both
her own and Kenneth's, which Lord Courtauld-Thomson preserved and sorted. This collection is stored at Dorneywood, the
house he left to the nation. I wish here to express my gratitude
to Mr. John Fletcher and Mr. John Wiltshire, who not only
allowed me to remove original documents and examine them
at my leisure, but also gave me every kind of practical advice and
help in my search. This book is primarily based on the Courtauld-
Thomson Collection, and I am deeply indebted to the Executors,
both for permission to reproduce evidence from this source, and
for allowing me free access to it in the first place. And I am
grateful to the Secretary of the University Chest Office, Oxford,
for permission to print hitherto unpublished Kenneth Grahame
writings.

Many others have generously come to my assistance in various
ways. To my publishers, and in particular to Mr. John Grey
Murray, I am indebted for the use of a room in Albemarle Street
where I could research at leisure, and constant support and encouragement at every stage of my work. To Mr. Roger Lancelyn
Green I owe an especial debt: though he had long cherished the
idea of writing about Grahame himself, he most generously put
all his knowledge at my disposal when I asked for his help, and
has allowed me to reproduce (with minor additions and modifications) the bibliography of Grahame's works which he originally

published in *The Times Literary Supplement* on 9th June 1945.

I am also profoundly grateful to Mr. Austin Purves, Jr., Mr. Dale Purves, Mr. Edmund R. Purves, Mr. John C. Purves, and Mr. Pierre M. Purves in America, all of whom wrote to me at great length and in most meticulous detail of their family friendship with the Grahames. To Mr. Pierre M. Purves I am further indebted for most generously sending me photostats of Grahame's correspondence with his father, Austin Purves, which revealed passages omitted by Chalmers in his biography.

The late Mr. L. A. G. Strong most generously allowed me to make use of his privately printed *Memoir* of Lord Courtauld-Thomson, especially in connection with the Fletcher Moulton case; his researches have eased mine considerably.

To Mrs. Margery Newnham Davis I owe a special debt of gratitude: her voluntary help in secretarial matters has gone far beyond even the demands of literary *pietas*. Besides typing by far the larger part of my MS, she has helped me throughout with information, advice, encouragement, and occasional most welcome criticism.

I am grateful to all those who have allowed me to reproduce letters in their possession: Mr. Charles E. Feinberg, Mr. Richard G. Hubbard, the Rev. K. H. Jocelyn, Mr. Alan W. Lidderdale (who also took me on a delightful expedition to Cookham Dene), Mr. Kerrison Preston (the late Graham Robertson's literary executor), Mr. Pierre M. Purves, and Miss Foy Quiller-Couch. For this, and much other help they have given me during my researches, I wish to express my thanks here.

I wish to thank, also, those many correspondents and witnesses who, by answering my queries, allowing themselves to be interviewed, and sending me unsolicited material, helped to piece together the mosaic of Kenneth Grahame's life, work, and background. These include the following: Lady Arundel; Dr. Geoffrey Best, of Trinity Hall, Cambridge; Mr. E. E. Bissell; Mrs. Esther Boumphrey; Mr. Spencer Curtis Brown; Mr. Cyril Caddy; Mr.

John Connell; Miss J. L. G. Crookston; Mr. A. W. Dascombe, the present Secretary of the Bank of England; Mrs. Anna Debenham; Miss Kay Dick; Mrs. Ellershaw; Mr. Malcolm Elwin; Dr. Anthony Feiling; Professor Sir Keith Feiling; Mr. Lawrence Forbes; Mr. Iain Fletcher, of the Faculty of Arts, Reading University; Dr. Philip Gosse; Miss Hilda K. Grahame; Mr. John K. Grahame; The Hon. C. Hope-Morley, the present owner of The Mount, Cookham Dene; Mrs. Beatrice Horton; Mrs. Florence Image; Mrs. Kay Ingles; Miss Marjorie Ingles; the Keeper of Western MSS, Bodleian Library, Oxford; Miss Pamela Hansford Johnson; Mrs. Ruth Lichtensteiger; Sir Compton and Lady Mackenzie; The Rev. J. A. B. Mercier; Miss Enid Mitchell; Mr. A. E. Morgan, Warden of Toynbee Hall; The Hon. Hugh Fletcher Moulton; Mr. Frederick Muller; Lt.-Col. Arthur Newland; Mr. Maxfield Parrish; Mrs. Elsie Ricardo; Lady Rose; Mr. Ernest H. Shepard; Mr. H. A. Siepmann; Mr. and Mrs. L. Smith, who devoted so much time and ingenuity to obtaining such excellent photographs for me; Miss E. A. Soper; Mr. Frank Swinnerton; Miss Barbara Euphan Todd; Miss A. S. Watts; Mrs. Kathleen R. West; Mrs. M. Hesketh Williams; Mr. J. Alan White, Managing Director of Messrs. Methuen & Co., Ltd.; Mrs. A. Vere Woodman; and Mrs. Delia Wysard, who, besides giving me most valuable information, also entertained me most charmingly during my visit to Pangbourne.

For permission to quote copyright material I am greatly indebted to many authors, publishers, and executors, all of whom acceded to my requests with most courteous generosity. Quotations from Kenneth Grahame's *The Wind in the Willows* are made by kind permission of the Oxford University Chest and Messrs. Methuen & Co. Ltd., to whom I am further indebted for authority to quote from Patrick R. Chalmers' *Kenneth Grahame: Life, Letters and Unpublished Work*, Maurice Hewlett's *Letters*, A. A. Milne's Introduction to *Toad of Toad Hall*, and Elspeth Grahame's *First Whispers of 'The Wind in the Willows'*. For permission to quote both from Mrs. Grahame's book and from her unpublished papers, my thanks are also due to her Executors (Lord Knollys, Mr. John Fletcher, and Mr. Gerald Russell) and the Dorneywood Trust: to them I owe a further debt of thanks for allowing me to quote from the late L. A. G. Strong's privately printed *Memoir* of Lord Courtauld-Thomson. Grahame's unpublished papers are reproduced by kind permission of Messrs. Curtis Brown Ltd.; to them, and to The Bodley Head, I am doubly grateful for permission to quote from all Grahame's published work with the exception of *The Wind in the Willows* and 'The Fellow That Goes Alone': the former is acknowledged above, and for the latter I am indebted to the Editor of the *St. Edward's School Chronicle*.

For permission to quote from other copyright material my grateful thanks go to the following: The Bodley Head, for Oscar Burdett's *The Beardsley Period* and Evelyn Sharp's *Unfinished Adventure*; Dr. David Daiches and New Directions, for Dr. Daiches' *R. L. Stevenson* (copyright 1947 by New Directions. Reprinted by permission of New Directions); Mr. J. E. Buckley and Princeton University Press, for Mr. Buckley's *W. E. Henley*; Mr. E. D. H. Johnson and Princeton University Press, for Mr. Johnson's *The Alien Vision of Victorian Poetry*; The Cambridge University Press, for Kenneth Grahame's Preface to *Poetry for Children*, and F. J. H. Darton's *Children's Books*; Messrs. Jonathan Cape Ltd., for two quotations from A. E. Housman's poems; Messrs. Constable & Co. Ltd., for J. L. Lowes' *The Road to Xanadu*; Mr. Spencer Curtis Brown, for his father's, A. Curtis Brown's, autobiography, *Contacts*; Mr. Frank Dancaster, Editor of *The Old Lady*, for two articles by W. M. Acres and W. B. Hillkirk, originally published in that periodical; Mr. Angus Davidson and Messrs. John Murray (Publishers) Ltd., for Mr. Davidson's *Edward Lear*; Mr. C. Day Lewis and Messrs. Jonathan Cape Ltd., for extracts from Mr. Day Lewis's sonnet-sequence *O Dreams, O Destinations*; Mr. T. S. Eliot, O.M., Mr. Louis MacNeice, and Messrs. Faber & Faber Ltd., for extracts from Mr. MacNeice's 'Eclogue for Christmas' and Mr. Eliot's 'Burnt Norton' and 'The Waste Land'; James Nisbet & Co. Ltd., for the Hon. Hugh Fletcher Moulton's *Life of Lord Moulton*; Messrs. William Heinemann, Ltd., for Jane E. Courtney's *Recollected in Tranquillity*; Messrs. Gerald Duckworth & Co. Ltd., for Constance Smedley's *Crusaders*; Mr. Graham Hough and Messrs. Duckworth, for Mr. Hough's *The Last Romantics*; Messrs. Macmillan & Co. Ltd., for W. B. Yeats' *Autobiographies* and *Collected Poems*; Mr. John Marlowe and The Cresset Press, for Mr. Marlowe's *The Puritan Tradition in English Life*; Mr. Frank O'Connor and Messrs. Hamish Hamilton Ltd., for Mr. O'Connor's *The Mirror in the Roadway* and *Domestic Relations*; Mr. Kerrison Preston and Messrs. Hamish Hamilton Ltd., for Graham Robertson's *Letters*; The Oxford University Press, for R. C. K. Ensor's *England, 1870–1914*, R. G. Collingwood's *The New Leviathan*, and the first stanza of Gerard Manley Hopkins' 'Duns Scotus' Oxford', published in *Poems of Gerard Manley Hopkins*; Mr. Alan Pryce-Jones, for his article 'Kenneth Grahame', published in *The London Mercury*, and also, in his capacity as Editor of *The Times Literary Supplement*, for permission to reproduce Mr. Roger Lancelyn Green's bibliography of Grahame; Messrs. Routledge & Kegan Paul Ltd., for Esmé Wingfield-Stratford's *Victorian Sunset* and *Victorian Aftermath*; Mr. R. S. Thomas and Messrs. Rupert Hart-Davis Ltd., for Mr. Thomas's 'The Last of the Peasantry', published in *Song at the Year's Turning*; and Professor Lionel Trilling and Columbia University Press, for Professor Trilling's *Matthew Arnold*.

Chapter VI of the present work, 'The Rural Pan', first appeared, in a modified form, in *The Cornhill*, and I am grateful to the Editor for permission to reproduce it here.

This book was written, and much of the secondary research leading up to it conducted, in the Reading Room of the British Museum and, latterly, the Cambridge University Library. I would like to thank the staff of both those admirable institutions (who all too seldom receive the credit they so richly deserve) for their consistent courtesy and helpfulness. Without the facilities offered by these two great libraries, and—hardly less important—the Newspaper and Periodical Library at Colindale, this book could hardly have been begun, let alone brought to completion.

Lastly, I owe more than I can well express to my wife, who from the very beginning has encouraged and supported this project, and to whose kindly yet penetrating criticisms any virtues it may have are largely due.

Go, said the bird, for the leaves were full of children,
Hidden excitedly, containing laughter,
Go, go, go, said the bird: human kind
Cannot bear very much reality.

T. S. ELIOT: Burnt Norton

And perhaps we have reason to be very grateful that, both as children and long afterwards, we are never allowed to guess how the absorbing pursuit of the moment will appear not only to others but to ourselves, a very short time hence. So we pass, with a gusto and a heartiness that to an onlooker would seem almost pathetic, from one droll devotion to another misshapen passion; and who shall dare to play Rhadamanthus, to appraise the record, and to decide how much of it is solid achievement, and how much the merest child's play?

KENNETH GRAHAME: The Golden Age

KENNETH GRAHAME
A Biography

INTRODUCTION

Since its first publication in 1908, *The Wind in the Willows* has achieved over a hundred editions, and an average annual sale of about 80,000 copies. *The Golden Age* and *Dream Days* have established themselves as minor classics of childhood. Yet their author remains a shadowy figure to the general public. The most that is normally known about him is that he was 'something to do with the Bank of England'. This ignorance is mainly due to the curious fact that hardly anything has been written about him. The biography by Patrick Chalmers, produced a year after Grahame's death in 1932, has been long out of print, and is far from being a satisfactory account. The only other book about Grahame is a Sorbonne thesis by Mlle D. M. Fyrth, which appeared in 1937 and is virtually unobtainable in this country. My first aim in writing the present work, therefore, was simply to fill an inexplicable gap, and, incidentally, to pay tribute to an author who has always occupied a special place in my affections.

But I found, as I explored Grahame's life and times more deeply, that I was committed to a larger and more complex task than I had ever envisaged. In the first place, the mass of documentary evidence provided by the Grahames' letters and family papers profoundly modified the picture which Chalmers presented, and which was accepted—though with reservations—by Mlle Fyrth. Secondly, my original assumptions about Grahame's literary position and aims, in the widest sense, had to be radically revised. My researches led me into social, religious, and even political fields not normally associated with a writer of Grahame's proclivities. It became clear to me that, far from being simple, he was extremely subtle and complex; that he was not, in the normal sense of the word, a children's writer at all; and that he crystallized, in his life and writing, many profoundly important changes which affected English society towards the close of the nineteenth century.

Grahame described himself as a 'mid-Victorian'.[1] This indicates, as it were, his natural centre of gravity. We are inclined to forget that he was a young man before 1880, and middle-aged by the turn of the century. He was, therefore, caught up emotionally in the events connected with Mid-Victorianism—the Industrial Revolution and its by-products, middle-class mercantilism and the collapse of agricultural society, scientific evolution and religious doubt. Like many other sensitive young men, he watched the decay of rural England with bleak horror, having been born early enough to understand just precisely what was being lost as railways and factories multiplied over the ravished countryside. He felt the tyrannous emptiness of a society which was rapidly losing all spontaneity, and which combined the pursuit of money with a rigid and authoritarian moral code.

Despite this, however, he (like many others in similar case) not only continued to honour the obligations imposed by the hierarchy of family and society, but in some sense actively needed them; and thus two powerful elements were permanently at conflict in him. He compromised: outwardly he conformed with his society. But his inner self took revenge in satire and fantasy: at first openly, then by more oblique and subtle methods. Like Lear and Carroll, he found relief in the world of childhood, the animal fable, the potent symbols of fantasy. It was a compromise which many of his contemporaries had to make.

There is a key passage in Frank O'Connor's recent study of the modern novel[2] which exactly epitomizes Grahame's position:

> He is a fascinating example of historic schizophrenia, standing on the frontier of two cultures, watching traditions older than the Celts, whose barrows topped the neighbouring hills, disappear as the extending railway line brings in the latest music-

hall song, the latest melodrama, the latest scientific theory. When two cultures clash in this way, what happens at the time is not that the more sophisticated one triumphs, but that the less sophisticated takes refuge in the depths of the heart . . . what takes place in the conscious part of a mind like that is the spread not of sophistication, but of naiveté . . .

Those words were used by Mr. O'Connor not of Grahame but of Thomas Hardy; yet they are equally applicable to Grahame, and indeed remind us how general the problem was, how widespread its ramifications through the whole changing structure of society. That is one reason why I have chosen to study it through the development, achievement, and tragedy of a single man, whose life and work reveal the larger pattern of their age.

Grahame himself both mistrusted literary criticism and did everything he could to discourage biographers: I cannot imagine that he would have approved of my investigations, which inevitably explore his life and work in great detail. His idea of an ideal biography was the kind of discreet *curriculum vitae* to be found in *Who's Who*;[3] and of critics—whom he described as 'literary resurrection-men'—he wrote in 1891: 'Of all forms of lettered effusiveness that which exploits the original work of others and professes to supply us with right opinions thereanent is the least wanted '.[4] In this book I have played a double rôle which my subject would have been the first to resent; I can only plead to his amiable ghost that my first concern throughout has been to see justice done to him.

Partly through the lack of personal documents such as diaries, partly because Grahame was an essentially autobiographical writer, I have frequently (though with great caution) used his published work to explain or illuminate some aspect of his personality. I am well aware that such methods often produce what Mr. Graham Hough, in his study of D. H. Lawrence, described scathingly as a 'mixed critico-biographical stew'.[5] Nevertheless, given the combination of author and period, it is hard to see what other method could adequately place Grahame against that background of social change which so profoundly affected him. His life, his writing, the ideas he absorbed, the code against which he rebelled, his private Hesperidean myth, all are interwoven and interdependent; it is impossible to separate them without distorting the total picture. My intention has been two-fold: to illuminate certain aspects of the late nineteenth century through the example which Kenneth Grahame affords and, con-versely, to explain Grahame himself in terms of the society which produced him. If I have succeeded even partially in either of these aims, I shall be well satisfied.

In July 1913, five years after he published *The Wind in the Willows* and retired from the Bank of England, Kenneth Grahame sent a short essay to his old school magazine for its Jubilee Com-memoration Number.[6] It gathers together so much that forms the very essence of his nature that we can treat it as a species of personal testament. In any case it forms a natural point from which to begin our picture of him. He called it, characteristically, 'The Fellow that Goes Alone'; and since it has never been re-printed, I quote it here in its entirety:

Those who have browsed among the pages of Caxton's *Golden Legend*—a story-book of much fascination—may re-member how it is told, in a passage concerning the boyhood of a certain English saint—Edmund, Archbishop and Confessor—that on a day when the boy was by himself in a meadow, 'sodeynlye there apperyd tofore hym a fayr chylde in whyte clothynge which sayd, "Hayle, felowe that goest alone"'.

Local considerations themselves should make us cherish the memory of this Edmund with a certain tenderness; for he was born at the pleasant town of Abingdon, that sits among its lush water-meadows and almost catches the chimes down the stream from the not so distant Oxford towers; and he 'went to Oxenforde to scole', as of course a good saint should; and many a time he must have ridden out over Grandpont and along the old raised 'Cawsy'—still there under the road—to visit his home and his good mother who was thought worthy to have inscribed on her tomb that she was the 'flower of widows'. Also he 'dwellyd long after at Oxenforde' and 'Teddy', the last of the old Halls, is said to perpetuate his name. But specially we should envy him his white vision in the meadow; for which he should be regarded as the patron saint of all those who of set purpose choose to walk alone, who know the special grace attaching to it, and ever feel that somewhere just ahead, round the next bend perhaps, the White Child may be waiting for them.

For Nature's particular gift to the walker, through the semi-mechanical act of walking—a gift no other form of exercise seems to transmit in the same high degree—is to set the mind jogging, to make it garrulous, exalted, a little mad maybe—certainly creative and suprasensitive, until at last it really seems to be outside of you and as it were talking to you, while you are talking back to it. Then everything gradually seems to join in, sun and the wind, the white road and the dusty hedges, the spirit of the season, whichever that may be, the friendly old earth that is pushing forth life of every sort under your feet or spell-bound in death-like winter trance, till you walk in the midst of a blessed company, immersed in a dream-talk far transcending any possible human conversation. Time enough, later, for that—across the dinner table, in smoking-room armchairs; here and now, the mind has shaken off its harness, is snorting and kicking up heels like a colt in a meadow. Not a fiftieth part of all your happy imaginings will you ever, later, recapture, note down, reduce to dull inadequate words; but meantime the mind has stretched itself and had its holiday. But this emancipation is only attained in solitude, the solitude which the unseen companions demand before they will come out and talk to you; for, be he who may, if there is another fellow present, your mind has to trot between shafts.

A certain amount of 'shafts', indeed, is helpful, as setting the mind more free; and so the high road, while it should always give way to the field path when choice offers, still has this particular virtue, that it takes charge of you—your body, that is to say. Its hedges hold you in friendly steering-reins, its milestones and finger-posts are always on hand, with information succinct and free from frills; and it always gets *somewhere*, sooner or later. So you are nursed along your way, and the mind may soar in cloudland and never need to be pulled earthwards by any string. But this is as much company as you ought to require, the comradeship of the road you walk on, the road which will look after you and attend to such facts as must not be overlooked. Of course the best sort of walk is the one on which it doesn't matter twopence whether you get anywhere at all at any time or not; and the second best is the one on which the hard facts of routes, times, or trains give you nothing to worry about. And this is perhaps the only excuse for the presence of that much-deprecated Other Fellow—that you can put all that sort of thing on to him. For the world is fortunately well-furnished with fellows who really like looking up Bradshaw, and paying bills, and taking charge generally; and it is wise to keep some such a man within easy hail. But spiritually he will be of little use, even if he were the angel that walked with Tobias.

Much converse will he have, too, with shy bird and furtive little beast, the fellow that walks alone. I seem to have noticed a different expression in the eye of bird or animal at one's solitary approach, from the way it looks at you when there are two or three of you about. In the first case it seems to say wistfully, 'This *may* be a pal!' In the second, 'This is certainly a conspiracy!' and acts accordingly. As for adventures, if they are the game you hunt, everyone's experience will remind him that the best adventures of his life were pursued and achieved, or came suddenly to him unsought, when he was alone. For company too often means compromise, discretion, the choice of the sweetly reasonable. It is difficult to be mad in company; yet but a touch of lunacy in action will open magic doors to rare and unforgettable experiences.

But all these are only the by-products, the casual gains, of walking alone. The high converse, the high adventures, will be in the country of the mind.

Echoes of that essay will return to us at every stage of Grahame's career. With it fresh in our minds, then, let us begin at the beginning, exactly a century ago.

I

DRAGONS AND PTERODACTYLS
1859-1867

Children look down upon the morning-grey
Tissue of mist that veils a valley's lap:
Their fingers itch to tear it and unwrap
The flags, the roundabouts, the gala day.
They watch the spring rise inexhaustibly—
A breathing thread out of the eddied sand,
Sufficient to their day: but half their mind
Is on the sailed and glittering estuary.

C. DAY LEWIS: *O Dreams, O Destinations*

Vitality—that is the test; and, whatever its components, mere truth is not necessarily one of them. A dragon, for instance, is a more enduring animal than a pterodactyl. I have never yet met anyone who really believed in a pterodactyl; but every honest person believes in dragons—down in the back-kitchen of his consciousness.

KENNETH GRAHAME: *Introduction to A Hundred Fables of Æsop*

We are so apt to associate Kenneth Grahame in our minds with everything that is rural and English—the Berkshire Downs, Oxford, the lazy reaches of the Thames round Cookham and Pangbourne—that we sometimes forget he was a thoroughbred Scot by birth. This provides one key to his character; like his compatriot Robert Louis Stevenson, he observed England essentially from the outside, and loved her more because he could never take her quite for granted. There was always for him in England,

7

as in Italy, an element of that romance which is bred from unfamiliarity, the lure of the alien tradition.

During the nineteenth century the name of Grahame was a synonym, north of the Border, for solid respectability. Holders of it were liable, as like as not, to be advocates or accountants, though there was an occasional minister among them. When they broke into print, which was seldom, their books tended to be severely functional. In 1817 we find James Grahame, Advocate, penning his *Defence of Usury Laws*. In 1867 a namesake of his (an accountant this time) published *Financial Fenianism and the Caledonian Railway*. Yet a third James Grahame, also an accountant, produced in 1890 *Tables of Silver Exchanges*, and two years later *Mr. Goschen's One Pound Note*. These books at least suggest a traditional background for the career in the Bank of England which Kenneth Grahame grudgingly undertook: he was very much in the position of the eldest son in an Army family who is compelled to swallow his pacifist convictions.

As far as literary antecedents are concerned, the evidence is more scanty. In a letter to Elspeth Grahame written after Kenneth's death, Colonel John Grahame (who drew up his pedigree for Chalmers) wrote: 'The literary talent so eminently possessed by Kenneth would appear to have existed most strongly in the White-hill family; at all events James Grahame was a poet of no mean order, with a wonderful spirit of imagination, whilst the *History of America* written by another James, his nephew, son of Robert Grahame of Whitehill, is, I understand, still a classic work in America'.[1] The poet referred to is, of course, the author of that lugubrious work *The Sabbath* (1804), Kenneth's great-grand-uncle, who provoked Byron's spleen in *English Bards and Scotch Reviewers*. 'The Sabbath bard', as Byron put it,

> Breaks into blank the Gospel of St. Luke,
> And boldly pilfers from the Pentateuch;
> And, undisturbed by conscientious qualms,
> Perverts the Prophets and purloins the Psalms.

'The family', Kenneth wrote, 'never repeated the experiment, and I have never read his works.'[2] James Grahame's spiritual (if not direct) descendant was clearly Mrs. Frances Grahame, who in 1866 wrote a rousing 'temperance tale' entitled *The Curse of the Claverings*.

Such, temperamentally, were the Grahames: devout Calvinists, with a disposition towards the legal and financial professions. Yet there is always a hint, however conscientiously repressed, of artistic interests. A contemporary of Kenneth's, a distant connection named George Grahame, actually became an art critic, and in 1895, the year *The Golden Age* was published, produced a book on Claude Lorraine; while Kenneth's own father, James Cunningham Grahame, gives every sign of having been a poet *manqué*.

Cunningham Grahame was born on 20th July 1830. He became an advocate, and apparently a popular one: a witty speaker whose *bons mots* were cherished in Parliament House. But he lacked the drive and ambition which then, as now, were essential to an Edinburgh lawyer. He was something of a hedonist, an easy-going *bon vivant*, and already, before tragedy overtook him, a heavy drinker.[3] On 13th March 1855 he married Bessie Ingles, the beautiful daughter of David Ingles of Hilton, Lasswade, and brought her to his home at 32 Castle Street, opposite the site of Sir Walter Scott's former house.[4] Here, during the next five years, she bore him three children: Helen in 1856, Thomas William ('Willie') in 1858, and Kenneth in 1859. Their early married life was extremely happy. They entertained a good deal, and moved in the best Edinburgh society: Cunningham Grahame could claim and substantiate a double line of descent from Robert the Bruce. His branch was 'presumed to be a Cadet of the Earls of Montrose', and his ancestors included Earls of Strathearn and Menteith.[5] His dinner menus had a strong Nationalist flavour about them; yet, like the Lord of Abbotsford, when it came to drink his preference was not for whisky, but claret, of which he was a well-known connoisseur.

Kenneth was born on the morning of 8th March, and Dr. James Simpson—'the Beloved Professor of chloroform fame'[6]—attended the birth. When we have surveyed the adult Grahame's life and opinions, we shall be able to see how symbolically appropriate it was that his life should have begun in the year that it did. 1859 was a time of change, a watershed dividing the old era from the new. During those twelve months there appeared not only Darwin's *Origin of Species* but also J. S. Mill's *On Liberty*: what Trevelyan described as the 'revolt against the tame acceptance of conventional opinions' had begun in earnest. Leigh Hunt, De Quincey, and Macaulay died; Dr. Livingstone reached Lake Nyasa; Mr. Gladstone was Chancellor of the Exchequer. The same thrifty, ambitious, materialistic business-men who made a best-seller out of Samuel Smiles' newly published *Self Help* also welcomed Landseer's lions to Trafalgar Square.[7] Patriotism and trade were indissolubly linked, and the foundation of the Volunteers that winter was prompted as much by concern for investments as a direct war scare. In the purely literary field two poems crystallized the official and 'irresponsible' elements of intelligent society: on the one hand Tennyson, with the first *Idylls of the King*, on the other Edward FitzGerald's translation of the seductively *fainéant* Omar Khayyám.

There is, indeed, more than a hint of the Persian poet's philosophy about Cunningham Grahame himself. He made a sufficient income without over-exertion; and for the rest there were his family, his many friends, the pleasures of Edinburgh society. Yet, as his subsequent behaviour showed, his was a far from tranquil nature; like many Scots he possessed a deep streak of pessimism, and his black moods were akin to fashionable modern *Angst*. It must have been some such mood which drove him to apply for a post which uprooted his family from Edinburgh. In May 1860, when Kenneth was little more than a year old, his father was appointed Sheriff-Substitute of Argyllshire, an unprecedented alien in Campbell country. The move took place at once.

The Sheriff-Substitute's seat of office was, naturally, at Inveraray, below the hill and not far from the Castle of the Dukes of Argyll. But Cunningham Grahame decided to build his own house there: and for three years the family lived in temporary quarters down Loch Fyne, first at Ardrishaig, later in Lochgilphead. The Campbell workmen were clearly in no hurry to oblige a foreigner.

Kenneth's earliest memory, he declared in after years, was of 'shiny black buttons, buttons that dug into dusty, blue cloth', probably the upholstery of the railway carriage in which he travelled from Edinburgh.[8] He also recalled the little paddle-steamer that delivered them to the quayside; and I suspect that a striking image from *The Wind in the Willows* may have been prompted by the first night he spent in this new and unfamiliar home, 'a child that has fallen happily asleep in its nurse's arms, and wakes to find itself alone and laid in a strange place, and searches corners and cupboards, and runs from room to room, despair growing silently in its heart'.[9] But he soon settled down happily to this new life; indeed, the wild skies and hills that ringed Loch Fyne, and more still the ever-present sea, left a powerful impression on his memory—'wind-shaken water, whip and creak and rattle of shrouds, flap of idle sails in halcyon spells, cry of gulls at pasture on the pale acres that know no plough . . . a certain haunting smell of tar and weed'.[10] Those were the happy years, years spent 'among the gleaming lochs and sinuous firths of the Western Highlands, where, twice a week maybe, the strange visitant crept by headland and bay, a piece of the busy, mysterious outer world'.[11]

Here the young boy found what he was always in after-life to cherish: tranquillity. Here—already a little aloof from his brother and sister—he would wander along the beach, where the 'big blacksided fishing-boats' lay, or loaf on the pier, 'with its tranquil "lucid interval" between steamers, the ever recurrent throb of paddle-wheel, the rush and foam of beaten water among the piles, splash of ropes and rumble of gangways'.[12] The local policeman was courting his nurse-maid; so from time to time, as a treat, he would be rowed out into the bay, golden sea-weed shimmering fathoms below, and look at the white yachts lying at anchor. It is not surprising that he hated the occasional trips away from this magic place to Edinburgh or elsewhere, and conceived a lively scorn for trains. Neither friendly porters nor the coat of arms emblazoned on the carriage door could endear this 'ungainly rattle-trap' to him; his only consolation was 'when suddenly it rattled past some dingy town, [and] over the reeking house-tops there appeared a tangled tracery of masts, while a delicate waft of tar and harbour-mud breathed of the authentic, unsuspected Paradise at hand'.[13]

Between Ardrishaig and neighbouring Lochgilphead, where they found better accommodation after a year or so, the Grahames spent the years 1860–2. Willie and Kenneth made friends with local fishermen, who carved model boats for them; there were cairn terriers at home, and gingerbread to be bought on the pier, and the fascinating spectacle of Highland girls baiting hooks with lug-worms. Kenneth's father would sometimes walk the harbour with him, quoting scraps of poetry, as he gazed at the masts and brown sails; it was here that Kenneth first heard, soon after its publication, a poem that was to haunt him all his life, Longfellow's 'Sea Memories'.[14]

> I remember the black wharves and the slips
> And the sea-tides tossing free;
> And the Spanish sailors with bearded lips
> And the beauty and mystery of the ships
> And the magic of the sea.

In that remote spot the events of the outer world must have seemed immeasurably distant, almost irrelevant: Garibaldi's final triumph, the American Civil War, even the terrible Lancashire cotton famine. Perhaps only the death of the Prince Consort had any reality for the isolated family. Here, without doubt, Grahame first acquired that habit of solitude which he was to preserve throughout his life. We may suspect too that the Hesperides of which he so often and wistfully wrote derived at least in part from the dour yet romantic background of Loch Fyne, fjord-deep between tall dark hills, unchanging, hardly touched by the disease (as he saw it) of modern industrialism, instilling its own slow sea-rhythm into his childish consciousness.

The new home at Inveraray was ready in May 1863: a big house of Scottish granite, backed with pinewoods, and looking out over the loch. The Grahames were automatically invited, after a suitable interval, to dine at the Castle, and Bessie Grahame described the occasion in a letter to her mother:[15] the Malcolms and MacNeils who were their fellow-guests, the silent young man whom she took (on account of his silence) to be a curate. We get the impression of a quick humorous eye, a highly vivacious personality. At any rate, Mrs. Grahame charmed the Duchess. Not only was she invited to bring her children visiting the very next afternoon, but was offered the services of a Ducal gardener 'to help with the flower-beds at the new house'. There is no record of how she was impressed by the rococo splendours of the Castle itself; nor does she refer to the fact that at the time of this dinner-party she was about four months pregnant.

The Grahames' last child, Roland, was born on 16th March 1864, nearly five years after Kenneth. A day or two later his mother collapsed under a virulent attack of scarlet fever. Complications set in—scarlet fever was at that period still a highly dangerous disease—and on 4th April Bessie Grahame died. Her last, characteristic, words were: 'It's all been so lovely'. The same day Kenneth caught the infection, and for several weeks his life, too, was despaired of. Cunningham Grahame wrote to his own mother in Edinburgh, and the old lady came West to nurse her grandson.[16] When the feverish five-year-old child grew fretful, and toys were useless, she could sit by his bedside and tell him stories of her own long-ago childhood in London. Those were the days before the coming of the railways: the horse-drawn Edinburgh Mail took four days to reach London. Its arrival 'was something of an event. Well, there were the usual business letters for the father and the long letters of gossip—Edinburgh and Glasgow gossip—crossed and re-crossed for the mother, and there was besides a dumpy package tied up with string, bearing the label of the well-known publishing firm of Ballantyne, and on this the girl, my grandmother, fell with a shout of triumph, for she knew it could be nothing else but an early copy of the very latest Waverley Novel.' [17] It was towards the end of his life, in a public lecture, that Grahame produced this vignette, out of the depths of his memory—the young girl from another era (unrecognizable in the old lady he himself recalled) stretched on her bedroom hearthrug and reading Scott, page after page, till her candle guttered and daylight shone through the closed shutters.

Slowly, very slowly, the young Kenneth passed his crisis and began to mend. But the disease had weakened him permanently, leaving behind a characteristic legacy of recurrent bronchial complaints. In all other respects he was healthy enough; in fact he was to prove something of an athlete. But throughout his life his chest remained alarmingly vulnerable to any change of weather, and at least once, in the year of his marriage, he was again very near the point of death. It is, perhaps, not surprising that after such a childhood experience he developed so tenacious and full-blooded a love of the visible natural world. He was never consumptive, as Richard Jefferies was, but he acquired something of the consumptive's intense interest in what can be seen, felt, tasted, absorbed: sunlight, good food and wine, Mediterranean landscapes, the small intricate life of field and hedgerow.

Cunningham Grahame was shattered by his wife's death. Like many essentially weak men, he was ill-equipped to absorb emotional shocks, and had clearly used his devotion to Bessie as a safeguard against aimless self-indulgence: her going seemed to destroy any vestige of ambition or responsibility he possessed. Plainly his attitude to her did not extend to his children; as soon as was decently possible he made arrangements for them all to go south, to live with their maternal grandmother at Cookham Dene in Berkshire. A letter of Helen Grahame's suggests that he made little financial provision for them. He probably had always resented his children for diverting even part of Bessie's affections from himself; in a man of his type, intelligent, weak-willed, emotionally immature, the phenomenon is well known. Roland at least he may well have seen, in his misery, as the direct cause of her death; they were all an intolerable reminder of what he had lost, to be pushed out of sight and forgotten. When they were gone he himself remained at Inveraray, indifferent to the shocked whispers of his neighbours, alone in the great granite house with his cellar of claret and his black self-pity.

Not once in all his published work does Kenneth Grahame mention either his mother or his father; yet their absence can be felt in nearly everything he wrote. At the beginning of *The Golden Age* comes the one direct hint, a notable and characteristic understatement: 'Looking back to those days of old, ere the gate shut to behind me, I can see now that to children with a proper equipment of parents these things would have worn a different aspect'.[18] From the loss of his mother he never, in fact, altogether recovered: his attitude to his wife was at least in part that of a son. His father he seems to have excluded from his emotions altogether; twenty years later the diary entries made on the day of Cunningham Grahame's death display a cold, clinical indifference. But for the moment the child's natural resilience was uppermost. On the way south, in Stirling, he was preoccupied to the exclusion of all else by a large rubber ball in a toyshop, and before he reached Cookham Dene was speculating wildly on the superlative, ideal qualities of this new grandmother. The reality, as he hinted many years later, he found 'a slight disappointment. Of course by this time we are well aware of the superlative and abiding charm of our grandmothers; or else we have learnt by sad experience not to expect very much from any of our relations.'[19]

Granny Ingles, of The Mount, Cookham Dene, was certainly a formidable character; 'a strong-minded woman and had her own way as far as she could', her grandson Reginald recalled in after years.[20] And Helen, with that brisk meiosis so characteristic of the ex-matron, wrote in 1936: 'I don't suppose she could be described as a child-lover'.[21] This was, perhaps, not entirely just, and indeed Helen herself modifies her verdict: 'It was hard no doubt at the age of sixty, having brought up her own family of five sons and a daughter to have us landed upon her, enough to try anyone's temper . . . our grandmother's income was a small one and if our uncle had not helped us I don't know what would have become of us'. Mrs. Ingles had certainly been highly attached, in an authoritative sort of way, to her own children. Most of her sons had careers in the Armed Services, and her granddaughter Bessie Luard (who thought her 'a very wonderful woman') recalled having heard 'my Father often say in joke that she sat on the steps of the Admiralty and the War Office till they did what she required for her sons'.[22] All sources of evidence agree that she was, in her own way, very sociable and an excellent talker, who used to tell her adopted brood 'stories about Wallace and Bruce—as Scottish history'. She was a Presbyterian, but for some inscrutable reason of her own always went to the Church of England Low Church—whether in support or defiance of her curate son David we do not know. As he lived at The Mount with her till his marriage in 1866, we may perhaps take the charitable view.

It is important, in view of Kenneth's later developments, to get as clear a picture as we can of the family atmosphere that prevailed at The Mount during those formative years. It was the opinion of Reginald Ingles (which we may well share) that Mrs. Ingles 'would have had some considerable influence on the characters of the Grahames'; but just what that influence was it is harder to determine. Helen admitted that 'she was not strict except about our table manners', but Helen herself by this time was already being enrolled as an adjutant to Authority, and probably found the disciplining of her unruly younger brothers a congenial task. Nevertheless, her summing-up—'if she treated us with "kindness according to the needs of the flesh" as Kenneth says[23] we could not expect more'—seems to reach the heart of the matter.

However strictly the family obligation might be honoured, the four Grahame children must have strained the charity of a not particularly well-off woman in her sixties. She did her duty by them, in the outward sense; but she could not summon up the emotional warmth on which children so desperately depend. She was clearly a strong-willed and autocratic woman, used to getting her own way, and impervious to argument. The financial burden which her grandchildren represented cannot have sweetened her temper towards them; and her Presbyterian conscience may well have been satisfied by the more material aspects of parental care. But there is no reason to suppose that the young Grahames suffered the kind of childhood that Kipling or even 'Saki' did. There was no cruelty in the positive sense, merely emotional deprivation of a rather subtle kind, and in the background a nagging sense of money-trouble.

There is, too, much to suggest that in ways those short years at The Mount were among the happiest of Kenneth's life. Certainly they made the most profound impression on him. In 1907, a year after he had returned to Cookham Dene as a married man, with a son of about the same age as he himself had been in 1865, Constance Smedley records him as saying:[24] 'I feel I should never be surprised to meet myself as I was when a little chap of five, suddenly coming round a corner. . . . The queer thing is, I can remember everything I felt then, the part of my brain I used from four till about seven can never have altered. Coming back here wakens every recollection. After that time I don't remember anything particularly.' This notion of the dissociated self, almost of a childish Doppelgänger is, as we shall see later, one of the main elements in Grahame's method of composition: he invests two characters with conflicting aspects of his own personality, and sets them off against each other. Frequently one is an adult, the other a child.

What was it about The Mount which affected him so powerfully? Certainly not (except in an adverse sense) his long-suffering relatives; more probably, following the best romantic tradition, it was the place itself and the countryside round it. All through his adult life this exiled Scot never strayed far from the soft hills and rich soil of Berkshire, so different from the sea-lochs and granite he had known as a child in the Western Highlands. It was as if he deliberately sought out the warm, friendly, tolerant south as an antidote to that repressive puritanism he always associated with his own background.

To such a child his first glimpse of The Mount must have been unforgettable. For all Mrs. Ingles' penuriousness, it remains by any standards a beautiful and spacious property.[25] The house was originally a hunting-box, and a great tree in the grounds, 280 years old, marks the former edge of Windsor Forest. The gardens and orchard cover several acres; the eye travels over wide lawns and trim yew hedges to a glimpse of Cliveden on a distant hillside. Round the house stand magnificent copper beeches, and the garden descends in terraced levels, decorated with flagged lily-ponds, low Italian walls, and ponderous stone flower-pots. The orchard is wild enough to contain any number of buffalo or pirates, while the house itself might have been specially made for children. The leaded windows, the old Dutch tiles, the heavy beams made out of ships' timbers, the twisting staircase leading up to a dusty, vaulted attic under the eaves—all must have been a paradise through which the young Grahames roamed in a private dream, only occasionally bothered by the claims of their latest governess or tutor.

As Kenneth lost sympathy with this new adult world, so he (and to a lesser extent his brothers and sister) retreated more and more into their own 'countries of the mind'—a course recommended by Marcus Aurelius, whose *Meditations* Kenneth later came to know and love, and who, like him, divided his life between public action and private ideals.[26] The conditions were perfect for the incubation of just such a dream-world as was to haunt Grahame for many years to come. The imaginary City which recurs again and again in his work (most notably, perhaps, in 'The Roman Road') was first built in that roomy attic at The Mount, known to the children (whose private domain it became) as 'the Gallery'. Chalmers writes:[27] 'The City was . . . kept strictly in the Gallery. Except on Sunday. On Sunday it became mentionable beyond the Gallery door, but only upon the way to church, but only if out of earshot of elder persons. Then, on the dusty church-ward mile, the previous week passed under close review; then all mortals encountered, Sunday to Saturday, in a world of workaday, were weighed in the balance. Those found worthy were forthwith proposed and elected freemen of the City. Those found wanting—was there not a savage pleasure, in excluding them, in having the golden barriers clash to. . . ?' The natural inclination which children have to form a world of their own was here intensified by the feeling the Grahame children must have had of *not belonging*: they were thrown, in several senses, on their own resources.

This general atmosphere tallies so exactly with that of *The Golden Age* and *Dream Days* that it is essential to clarify how far the two books can be admitted as biographical evidence.[28] We cannot, obviously, treat them as pure autobiography, though there is no doubt that they are largely based on the Grahames' life at Cookham Dene. In the first place, it is impossible even to equate the fictional characters, consistently, with real-life prototypes. There is no attempt to portray Mrs. Ingles (unless some of her massive self-assurance has filtered into Aunt Eliza); and if

Selina is Helen, as might plausibly be supposed, who is Charlotte? Perhaps Helen was the model for both, at different ages; we cannot be sure. But even this takes us straight into the realm of pure fiction: a conclusion more than reinforced by the genesis of Harold's 'death-letter' in *Dream Days*. On the autobiographical assumption, Harold is Roland; but in fact the 'death-letter' was composed thirty years later, about 1894, by Anthony Feiling. Grahame was a frequent visitor at the Feilings' house at Amwell Bury and was obviously on the look-out for fresh material, which the young Tony and Keith Feiling were only too glad to supply.[29] Not only the 'death letter', but also Harold's idiosyncratic penchant for 'playing clubmen' derive from this source. The latter appeared in 'Snowbound' in 1893, while the former was quoted *verbatim*, in 'Mutabile Semper', in April 1896. Now if Harold is a portrait of Tony Feiling, we cannot trust *The Golden Age* (without corroborative evidence) to tell us anything precise about the Grahames' own childhood. But in fact Harold, like most of Grahame's characters, is something more elusive still: a composite portrait. We can isolate a derivative strand here and there; but the children of *The Golden Age*, in so far as they have a distinctive personality of their own, are the products of Grahame's own mind, which in its creative processes somewhat resembles that of Coleridge. Even when he comes nearest to direct portraiture he adds and embellishes, often with touches drawn from himself.

The best point from which to start, then, is the anonymous narrator; though even here we must make allowances for Grahame's desire to idealize his childhood self. In 1931 he wrote to a curious enquirer: 'The "boy" somehow never had a name, so I suppose at this late period he must just go on being anonymous'. But at the time of composition he had been less reticent, as Helen Dunham recalled after his death in a letter to his wife: 'We first met in 1896, after *The Golden Age* had come out. . . . I remember speaking to Mr. Grahame of "The Roman Road"—

and he said: "Ah, I'm glad you like that, because it was more or less myself", and when I said something of having been afraid that he might grow up, he said "No—I don't think I shall—I've just been writing about a circus and I found I didn't feel a bit grown up".'[30] We can assume, then, that in a broad sense the 'I' of *The Golden Age* and its sequel at least represents Grahame's early attitude to life as he himself later recalled it.

This boy has a strongly marked and individual character. He simultaneously resents and envies the arbitrary power exercised by his elders. He has the emotional precocity often to be found in orphans, foster-children, or young D.P.'s. His tendency to solitariness is pronounced, and causes him some twinges of conscience; these children live by a positively hierarchical common code, and the individualist is not encouraged: 'I waited until they were both thoroughly absorbed, and then I slipped through the hedge out of the trodden highway, into the vacant meadow spaces. It was not that I was unsociable . . . but the passion and the call of the divine morning were high in my blood.'[31] This is the authentic Wordsworthian note; Kenneth was to wander 'lonely as a cloud' for the rest of his life. From the beginning his love of Nature—that ambivalent abstraction—was considerably higher than his love of humanity: a point brought out a few lines later in the passage I have quoted, where he writes: 'They could not but jar and seem artificial, these human discussions and pretences, when boon nature, reticent no more, was singing that full-throated song of hers that thrills and claims control of every fibre'. Humanity and Nature, in fact, are not only separate entities, but in opposition.

The *alter ego* of *The Golden Age* also goes out of his way—beyond the normal derision natural to a young boy—to mock and sneer at girls in general and the whole network of personal social relationships they involve one in. Girls are the inferior sex in every way. 'I can't make out what they find to talk about', Edward complains, and the Narrator replies: 'What they'll be when they're men'. His own infatuation, in 'Mutabile Semper',

21

provokes him to a devastating piece of satire, all the more effective for its feather-light obliquity. The girl in question is made to reveal in turn her squeamishness, her passion for worming out secrets and then giving them away, her shameless capacity for emotional blackmail. She is house-proud, materialistic, and possessions-conscious; bossy and egotistic; sharp-tongued, authoritarian, flirtatious. She has all the ghastly feminine failings known to mankind, and unrolls them in the space of ten pages. The largest concession this premature misogynist will make is that 'when you have girls about the place, they have got to be considered to a certain extent'.[32]

Other characteristics can be gathered from chance allusions. He is indifferent to the morality of property-rights, but suffers guilty qualms at the sight of a village whipping-post; he likes to strum at random on a piano because scales are associated with adult discipline; he supposes that sundials wind up, and, like Candide, tends to take the worn clichés and metaphors of his elders at their literal face value. He dislikes the moral precepts with which they hedge anything to do with money. He is liable to periodical fits of violent depression and pessimism. He hates all 'courtesies, welcomes, explanations, and other court-chamberlain kind of business'[33]—a trait which he later passed on to Badger. He is naturally generous, and (though loath to admit it) genuinely attached to his brothers and sisters. He is conscious of an occasional temptation to act as a buffer between them and the grown-ups, to play the 'Blameless Prig'. He is an expert on the fauna of the American continent, and a willing but incompetent hand with a paint-box. His natural temperament is conservative; he has an absolute passion for stability, discipline, the sense of a fixed order in life; and his worst fits of brooding and misery are provoked by such occasions as the departure of a governess, or Edward's metamorphosis into an alien schoolboy—when he is left to contemplate the 'raw new conditions of our changed life'. The acuteness of his misery can be gauged from the fact that it is for him something physical—it leaves a dull bruise, it is like a beating, it gives one 'a dull, bad sort of pain low down inside', a pain which can even resemble 'a corporeal wound'.[34]

Some of these qualities may derive from adult *arrière-pensées*; but in general they square very well with what we know about the conditions of the Grahames' existence at Cookham Dene. They suggest how violent in fact was the emotional wrench that uprooted these children from their family atmosphere and transplanted them to the thin soil of relatives' charity. Nevertheless, the 'Olympians' that Kenneth actually knew were far from being monsters; at the worst they were unimaginative and irritable. There is every reason to suppose that he later fictionalized them almost completely in order to extend his satirical attack to a specific class of contemporary English society.[35]

Who, in fact, among his relations was he in constant contact with during this period? His grandmother, indeed, was omnipresent; but the only other relative that we know to have actually *lived* at The Mount (and even then for two years only) was her son David, Bessie Grahame's twin brother. The Rev. David Ingles was in his early thirties, a graduate of Edinburgh Academy and Trinity College, Cambridge, where in 1860 he had acquired a rowing Blue. His previous curacy had been at Stoke-on-Trent; he was appointed to Cookham Dene in 1864—an appointment which suggests that Mrs. Ingles could charm the ecclesiastical authorities no less than the War Office. He lived with her and the Grahame children till his marriage in 1866. Helen Grahame recalled that he 'made a great deal of us, taking us on the river and to see his friends at Bisham and elsewhere'.[36] Perhaps it was from Uncle David that Kenneth first acquired his passion for 'messing about in boats'; and I suspect that his amiable personality may have partly inspired the original curate of *The Golden Age*—if not his successor, the egregious Mr. Hodgitts:

> He could receive, unblenching, the information that the meadow beyond the orchard was a prairie studded with herds

of buffalo. . . . He neither laughed nor sneered, as the Olympians would have done; but, possessed of a serious idiosyncrasy, he would contribute such lots of valuable suggestion as to the pursuit of this particular sort of big game that, as it seemed to us, his mature age and eminent position could scarce have been attained without a practical knowledge of the creature in its native lair . . . I trust he is a bishop by this time. He had all the necessary qualifications, as we knew.[37]

Apart from these two, we cannot be certain that there were any relations in residence during the Grahames' time at Cookham. It is possible that some unmarried cousin or niece of Mrs. Ingles was attached to the household, but, if so, their presence is not recorded. Visitors were frequent enough—Uncle Jack Ingles, 'our sailor Uncle Jack, came and went and was wildly welcomed',[38] and Uncle John Grahame also appeared, though perhaps his reception was a trifle cooler—but visitors are not *bona fide* Olympians. Their flittings are recorded in *The Golden Age*, and still leave an irreducible, permanent core of Auntdom behind.

Who were these aunts, who constitute the Olympians at their most intolerable? Supposing our evidence to be correct, did Grahame invent them? But this raises a further problem. If, as the record suggests, his individual relatives were on the whole kindly disposed towards him, why did he wish to attack them at all? Whom, in fact, *was* he attacking? There can be no doubt about his resentment and hatred of relatives as a class; however hard he tried to disguise it as comedy, there are times when this resentment rises almost to pathological levels—openly in *Pagan Papers*, with greater art and discretion in *The Golden Age* and *Dream Days*. Perhaps it was provoked simply by emotional stupidity, unimaginative treatment, the unwillingness or inability of these adults to enter into a child's world. The core of Grahame's complaint really seems to be that they allowed the young no seriousness, no dignity, no warmth or colour, no *meaning* in life. For a foster-child such treatment would have been doubly destructive.

Whatever the cause, Grahame hit back, thirty years later, with every weapon at his disposal. The Olympians in general were materialistic, dull, anaemic, listless, wilfully stupid, stickily sentimental, stereotyped in their thought, unambitious in their actions. Their position of authority was an accident of which they entirely failed to take desirable advantage, but used as a weapon to enforce their unfair and grossly arbitrary decisions. They were hypocritical over religious observances, the slaves of meaningless social conventions, and liable to break promises. They had an inexplicable habit of talking to each other at the same time. Children they regarded 'with indifference (an indifference as I recognize, the result of a certain stupidity) and therewith the commonplace conviction that your child is merely animal'.[39]

A modern reader will not be surprised to find that these spiritual oafs provoked elaborate revenge-fantasies, which culminated in visions of a triumphant child bestowing charity and forgiveness on the by now contrite aunt or uncle concerned.[40] (It is interesting, however, to compare Grahame here with 'Saki': the latter, in 'Sredni Vashtar', allows his fictional revenge-fantasy to become fictional fact, when Conrad's aunt is bitten to death by the giant pole-cat ferret. Grahame never takes this final step.) The fantasies first appear in *Pagan Papers*, are absent from *The Golden Age*, but recur in *Dream Days*. They involve, *inter alia*, skinning alive, shooting, mass-murder, and walking the plank.

The most concise statement Grahame makes anywhere about his personal objections to relatives as such is in a piece called 'Justifiable Homicide', written in 1891, where he puts forward humorous arguments (reminiscent of De Quincey's 'Murder as One of the Fine Arts') for their extinction. They are abominably stingy; they 'have crammed their victim full of precepts, rules of conduct, moral maxims, and most miscellaneous counsel; all which he intuitively suspected at the time, and has ascertained by subsequent experience, to be utterly worthless'. This summing-up, while it largely confirms the evidence of the other books, adds one very interesting fact: Grahame resented meanness over money in adults. Perhaps he looked on half-crowns as a tangible substitute for that affection which the Olympians could not give, a substitute which they were in duty bound to provide. Yet, ironically, it was one of the few unlikeable traits which in after years he himself acquired: something more than good Scots thrift. We always tend to condemn our own weaknesses most violently in others.

The governesses and tutors who appear at intervals throughout the two books of childhood may possibly have been drawn from life; Miss Smedley rings true, and I would very much like to believe in the aesthetic young man who prattled of fashionable artists and belonged to a Psychical Society. But again, Grahame uses them ultimately as pegs on which to hang a general moral protest against the uselessness of this kind of education *per se*:

> In the matter of general culture and attainments, we youngsters stood on pretty level ground. True, it was always happening that one of us would be singled out at any moment, freakishly, and without regard to his own preferences, to wrestle with the inflections of some idiotic language long rightly dead; while another, from some fancied artistic tendency which always failed to justify itself, might be told off without warning to hammer out scales and exercises, and to bedew the senseless keys with tears of weariness or of revolt. But in subjects common to either sex, and held to be necessary even for him whose ambition soared no higher than to crack a whip in a circus-ring —in geography, for instance, arithmetic, or the weary doings of kings and queens—each would have scorned to excel. And, indeed, whatever our individual gifts, a general dogged determination to slink and to evade kept us all at much the same dead level—a level of ignorance tempered by insubordination.[41]

It is basically the same complaint: an adult attitude that is stupid, convention-ridden, blind to the mystery and excitement and impalpable wonder of life.

The exceptions to this dreary rule are delineated with loving care; and none more memorably than the ancient, absent-minded, gentle rector, 'a bachelor, eccentric, learned exceedingly, round whom the crust of legend was already beginning to form; to myself an object of special awe, in that he was alleged to have written a real book'.[42] His essential, as opposed to his incidental, virtue as far as Grahame is concerned is his all-embracing and charitable tolerance. He accepts everyone on their own terms and sees good in the most unlikely places: there is a flavour of Browne's *Religio Medici* about him. He encourages strumming; he would probably have appreciated the negroes, monkeys, and crocodiles with which the young Grahame decorated his textbooks, and still more the Gryphon pursuing the Arimaspian along the margins of Milton.[43] The model for this portrait may well have been George Hewitt Hodson, the eccentric and scholarly vicar of Cookham Dene, who was, among other things, the brother of Hodson of Hodson's Horse. He had formerly been a Fellow of Trinity College, Cambridge, and remained a distinguished classicist: but his one book was an edition of his brother's letters from India. His introduction hints at a penchant for romantic tales that would have entranced the six-year-old Kenneth.[44] Another clergyman who may have contributed to the final picture was Conyngham Ellis, an ancient Irishman ordained late in life, and in 1866 Vicar of Cranbourne near Windsor: but this is slightly to anticipate events.[45]

In December 1865 one of the chimneys at The Mount fell in a heavy gale, and old Mrs. Ingles became nervous about the others. It was at this point that Uncle John Grahame, Cunningham Grahame's brother, persuaded her to move to a different and considerably smaller house. John Grahame was a Parliamentary Agent, a partner in the firm of Grahame, Currie and Spens; and it is clear from a letter of Helen Grahame's that he had made himself at least partially responsible financially for the *ménage* at The Mount.[46] It seems probable that he had been exerting pressure on Mrs. Ingles for some time, and found that the chimneys did the trick.

At all events, in the spring of 1866 Mrs. Ingles and her brood of grandchildren left The Mount and its spacious acres for Fernhill Cottage, Cranbourne. Once again, after putting down tentative roots in Berkshire soil, Kenneth and the rest were (as it seemed to them) arbitrarily transplanted once more, as if they were part of the luggage, without feelings or free will. To a child with Kenneth's passion for the fixed order of things such migrations—and the half-knowledge that they were forced by financial pressure—must have been profoundly disturbing.

Nevertheless there were compensations. The cottage was leased from Mr. Algernon Gilliatt, who was a cousin of Uncle David's newly-married wife Anna, and became a close friend of the family while they remained there. It was at Cranbourne, too, that David Ingles introduced the Grahames to a man who was to influence the course of Kenneth's life irrevocably: William Lidderdale, the future Governor of the Bank of England. Helen writes: 'Mr. Lidderdale's only connection with Cranbourne was that his wife's mother Mrs. Busk lived at Ascot Place, Winkfield, about two miles away. The Lidderdales used to come to stay with her in the summer and we went over to see our old nurse Ferguson and the Lidderdale children. But Mrs. Busk was an old friend of Grannie's and we were always at Ascot Place.'[47]

By this time Kenneth's literary tastes had begun to show themselves, chiefly in his disconcerting habit of chanting such infectious stuff as *The Lays of Ancient Rome* on walks through the pinewoods. Conyngham Ellis may have fostered this tendency, though Helen asserts, oddly, that Kenneth never had lessons in Cranbourne. She herself seems to have viewed her brother from this moment on with some suspicion. 'It was at Cranbourne', she writes, 'that Kenneth began to spout poetry, first Shakespeare, then Macaulay's *Lays*, then Tennyson', as if such behaviour was somehow reprehensible. In later years she was to observe to enquiring friends: 'Oh, we don't go in for Kenneth, you know'.[48] Yet Helen herself wrote some charming occasional verses—in private. The family tradition of the Grahames did not encourage literature: they believed in pterodactyls, not dragons.

Kenneth seems to have struck most response at this period from his cousin Reginald Ingles, who was several years his junior. Major Ingles recalled of his visits to Fernhill Cottage that Kenneth 'was the nice one, who was always kind, and who we were always delighted to see—and to go out with, who never ticked us off, and was always ready to help one in little things. . . . Willie and Helen we did not like very much. . . .'[49] Already, it seems, Kenneth was becoming isolated from those he most needed emotionally.

Then came a fresh surprise, which momentarily raised Kenneth's hopes only to disappoint them once more. In that same summer of 1866 an unexpected letter reached Cranbourne from Inveraray: James Cunningham Grahame had suddenly decided to summon his family home. We cannot be certain of his motives. He may have felt a genuine fit of remorse and affection; he may have supposed that the presence of children would help him to fight his crippling alcoholism. At the lowest level, it may have been a move to make some show of social respectability, and so safeguard his official position.

At all events, the children left Fernhill Cottage and travelled north once more, as Kenneth recalls in 'The Romance of the Rail', 'through the furnace-lit Midlands, and on till the grey glimmer of dawn showed stone walls in place of hedges, and masses looming up on either side; till the bright sun shone upon brown leaping streams and purple heather, and the clear, sharp northern air streamed in through the windows'. They went with excitement and high hopes; but it was useless. Their father's resolution soon spent itself when they were present in the flesh, and by now, too, the time had almost been reached when through his heavy drinking he would no longer be fit for the duties of a Sheriff. It is not difficult to imagine what lay behind his son's words: 'Return, indeed, was bitter; Endymion-like, "my first touch of the earth went nigh to kill"'.

For nearly a year they stayed at Inveraray, witnesses to their father's slow moral and physical disintegration; then Cunningham Grahame resolved the dilemma himself. He resigned his post in the spring of 1867, and went abroad. For twenty years he scraped a wretched living in France, probably by teaching English, and died alone in a cheap Le Havre apartment house. As far as we know none of his children saw or communicated with him throughout the whole of those twenty years. But Kenneth, at least, could not rid himself of the vain dream with which he had travelled north: '"We are only the children who might have been", murmured Lamb's dream-babes to him; and for the sake of those dream-journeys, the journeys that might have been, I still hear with a certain affection the call of the engine in the night'.[50] Not for the first time in the young boy's life there had been an ugly split between hope and fulfilment, dream and reality. He was eight years old. Who can blame him if he clung with desperate and increasing intensity to the dream?

II

THE SPELL OF OXFORD
1868-1875

The Half-Way House to Rome—Oxford.
Punch, vol. xvi, p. 36 (1849)

Towery city and branchy between towers;
Cuckoo-echoing, bell-swarmed, lark-charmed,
   rook-racked, river-rounded;
The dapple-eared lily below thee; that country
   and town did
Once encounter in, here coped and poisèd powers.
        G. M. HOPKINS: *Duns Scotus' Oxford*

When, many years later, Kenneth Grahame came to create the idealized picture of his childhood, his main object was to preserve something essentially transient from oblivion, a talisman against time and change. Each successive blow at his sense of permanence and stability drove him further in upon himself. In *The Golden Age* and *Dream Days* he set down the vision he had had before, like Traherne, he was 'corrupted by the dirty devices of this world';[1] they are his bulwark, the fragments he has shored against his ruins. The quality he values above all is timelessness. Time destroys legends, puts children beyond the reach of fantasy, gives no warning of coming bereavement. 'Time Tryeth Trothe', runs the inscription on the sundial in *The Golden Age*. Autumn brings 'changing lines and chill forebodings', humans cannot bear to look into the future.[2]

31

Nothing made a deeper impression on Grahame's mind than the beginning of his school-days: they mark the close of an era. Henceforward dream and reality are separated for ever, and the precarious private world the children had created exists only in memory. Once again it is an adult decree which shatters their defences. In 1868 (probably at Uncle John Grahame's urging) 'the word had gone out, the school had been selected; the necessary sheets were hemming even now, and Edward [*i.e.* Kenneth and Willie] was the designated and appointed victim'. At that grisly farewell scene on the station platform the narrator recalls: 'Fortunately I was not old enough to realize . . . that here on this little platform the old order lay at its last gasp, and that Edward might come back to us, but it would not be the Edward of yore, nor could things ever be the same again'. (It is interesting that Grahame describes *from the spectator's viewpoint* a departure in which he himself was involved: as if in fact his true self was being left behind.) And indeed he is only too well justified in his forebodings; when Edward does come home after one term he is translated into an alien being 'ragged of attire and lawless of tongue, a scorner of tradition and an adept in strange new physical tortures, one who would in the same half-hour dismember a doll and shatter a hallowed belief'.[3]

Here, in fact, is the first whiff of the Olympians' own world; arbitrary, pragmatic, unimaginative, custom-bound, and strongly hostile to the pleasures of fantasy. Because it is laid down by immutable decree, this ordeal of school is unavoidable: henceforth one must live in the enemy's camp, wear his colours and mouth his public shibboleths. What is more insidious is the possibility that one may come to believe in them—'can it be that I also have become an Olympian?'[4] Though the inner self clings to its old truth still, and the double personality preserves its countries of the mind, a permanent conflict has been set up. The pleasures of maturity, as Grahame made very clear in his two childhood books, have their own peculiar seductiveness for the youthful imagination.

It was 'on or about Michaelmas Day, 1868', Grahame wrote in 1932, a few months before his death, when 'a bright and eager (sullen, reluctant, very ordinary-looking) youth of nine summers sprang lightly (descended reluctantly, was haled ignominiously) onto the arrival platform of the Great Western Railway Station at Oxford'.[5] During the weeks of anticipation dread had been mixed with hopeful excitement. 'According to some it meant larks, revels, emancipation, and a foretaste of the bliss of manhood. According to others—the majority, alas!—it was a private and peculiar Hades, that could give the original institution points and a beating.'[6] Certainly at first the majority seemed to have been the more accurate prophets. St. Edward's School had only been recently founded, and somewhat anarchic conditions still prevailed there. The Headmaster, Mr. Fryer, 'would hide pence and halfpence and turn us all out in the dark to look for them. . . . Pits were dug and filled with mud and water, and over them, and into them, the unsuspecting ones were lured.' The upper boys were liable to go on strike; one, who was believed to wear a corset as a protection against caning, 'being told to report himself to the Head seized the easel and announced aloud that he would knock the Head down with it'.[7] Notwithstanding this, St. Edward's was a highly religious foundation; about one boy in seven took orders, and twenty masters were ordained during residence. 'We can at least claim', the Jubilee Number of the school magazine announced, 'that the so-called "gentleman-at-large"—a dangerous sort of wild beast—is a negligible quantity in the total of our results. The O.S.E. are almost without exception workers.'[8]

It was not, perhaps, an entirely sympathetic atmosphere; and Grahame has left us a picture of 'a small school-boy, new kicked out of his nest into the draughty, uncomfortable outer world, his unfledged skin still craving the feathers whereinto he was wont to nestle. The barrack-like school, the arid, cheerless class-rooms, drove him to Nature for redress; and, under an alien sky, he would go forth and wander along the iron road by impassive fields, so like yet so unlike those hitherto a part of him.'⁹ The discipline in this respect was easy-going. Within certain limits boys were allowed to wander where they liked, and Grahame took full advantage of this: there was, as he noted, no games tyranny.¹⁰

At first he was very much a hermit-crab *sans* shell, clearly unused to the conventions prevailing in such an establishment. His initial encounter with Authority was highly comic, however: it took the shape of 'a round and rosy young man with side-whiskers who desired, he said, to record my full name for some base purpose of his own. When he had got it he tittered girlishly and murmured, "What a *funny* name!"' But within a day or two of his first arrival Kenneth had a taste of discipline fiercer and more arbitrary than his domestic Olympians could ever have conceived:¹¹

> The junior form, or class, was in session, so to speak, and I was modestly occupying that position, at the very bottom, which seemed to me natural enough, when the then Head-master entered—a man who had somehow formed an erroneous idea of my possibilities. Catching sight of me, he asked, sternly, 'What's that thing doing down there?' The master in charge could only reply that whether it was crass ignorance or invincible stupidity, he wotted not, but there it was. The Head-master, who was, I was persuaded, a most illogical man, and could not really have studied that immortal work, the *Republic* of Plato, in which the principles of ideal justice are patiently sought out, merely remarked that if the thing—meaning me—was not up there or near it, pointing to the head of the form, before the close of work, it was to be severely caned; and left the room.

It is pleasant to record that the rest of the form achieved undreamed of heights of stupidity in order to avert the worst; but Kenneth, who was unused to being 'savaged by big, beefy, hefty, hairy men called masters',¹² promptly burst into tears of horror and bewilderment. 'What maggot had tickled the brain of the Headmaster on that occasion', he wrote, 'I never found out.

Granny Ingles   Kenneth Grahame as a new boy
          at St. Edward's School

The Mount, Cookham Dene

Schoolmasters never explain, never retract, never apologize.' He was, as he himself admits, a little chap, and unused to physical punishment. He had been doing his best, 'and at home I had not been considered an absolute fool'. Now he had run full tilt into the public school tradition of arbitrary assault. It was a salutary shock, and he quickly adapted himself to this new, unbelievable world, horseplay and all. But he never jettisoned his own basic beliefs; he merely learnt (as all his contemporaries of a similar disposition did) that in public they must either be concealed or presented indirectly. In 'Saturnalia' he started specifically: 'Whenever a child is set down in a situation that is distasteful, out of harmony, jarring—and he is very easily jarred—that very moment he begins, without conscious effort, to throw out and to build up an environment really suitable to his soul, and to transport himself thereto. . . . Of the herb called self-heal he has always a shred or two in his wallet.'

It is a tribute to his toughness, resilience and inner resources that he not only survived his seven years at St. Edward's, but did extremely well there in every way. After his rough initiation, he settled down to prove himself as conventional a public schoolboy as the best of them. He gained his 1st XV Colours for Rugger ('a useful forward; always upon the ball, lacks weight and strength'[13]); was Secretary of the 2nd XI at cricket; shot at Wimbledon; and spent his last four terms, from Michaelmas 1874 onwards, as Senior Prefect, or Head of School. He won prizes for Divinity and Latin Prose in 1874, and the Sixth Form Class prize in 1875.[14] It was a solid and respectable progression. Yet I suspect strongly that much of this performance was executed at least partially tongue in cheek. Grahame's first known appearance in print, at the age of fourteen, was with an essay entitled 'The Good and Bad Effects of Rivalry', which was printed in the school *Chronicle*,[15] 'to encourage care in . . . composition'. Even a St. Edward's master, writing in 1913, admits that this 'shows no promise of the exquisite prose that was to be in later years the delight of thousands'. What he fails to add is that it displays a breathtaking and calculated sanctimoniousness.

'. . . It certainly is a very difficult thing in practice to feel kindly towards a rival, and to anyone but to one who always bears in mind one of the chief duties of a Christian, to love one another, and keeps a good control over himself, it is a very difficult thing . . .' writes the future author of *Pagan Papers*, who knew, no less than Stalky, what would please the muscular Christians set in authority over him. Nowhere else does he display anything but amused contempt for the official creed as practised in the 'days when one was young and Godless, and went to church'. Of his elders he observed: 'No irresistible Energy haled them to church o' Sundays; yet they went there regularly of their own accord, though they betrayed no greater delight in the experience than ourselves'.[16] He constantly attacks the empty social formula which the Victorian Sabbath had become, the aesthetic tastelessness of the services: but his most biting satire is reserved for Puritanism— hell-fire preachers, missionaries, Original Sin, the discipline of 'barbed-wires and Sunday schools'.[17] The 'Rivalry' essay, examined in this context, reminds me of Mark Twain's comment on Margaret Fleming, Scott's 'Pet Marjorie': 'Under pressure of a pestering sense of duty she heaves a shovelful of trade godliness into her journals every little while, but it does not offend, for none of it is her own . . . it is the most innocent of hypocrisies'.[18]

Grahame tells us, in pretty clear terms, that he still, throughout this period, kept his secret world of the imagination active. The dreamy, unresponsive 'Smith' he describes so meticulously in 'Ideals' is not merely idle or stupid, nor even preoccupied with cricket averages or ways of making money: 'his mind is up and away, in a far, far better world than this, a world wherein matters are conducted as they should be, and where he is undoubtedly the best man there and is being given a fair chance at last. He is, in fact, pursuing his ideals.'

Even so it was impossible for Grahame to preserve a completely orthodox front; the anti-authoritarian streak in him was too strong. He found a convenient and legitimate outlet in the Debating Society, where his most outrageous opinions could pass as cheerful coat-trailing. He 'considered a lawyer was only doing his duty when he defended a client whom he knew to be guilty'. He supported cremation, a more provocative thing to do then than now: but 'the hideous utilitarian phantom was banished by a large majority'. He bombarded the House with statistics on Free Trade, and 'thought the custom of duelling had gone far to sustain the honour of the country'. Only once, in 1875, did he show his hand on a religious topic, but then he by no means minced his words. In a debate on the relative merits of Queen Elizabeth and Queen Mary, we read:

> K. Grahame, who was on the opposition side of the house, said there was nothing to choose between the characters of the two Queens. One was a bigoted Catholic, the other a spiteful Protestant. He read to the house a passage from a work entitled 'The Student's Hume', but did not justify the opposition view of the question by drawing any deductions from his quotation.

Even in 1875 Hume, who explained moral principles in terms of habit and social custom, and supposed that religion arose 'from the incessant hopes and fears which actuate the human mind', would have been fairly strong meat for an orthodox Anglican schoolmaster. Perhaps wisely, the young empiricist only released this broadside in his last term.[19]

At the same time, that is when he was in the Sixth, he was devoting a good deal of his time and energy to the *Chronicle*, which had been started by a contemporary of his, Trant ('Tichy') Chambers.[20] Chambers edited it, and Grahame supplied many original contributions, all unfortunately anonymous. We can hazard a guess, but no more than a guess, at the identity of some of them. 'The Dress and Manner of the Man', for instance, agrees very well with Grahame's early dandyism. 'Tomorrow,' he told a friend on the eve of Gaudy Day, 'tomorrow I shall be superb.'[21] It is a touch worthy of the young Beerbohm. 'On the Road', too, strikes a note we shall find recurring again and again later: 'Let us then have done for a while at least with the hurry-scurry of artificial locomotion, with railway, coach, or bicycle, to wit, and use our natural powers of movement'.[22]

It is interesting and characteristic that Grahame's memories of his school-days are far more concerned with visual impressions of places and objects than anecdotes about his contemporaries. 'Misty recollections of friends—clear and distinct of desk, stair, cistern, room' he noted.[23] He shows a lively curiosity about the old school building in New-Inn-Hall Street, which was abandoned for a better site, known as Summertown, in 1873:

> On the left, or west side, first you had the buildings com-posing the Hall itself, the 'Tavern' of Verdant Green's days, where the buttery was open all day; then the grounds and solid Georgian vicarage of St. Something-le-Baily . . . —a pleasant jumble. On the right or east side were two little two-storied white gabled houses, of the sort common enough in Oxford then, and of which a few specimens still remain, running up to the old, fifteenth-century, back gate of Frewen Hall. Then came St. Edward's, a stone-built mansion of two stories, reaching to the end and then 'returned', as architects say.[24]

Here, in this pleasant Queen Anne house, Kenneth Grahame spent five of his seven years at school. Everything, 'in those troglodyte days', as he put it, was very primitive. There was no Sixth Form, merely Big Boys. The house was obviously over-crowded: the boys slept five or six to a bedroom, and conditions upstairs were 'rabbit-warrenish'. The matron, Mrs. Reece, seems to have been a kindly soul, and in sympathy with the boys rather than the masters. She used to come and help the smaller fry wash in the morning, and would occasionally smuggle a particularly dispirited urchin into the kitchen where (like Martha in *The Golden Age*) she proceeded to regale him with bread and treacle. If a master was heard approaching, a heap of dirty towels served as camouflage.

There were at that time few organized games, which may explain why the boys were allowed to spend so much of their free time exploring the neighbourhood. Most activity was centred on the playground, where the boys played Prisoner's Base, or even (in the very early days) rolled a heavy log about. 'Some of the fellows', recalled the Rev. J. C. Michel, 'dug out pits in which they buried boxes labelled "Gold", and we tried to imagine the feelings of the finders in after years.' This playground had once been a pleasant garden, and there still remained some flower-beds where, as Grahame put it, 'the horticulturally-minded were allowed, and even encouraged, to employ their grovelling instincts'. But for the most part it was now gravelled over, and used for gymnastics. Grahame adds an anecdote which shows how quickly he conformed with the new régime:

> Some sort of stable, or garden, gateway gave issue on the street northwards; but this was never used, and I only happen to remember it because on my first Guy Fawkes Day we boys attempted a private bonfire, thinking, in our artless way, that in Oxford bonfires were the rule rather than the exception. The authorities, however, thought otherwise, and firemen and police battered at the stable gate aforesaid till explanations ensued and till, I suppose, somebody was squared as usual.[25]

After the move to Summertown, a more organized curriculum was introduced, in which games played a larger part. Grahame, as we have seen, showed himself an excellent all-round sportsman; but he probably looked back with nostalgia to the more leisured days at New-Inn-Hall Street, a supposition confirmed by the fact that he nowhere gives a description of life at Summertown. The well-ordered White House cricket ground, for instance, could never replace in his estimation those hilarious games played on Port Meadow. The sole advantage Port Meadow possessed as a cricket pitch was an absence of boundaries:

> If an ambitious and powerful slogger wanted to hit a ball as far as Wolvercote, he could do so if he liked; there was nothing

to stop him, and the runs would be faithfully run out. The chief drawback was that the city burgesses used the meadow for pasturage of their cows—graminivorous animals of casual habits. When fielding was 'deep', and frenzied cries of 'Throw her up!' reached one from the wicket, it was usually more discreet to feign a twisted ankle or a sudden faintness, and allow some keener enthusiast to recover the ball from where it lay.[26]

It is a scene which would have delighted A. G. Macdonell.

But nothing, not even Port Meadow cricket, could compare with the delights of 'exploring, exploring, always exploring, in a world I had not known the like of before'. Inveraray and The Mount had contributed their share to Grahame's undiscovered City; now it was Oxford's turn, and Rome would come later. On a page of notes for the memoirs he never began Grahame scribbled, apropos his schooldays: 'What one took away: the Spell of Oxford'; and another fragment he left pays the city a tribute that is a queer foreshadowing of Hopkins:

In that gracious grey old city of our abiding, well-watered, of pleasant approach by bridge that bestrode the brimfull river or causeway through standing water lily-starred, grey straying side-streets looped or nestled all along the four noble thorough-fares rich in tower and steeple—the home of restless jackdaws forth-issuing day-long; the organ-mouth of bell-music vocal through daylight most passionately appealing at the quiet close of evening. . . .[27]

Oxford in Grahame's schooldays was indeed a fascinating lure for an imaginative boy: perhaps more so than today. To begin with, all the streets (except the newly macadamized High) were still paved with mediaeval cobbles: even the Broad and St. Giles. This was not only picturesque; it discouraged traffic. The few ancient hansoms and flies were mainly in demand for the beginning and end of term, to make the long trip between the colleges and a decently secluded railway station. There were no bicycles, and—if one can imagine Oxford without them today—no cars. Morris-Cowley still lay in the womb of time. As R. W. Macan pointed out:[28] 'Unless you were wealthy and kept a horse, you trusted mainly to your own legs for locomotion. Pedestrianism was still the joy of the reading man in the Oxford of the "seventies". But then, he still had the unravished country of the Scholar Gipsy to wander over, with or without a companion. . . . Oxford was still a duodecimo city in those days. The country began just beyond the bridges.'

In this mediaeval paradise Grahame wandered, hour after hour, rapturous and obsessed. With no one to ask questions, as at home, or make 'tedious talk of delphiniums and greenfly and such', he strolled in and out of the Fellows' Gardens; he sampled the Arabian Nights' catholicity which, then as now, characterized the Market. 'It seemed', he recalled, 'to have everything the heart of man could desire, from livestock at one end to radiant flowers in pots at the other.' He window-gazed in the High, lingering at the smart tailors' displays. Before he was ten he knew by heart 'all the stately buildings that clustered round the Radcliffe Library', even finding time for wonder at the 'exceeding nigritude and decay' of the Sheldonian Caesars, and the general blackness of the University buildings; this, he thought, 'might have been put on with a brush, in a laudable attempt to produce the "sub-fusc" line required in the attire of its pupils'. He would have been especially delighted by the archaic methods employed to lay the dust in the High:

> A copious tap [Macan writes[29]], turned on at Carfax, sent water down the street in two streams, one in each gutter. On either side a municipal *Aquarius*, armed with large wooden shovel and encased in long boots, advanced down the street, and with a tarpaulin contraption every thirty or forty yards dammed the stream into a pool, and with his shovel flung the water half-way across the street, careful to avoid drenching his *vis-à-vis*, diagonally and similarly engaged.

Brasenose Lane held flesh-creeping delights; in this gloomy *couloir* Grahame and his friends were shown the precise window at which a horned and hoofed Devil appeared, one Sunday night, to the members of the Hell Fire Club. Here a stray reveller witnessed the fearful scene: Old Nick caused the blackest sinner to collapse in convulsions on the floor, and extracted his soul slowly through the bars (says Grahame, with all the relish of anti-climax) 'as a seaside tripper might extract a winkle from its shell with a pin'.[30] It was a tale precisely calculated to tickle the boy's anti-Puritan instincts; yet he remained (like Stevenson) enough of a Scots Calvinist to get a genuine *frisson* out of it.

During his second year at school, in 1869, Grahame visited St. Giles's Fair. It was the first fair of importance he had ever seen, and stirred in him a passion for the world of circus and fair-ground which persisted all his life. Freaks were then the mainstay of the show: Grahame recalled 'giants, dwarfs, fat ladies, tattooed ladies, mermaids, six-legged calves and distorted nature of every variety'. Not possessing enough pocket-money to investigate the side-shows for himself, he wandered down the rows of painted booths, drinking in their wildly imaginative advertisements, which depicted 'the object within under conditions and in surroundings hardly quite realizable, one was tempted to think, within the limitations of a caravan. There mermaids combed their hair on rocks, or swam lazily about in warm tropic seas; there boa constrictors wound themselves round the bodies of paralysed Indian maidens, in the depths of Amazonian jungles.'[31]

Perhaps he had the best of the bargain. For him the mermaids remained mermaids, the jungles were truly parrot-haunted, and the lagoons through which he swam in imagination were golden and tropical. It is faith, not money, which can move mountains: the bystanders who paid their sixpences and went inside soon re-emerged disillusioned, their faces set in what *Uncle Remus* describes as 'a spell ob de grins' at having been so easily caught. What *they* saw were 'clumsy fakes, dried fish, abortions in bottles, mangy and sickly animals cooped in packing-cases'. The whole story crystallizes, in precisely applicable terms, just that conflict of dream and reality which continued to haunt Grahame's imagination. There is no doubt (though he makes no comment) who he thought was happier, wiser, and ultimately better off: the penniless boy with a spirit as free as Ariel's, or the prosaic spectators who could only understand 'reality' at one level, and whose transactions were all conducted on a cash basis.

There were, too, other more strictly indigenous spectacles than fairs. In 1870, for instance, Oxford celebrated a particularly sumptuous Commemoration of Founders and Benefactors. The new Chancellor, Lord Salisbury, was there, with diminutive but impeccably blue-blooded pages to hold up his train; there was a Gala Ode composed by the Professor of Poetry and set by the Professor of Music; there was a recitation of the Newdigate Prize Poem, and honorary degrees for such notables as the P.R.A. and Mr. Matthew Arnold. Oxford can muster some impressive pageantry and processions for such occasions, of a kind to impress a boy already (without knowing it) in love with Pre-Raphaelism. A more unique sight, perhaps, was Professor Ruskin teaching Balliol undergraduates how to dig roads; an experiment which, though conducted in the same spirit as William Morris's weaving, was somewhat less successful.

Nevertheless, the spirit of Arnold, Ruskin, and Morris was powerful enough at Oxford in the seventies to captivate an impressionable schoolboy, already soaked in Virgil and Horace. And there was too, perhaps a more potent influence than any other, what Mr. T. S. Eliot calls 'a strong brown god'—the River.[32] As Grahame wrote:

> The two influences which most soaked into me there, and have remained with me ever since, were the good grey Gothic on the one hand and, on the other, the cool secluded reaches of the Thames—the 'stripling Thames', remote and dragon-fly haunted, before it attains to the noise, ribbons and flannels of Folly Bridge. The education, in my time, was of the fine old

crusted order, with all the classics in the top bin—I did Greek verse in those days, so help me! But these elements, the classics, the Gothic, the primeval Thames, fostered in me, perhaps, the pagan germ that would have mightily shocked the author of *The Sabbath*.

'The classics, the Gothic, the primeval Thames': they form an interesting trilogy. Grahame, of course, over-simplifies the problem: it is hardly necessary to say that many Oxonians survived these pleasant hazards without having their faith unduly disturbed, and that the roots of Grahame's paganism are to be sought at a deeper, more personal, level. What he has picked on, in fact, are his particular *pleasures*—equally illuminating, but not quite the same thing.

Grahame's classical learning is very sketchy: much of it consists of well-worn tags, and a good deal more probably reached him by way of Lang, Morris, or Arnold. What he felt was a romantic passion for antiquity, not a specific affection for great, ancient authors as such. He used the world of Greece and Rome simply as an adjunct to his own myth: it is no coincidence that the three works he does show signs of having studied closely are Virgil's *Georgics*, Horace's *Satires*, and the *Meditations* of Marcus Aurelius. It is curious that he does not appear to have read Herodotus—an author who, one supposes, would have appealed to him strongly. On the other hand, he was familiar enough with Homer to parody him, as we shall see later.[33] Many of his quotations he lifted direct from well-read English authors.[34]

His predilection for Gothic, too, he seems to have acquired, like many of his tastes, at second hand. Its primary inspiration was almost certainly Ruskin's famous chapter in *The Stones of Venice* on 'The Nature of Gothic',[35] where Ruskin discusses the fascination of 'tracing out this grey, shadowy, many-pinnacled image of the Gothic spirit within us and discerning what fellowship there is between it and our Northern hearts'—a theme which left its mark on Grahame's early essays. From this source, too, probably derives that half-mystic distinction Grahame is always drawing between the Nordic and Mediterranean temperaments: ice and fire, melancholy and happiness, Puritanism and liberalism, Death and Life. 'It was but now,' he writes, 'as I sprawled in flowers, that I began to realize how the mind may starve and pine in glacial surroundings.' It was a realization brought abruptly to the surface of his mind by the warming influence, even though indirect, that Oxford and Oxford ideas provided.

But Ruskin (as we shall see more clearly in Chapter XI) had a subtler and more extensive influence on Grahame than has generally been realized. Grahame's obsession with the antithesis of man and machine, his weakness for near-pantheism, his pre-occupation with things so diverse as the frescoes of Giotto or Pinturicchio and the external symbolism of the Roman Catholic Church—all these stem from Ruskin. So too do his romantic mediaevalism and the vision of the New Jerusalem which he shared with William Morris. It is a striking vindication of Mr. Graham Hough's thesis, that 'the new ideas about the arts and their relations to religion and the social order all seemed to originate somewhere in the dense jungle of Ruskin's works'.[36]

But the influence of the River was something altogether more basic and arresting. Its rhythm, as Mr. Eliot says, was present in the nursery bedroom,[37] and to his last days Grahame preserved a deep, not entirely articulate passion for 'this sleek, sinuous, full-bodied animal, chasing and chuckling, gripping things with a gurgle and leaving them with a laugh . . . glints and gleams and sparkles, rustle and swirl, chatter and bubble'. The river is in one sense a symbol of life, in another an emblem of constancy: it is faithful and steady-going, it never 'packed up, flitted or went into winter quarters'.[38] It is also the last natural refuge from speed and mechanization; a system of toll-gates and locks ensures leisurely progress, free from dust and clatter, to the quiet upper reaches by Lechlade or Abingdon. The roads have been ruined; the River remains what it was.[39] All running water affected Grahame almost hypnotically: he could stand and stare at it for hours.

It seems possible too, from his own account, that Grahame, while still a schoolboy, contrived to indulge his lifelong passion for 'messing about in boats'. The exploration of the Thames to which he alludes is unlikely to have been conducted entirely from the landward side. There is a fragment of MS. in which he pictures himself gliding lazily through Oxfordshire harvest hayfields in a canoe—a craft which he would have disdained later, when he had become a sculling enthusiast. As his introduction to sculling was accomplished by F. J. Furnivall, whom he met in 1876, the year after he left school, we can probably assume that some kind-hearted schoolmaster lent him a canoe while he was still at St. Edward's.[40] In this canoe we can picture the slight, dark-haired schoolboy paddling (as he described) past labourers busy about the harvest, and occasionally exchanging a cheerful word with them. One, 'who stood kneedeep in fragrant hay tossed up to him by moist helpers below, catching sight of my canoe . . . was fain to cheerily observe, "Ah, if I had lots o' money that's the way I should travel"'. The young Grahame retorted, enviously, that there were worse ways of going about than on a haycart, and that he (the labourer) didn't know how lucky he was to have spent so much time in such a pleasant occupation. 'Rejoinder he doubtless could have supplied—but the remorseless stream bore me out of hearing. That is one of the special charms of the stream: the river of life has remorseless eddies and backwaters which forbid your escape from such disputes.'

So the canoe would drift on, between meadows thick with loose-strife, through the country where Arnold's Scholar Gipsy roamed:

> For most, I know, thou lov'st retired ground.
> Thee, at the ferry, Oxford riders blithe,
> Returning home on summer nights, have met
> Crossing the stripling Thames at Bablock-hithe,
> Trailing in the cool stream thy fingers wet,—

beyond Pinkhill and Eynsham Lock and Wytham Great Wood, past Hagley Pool and the Trout Inn by Godstow Bridge, till Port Meadow and Osney Lock brought 'noise, ribbons and flannels' once more, and waters desecrated with 'lobster-claws, gold-necked bottles, and fragments of veal pie'.[41] Here we can leave him, leaning over New Bridge, where Cromwell's levies once tramped, and meditating on the Oxfordshire landscape: 'Typical of the country, which has changed not at all—and why should it —hay, and the rural Pan for ever'.[42]

During the Christmas holidays both Kenneth and Willie were often guests at Uncle John Grahame's London house in Sussex Gardens. They were taken to Drury Lane for the pantomime, together with Uncle John's children, Edward, Walter, Bessie, and Agnes. Mr. Bilson, Uncle John's head clerk, was given afternoons off to escort them to the Zoo, the Tower of London, and other such urban delights. Kenneth caused amusement, and a certain degree of raised eyebrows, by his somewhat precocious wit, probably sharpened in the Debating Society: 'Some dull family friends,' Chalmers writes, 'kindly folk who, of their garden's plenty, gave surplus vegetables to their neighbours, were on the agenda. "They have their points," declared someone at the dinner-table. "Have they?" said Kenneth doubtfully. "Well, dear," he was told, "they gave us this excellent asparagus." "*Pointes d'asperges*," Kenneth is said to have retorted as he helped himself.' Perhaps for this, perhaps for less definable reasons, he found himself from the beginning out of sympathy with Uncle John, a downright practical man who believed in hard work, physical exercise, and no nonsense. Agnes, however, liked him consider-ably: 'a tall good-looking boy of kind and charming disposition' is her description of him at this period.[43]

The Grahame boys seem not to have come near Sussex Gardens during the summer holidays. In August, when not at Cranbourne, they were often to be found in Portsmouth, where Uncle Jack Ingles was a Commander aboard H.M.S. *Hercules*. Reginald

Ingles, Uncle Jack's son, recalls a visit he made to the wardroom with Kenneth, when Uncle Jack gave them a sumptuous breakfast of omelettes (which Kenneth had never tasted before) and devilled kidneys; and afterwards turned them over to the gunnery-lieutenant, who failed to appreciate their calling his armament 'cannons'.[44] From the scanty evidence, one gets the impression that Granny Ingles found it somewhat overwhelming to have all four Grahame children in residence for the whole span of a holiday. She probably farmed them out, *privatim et seriàtim*, to the many relatives available—a process which may have supplied material, eventually, for *The Golden Age*.

At the beginning of 1875, Kenneth's last year at St. Edward's, Willie died. He had never been a particularly healthy child: he shared Kenneth's weak chest, but not his resilient general health. He had been forced to leave St. Edward's in 1871 because of chronic recurrent bronchial trouble; and during the Christmas holidays of 1874, which he and Kenneth were spending with Uncle Jack, he went down with severe inflammation of the lungs. Granny Ingles was hastily summoned, and doctors fought to save him: but on New Year's Eve he died without rallying. He was sixteen years old. The funeral was held early in January, and Willie was buried beside his grandfather in Highgate Cemetery, where many Grahames lie. 'Close by', Grahame noted laconically, when he visited the site on 22nd April 1887, 'is the grave of Rossetti's father, mother, and wife.'[45] Another bond had been broken; and yet more disillusion was to come. The Golden Age was fast dissolving in the stress of adult realities, and its memory became increasingly precious as time drew relentlessly on.

A LONDON PRELUDE
1876-1878

'And yet, (said I) people go through the world very well, and carry on the business of life to good advantage, without learning.' JOHNSON: 'Why, Sir, that may be true in cases where learning cannot possibly be of any use; for instance, this boy rows us as well without learning, as if he could sing the song of Orpheus to the Argonauts, who were the first sailors.' He then called to the boy, 'What would you give, my lad, to know about the Argonauts?' 'Sir, (said the boy) I would give what I have.'

Boswell's Life of Johnson

The dust of London fills the eyes and blurs the vision; but it penetrates deeper than that. There is a dust that chokes the spirit, and it is this that makes the streets so long, the stones so stony, the desk so wooden; the very rustiness of the iron railings about the offices sets the teeth on edge, the sooty blackened walls (yet without shadow) thrust back the sympathies which are ever trying to cling to the inanimate things around us.

RICHARD JEFFERIES: *Nature Near London*

It seems clear that, all through his school-days, Grahame assumed himself to be destined for Oxford. His natural aptitude for the humanities would, indeed, have gained him an easy entrance, and he would in all likelihood have done well enough there to emulate Lewis Carroll and become a don. Such an existence he would have found congenial above all others: in later years he envied his friend Sir Arthur Quiller-Couch, who so comfortably blended his academic and literary lives. The social aspects of Oxford also appealed to him; he once wrote to Sir Sydney Cockerell that 'as a manner of life I like Feasts and going on to rooms, and could contentedly spend most of my existence that way'.[1] And for the place itself, with its timeless air of mediaeval-ism, its pageantry, its scholarship, its colour and light and Gothic architecture, he had conceived a deep and abiding passion. Years afterwards he still took a particular pleasure in showing visitors round, and astonished them by the variety and exactitude of his knowledge.

We should not forget, either, that to an intelligent upper-class English boy of the period an Oxford education was taken for granted: it was a part of the natural order of things, as inevitable as moon, sun, and stars. Such an assumption is not altogether dead even today, and Grahame, with his passion for traditional English observances, must have leaned heavily on it—so heavily that (like most adolescents) he failed to reckon the financial cost which four years at Oxford would involve. Uncle John, however, was not an upper-class Englishman but a middle-class Scot, and therefore less indifferent to such mundane details. He informed his nephew bluntly that Oxford was out of the question. Kenneth pleaded with him desperately, promising to live, while up, with the strictest economy, to take a brilliant degree, to become a dis-tinguished member of a High Table, or one of the learned pro-fessions. But Uncle John, that dour and practical business-man, was adamant. Granny Ingles induced her son David to put in a word with Mr. Lidderdale, and Kenneth was in due course nominated to a clerkship in the Bank of England. There was a waiting-list, however: no vacancy would occur till 1879. Uncle John proposed that Kenneth should spend the two intervening years in his, Uncle John's, office at Westminster, and Kenneth had no option but to agree.[2]

This was the most crushing blow that Grahame suffered, perhaps, in his whole life; nothing else had such radical and far-

The Ridgeway, near Streatley
Fowey Estuary

reaching consequences. It not only meant that he was condemned to enter the Bank; it effectively deprived him of escape from it at a later date. To do any of the things which Grahame envisaged as his life's work—to pursue an academic career above all—an Oxford or Cambridge degree was absolutely essential. 'I think at one time', wrote his cousin, Annie Grahame, 'he hoped to get a post as Inspector of Schools, but whenever he applied for anything he was turned down through no fault of his own because he had never been to College and taken his degree. I've always thought it splendid of him to stick to his work at the Bank as he did.'[3] Chalmers claims that he was 'always too big for a less than philosophical view of life';[4] but the testimony of relatives, no less than his own early work, makes it plain that, for the first few years at any rate, he resented bitterly the uncongenial task thus forced upon him.

The nature of this resentment requires careful examination. Grahame's bitterness is not general but specific. He is not, like Housman, cursing 'whatever brute or blackguard made the world', he is damning his relatives. And he is not (when we go into the matter more closely) damning them, out of spite, for their unfortunate poverty; on the contrary, the burden of his complaint is precisely that they had the money, but refused to use it for his benefit. 'During his minority he has lain entirely at their mercy: has been their butt, their martyr, their drudge, their *corpus vile*. Possessing all the sinews of war this stiff-necked tribe has consistently refused to part: even for the provision of those luxuries so much more necessary than necessities.'[5] The phrasing of this passage suggests that Grahame was thinking of his late adolescence rather than his childhood; that the martyrdom and drudgery were the duties imposed on him as a clerk; and that the valuable luxury for which his elders would not provide was a university education. Now we have seen already that Granny Ingles, on Helen's testimony, was really poor. The inference is clear enough: Uncle John put his high-falutin nephew into a practical job to bring him to his senses, and teach him his rôle in society as a *de facto* orphan. It was not that he could not afford to send Kenneth to Oxford; he disapproved of such a step on principle.

If this conjecture be true, it makes Kenneth's attitude far more comprehensible. It explains why he was not only miserable but angry, why he indulged in such ferocious compensation-fantasies about his relatives, why he went out of his way to satirize the Olympians as materialistic, arbitrary, and mean. And the conjecture can be tentatively carried one step further. A peculiar characteristic of the Olympians is their readiness to break promises.[6] Is it possible that Kenneth made earlier enquiries, and was led to suppose that a special effort at school would be suitably rewarded? Certainly he worked like a demon in his last year, as the cluster of prizes and his position as Head of the Sixth amply demonstrate. To be told *then* that Oxford was out of the question —especially if he had a fair notion of Uncle John's financial resources—would indeed have given him adequate grounds for bitterness and resentment.

'Schoolboy hopes these,' he wrote in 'A Funeral',[7] 'comically misshapen, tawdry and crude in colour—let the pit receive them, and a good riddance! . . . It is time to have done with fancies and get back to a world of facts. If only one could! Well, one can but try. It will be easier, now that they are really buried all. Hail and farewell to the short-lived dead!' It is not surprising that relatives speak of strained relations between uncle and nephew; nor that old Dr. Kingdon, the Surgeon to the Bank of England (and not a man to suffer whimsy gladly), should have observed that Kenneth's uncle did not seem to understand the boy.[8] Indeed, the *mores* of his class and age entirely sanctioned Uncle John's attitude. As Mr. John Marlowe recently pointed out,[9] 'much of the energy and driving force of the Victorian middle class was derived from the feeling of servility which was associated with financial dependence. This attitude of mind meant that the whole subject of money and property became hedged about with a peculiar sanctity . . . a man losing his money was the equivalent of a woman losing her virtue.'

Both socially and financially Grahame was completely helpless. Even if it had occurred to him to disregard the decisions made on his behalf, he could have taken no effective action. But, given the assumptions governing his particular social class, there is no reason to suppose that the possibility of active rebellion even entered his head. Protest, unorthodoxy, disobedience—these were things to be released only through the disguising medium of the imagination. Grahame himself would have been horrified at any suggestion that he should overthrow those traditional dogmas of family loyalty by which his life was regulated. In order to understand him we must recognize that this pull towards discipline, duty, obligation, and conformity was at least as strong as the anarchic individualism which complemented it; and that the tension set up by these two forces in conflict was an essential element in his creative process. When the tension slackens, and more particularly when the dilemma is finally resolved, the impulse to write dwindles and dies.

But in 1876 the emotional tug-of-war had only begun, and its effects were as yet incalculable. What it seems to have done right from the beginning was to establish a violent dualism in Grahame's mind, a dualism that invaded every aspect of his personality and work, and manifested itself in several distinct forms. One of the most interesting is the habit he developed of setting the two halves of his ego arguing; sometimes obliquely, disguised as separate characters, sometimes in open schizophrenia. In the latter category comes a passage describing how, day-dreaming of lotus-land, his thoughts

> flew back to the far-away northern island, arena of strife and all the crowd of petty vexations. Now, how small they all seemed! How simple the unravelling of baffling knots! How orderly and easy the way to meet them and brush them by! So that I,

sitting there in the South, seemed to be saying to my struggling self in the North, 'If I were you, how easily would I make my way through these petty obstacles! And how helpless and incapable you are in a little strait!' And myself in the North, put on defence, seemed to reply: 'And if I were you, so would I—with your fuller knowledge, fuller strength. As it is, perhaps on the whole I do my best.' And myself in the South, in justice forced to assent, returned, 'Well, yes, perhaps after all you do your best—a sorry best, but as much as can fairly be expected of you.' Then I woke, startled at the point to which my dream had led me.[10]

Elsewhere [11] he conducts a sprightly argument between the Self and the Subconscious Ego; and one of the themes discussed (under the heading of '"approve" or "not approve"') is his longing to 'proceed to your M.A., pay your fees, and in due course settle down in a College living'. The Self comments on this: 'Well, if you do, you must be prepared to justify yourself. If there is to be no "approval" or "disapproval" but allowance and acceptance instead [i.e. if the social and moral puritan ethic is finally rejected] be prepared to justify that allowance and acceptance.' Throughout his work, in one shape or another, the moral conflict recurs. Grahame was not (as has sometimes been supposed) a wistful anarchist who lacked the courage of his convictions; the division, the battle, was in himself. Only half his nature fought against the things he satirized; a fact recognized by a reviewer of *Pagan Papers*,[12] who observed that while posing as an unregenerate child of Nature, he had every appearance of respectability.

The climate of the age encouraged this split approach to life, and Victorian literature is full of it: the result was what Holbrook Jackson described as 'a glorification of the fine arts and mere artistic virtuosity on the one hand, and a militant commercial movement on the other'.[13] Stevenson summed it up in a strikingly relevant phrase: 'Shrilly sound Pan's pipes; and behold the banker instantly concealed in the bank parlour'.[14] Arnold had crystallized the attitude of the opposition, locating the evil in industrialism,

purely material ideals, the repression of instinct, the spiritual
sterility that was a direct product of a puritan cash-morality. He
saw, too, the force of repressive public opinion and the dualism
it was liable to produce:

> Put quite simply, Arnold felt that the temper of Victorian
> society was destructive of individual integrity and wholeness of
> being. . . . Whether the social mask be worn instinctively to
> hide an inner vacuity, or whether it be deliberately assumed to
> shield a central core of sensitivity, the penalty is the same: dis-
> integration of individuality, estrangement not only from one's
> kind, but from oneself as well.[15]

The age that produced Grahame's *The Golden Age* also threw up
Stevenson's *Dr. Jekyll and Mr. Hyde*.

The result of this atmosphere was to produce a pregnant contrast between the business-man and the country vagabond, entirely
to the latter's advantage; and a whole crop of stories appeared in
which stockbrokers and similar urban figures broke loose, lost
their memories, vanished, hit the trail, went West or South,
kicked over the traces, and in various ways displayed a pretty
blend of fugal neurosis and resurgent natural instincts. This
literary symptom of the current social malaise is well represented
in Grahame's work. Rat, in 'Wayfarers All', is so painfully
affected by the Call of the South that his eyes change colour, and
he displays other interesting hysterical symptoms. A bespatted
member of the Baltic Exchange disappears to Italy periodically
via the National Gallery, and suffers amnesia on his return. A
character called Fothergill 'dies to Bloomsbury' by buying a
Whitechapel barrow complete with donkey, on which 'he passed
out of our lives by way of the Bayswater Road', to end up, not
surprisingly, on the Berkshire Downs. Yet another stockbroker
('a good portly man, i' faith: and had a villa and a steam launch
at Surbiton') disappears from home and business, to be found
weeks later in ragged country clothes, by a Hampshire river-bank,
tickling trout with village urchins; 'and when they would have

won him to himself with horrid whispers of American Rails, he answered but with babble of green fields'. Nevertheless, inevitably, Throgmorton Street gets him back in the end. He has had his fling; but the social fabric must be preserved.

Not nearly enough has been made of Grahame's successful career at the Bank of England. To the individual, the anarchic artist in him, it must have been the equivalent of selling out to the enemy for a handful of silver. The Bank was the very nerve-centre through which operated the speculators and big business firms to whom industrialism was the breath of life. It was the Bank that in 1842 decided to lend up to £250,000 on railway development—a sum which by 1851 had swollen to £3,070,000 in debentures spread among eleven railway companies. As Sir John Clapham observes, 'over 9000 miles of line were authorized and nearly 1900 miles opened in Britain between 31 December 1843 and 1 January 1848'. It was the Bank he served for so long which directly supported what Grahame described as 'the iron tetter that scurfs the face of our island [and] has killed out the pleasant life of the road'. It is easy to see how bitter the internal conflict, in his early years at least, must have been.

Yet there was no breaking away from the prescribed order of things. Grahame was enough of a child of his time to accept unquestioningly the bonds against which his spirits chafed. Besides, he had banking in his Scots blood; there was always present in his character an element which, far from opposing middle-class mercantilism, was largely identified with its interests, and which became increasingly predominant as time went on.

Only Stevenson, of all those who set down their Hesperidean dreams on paper, made them finally come true in the fullest sense. For Grahame there is always the tension—between Freedom and Order, Pleasure and Duty, Home and Abroad, Dream and Reality. It is the tension, in fact, that stimulated him, he persuades himself, in an essay written when he was thirty-six and already well on the road to success both as banker and writer:

The most of us prefer to fight on—mainly, perhaps, from cowardice, and the dread of a plunge into a new element, new conditions, new surroundings—a fiery trial for any humble, mistrustful creature of use-and-wont. And yet it is not all merely a matter of funk. For a grim love grows up for the sword-play itself, for the push and the hurtle of battle, for the grips and the give-and-take—in time, for the fight itself, whatever the cause. In this exaltation, far from ignoble, we push and worry along until a certain day of a mist and a choke, and we are ticked off and done with.

It is a revealing apologia, and reminds us of the long line of Edinburgh divines, advocates, and accountants which formed Grahame's ancestry. But he had been vouchsafed his vision, and had denied it—or was robbed of it by circumstance. Over and over again comes the bitter confession of failure: 'To know what you would like to do is one thing; to go out boldly and do it is another—and a rarer; and the sterile fields about Hell-Gate are strewn with the corpses of those who would an if they could'.[16]

It may be doubted whether Uncle John could have chosen a profession for Kenneth which more aptly symbolized everything against which the boy's instincts rebelled. Yet we should not condemn his action out of hand. By his own lights he acted for the best. Oxford, it should be remembered, did not enter into the Grahames' scheme of things. The academic life meant nothing in their tradition. Like most middle-class Calvinist families, they either served God or Mammon, and occasionally defied Holy Writ by doing both: especially when practising at the Bar. To John Grahame his nephew's request must have seemed not only fanciful but reprehensible, mere dilettantism. Besides, it was high time the boy was earning his keep. So he probably argued, bewildered and annoyed at the trick Nature had played by placing this literary cuckoo in a solid, respectable Scots nest.

What passed between the two of them at that crucial interview will never be known. But at all events things were arranged in such a way that Kenneth was not obliged to live with Uncle John till he found his own feet in London. Another of his father's brothers, Uncle Robert, offered him accommodation in his own house, Draycott Lodge, and Kenneth gratefully accepted. No doubt John Grahame, too, was relieved at not having so reserved and enigmatic a boy under his roof as a permanent guest. He probably saw quite enough of him during working hours at Westminster.

Robert Grahame was a merchant who had spent much of his life abroad in Manila. His wife Georgina was later to write, anonymously, a charming book called *In a Tuscan Garden*, which described life in their summer villa near Florence, and contains references to Kenneth's visits. They had one daughter, Annie, with whom Kenneth struck up an immediate friendship; and this continued for many years, long after Kenneth had moved elsewhere. He remained at Draycott Lodge till his entry into the Bank; it was conveniently handy for Westminster, an old-fashioned house between the King's Road and Fulham. In 1876 Fulham was still a small village in the midst of market gardens; since then the market gardens have vanished, and Draycott Lodge with them.[17]

If Kenneth had to live in London, Chelsea and Westminster were far more pleasant than most districts; but what stuck in his throat was having to live in London at all. It was a penance he endured as well as he could, and indeed made the best of: but a penance it remained. Eighteen years later, in *The Yellow Book*, side by side with Grahame's own 'Roman Road', John Davidson wrote a ballad of a thirty-bob-a-week clerk which exactly caught the mood shared by Grahame and thousands more urban workers, now as then:[18]

> For like a mole I journey in the dark,
> A-travelling along the underground
> From my Pillar'd Halls and broad suburban Park
> To come the daily dull official round;

And home again at night with my pipe all alight
A-scheming how to count ten bob a pound.

We shall meet that mole again; but it is not till 1908 that he
finally bursts into the light and enjoys the sunny, uninterrupted
pleasures of total irresponsibility.

The prevalent attitude of writers to London ever since the
Industrial Revolution (and often before: consider Johnson's
diatribe) had been one of moral and physical disgust, symbolized
by Cobbett's clinically exact image of the 'Great Wen'. The
agricultural slump was largely caused by the draining of countrymen into the towns for higher wages, and accelerated by the
import of cheap American grain. Add to this the impact of the
railways, the spread of the suburbs, and the passing of the Union
Chargeability Act in 1865 (which 'finally detached the labourer
from his place of settlement . . . and created mobility of labour'):
the result was the end of village life (as Hardy, Rider Haggard,
and Richard Jefferies all perceived) and, in Dr. Trevelyan's words,
'the general divorce of Englishmen from life in contact with
nature, which in all previous ages had helped to form the mind
and the imagination of the island race'.[19]

To intelligent and sensitive writers who knew the full meaning
of this upheaval, who could gauge just what intangible element
was being lost for ever from English life, and at what cost, London
stood as the visible symbol of the Enemy, the Destroyer. Its
swarming slums, its granite pavements, its foul fogs and polluted
air, its counting-houses and banks, its prostitutes and gin-palaces,
its ceaseless noise, all summed up the new way of life which was
spreading like a cancer to engulf the old in the sacred name of
Progress.

Mr. Lionel Trilling, in his study of Matthew Arnold, takes this
point somewhat further.[20] He reminds us that Victorian London,
with its terrible contrasts of poverty and wealth, 'is not merely
a symbol, it is the actual product of the nineteenth-century
economic life, of the uncontrolled development of manufacture.

And just as the latter-day Greeks and the imperial Romans felt deracinated in their great cities, so the modern men feel that their roots lie elsewhere, and, like the ancients, yearn back to nature in idyll and in pastoral.' Horror and nostalgia form the twin keynotes of the literature devoted to the subject, from Morris's *Earthly Paradise* to Henley's virulent and hysterical *London Voluntaries*, with its 'hangman wind' and 'excremental humours':

> A cave of cut-throat thoughts and villainous dreams,
> Hag-rid and crying with dirt and cold and wet.
> The afflicted City . . . seems
> A nightmare labyrinthine, dim and drifting . . .
> Wherein the lamplight, scattered and sick and pale,
> Shows like the leper's living blotch of bale:
> Uncoiling monstrous into street on street
> Paven with perils, teeming with mischance.[21]

In this Goyaesque sub-world grim new forces were stirring, that fed on poverty and despair. In 1867 the first volume of *Das Kapital* appeared; in 1871 an engineering strike paralysed northeast England; in 1875 the right to picket and strike was firmly established by law, in an Act that was also concerned with 'Improving Artisans' Dwellings'. Everywhere there was change, unrest, disruption of tradition. Grahame could hardly have enjoyed the atmosphere of this London, so far removed from Dunbar's 'Queen of Cities all'. But he had no choice in the matter: and London became his home (though he escaped from it whenever possible) for the next thirty years. It was only two years before his retirement that he escaped permanently to Berkshire and the quiet backwaters of the Thames.

Nevertheless, if he was unhappy in London, he took some trouble to conceal the fact. He dined with Uncle John at Sussex Gardens on every second Sunday, both before and after he went into the Bank; and to him he presented a front of Stoic cheerfulness and determination over the *fait accompli* of his career which won the older man's admiration. 'Pluck and steadiness' were the words Uncle John chose to describe Kenneth's attitude; and his cousin Agnes recalled of these occasions that 'it was a pleasure to see him come into the room, he looked so happy and pleasant. He was neither too talkative nor too reserved.'

Already the public mask was slipping into place, the gap between appearance and reality widening. 'I have never heard him talk about himself', Agnes added, and we can see this reticence as characteristic of something more than modesty.[22] The nearest Kenneth came to telling the truth about himself was, paradoxically, in his published work. Through this stylized *persona* he could speak more honestly than when he wrote as himself, even as a diarist or in his love-letters. As Mr. David Daiches observed of Grahame's master Stevenson (whom his private self in many ways also resembles) 'his essays became more and more a sort of mental overflow into which he put expressions and confessions that arose directly out of the development of this inner mental life'.[23]

Certainly there was no apparent rupture during this difficult period between Kenneth and any of his relatives. Christmas 1876 found him, together with Roland, staying at Halstead Vicarage in Essex, where Uncle David and his family had migrated two years previously.[24] Granny Ingles was a frequent visitor there also. The following September was spent in Scotland, where Uncle John had rented a holiday house near Pitlochry. Besides Agnes and Walter, his own children, and Kenneth, Helen, and Roland, he had also invited his niece Annie—Uncle Robert's daughter—who wrote of this visit: 'We certainly didn't bother ourselves about politics or anything abstruse [presumably a reference to Uncle John's profession]—but I had been reared on old Scotch ballads and stories and folklore which appealed to Kenneth also, and later on at any rate formed a bond of union between us'. The holiday was apparently a success; at any rate it was repeated, probably in 1881, and on this occasion, Annie remembered, 'Kenneth brought with him a copy of *Uncle Remus* which had just come out, I think;—at any rate none of us had ever heard of it;—and he was continually reading and quoting from it.'[25]

While he was attached to the firm of Grahame, Currie, and Spens—the attachment, to judge by Cousin Agnes' recollections, was a decidedly vague one[26]—Kenneth occupied some of his time in learning shorthand.[27] Perhaps his aim was to become a parliamentary reporter, like one of his favourite authors, Dickens; if so, the attempt to break away from the prescribed *cursus honorum* was frowned upon, even by a parliamentary agent. Authors, in Uncle John's opinion, were *flâneurs*, not really gentlemen, and liable to immorality: Mr. Dickens' private life was no example to follow. The boy was obviously leading too sedentary a life; it was making him liverish and unsettled. The best thing he could do would be to join the Volunteers—plenty of good hard drill.[28]

Kenneth, as usual, took up the suggestion without fuss, and worked at it with dogged conscientiousness. Besides, at least half his own nature was highly suspicious of journalism and professional authors; to the end of his life he held that writing was a gentleman's spare-time occupation, not to be contaminated with money or deadlines or hack-work. This did not (as Wilfred Gibson once observed) prevent him habitually bargaining for unusually good terms, even with the publishers of his first book: he was, after all, a Scots banker as well as an English essayist.

The Volunteers as a body had been founded, as we have seen, in 1859, and had since grown and proliferated considerably. Kenneth and Roland naturally joined the London Scottish, and there is a photograph of Kenneth at this period in uniform, grey kilt, ornate bonnet and sporran, belt and swagger-stick. He has grown a small military moustache to go with the part, and sits facing the camera with military self-assurance—hands on spread knees, the swagger-stick between, bonnet cockily askew. But the eyes are remote and defensive, the face set in blank expressionlessness; one senses the mask again. Kenneth threw himself into drill, and boxing, and fencing, with abandon: such activities kept him healthy and occupied. (In that sense Uncle John had been quite right.[29]) Later he became a sergeant; and there is a delightful story of his leading a most unorthodox sort of charge in Hyde Park.

It came about in this way. Kenneth and Roland were regular guests at the Lidderdales', and had made great friends with their two baby daughters. (The connection was strengthened by the fact that the Grahames' old Scots nurse, Ferguson, had now moved on to the Lidderdale household; possibly as a *quid pro quo* on Granny Ingles' part in acknowledgment of Kenneth's nomination.) One day when they were drilling in the Park, Ferguson wheeled the Lidderdale girls over to watch, in their large, shiny double perambulator. This was more than Sergeant Grahame could resist; when he recognized his admirers, he

> ordered a complimentary charge to be made on the perambulator. His platoon, flourishing its muskets, therefore advanced with leaps, bounds and loud cheers. The two objectives in the perambulator were enchanted. Not so their guardian, who thought that her Master Kenneth had 'gone gyte'.[30]

Kenneth seldom 'went gyte', as we shall see; and when he did let himself go in this way it was more often than not with children, who could be relied on not to mistake his mood.

London offered other compensatory pleasures to the imaginative. Grahame had discovered Soho, as we might expect, immediately on arrival. He developed a passion for wandering through the Italian quarter, fascinated by the exotic little restaurants, the unfamiliar but beautifully cadenced language, the warmth and friendliness of the atmosphere. It offered him something more than cheap but delicious wine and food; it kindled that passion for the south which sustained him steadily throughout his long years in the City, and led him on those first breathtaking pilgrimages he made to Florence and Rome during his summer vacations. He formed the habit of dining in Soho once a week if he could afford it; and at one of these dinners he made the acquaintance of a most remarkable man, a huge, grey-bearded, heavily-muscled lion of about fifty, who attracted Grahame's attention by his Johnsonian dogma and Rabelaisian wit. Their eyes met over a joke; the stranger invited Grahame to join his party; and they finished the evening (after putting away a good deal of cheap red wine) by solemnly exchanging cards. The stranger's name was Furnivall, and the meeting took place towards the end of Grahame's first year in London.[31]

Frederick James Furnivall has been aptly described as a 'living and talking library, more comforting, indeed more delightful and cheering, than a visit even to the British Museum'.[32] His interests were certainly wide. He read mathematics at Cambridge, was later called to the Bar, but abandoned both when he became involved in the Christian Socialist Movement led by F. D. Maurice. He also developed an early interest in music and philology, and in 1849 began a long friendship with Ruskin, which lasted till the latter's death. He 'lectured on English poetry from Chaucer to Tennyson', and in the sixties began exploring early and middle English literature, particularly the Arthurian romances. His editing labours soon crystallized in the founding of the Early English Text Society, with Tennyson and Ruskin among the first subscribers. Some three years before his meeting with Grahame he had also launched the New Shakespere Society, which became especially associated with dating Shakespeare by metrical tests. This practice called out a good deal of petulant ridicule from predominantly aesthetic critics, culminating in a pamphlet entitled *Furnivallos Furioso*. The epithet was, perhaps, not entirely unjustified.[33]

The oddly assorted pair took to each other instinctively. Furnivall was everything that the Olympians were not: a wild man of letters, a prodigious scholar, a natural odd man out, a Bohemian, a drinker, a savant who held court on the first floor of the New Oxford Street A.B.C., who took slum children to Kew Gardens, marched round London in red shirt-sleeves, and was likened by one country wag to the Prophet Jeremiah. When a stranger wrote to ask when the E.E.T.S. edition of Boëthius' *De Consolatione Philosophiae* would appear, he replied to the effect that he really could not say, and would the enquirer undertake to edit it himself?[34] Once he started talking 'the difficulty was to stop his flow of speech, as many a chairman found to his dismay. He was irrepressible. Relevance never troubled him.'[35] Strangest of all, and a supreme attraction as far as Grahame was concerned, he was a champion sculler, and devoted to the life of the river; yet, paradoxically, he had never learnt to swim.

As early as 1845 he had devised and helped to build two sculling boats of a new and radical design. Sir Sidney Lee records that 'a wager boat on Furnivall's lines was soon built for the champion sculler, Newell'.[36] From 1861 onwards Furnivall ran a highly successful working man's rowing club on the Thames. He conducted a ferocious campaign against the Amateur Rowing Association for excluding artisans from the 'amateur' class in sculling; his vitality won him as many friends as his tactlessness made him enemies. Warm-hearted, fiery-tempered, humane, irreligious, a scholarly radical and radical scholar, he was exactly the fermenting influence which Grahame needed. The debt was acknowledged, many years later, in an oblique portrait, or rather, two half-portraits, as we shall see: in what form, the percipient may guess from Miss Jessie Currie's picture:[37]

When I took a studio at No. 4 St George's Square, Primrose Hill, the outgoing tenant said, 'Let me introduce you to Dr Furnivall. He will ask you if you can scull. If you say "No", he will take you up the river to teach you. If you say "Yes", he will take you up the river to keep you in practice. He will take you anyhow.' . . .

I could not help smiling as, after a little enquiry about my work, he [Dr. Furnivall] asked, 'Can you scull?' When I answered 'Yes', his whole face beamed. 'How jolly!' he exclaimed. 'I hope you will often come up the river with us.'

. . . I met him shortly after nine o'clock on the appointed

morning, as he was coming out from his house. Two large
string bags were slung over his left shoulder—one hanging in
front, the other behind. These, with a third bag in his right
hand, were all full of good things to eat. . . .

Back at Richmond the club boats went on to Hammersmith,
but the Doctor would take his party to the station by queer
narrow back streets, in one of which there was a quaint little
'tuck-shop'. Into this he would suddenly disappear, and those
of the party who did not know that the floor of the shop was
two steps below the level of the street, literally dived after
him. . . .

Xanadu, as Professor Livingston Lowes discovered, can be
reached by many strangely devious routes; and much hetero-
geneous material and experience sinks into the well of the subconscious before the creative spring brings it up once more,
almost—but not quite—unrecognizable.

Grahame joined the New Shakespere Society on Friday 9th
June 1877, and the records of the Society show that his cousin
Annie, who shared his literary interests with such sympathy,
became a member at the same time.[38] For three years he attended
the Friday meetings at University College in Gower Street; and
then in 1880 Furnivall invited him to become Honorary Secretary
of the Society. He accepted, and continued to discharge this office
till the Society's final dissolution in 1891. During all this time he
never once delivered a paper or voiced a personal opinion on any
subject, which must constitute something of a record. He may
well have been walking warily, like Agag, to keep out of the way
of the polemical brickbats buzzing round his President's head; for
about the time Grahame became Secretary the quarrel with the
aesthetes was assuming vast proportions. Swinburne, who at first
supported Furnivall, had suddenly made a *volte-face* and published
a satirical skit on the Society; Furnivall replied with a fine piece of
invective, and was soon referring to Swinburne, in print, as 'Pigs-
brook'. By 1881 complaints were reaching Browning, the senior
vice-president of the Society, of Furnivall's 'coarse and imperti-

nent language'. Furnivall went on exactly as before, and many of the Society's more distinguished vice-presidents (though not Browning himself) resigned. From this scandal the Society never fully recovered, though it struggled on for another decade.[39]

Grahame's specifically literary debt to Furnivall is obvious and considerable. It embraces his close acquaintance with (at one end of the scale) Malory, Hakluyt, the Arthurian romances, and above all Shakespeare; and (at the other) his passion for Browning, Shelley, Ruskin, and Morris. Furnivall founded both the Browning and Shelley Societies, and would probably, given the chance, have extended his organizing activities to his other favourites. So, too, it was through Furnivall's agency that Grahame gained his *entrée* to the outer circle of that literary society which revolved round Tennyson and Browning, and first met the bright young men and women who were later to be his fellow-contributors to the *National Observer* and *The Yellow Book*. And at some point during their early acquaintance Grahame showed Furnivall, very tentatively, his own unpublished jottings, and asked his advice on what to do with them.

It seems fairly clear that he had been writing, in private, ever since his first anonymous contributions to the *St. Edward's School Chronicle*, though without any definite idea of publication. Mostly he composed poems; but there is a hint that he may also have tried his hand at political journalism. About the time that he was practising his shorthand and listening to the professional gossip in Uncle John's office—gossip, be it noted, of a strong Tory flavour— a series of articles began to appear in the *Chronicle* entitled 'Passing Events', and signed simply 'Old Boy'. Four were published in all, between February and July 1878. They were written in just that blend of smooth political cliché and schoolboyish enthusiasm we might expect from a clever, imitative nineteen-year-old in Grahame's position. The first, after an assured analysis of the Russo-Turkish war, and a rap over the knuckles for Stanley about atrocities, suddenly turns to a lament for the recently dead cartoonist, George Cruickshank; the third discusses the awful likelihood of whisky or tobacco being taxed; while the last is a most fulsome tribute to Disraeli on his return from the Berlin Congress.[40] 'Old Boy' was thereupon replaced, in the December issue, by a correspondent of more Liberal convictions.

It is impossible to prove that 'Old Boy' was Kenneth Grahame, but there is at least strong circumstantial evidence suggesting that he may have been. Grahame was associated with a parliamentary agent who was a strong supporter of Toryism in general, and Lord Beaconsfield in particular. He was probably trying to equip himself for a new career as a political journalist: there is no other conceivable reason why, placed as he was, he should take the trouble to teach himself shorthand. The temptation to try out his paces on the school magazine—and perhaps convince Uncle John by a virtuoso display of political expertise—must have been overwhelming. But apparently neither Uncle John nor the editor of the *Chronicle* was over-impressed; and as we know, the project (if it was ever seriously considered) soon fell through. The New Year, bringing Grahame's final committal to the Bank, drew steadily closer. The last card had been played and lost.

What he showed Furnivall, however, was something very different. In a 'small ledger book, no doubt originally bound for the baser uses of the Bank and its balances'[41]—and therefore not begun before 1879—he had taken to scribbling down odd quotations that caught his fancy, short anecdotes, scraps of highly personal prose,[42] and a series of poems composed by himself. This ledger disappeared at some time after Mrs. Grahame's death in 1946, and all efforts to trace it have failed. We can, nevertheless, form a fairly clear picture of its contents, since Chalmers quotes from it liberally, and Mr. Roger Lancelyn Green (who also examined it, albeit hurriedly and under difficult conditions) has made notes of the poems. He describes them (with reservations) as '*very* artificial in type, rather the pretty-pretty Dobson kind of thing',[43] an opinion on the whole confirmed both by the extracts

Chalmers prints, and by such complete poems as survive in various periodicals.[44] In the circumstances it is not surprising that Furnivall, while recommending Grahame to send his work to editors, strongly advised him to give up poetry and stick to prose. Posterity has confirmed his purely literary verdict: but the biographer may be grateful that some at least of these poems survive.[45]

As far as we can judge, the extracts printed by Chalmers, in whatever form, tally exactly with Grahame's inner moods during this period. Solitude is evoked by the twice-repeated quotation from Caxton's *Golden Legend* about the 'felowe that goes alone'. Pagan pessimism is served by Herrick:

> Born was I to be old
> And for to die here;
> After that, in the mould
> Long for to lye here.

That, of course, is only the first half of the poem; and I suspect that Chalmers, not Grahame, was responsible for suppressing the last four lines, which entirely suit Grahame's character:

> But before that day comes
> Still I be Bousing;
> For I know, in the Tombs
> There's no Carousing.

From Matthew Arnold's 'Lines written in Kensington Garden' the young clerk drew a stanza which exactly echoed his own dilemma:

> In the huge world which roars hard by,
> Be others happy if they can!
> But in my helpless cradle I
> Was breathed on by the rural Pan.

He must have pondered, though he did not quote, the verse with which this poem ends:

> The will to neither strive nor cry,
> The power to feel with others give!

Calm, calm me more! nor let me die
Before I have begun to live.

Then, with seasonal cheerfulness breaking through, he turned to
Horace. The familiar Ode—it was also one of Housman's favourites—deals with melting snow, spring, the beginning of the boating season: all things dear to Grahame's heart, the obverse of the
dark yearning drawn by Arnold:

Solvitur acris hiems grata vice veris et Favoni,
     trahuntque siccas machinae carinas.

This Grahame loosely paraphrased in a rhymed triplet (it is his
only known translation) as follows:

Gone are the snows and April come is she;
The West Wind blows and, down loud beaches, we
Once more our prows propel to their blue sea.[46]

'Boats,' he wrote, many years later, to a little girl who had sent
him a letter about *The Wind in the Willows*, 'boats are the only
things worth living for—any sort.'[47] Yet, just as Herrick's poem
balances the gloomy and cheerful aspects of the pagan attitude, so
Horace's picture of spring-time pleasures, with its dancing nymphs
and myrtle-wreaths, suddenly dissolves into a ghastly warning of
death's inevitability, the transience of all human desires and
affections, the *vitae summa brevis*.

Grahame's own contributions to the ledger show considerable
range of mood. At one extreme is his pessimistic poem 'As You
Like It', which was published in the *National Observer* in 1891,
and partly reproduced by Chalmers. The first stanza runs:

Life's a jungle, life's a dance,
See the mummers everywhere
Hopping, tossing bells in air—
How the hobby-horses prance!
     I advance
Somewhat sick the round to share.

This image of 'life' as a shadow-show played out by mummers recurs elsewhere: 'our daily round', Grahame wrote in 'Concerning Ghosts',[48] 'is passed among such gibbering simulacra that to foregather with a ghost would be a mild but very real and pleasant relief'. Appearance and reality, in fact, are becoming inverted, or, from another viewpoint, acquiring Platonic values. The 'real' is a permanent disappointment when measured against the 'ideal'; dreams are the only true ideals; Fairyland has probably invented us rather than *vice versa*.[49]

There is (as nearly always) a flicker of cheerful irreverence running through even the most pessimistic of Grahame's utterances, and the tone of this poem is subtly modified by recognition that it probably derived in part from a song of W. S. Gilbert's in *The Gondoliers*:

> Try we life-long, we can never
> Straighten out life's tangled skein,
> Why should we, in vain endeavour,
> Guess and guess and guess again?
> Life's a pudding full of plums,
> Care's a canker that benumbs.
> Wherefore waste our elocution
> On impossible solution?
> Life's a pleasant institution,
> Let us take it as it comes!

Occasionally, too, Grahame tries his hand at the consciously humorous anecdote, somewhere between *Punch* and the *Dolly Dialogues*. It does not show him at his best: it is written (as Mr. Alan Pryce-Jones observed of *Pagan Papers*) 'in that irritatingly facetious style which is the chief objection to trying to be funny in English':[50]

> T'other day I was about to cross the Channel—the usual crowd at the quay. A lady approached me in evident distress—a pretty woman too. 'Sir,' she said, 'my husband disappeared from my side ten minutes ago and I can perceive no trace of him—and now my black poodle has slipped his collar and

escaped!' 'Madam,' said I, severely, 'you are most unreasonable. I can supply the place of your husband to a limited extent, but I'll be hanged if I'll play at being a black poodle for anyone.'

Apart from this, there are several biographically suggestive love poems which will be considered separately in Chapter IX, and two fragments of rather Elia-like speculative prose. One of these, the split-ego discussion on Pleasure in the South and Duty in the North, we have seen earlier in this chapter; the other is a revealing passage on Friendship. The dead, says Grahame, are dearer than the living, 'for though, through circumstance and the sorry, sordid rubs of life, the former may start away, or pale and change till they are perhaps even actively hostile, derogatory, scornful, and love sickens and grows cold, still the dear dead always approve; their sympathies are sure'. And not only the dead, we can deduce. Children grow up, change, forget their old nature, die (in a sense) from what they were. But once they are caught and set down in words, they are fixed for ever, like the figures on Keats' Grecian Urn, in a pose which preserves that ideal moment.

Yet Grahame cannot bear the thought that these idealized companions have failed as adults; and so he transfers the failing to himself: 'The friends of our youth . . . live somewhere yet in the flesh, might be seen and talked with, if we would. But we will not have it, at least yet. Because of the very height of the ideals we shared together, we cannot face them yet, while not one solid step has been made.'[51] To confront remembered dream-children with their real, changed, adult counterparts is a perilous proceeding; and we shall see Grahame more and more uneasy, as time passes, when in the company of his brother and sister. His family were never quite able, or eager, to live up to the private ideal he set them.

How many of these fugitive pieces had been written when Grahame showed Furnivall the ledger we cannot be certain: probably not many, since London editors first began to accept his known work in 1888, and some poems from this source were published as late as 1891–2.[52] It is interesting (and squares with all we know of them) that Grahame had found no one in his own family to whom he was willing to show his prentice work, or who could be expected to take any interest in it: nor, apparently, was there any like-minded spirit at the Bank or among his colleagues in the Volunteers.[53] If he let Cousin Annie share his secret, he certainly did not admit the fact to Furnivall: but since they had been drawn together by their literary interests, it seems likely enough that the ledger had passed through her hands before the Doctor pronounced on its contents. At any rate, from this time forward, Grahame began to submit essays, articles, even stories for publication: and it is possible that some of these early pieces actually appeared in obscure periodicals and have not been traced. Trant Chambers, for instance, referred to 'a pretty little storyette of yours about an aristocratic little girl who made friends with a poor little lad, who subsequently died'.[54] For several years—perhaps not entirely surprisingly if this is a fair sample—'five out of six of my little meteorites', as Grahame put it, 'came back to me'.[55] Meanwhile the material world had closed in on the would-be author, and diverted much of his time and energy into more practical channels. The Olympians, for the time being at least, had the upper hand.

ULYSSES IN
THREADNEEDLE STREET
1879-1887

Unreal City,
Under the brown fog of a winter dawn,
A crowd flowed over London Bridge, so many,
I had not thought death had undone so many.

T. S. ELIOT: The Waste Land

I should like to rise and go
Where the golden apples grow:
Where below another sky
Parrot islands anchored lie.

R. L. STEVENSON:
A Child's Garden of Verses

Kenneth Grahame entered the Bank of England as a gentleman-clerk on 1st January 1879, and Threadneedle Street welcomed him with the thickest, yellowest fog that had been seen that winter. Since he had acquired the habit of walking to work (partly for economy's sake and partly for the exercise) he had found it advisable to move his lodgings somewhat nearer the City. From Draycott Lodge, with its clear air and market-gardens, he transferred himself to a 25s.-a-week flat in Bloomsbury Street, which he later shared with Roland when the latter also entered the Bank. On that first morning, conscientious as ever, the new clerk allowed himself ninety minutes to walk a mile and a half through the fog. He arrived in Threadneedle Street on the stroke of ten, and found himself alone in his department, with no superior to report to. 'An hour later', writes Chalmers—a banker himself—'he was to learn from a youthful colleague, in a frock-coat and flourishing whiskers, the first principle of Finance. Which is that a London Particular excuses all things dilatory in a banker and especially is it indulgence, extenuation and ample justification for an extra hour in bed and a leisurely breakfast.'[1] It was a lesson which Kenneth was quick to learn.

He had acquitted himself with distinction in the entrance examination, and his English Essay paper actually gained full marks—a unique achievement, without precedent in the Bank's history, and never afterwards to be repeated. The subject was 'India', and it would have been interesting to see how Grahame approached the subject: but despite its quality the essay was not preserved.[2] We may hazard a guess that its political sentiments were as acceptable to that most conservative of institutions as its literary style: Grahame's views on coloured people were not so much hostile as comfortably superior. Miss R. M. Bradley, daughter of the then Dean of Westminster, recounted how 'he once startled a lunch-table at which the habits of a European potentate then visiting London were under discussion, by announcing "Well, he's a Black", as if that settled the matter. On being asked to explain so inaccurate a statement, he replied blandly: "I divide the whole population of Europe into English people and blacks".'[3] She added in explanation that, despite his wide travels in Southern Europe, this was no pose; he perversely expected a different code of manners from his own countrymen.

There has been a general tendency (largely fostered by Grahame's own early essays) to regard his sojourn at the Bank as an unrelieved grind, the mere means by which he earned a living; and thus to disregard this aspect of his life entirely when considering his literary work. The unspoken inference is, of course, that the two had no connection. A more misleading assumption could hardly be made. When a man spends nearly thirty years in a given profession it leaves its mark on him; and when he is appointed to one of its three highest offices while still under forty we cannot suppose that he treated it as nothing but a bread-and-butter chore. On the one hand, there was banking in Grahame's blood; and on the other, there was much about the Old Lady of Threadneedle Street that was calculated to appeal to the romantic side of his nature. To the spirit of finance, and the disfiguring urbanization it bred, he remained profoundly hostile; but the Bank itself, the visible manifestation of a great and ancient tradition, with its ritual, its liveries, its vaulted strong-rooms packed with gold—that was a different matter entirely.

One of the Bank's first women employees, Miss Jane Hogarth, left a most vivid picture of it about this time:[4]

> The Bank was full of eighteenth-century, and even earlier, survivals, the dress of its gate porters, the 'nightly watch' going round with Guy Fawkes lanterns (I once asked them, when I met them at four o'clock on a summer Saturday afternoon, why they did this and they seemed hardly to know, except that it was an immemorial custom); the company of Guards coming in at sunset, their sentinels stationed in the courtyard . . .; the Bank cats which a parsimonious Governor put down by docking their 'allowance'; the great bars of gold and silver in the fortress-like bullion vaults, brought in from Lothbury under guard through an archway which looked as if it ought to have a portcullis; the almost human gold-weighing machines, which spat out light sovereigns sideways and let the rest fall in a steady stream into copper vessels like coal pans—all the significant evidence of Britain's wealth and British solidarity, so picturesque, so historic, so reassuring, and, in the long run, so unbearably tedious.

Grahame, I suspect, felt much about the Old Lady as Miss Hogarth did: she fascinated him with her ritual, her stability, and her treasure-trove, but finally—and probably long before the end

—bored him by her very immutability and solid assurance. Yet in those earlier, creative years, though he may (as he himself represents) have been a galley-slave, part of his nature at least rejoiced in its chains; and they did not, when all is said, chafe very heavily. Bankers' short hours are proverbial, and even the Old Lady's most junior employees enjoyed a surprising amount of leisure.

The general atmosphere of day-to-day life in the Bank at this period—certainly in the lower échelons—was not by any means so prim, stuffy, or Gladstonian as we might suppose. Eccentricity was common, and rowdyism not unknown: the clerks behaved surprisingly like medical students of the Bob Sawyer vintage, and many of their superiors could have sat for Leech or Boz. The Old Lady, in fact, was so ultra-conservative in her traditions that by 1880 a distinct whiff of the Regency still lingered about her. Allan Fea, who became a clerk two years after Grahame, and first worked in the Private Drawing Office, paints an extraordinary picture of the Bank as it then was—an aspect of Threadneedle Street which the official histories tend to overlook: [5]

> In 1881 [he writes] the Bank was very different from the orderly place it is now, and the above-mentioned department [*i.e.* the Drawing Office] was one of the rowdiest of the lot. The pandemonium was a little startling to a novice—jokes shouted from one end of the office to the other; the singing of a line from some popular song winding up with 'Amen' in a solemn cadence of about a hundred voices. If you were not good at dodging you were liable at any time to have your hat knocked off your head by a flying Pass-book. . . .

Such horseplay was mild in comparison with some of the extra-curricular activities in which the clerks indulged. Drunkenness was extraordinarily prevalent: it was 'by no means uncommon in the eighties to see fellows in the washing-places trying to sober themselves with douses of cold water, or lying prone upon a table for a while, ere they dare return to their desks'.[6] It was not so long since fighting dogs had been chained by those desks, waiting for after-hours bouts down in the lavatories. Some clerks ran small farms outside London, and turned up stinking of the midden; others used to buy their meat in bulk at Billingsgate, and leave it lying about the office: 'it was a very ordinary thing' recalled Fea, 'for the householders in an office to carve up half a sheep downstairs in the washing department'.[7]

Though many of the clerks had private means, and entered the Bank for purely vocational reasons,[8] there seems to have been a scattering of extraordinarily rough diamonds about when Grahame entered on his apprenticeship. (There was an old tradition that till the seventies the Bank had advertised vacancies by a notice on the railings outside; that anyone could apply; and that once a butcher had left his meat with the porter, gone in, and found himself a clerk five minutes later.) Table-manners were appalling, and one man had such objectionable habits of hawking and spitting that the head of his department ordered—not a reprimand, but a free daily issue of sawdust to be scattered round his desk. One elderly superintendent detested elegance, 'frills', or dandyism of any sort, and it may well have been of the sartorially impeccable Grahame that he observed: 'Take a hape and dress 'im in purple and fine linen: what is 'e but a bloody monkey still!' The clerk's *réplique*, some weeks later, is also in character: when the old man went to a funeral, his junior suggested that he 'had gone to pay his tribute by dropping an H on his friend's tomb'.[9]

I suspect that a good deal of Grahame's distaste for his job during the early years may have been due—curiously enough— not to the air of starched Victorian rectitude which one normally associates with banking in the eighties, so much as this atmo- sphere of crass and Philistine licence. Paganism was one thing, this kind of behaviour (as Grahame made clear in 'The Rural Pan'[10]) quite another; Pan and Mercury have little in common, and Grahame's Calvinism was strong enough still to gag at these swillings and oafish crudities of behaviour. On the other hand, he must have relished the more harmless eccentricities in which the Bank abounded; the ancient and decrepit stockholders who appeared on dividend day (including one old lady who asked the cashier to make it as much as he could); another old lady, Amelia Macabe, who dressed like a girl, with a hat like 'a strawberry basket trimmed with white muslin', and distributed booklets of her own poems among the clerks; the raffles before pay-day, at which one enterprising young fellow auctioned his uncle's cremated bones; the strange nick-names—'Job Lot', 'The Dead Horse', 'The Dook', 'The Stiff 'un', 'The Ghost', 'The Maiden Aunt', or 'The 'Orrid Old 'Og'—which the clerks bestowed on each other and their chiefs. (In view of his known passion for the stuff in later life, it is tempting to guess that it was Grahame who was referred to as 'The Ice-Cream Man'; but it was more probably someone with an Italianate name. We hear of a psychic department head named Sperati: it may have been him.[11])

There were, too, plenty of loopholes for escape during working hours. Business was often very slack, and always slack enough to allow time for shopping after lunch—a leisured lunch taken at one of those famous old chop-houses, long since destroyed: the Bay Tree, with its open grill and comfortable pew-seats, where you could get the best steaks in the City; Baker's, whose old-world waiter seemed to belong more to coaching times than Victorian London; Birch's, with its punch and cheese-cakes; Thomas's, where huge chump chops were served off pewter. Full and cheerful, the clerk with his wits about him could always manufacture some errand or other which would leave him free for an hour or two. He might explore the by-ways of old Holborn[12] while officially collecting money from some counting house or other; he might take a 'penny steamer' up to Westminster or down from the Old Swan Pier to Wapping and Shadwell. How even the minimal amount of work required actually got done it is difficult to imagine.

Over the week-ends Grahame's beloved Thames was within fairly easy reach. Fea recounts how one of his seniors, a rowing enthusiast, took him exploring between Henley and Mapledurham,[13] and it seems clear, from chance allusions scattered through *Pagan Papers*, that Grahame also escaped to the peace of the river and the Berkshire countryside whenever he could.[14] Oxford, on the other hand, he never revisited for ten years after he left school: we have his own word for this.[15] Perhaps he could not bear to go near a place that had held out such hopes to him, and won his affection so entirely, only to fade like a mirage when he stretched out his hand to touch it; the wound of disappointment, however well concealed, remained raw and aching.

But as time passed Oxford, too, became incorporated in his private myth. 'During (say) the last five years of those ten', he wrote [*i.e.* from about 1880 to 1885], 'I constantly at night ran down to a fairy Oxford—the real thing, yet transformed, and better, because the Gothic was better—a maze of lovely cloisters and chapels and courts. I used to spend a long day there and come back next morning. At the end of those ten years I happened to revisit the real Oxford several weeks in succession—I spent several weekends there—and at once the fairy Oxford vanished, and is only just beginning to return now, [1896] when I have not seen the real thing for two years. I like the fairy one better!'

This is a curiously prophetic passage; it confirms what one suspects of Grahame's art—that it throve best on deprivation, nostalgia, the ideal never quite attained. When all the barriers were down—when the Eternal City was simply Rome, that could be visited during any month of the year, when there was no compulsion to stay aboard the galley and toil at the oar—then the imaginative impulse failed: reality had displaced it. Grahame needed his bench and shackles: the more illusory they proved in fact, the more vigorously he depicted them in print. Elysium once attained turned out to be, if not commonplace, certainly an anticlimax. He knew the danger himself. 'Think of living in Italy,' he remarked during his first visit to Florence, 'when you might have it to go to.' [16]

Meanwhile London offered not only pleasures but a panorama of life which, for the observant eye, contained its own drama and aesthetic appeal. Grahame discovered (as Louis MacNeice also did half a century later) that

> . . . yet there is beauty narcotic and deciduous
> In this vast organism grown out of us. [17]

Standing in Trafalgar Square he watched the flash and tumble of pigeons, sunlight flaking from their opalescent wings, or a crocodile of schoolgirls tripping by, with restless eyes, glancing ankles, a susurrus of chatter—'and oh, that wave of red hair that flaps on one cool white neck!' Close by the steps of the National Gallery, then as today, a pavement 'screever' was busy with his gaudy chalks. Above, a sky of crystalline blue, and the year's first real sun alchemizing the sooty London wilderness: the young clerk stared entranced, and later caught the scene perfectly in a short essay called, appropriately enough, 'Pastels': [18]

> The buses whirl up and recede in vivid spots of red and blue and green; tawdry house-fronts are transmuted into mellowest shades of blue-grey and tawny; or, freshly-painted, throw up broad masses of dazzling white. A butcher's cart, a child's Tam-o'-Shanter, a mounted orderly jogging from Pall Mall—all join in the conspiracy of colour; and woman everywhere, realizing what she was created for, flecks the canvas with pigments unknown to the dead and buried year. The artist, meanwhile . . . rubs in the white round the widow's cap, brings out the high lights on the greensod, and adds corners of the proper droop to the mouth of the orphan in his old masterpiece—'Her Father's Grave'.

The pavement artist's activities seem to have fascinated Grahame beyond measure, and he describes the pictures in detail: a cut half-salmon ('with special attention to the flesh-tints at the divided part'), the Charge of Balaclava, the portrait of Lord Wolseley that could be transformed at need, by the addition of a beard, into the Duke of Saxe-Coburg. 'It has always been my longing', Kenneth wrote to his friend Graham Robertson, 'to have been able to draw and paint'—but the kind of painting he had in mind was something very like the screever's work, itself first cousin to that of the school-room. These bold chalk pictures, like Mrs. Percy Dearmer's illustrations, must have recalled his own childhood: [19]

> Surely the 'manner' of this artist was my own 'early manner' —those broad, simple spaces, that large handling of primary colours? My tongue begins to protrude again as I look at them (this was a part of the early manner). Again the obstinate lid of that paint-box jams and slides a little, and jams again in its old way . . . and the potent old smell asserts itself once more.

At all events Grahame seems to have stayed there, absorbed in the scene, while 'the afternoon haze mellowed everything with an illusion of its own', putting him in mind of old-world châteaux and pre-Revolutionary France; till darkness fell, the red tail lamps of hansoms dotted the gloom, and the pavement artist departed in search of the nearest four-ale bar. If he moved at all it was into the National Gallery itself, a favourite haunt of his. Like the Baltic stockbroker he describes in 'The Iniquity of Oblivion', he 'only went in to be amused, and was prepared to take his entertainment from all schools alike, without any of the narrow preferences of the cultured'. ['Did the British artists in Suffolk Street', he remarks laconically in his diary entry for 22nd April 1887.] 'From the very first, however, the Early Tuscans gripped him with a strange fascination, so that he rarely penetrated any further.' Elsewhere he recalled that

> before the National Gallery was extended and rearranged, there was a little 'St. Catherine' by Pinturicchio that possessed my undivided affections. In those days she hung near the floor, so that those who would worship must grovel; and little I grudged it. Whenever I found myself near Trafalgar Square with five minutes to spare I used to turn in and sit on the floor before the

object of my love, till gently but firmly replaced on my legs by the attendant.[20]

Grahame never, as he says, strayed down the tortuous by-ways of Art; but he acquired a wide working knowledge of many artists' works, from Carpaccio or Botticelli to Watteau, Fragonard, and Lancret. He had a then unfashionable obsession with Blake, disliked the Manchester School heartily, and (presumably under Ruskin's influence) considered the Northern and Flemish schools influenced by the 'toil and stress of weather'. He praised the realism and modernity displayed by such artists as Turner or Frith[21] —when their work is compared with the equivalent writing of the time we can see his point—and believed, characteristically, that one of the main purposes in art was to save the past from entire oblivion:

> When, wandering through some gallery [he observed in a lecture] we come suddenly on the depicting of some once well-known and loved piece of nature or architecture, now swept away by so-called improvements or developments, we must have felt some glow of gratitude to the painter, over and above any joy in his work, for having fixed and recorded, for practically all time, a beauty now in itself vanished for ever.[22]

Yet not all his reactions followed this simple and practical pattern. The Italian Primitives seem to have moved him so strongly that he refers to the sensation as a 'possession'. Grahame was shy of self-analysis: 'the man', as he says on this occasion of his thinly disguised *alter ego*, 'was not apt in the expression of subtle emotion', and steered away from it in panic wherever possible.[23] We cannot do more than guess *what* he experienced in the National Gallery when looking at the Primitives; we only know that his feelings reached an unusual peak of intensity and awareness. The peculiarly spiritual quality which early Italian painting displays makes it likely that there was, in the widest sense, a religious element involved. Calvinism and social Anglicanism between them had dammed Grahame's natural spring of faith at the source; what he suffered from, paradoxically, was severe religious repression, which sometimes found very odd outlets. For so resolutely commonsensical a pagan he appears surprisingly familiar with obsessive, hysterical, and generally abnormal emotional states: there is even a hint, in 'The Piper at the Gates of Dawn', that he underwent at least one intense visionary experience of a semi-mystical nature.

But such moments of awareness or self-exploration were comparatively rare, and there were less demanding amusements available than the National Gallery. Grahame's tastes were well-marked: the circus, the freak-show, the illusionist, anything instinct with fantasy, oddness, the romantic or the macabre. He was fascinated by the Crystal Palace, and visited it frequently;[24] and he almost certainly went to the old Polytechnic, where there were Haunted Castles, strange scientific experiments, a genuine 'Pepper's Ghost', and blood-curdling performances of such immortal works as 'The Mysteries of Udolpho' and 'Baron Münchhausen', complete with electrical effects. A Miss Alice Bath, as Allan Fea tells us,[25] often figured in these scenes, and appeared as 'Undine, the Spirit of the Fountain': an ingenious arrangement of a large glass shade with a hose playing on the top. There was also the life-sized acrobat, 'Leotard', 'who performed stiff-jointed exercises and evolutions as he swung across the Central Hall'—and gave his name to a smaller, more domestic version who appears in Dream Days. Grahame found mechanical toys of any kind irresistible:[26]

He was an acrobat, this Leotard, who lived in a glass-fronted box. His loose-jointed limbs were cardboard, cardboard his slender trunk; and his hands eternally grasped the bar of a trapeze. You turned the box round swiftly five or six times; the wonderful unsolved machinery worked, and Leotard swung and leapt, backwards, forwards, now astride the bar, now flying free; iron-jointed, supple-sinewed, unceasingly novel in his invention of new, unguessable attitudes. . . .

There were Hengler's Circus and the Egyptian Hall, the Lowther Arcade, the Thames Tunnel, and at Christmas the old Soho Bazaar; there was Westminster Aquarium, 'which so soon degenerated into an incongruous exhibition of stewing crocodiles, fasting men and boxing kangaroos', and the Zoo, where in those days a handsome old French sailor looked after the seals, and was rewarded at dinner-time by smacking (if somewhat fishy) kisses from the occupants of the pool. London, despite everything, had its attractions.

It was early in 1882 that young Reginald Ingles, at the age of sixteen, began to visit Kenneth and Roland in their Bloomsbury Street lodgings. (Uncle Jack, now a captain, was on a long course at Greenwich, and he and his family were living in Blackheath.) Kenneth went out of his way to make the younger boy at home; late in life Major Ingles recalled that his cousin 'always treated me just as an equal, though I know now that I was rather young and foolish'. This instinctive, unforced sense of equality was one of Kenneth's most deeply ingrained assumptions: we meet it again and again in his work. As far as Reginald Ingles was concerned, it meant pleasant visits to *Faust* at the Lyceum, or dinner at Kenneth's favourite Italian restaurant in Soho, where they 'had about ten courses for 1s. 6d. and drank Chianti out of a basket bottle'; or long hours of talk in the evening, when the air would grow heavy with the smoke of Honey Dew and the smell of fresh-ground coffee-beans. Kenneth was fussy over his coffee, always insisting on making it with an earthenware strainer; occasionally his tidy nature must have protested at his visitor's clumsiness, but good manners, somehow, always prevailed:

> I remember Kenneth lending me a long churchwarden clay pipe with red sealing-wax on the stem. It was one of his treasures. . . . But I unfortunately broke the bowl off by tapping it on the fire-grate to knock the ash out. Kenneth, though he looked just slightly annoyed, was awfully nice about it and said that it did not matter a bit.[27]

According to Major Ingles, Grahame was certainly writing in 1882, but whether or not with any success is uncertain from the way he phrases it: 'I think at that time he used to write a little to [sic] magazines and some literary pages'.[28] He had begun that habit of walking-tour holidays which he only abandoned when he later went abroad regularly; and despite his drill and fencing, he had, during this period, two severe illnesses, 'what they called in those days inflammation of the bowels—one time I believe he was very bad and nearly died'.[29] Despite his fine physique, it is clear that Grahame was never a completely well man all his life.

Partly because of his health, partly through that instinct for solitude which was so strong in him, he soon after this left Bloomsbury for a top-floor flat at 65 Chelsea Gardens, off the Chelsea Bridge Road. Probably there was already some slight clash of temperament between Roland and himself; if so, he would have wanted at all costs to avoid an open quarrel. But more urgent, certainly, was the need to find what he had never truly possessed, a place of his own. His life since childhood had been rootless and transitory, never more than a year or two in any one place. There had been no real ties of domestic affection to bind him to any of them. The result of this was a psychological characteristic that recurs throughout his work: a strong but unanalysed homing-instinct towards an ideal home that had never in fact existed. This instinct acts as a counterbalance to Grahame's equally strong wanderlust: they maintain an uneasy balance of tension.

Grahame's domestic longings crystallized themselves in a persistently recurring dream which he later noted down in some detail. To judge by his letter to Helen Dunham—who confessed to a similar experience—he seems to have investigated the possible causes of his dream with great care. 'I'm not surprised at all', he wrote, 'that you too have a room. Scientific people deny the repetition, and say that the one dream has along with it, and as part of it, a confused sense of many previous ones—that it is a mirage, in fact. But *we* know better.'[30] Here is the dream as he remembered it:

> First, there would be a sense of snugness, of cushioned comfort, of home-coming. Next, a gradual awakening to consciousness in a certain little room, very dear and familiar, sequestered in some corner of the more populous and roaring part of London: solitary, the world walled out, but full of a brooding sense of peace and of possession. At times I would make my way there, unerringly, through the wet and windy streets, climb the well-known staircase, open the ever-welcoming door. More often I was there already, ensconced in the most comfortable chair in the world, the lamp lit, the fire glowing ruddily. But always the same feeling of a home-coming, of the world shut out, of the ideal encasement. On the shelves were a few books—a very few—but just the editions I had sighed for, the editions which refuse to turn up, or which poverty glowers at on alien shelves. On the walls were a print or two, a woodcut, an etching—not many. Old loves, all ot them, apparitions that had flashed across the field of view in sales-rooms and vanished again in a blaze of three figures; but never possessed—until now. All was modest—O, so very modest! But all was my very own, and, what was more, everything in that room was exactly right.

It is characteristic of Grahame that his wish-fulfilment dream should invent a past as well as a future: that the ideal room should not only be perfect but *familiar* (even down to little details like the oak balustrade on the stair) though in fact he had never known anything resembling it. To make the illusion yet stronger, he played an elaborate charade with himself, based on the assumption that the room *did* exist, that he *had* been there, and only unaccountable absentmindedness prevented his remembering the circumstances. He would consult his accounts for details of rent-payment; but found, conveniently, that he did not keep accounts. (This was a plain evasion: he kept meticulous accounts, as we would expect. But the next sentence gives away the truth: 'statistics would have been a mean prosaic way of plucking out the heart of this mystery'—especially when there was nothing to pluck out.) There followed investigations in the back streets of Bloomsbury and Chelsea, but, naturally, without result. If only there were some clue, 'some touch, scent, sound, gifted with the magic power of recall': but no clue presented itself. And again the strange split in Grahame's mind, so consciously conceived, is presented in an arresting image:

> It waits, that sequestered chamber, it waits for the serene moment when the brain is in just the apt condition, and ready to *switch on the other memory* even as one switches on the electric light with a turn of the wrist. Fantasy? well—perhaps. But the worst of it is, one can never feel quite sure. Only a dream, of course. And yet—the enchanting possibility! [*Italics mine.*]

Once again, and not for the last time, we have seen the genesis of a theme that was only to be developed fully in *The Wind in the Willows*.

Meanwhile the flat in Chelsea Gardens served as some kind of substitute, and at least had the virtue of inaccessibility. 'It was like climbing the stairs of a lighthouse,' one visitor recalled. 'There was no lift and the dirty stone staircase swept up in endless spirals.'[31] As some compensation Kenneth had a superb view out over the Thames and Battersea Park; and he was already, within his limited means, beginning to stamp his personality on his rooms—a few prints, and one or two pieces of good furniture acquired from friendly relatives, or bought cheap in the Portobello Road. Chief among these purchases was a Chippendale bureau which, so tradition had it, once belonged to the Duke of Wellington; and this bureau sheds an interesting side-light on his methods of composition. After his death a secret drawer was discovered in it, which contained a small hoard of odds and ends: 'a set of Maundy Money, a handful of small sea-shells, minute models of *filets-bleux* (Breton fishing-nets), the Rules of Roulette (in miniature), a coloured prayer-card of Tobias and the Angel, &c.'[32] Now this is almost certainly the bureau which figures in

The Golden Age, and which also contains a secret drawer with treasure-trove;[33] but since Grahame bought it while he was living in Chelsea Gardens, it follows thát he used the experience to enrich the memory of his childhood, that it was transferred from another setting. Similarly with the sumptuously illustrated volume in 'Its Walls Were as of Jasper': it was composed (Grahame himself wrote) 'of several books, or rather memories of them—a little town or two—and some early Italian pictures'.

There is one curious passage in 'The Secret Drawer' which confirms this duality. The fictional narrator, a nine-year-old boy, suddenly breaks off in the middle of persuading the boudoir bureau to give up its secret, and reflects: 'Was it any good persisting longer? Was anything any good whatever? In my mind I began to review past disappointments, and life seemed one long record of failure and of non-arrival.'[34] Such sentiments are startlingly out of key in the story, even when one has accepted Grahame's technique of moving to and fro contrapuntally between his adult and childish outlook; but in their proper context—a depressed young clerk furnishing his flat—they are only too appropriate. This is one of the clearest instances of Grahame's failing to disguise his source-material; in general he very carefully obliterated all tell-tale clues.

An interesting example of the process at both stages has survived. During his early years at the Bank Grahame took considerable interest in the legends of eccentricity which the older hands recounted. He went to the trouble of grubbing about in the official records in order to supplement oral tradition, and was sometimes richly rewarded. Of one former Bank employee he wrote:[35]

> In his office there was the customary 'attendance-book', wherein the clerks were expected to sign each day. Here his name one morning ceases abruptly from appearing; he signs, indeed, no more. Instead of signature you find, a little later, writ in careful commercial hand, this entry: 'Mr. —— did not

attend at his office today, having been hanged at eight o'clock in the morning for horse-stealing'.

Now we should not have known for certain that this episode referred to the Bank (though we might have guessed it) had we not possessed both original draft and published version of another anecdote relating to 'the same establishment'. These are so revealing when compared that they are worth quoting at length. The first is from the 'ledger diary', and shows the original germ of the idea:[36]

> A certain old clerk in one of the pay departments of the Bank of England used to spend his yearly holiday in relieving some turnpike-man of his post and performing all the duties pertaining thereto till recalled to Threadneedle Street. This was vulgarly supposed to be an instance of slavery to one's accustomed work—of 'pay and receive'—and spoken of pityingly. But that man doubtless knew what he wanted, knew one way of seeing Life. And what better way? And if all he was good for was to pay and take payments at least he recognized the fact, accepted it, boldly built thereon and went for it in its best shape.

This fragment was afterwards worked into an essay called 'The Eternal Whither', published in the *National Observer* on 9th July 1892. By then the text had been modified in several ways. The exact location had been carefully concealed, the style has become far more prolix and ornate, and—perhaps most significant of all— the final stoic resignation had been completely reversed:[37]

> There was once an old cashier in some ancient City establishment whose practice was to spend his yearly holiday in relieving some turnpike-man at his post, and performing all the duties appertaining thereto. This was vulgarly taken to be an instance of mere mill-horse enslavement to his groove—the reception of payments; and it was spoken of both in mockery of all mill-horses and for the due admonishment of others. And yet that clerk had discovered for himself an unique method of seeing Life at its best, the flowing, hurrying, travelling, marketing

Life of the Highway; the life of bagman and cart, of tinker and pig-dealer, and all cheery creatures that drink and chaffer together in the sun. He belonged, above all, to the scanty class of clear-seeing people who know both what they are good for and what they really want.

And here Grahame adds a sentence which we have already seen:

To know what you would like to do is one thing; to go out boldly and do it is another—and a rarer; and the sterile fields about Hell-Gate are strewn with the corpses of those who would an if they could.

The first version is perhaps more honest than the second, which seems to be propagating a carefully cultivated personal myth; yet who can tell, when dealing with Grahame, exactly where the borderline between myth and actuality can be drawn? He came to see himself as Ulysses in Threadneedle Street, the romantic wanderer pinned down to an urban routine by duty and necessity, the defeated rebel; but later in life, at least, he quite consciously urged the use of 'the countries of the mind', of day-dreams and fantasy, as a psychological therapeutic for those exhausted by the workaday world which they must accept whether they will or not:[38]

Life has only one side to it, and can only be lived in one way; but, as we all know, that way demands constant re-actions and recuperations. Accordingly, from time to time we go to the hill-tops, or to sea-coasts, or into retreats, or we (some of us) go on the spree, as it is vaguely but pleasantly called. It is all the same—all re-action in one form or another. Well, dreams are but re-action from life, and the easiest, the most accessible form of healing re-action that there is. For your hill-top may disappoint you, and your sea-coast be too stuffy or too expensive, but the mountain air of dreamland is always recuperating, and there Apollo and all the Muses, or at least Pan and his attendant Fauna await you.

It is double-edged advice, and possibly a retrospective rationalization of behaviour that in fact had sprung from less carefully calculated motives. The Hesperides, the Golden City, the Fortunate Isles and the imagined South of the early essays and stories are a desperate refuge rather than a casual holiday resort. As Grahame grew older, two complementary tendencies became more marked in him: his inner self expressed its emotions with increasing obliquity, hiding behind an ever-thickening hedge of symbol and allegory, while his conscious mind carefully reduced its past to logical, unemotional, often flippant proportions. It was a double form of self-protection.

His life between 1882 and 1887 fell into a well-ordered routine. There was the ferry-steamer to and from work, boarded at Chelsea Embankment or London Bridge;[39] evenings visiting relatives, or dining in Soho, or drilling with the London Scottish; the business of the New Shakespere Society, and Furnivall's always stimulating company. In 1884 he added a new interest to the others: perhaps at Furnivall's suggestion he undertook voluntary work at the newly founded Toynbee Hall, in Stepney.

He is not listed among the distinguished lecturers who addressed the East End poor on English literature or current affairs; his was a more practical bent. He took the chair at sing-songs, and even sang himself; he fenced, boxed, and played billiards with the young toughs of Whitechapel and the Commercial Road. His one encounter with a literature class was mildly disastrous: he undertook to address a particularly rowdy group of girls. Perhaps his flustered good looks were irresistible; at any rate, almost before he could open his mouth, his audience mobbed him cheerfully, smothering him in kisses, 'at the same time chanting, to the tune of *Men of Harlech*, "What is one among so many?"'[40] Grahame's only comment on this episode was that it considerably increased his affection for the London Scottish.

Sidney Ward, a colleague of his in the Bank, also did similar work at Toynbee Hall, and reveals in his reminiscences that Kenneth took some interest in Canon Barnett's early exhibitions of modern art, which were held in what has now become famous as the Whitechapel Gallery. But even so, Ward remarked—and we recognize the trait at once—'he liked a solitary life as a bachelor, with his books and writing, so that, friends as we were, I never saw a great deal of him outside our office life. He was probably the better pleased to see me because I didn't dig him out too often.'[41]

His reticence was absolute unless he chose to reveal something of his inner thoughts; Dame Henrietta Barnett, Canon Barnett's widow, made the best of a bad job after the event: 'I had always guessed something of the beauty and poetry of his character,' she asserted, 'even though the Mr. Grahame that I best knew seemed outwardly but a young City man with a dutiful consideration for his poorer neighbours. . . .'[42] Perhaps he had; yet it is worth recording that as late as 1898 a director of the Bank purchased *The Golden Age* under the impression that it had something to do with bimetallism.[43] Lewis Carroll and Stephen Leacock were liable to suffer a similar fate; with the trifling exception that they really had written books on mathematics and economics.

In August 1884 Grahame spent the first of several summer holidays at the Lizard, in Cornwall. He and Helen went together, and stayed with a friend of Helen's named Mary Richardson, whose brother Maunsell ('The Cat') was a famous gentleman-jockey. Helen must have fallen as deeply in love with the place as Kenneth did: when she retired from nursing she took a house at the Lizard and remained there till her death in 1940. Kenneth at once developed a passion for deep-sea fishing: he learnt to whiff for pollock and mackerel, and the difficult art of dealing with conger. (He maintained that 'the fun with a twenty-five pound conger only really began after you got it into the boat'.[44]) He became adept at baiting and hauling a mile-long sea-line, and at times he went out with the pilchard fleet, dressed like a local fisherman in rough warm blue jersey and peaked cap. On one of these occasions the Principal of Hertford College, Oxford, who visited the Lizard regularly and took a great interest in the fishermen, mistook Kenneth for the genuine article. Kenneth, poker-faced,

touched his cap and answered Dr. Boyd's somewhat patronizing questions in a fine Cornish burr; but the real locals, unable
to keep this joke to themselves, told the truth to the Doctor, who
came back to apologize in an agony of embarrassment. But
Kenneth (as he said a few moments later to Helen and Miss
Richardson, beaming with delight at the success of his joke) had
never been so flattered in his life. Fishermen were real people,
untouched by the canker of urbanization; it was a rare compliment to be taken for one of them.

Miss Richardson gives an interesting description of him at this
period, when he was about twenty-five:

> He was a tall (over six foot[45]) fine looking young man, a
> splendid head, broad and well-proportioned—carried himself
> well—a good healthy complexion, large widely opened rather
> light grey eyes, always with a kindly expression in them. Not
> exactly handsome but distinctly striking-looking—sensitive
> hands and mouth, rather short clever nose. . . . Distinctly
> reserved, until he trusted you—he seemed to me at times as if
> in his younger days he had been teased, and his boyish aspira-
> tions trodden on. . . .

This diagnosis exactly confirms the evidence given by Grahame's
own writings; and it is more than possible that he told Miss
Richardson something of his hopes and disillusioned ambitions.
She was clearly a sensitive and sympathetic girl.

So the Lizard, too, was gathered in to Grahame's private world
of release and romance, its memories cherished like those trinkets
in the secret drawer which were, in a sense, the symbol of this
larger myth which sustained him. Night fishing by lantern-light,
trolling off Kynance Cove, the great and mysterious sea-beast
which broke his line one stormy evening, the cargo of African
fleeces washed ashore for salvage—Kenneth went out to the wreck
with the coxswain of the lifeboat, his seventy-four-year-old fishing
companion Tom Roberts—the soft-spoken Cornishmen in whose
homes he came to be welcome: all were woven into a pattern of

remembered happiness, remote as a star, which warmed him through a London winter.

He remembered the swifts flying above the estuaries, the gorse and the gales and the pounding breakers—and especially he remembered the food: Cornish cream, 'thunder and lightning', pilchard pie, leek pasties. He haunted the Cornish bric-à-brac shops, too, and his Chelsea rooms were soon littered with ink-stands and candlesticks carved in serpentine. About this time his habit of collecting knick-knacks becomes generally noticeable. One of his manias was for those hollow glass rolling-pins with painted designs, known as 'Sailors' Farewells'; at a sale in 1920 he put up nearly forty for auction. The normal psychological explanation for this magpie practice is an urge to compensate for emotional deprivation, which fits well enough in Grahame's case, and is supported by his obsessional preoccupation with food.

It was in 1886 that Grahame first visited Italy: a momentous event in any sensitive northerner's life, doubly so for one who had his peculiar passion both for the South and for classical antiquity. He went with Helen to stay in the Villino Landau, near Florence, a 'little old farm-house' as Annie Grahame described it, which had been discovered by her mother and taken by Robert Grahame on an extended lease. It was a long, low, two-storied building, from which a paved courtyard sloped gently down to an old stone archway. Georgina Grahame was a passionately devoted gardener, and the whole place was a mass of madonna lilies, tea-roses, narcissi, jonquils, and sweet lemon plants.

> Towards the north [she wrote] we looked up to the highest point of the old Etruscan mother city; eastward were the Vallombrosa hills, and lying down below, veiled in the misty light of the hot June sun, were the domes and spires of Florence, with the blue Apennines rising beyond, to the far south. . . . So great an expanse of level ground is very unusual there, and it was the blending of the English with the Italian element of beauty that gave it so distinctive a character, and so great a charm.[46]

On the second Sunday in May Kenneth and Annie Grahame made an expedition to the Festival of the Madonna del Sarso in the hill country behind Fiesole. Annie describes this expedition to the Madonna in amusing detail, and concludes: 'We got back about 7 p.m., none the worse for the long day, which Kenneth had beguiled with delightful fairy tales'. His own? Perhaps; we cannot tell. At all events the genial air of Tuscany was working its magic on him, and it may be that his cousin's company, sympathetic as always, stirred him to inventiveness, as they walked those steep hill paths to the Madonna and her ancient Festival.

Characteristically, Kenneth had spent weeks before this visit acquainting himself with Florentine history and art; as a result he knew exactly what he was looking for and where to find it, an achievement which highly impressed Mrs. Grahame, who wrote of the visit in glowing terms as 'in more senses than one, a "Golden Age" visit', and added wistfully that 'such red-letter times do not come every day'.[47] Yet Kenneth was able to lift his nose from his Ruskin and Burckhardt long enough to observe and note down that 'the smells of Italy are more characteristic than those of the South of France',[48] a statement which time has done nothing to refute. It was during this visit, too, that he bought the little blue-and-white majolica plaque—one of Cantazala's reproductions of a Madonna and Child by della Robbia—which he some years later put up, like a modern L.C.C. memorial tablet, outside his house in Kensington Crescent: an echo of those disturbingly intense moments he had spent in the National Gallery contemplating the Italian Primitives.

Either that year or the next, Grahame also had his first sight of Rome: and though this was a Rome which has long since vanished, a Rome of the *contadini* that still preserved an authentic whiff of the atmosphere which Shelley knew, I suspect that, as well as delight, Grahame experienced a secret twinge of disappointment. The glorious dream-Rome of *The Golden Age* could be approached by no three-dimensional reality, however august, sunlit, and picturesquely ruinous; Grahame admitted as much, years afterwards, in a lecture delivered before the Keats-Shelley Literary Association—in Rome:[49]

> Which of us, even today, when about to visit some new far-distant city or country, does not form, sometimes deliberately but usually almost unconsciously, a picture of it, more or less vivid, beforehand? And do we not nearly always find in our past imaginings, when we take the trouble to refer back to them, just those two touchstones of the ideal—a fantastic unlikeness to the real thing, together with a special beauty nowhere to be actually found? I suppose that all of us here can remember our coming to Rome for the first time in our lives, and the preconception of the place that we brought along with us. Do we not all remember, when we reached Rome at last, the same two things—the absence of that strangeness which I have called the fantastic element and which somehow we cannot keep out of our imaginings, and secondly, the slight touch of disappointment that even the beauty of Rome was not just that particular beauty that we had caught a glimpse of through the magic casement of our idealism?

The warning was clearly given; and yet in after years it was ignored, and the vision lost. Grahame should have remembered that it was Stevenson who said that it is better to travel hopefully than to arrive.

On the eve of his departure for Florence, Grahame let himself become involved, in a minor capacity it is true, in a roaring theatrical scandal—a production of Shelley's *The Cenci*. Perhaps he had some idea of putting himself in a properly receptive mood for Italian culture; more probably he was incapable (like most people) of saying 'No' to Furnivall, who, as we might expect, was behind the occasion. Since the Lord Chamberlain refused to license *The Cenci*, the usual solemn mummery of a 'club production' was gone through. The play was produced by the Shelley Society on 7th May, at the Grand Theatre, Islington; it was

Browning's birthday, and with him in the audience were Lowell, Meredith, Shaw, Andrew Lang, and Sir Percy and Lady Shelley. Hermann Vezin played the Count, and Miss Alma Murray, Beatrice; Kenneth took the part of Giacomo, one of the Count's sons. Dr. Furnivall, somewhat mischievously, considering the incestuous subject-matter of the play, sent his housemaid to see it, and as Annie Grahame relates, 'being anxious to learn what impression it had made on her asked her what she thought of it. She said: "Mr. Grahame did look so handsome walking up and down the stage in his best clothes".' The result of the play was (as Furnivall had obviously hoped) a fine advertisement of the society; but there was also 'a howl of disgust from various critics, and a spirited controversy on the propriety of the play and Vezin's interpretation of his part, in the *Pall Mall Gazette*'.[50] During the subsequent uproar in the correspondence columns, Grahame was in all likelihood only too thankful to slip away to Italy. It was, as far as we know, the only time in his life that he ever appeared on a public stage: it was certainly the last.

The following year, 1887, marked the end of a major, if silent, influence in his life. On Sunday 27th February, he took a walk after lunch through Fulham and over Putney Bridge to Barnes Common, ending up at Hammersmith Bridge and returning along the towpath as far as Putney. He stayed out to tea with a friend, and on his return home found a telegram saying that his father had had a serious apoplectic stroke.[51] It was from Mr. Currie, a partner of Uncle John's, who had been in the Le Havre office when Cunningham Grahame first fell ill; he sent the wire, he told Kenneth afterwards, 'from a feeling of considerateness'—which at least suggests that Kenneth and his father had not previously been in any kind of communication. Shortly afterwards, however, a second telegram arrived, with the information that Mr. Grahame had died during the afternoon. Kenneth wired back to Currie to say he was coming, wrote to Helen, and the following night crossed from Southampton to Le Havre, where his father had died, and where all but the first two years abroad had been spent. He noted down the following account of that Tuesday's events:

> Mr. Currie met me, and we drove straight to my father's room, where I was able to see his face before the coffin was finally closed. He seems to have died quite instantaneously, no signs of life having ever shown themselves after those who heard the noise of his fall had reached his room and raised him . . . At three o'clock we drove to 32, Rue Bougainvillea where for want of room inside, the coffin was placed in the little turfed garden or yard outside the house, and Mr. Whelpton [the resident Methodist minister] read passages and prayers, chiefly those included in the Church of England Burial Service. . . . We then drove to the little cemetery of Sainte Adresse [52] on the heights overlooking the sea, near the lighthouses. With us were some clerks from Mr. C[urrie]'s office who had known my father . . . and the old landlady Madame Bazille, with her son and daughter-in-law. At the grave Mr. Whelpton completed the service—I bade adieu to the other mourners at the gate of the cemetery. After speaking to Madame Bazille I put a £5 note into her hand. This had been approved of by Mr. Currie, who spoke warmly of her affectionate care for eighteen years.

Next, Grahame went down to Mr. Currie's office, where his father's papers and books had been brought. The books, he notes, were mostly school-books—dictionaries, grammars, and so on—and he brought away a few only. He seems to have been disappointed in his search for private and legal documents, though with Mme Bazille's son he made a thorough search of his father's room. 'I made over the clothes to the Bazilles, and also the money in his purse—only 15 frs—Mme Bazille showed me a small photo of himself which he had given her, and which she wished me to take if I had not got one. I begged her to keep it.' There followed some routine business at the Mairie and British Consulate, after which Grahame, like any sightseer, went off for a tour of the docks with a man named Holmes, from Mr. Currie's office. He returned to London the following day.

Nowhere in these bleak, practical diary entries is there the least hint of regret, hatred, or strong emotion of any kind: merely a cold and businesslike indifference. The ritual had to be gone through, and Grahame went through it quickly, efficiently, and economically, even to the picking of the cheapest available cemetery. On the surface it does not seem that his father's death affected him one way or the other. Yet is it entirely coincidental that the following year he began to be published, and that from then on essays and stories poured from him in an ever-increasing spate? While he lived, Cunningham Grahame still exercised a psychologically inhibiting influence on his son, even from across the Channel; the prose style of Grahame as diarist is tight, spare, restrained—almost, one had said, repressed. But after his father's death there is an immediate sense of release, the blowing away of a black cloud. It was only in later years that Grahame personified the corollary of this psychological theorem—that a son who has been in opposition to his father will, after that father's death, eventually reproduce in himself many of the traits he has most rebelled against.

But for the moment, to judge by the scrappy entries in his April diary, Grahame's mood was one of relaxed cheerfulness. He went boating down to Kew, and, as we have seen, spent many hours at the Great Exhibition. He explored the back streets of old Chelsea, walked in Kensington Gardens, and dined at Blanchard's, Pagani's, and other of his favourite restaurants. One Friday he left the City soon after 11 a.m.—a short working day even by Bank of England standards—and spent several hours gallery-gazing. He visited Uncle John and his family in Sussex Gardens, and dined with Sidney Lee, then working on the *Dictionary of National Biography*, at his house in Lexham Gardens. He still either walked to work or went by boat; and on Monday 18th April, a day of bright sun and white frost on the ground, he 'got up at 6, and went a delightful walk by the river before breakfast'. Life was suddenly—he probably could not have explained how or why—opening out into a pattern of brighter colours, wider interests. He might well reflect with Baudelaire, whose *Fleurs du mal* were just beginning to percolate into the upper stratum of English literary awareness, that

> Derrière les ennuis et les vastes chagrins
> Qui chargent de leur poids l'existence brumeuse
> Heureux celui qui peut d'une aile vigoureuse
> S'élancer vers les champs lumineux et sereins.[53]

At all events, one day, his mind running on the Berkshire Downs in December, where 'the furrows still gleam unbroken, touched each, on the side the share has polished, with warm light from the low, red, winter's sun', he sat down and wrote a country essay[54] which he sent to the editor of the *St. James's Gazette*: and this time there was no rejection slip.

V

PAGANS AND PHILISTINES
1888-1893

Their writings, inspired by a whole-hearted hostility to the progress of industrial culture, locate the centres of authority not in the existing social order, but within the sources of individual being. . . . At the core of the malaise which pervades so much that is best in Victorian literature, lies a sense, often inarticulate, that modern society has originated tendencies inimical to the life of the creative imagination.

E. D. H. JOHNSON: *The Alien Vision of*
Victorian Poetry

Of the New Paganism . . . there is no necessity to take any very grave account, except as a thing which left behind it incomparable exercises in the English language. The New Paganism is no longer new, and it never at any time bore the smallest resemblance to Paganism.

G. K. CHESTERTON: *Heretics*

In June 1887 Queen Victoria celebrated her Golden Jubilee, and the London Scottish were on duty, as Kenneth wrote, 'during the whole short summer night prior to the Great Day'. They were later inspected by Lord Roberts, and Kenneth described the occasion, in which both he and Roland participated, as 'full of music, marching, and much true and affectionate loyalty and patriotism'.[1] Yet this picture of stable harmony was far from the whole truth. Enormous forces were beginning to disrupt the

Victorian class-structure, and as a Londoner Grahame could witness at first hand some of their uglier manifestations. In the Jubilee year itself jingoistic complacency was shattered by Bloody Sunday and the Trafalgar Square riots; and though few people, perhaps, saw a connection between the founding of the I.L.P. and that of the Arts and Crafts Movements, whose originators thought it 'more honest to learn to weave or make furniture than gamble on the stock exchange',[2] they were undoubtedly part of the same great protesting ferment.

Since Grahame's arrival in London, this atmosphere of opposition had become more violent and more articulate. At one end of the scale came the hierarchic social round, with its stilted compliments, its snobbish etiquette, its conversational clichés and elaborate sexual gambits;[3] at the other were the Salvation Army, the Irish Land Act, the first Rowton Houses, and the Fabian Society. In the middle Sir Gorgius Midas sat, coining money from sweated labour, lampooned in the pages of *Punch*, and pertinaciously buying his way into the higher échelons. Between these three class-divisions were basic fear, hatred, and distrust; but in a real emergency the rich and the privileged would always unite against the radical element. The days were passing when a tenant, suspected of trades-unionism, could be quietly ousted from his tenancy; in 1880 Richard Jefferies noted that 'respect for authority is extinct. . . . There used to be a certain tacit agreement among all men that those who possessed capital, rank, or reputation should be treated with courtesy. . . . But now, metaphorically speaking, the labourer removes his hat for no man. . . . The cottager can scarcely nod his employer a common greeting in the morning.'[4]

Things were indeed different now; when the first Fabian pamphlet appeared in 1884, a year after Marx's death, it contained these words:[5] 'We live in a competitive society with Capital in the hands of individuals . . . the time approaches when Capital can be made public property . . . the power is in your hands, and chances of using that power are continually in your reach'. Sometimes this movement was Utopian; Morris and Ruskin have been aptly described as artistic Luddites, and Robert Blatchford's *Merrie England* falls into the same nostalgic category.[6] Sometimes, more often as time went on, it was angry and violent. Anarchists proclaimed their intention of 'sending the privileged classes to heaven by chemical parcel post',[7] strikes and riots increased, political murders were not unheard-of, and an attempt was even made, in 1882, to assassinate the Queen.

'Everywhere,' as Esmé Wingfield-Stratford wrote, 'certainties were being called in question, sanctities were flouted, thought was beginning to slide down the inclined plane towards revolution. The movement might, as yet, be slow, but the acceleration was perceptible.'[8] Meanwhile, for the mercantile middle-class, material progress remained the watchword. By 1884 the railway companies were practically exhausted after four decades of cut-throat competition, leaving a legacy of deserted roads, ruined countryside, and disrupted local traditions. The industrial towns were spreading their tentacles further and further into hitherto rural areas, and the flow of labour away from the land continued unchecked. The counties in 1885 defied squire and farmer and voted Liberal; the following year came the Pall Mall Riots, with a furious mob looting the shops in Piccadilly.[9]

It seems clear in retrospect (though it was not probably realized at the time by either side in the struggle) that the privileged classes of the eighties and nineties were frightened as well as angered by such demonstrations; and that it was fear, the subconscious nightmare of the upsurgent mob, which hardened their resistance. Radical change of any kind—especially change which involved their rural economy—they regarded with the deepest suspicion. It was not only the county families (broadly speaking) who adopted this attitude of militant chauvinism; the intellectuals and writers largely followed them. As Osbert Burdett perciently observed,[10] they 'could not conceive society in other than aristocratic terms, and their preference for aristocracy persisted side by side with hatred of the plutocracy that apes it. Thus they became destroyers of the remnant of what they loved, without identifying themselves with the disruptive forces that were preparing the ground for a different society.'

Nostalgia, fear, anger, wish-fulfilment, escapism in the broadest sense: these were their driving motives. It was as if by taking thought they could alter the unwelcome pattern of their age, as if words were magic weapons which could break up the nightmare and bring back daylight once more. It was these brutal facts which underlay the whole drift towards fantasy, 'art for art's sake', the Celtic Twilight, the hair-splitting over Appearance and Reality, the *Looking-Glass* doubt as to who was in whose dream, the widening gap between the artist and a society which he hated and feared, yet could not wholly escape.

In one way or another nearly all the writers of the later Victorian period attacked the new radical trends; and even those who, like William Morris, actively supported radicalism still disassociated themselves from the industrial urbanization which produced it. This put them in an impossible position. Their 'ideal' society was aristocratic, rural, and pre-industrial. The actual society to which they belonged was a solidly materialistic and intolerant bourgeoisie. They were simultaneously committed to a doctrine of material progress, and debarred from any kind of progressive thinking, by temperament no less than social pressure: mechanical development.was accompanied by hardening of the religious and political arteries. They knew their civilization had taken the wrong turning, not in their brains but in their blood: every physiological instinct they possessed rebelled against the retreat from natural rhythms to the seasonless maelstrom of the metropolis.

Yet their protests did them no good, and not a little harm. When Morris spent his time weaving on a handloom, or turning out superb editions from the Kelmscott Press, or living in a pseudo-mediaeval revival of his own making, he was certainly at peace with himself, but he was out of step with his society. That is the tragedy of the post-industrial age: a man who satisfied his natural creative or pastoral instincts, who set out to be craftsman and maker, would by that act cut himself off from his fellows. He could fulfil himself, or he could conform with his society; but he could not do both, though both were essential to his well-being. The point had been reached at which they were mutually contradictory.

Different writers reacted to this situation in different ways. Some, like Kipling, tried to achieve the impossible task of reconciling the new industrial scene with the demands imposed by human instinct. But imperialism and machinery, Sussex and space-fiction, obstinately refused to blend. It was steam, not romance, that brought up the 9.15, aided by solid piles of gilt-edged investments and thousands of anonymous navvies who had sweated at the rape of the countryside.

The attempt to romanticize industrial phenomena by absorbing them into a traditional myth—whether Lionel Johnson's 'iron lilies in the Strand' (*i.e.* lamp-posts) or the pyloned landscapes of the thirties—is simply a form of self-protection. When reality reaches a certain level of repulsiveness, when the human psyche is outraged by external circumstances it is powerless to avoid, the remedy is often a carefully developed conviction (or convention) that the repulsive is in fact infinitely desirable. Kipling was a pioneer in this kind of social therapy, and it does much to explain his quite extraordinary popularity. He was not only the apostle of imperial benevolence, but a new Jacob who had wrestled with the Machine, and proclaimed it ally rather than foe: an ally, moreover, that looked kindly on the social order as it stood.

The easiest answer, of course, was to contract out of society altogether, as, under somewhat similar circumstances, the Epicureans had done in the ancient world. Pater was a leading example of this trend, which later embraced the vast majority of writers;

he considered art, literature and religion as 'a refuge, a sort of cloistral refuge, from a certain vulgarity in the actual world'.[11] The dangers of such a withdrawal are perhaps more obvious today than they were then. An art that cuts off its own roots soon withers away into sterile repetitiveness: nothing is more subtly destructive than a closed circle of artists feeding on each other. An excessive preoccupation with stylistic ornament, leading to rank growths of baroque decoration; a tendency to subordinate subject-matter to form, and to derive themes from the work of previous writers; an evaporation of moral seriousness into mere hedonistic froth; a species of emotional corruption induced by the necessary search for new sensation: these are some of the more obvious dangers inherent in the formula of 'Art for art's sake'.

Those writers who could not reconcile themselves with this *déraciné* aestheticism, and yet remained temperamentally opposed to the radical view, tended to throw their energies either into satire or the kind of swash-buckling romantic imperialism made popular by Disraeli. The satire ranged from hysterical denunciation of the proletariat by Coventry Patmore, in *The Unknown Eros*,[12] to more subtle denigration such as that employed by Anstey in his *Punch* articles, later collected as *Voces Populi*. These contrived to suggest that all demonstrations were run by 'roughs' or rich trouble-makers for their personal profit, and that the working classes as a whole were vicious, idle, cowardly, hypocritical, and stupid.[13] His Hyde Park Socialist declares:

> ' *We're* the honly class wuth bein' considered, feller-citizens! It's *hus* that repperesents the hintelleck, the henergy, the hability, the morality of the nation.' (*General chorus of* ''*Ear, 'ear!*') 'The Haristocracy and the Middle Classes—well, they've got jest enough er cunningness, (I won't call it hability), er *cunningness*, for to cheat us out er wot's ours.' . . . &c.

The imperialism represented the positive implications of this rather negative carping, and apart from Kipling its main exponent was that remarkable character W. E. Henley: poet, journalist, encyclopaedist, art-critic, playwright, essayist, lexicographer, anthologist and—last but not least—editor.[14] It was in this editorial capacity that he first met Grahame, whose 'little meteorites' had at last come to rest in the office of Frederick Greenwood, editor of the *St. James's Gazette*. James Payn at the *Cornhill* had fobbed his would-be contributor off, a month or two earlier, with a polite bromide: 'Your little paper', he wrote, 'is too short and slight for the *Cornhill*, but the humour it exhibits has struck me as being exceptional and leads me to hope that I may again hear from you'.[15] The *Cornhill* never had another piece by Grahame till the posthumously published 'A Dark Star' in 1933;[16] what is interesting about Payn's letter is its reference to *humour*, which seems hitherto to have excited no comment.

The two early essays which Greenwood published, 'By a Northern Furrow' and 'A Bohemian in Exile', though not without a quiet wit, could hardly be described as humorous, even by the standards of 1890. Presumably then, Payn had seen something else. But what? Grahame hardly qualified as a humorist (unless we count the anecdotes in the 'ledger-diary') till he struck the inspired vein that runs through *The Golden Age*—or so it would appear from the published record. But here we are reminded forcibly that a great deal of Grahame's journalism at this period was anonymous, and that without external evidence we have no means of discovering the full range of his interests. By a stroke of good fortune, however, one such essay, hitherto unknown, has now turned up. It shows that Grahame *was* a humorist, and a mildly scurrilous one at that; it also confirms his interest (which has been doubted) in contemporary and political affairs.

Sidney Ward, in his unpublished recollections of Grahame, gives this account of the episode: 'It was at the time of the great Parnell divorce, and the papers were full of sensational accounts of how the great man escaped from Mrs. O'Shea's house, through a window, when the Captain arrived unexpectedly. A day or two afterwards there appeared in the *St. James's Gazette* an alleged

"Conversation between a Balcony and a Waterspout". It was clever and witty and scurrilous and altogether delightful. I turned to K. G. and said: "I say, Grahame, did you see that gorgeous conversation between a balcony and a water-spout in the *St. James's* last night?" "Yes," said K. G., "I wrote it!'" [17] The issue in which it appeared was that of 19th November 1890, and it is here reprinted for the first time:

A PARABLE
(OVERHEARD AND COMMUNICATED BY OUR OWN CAT)

"Well, old fellow," said the Waterspout to the Verandah, "and how do you feel, now it's all over?"

"Very poorly indeed, thanks," said the Verandah mournfully. "Just look at my nice paint! I'm scratched and kicked all over."

"Paint, indeed!" said the Waterspout, with scorn; "what does paint matter? Now look at me. I'm all twisted and bent like a bayonet. If it hadn't been for our old friend the Fire-escape there, who took some of the work, I should have been old iron long ago."

"Well, it's splendid exercise," put in the Fire-escape meditatively; "*I* don't mind if he thinks it does him good. But, really, I didn't think he had it in him. He's a marvellous man!"

"Oh, *you* don't mind, of course!" remarked the Waterspout; "escaping is your business. But it's not mine, and I don't want to take it up. And now my old friend the sparrow, who's built in me these five years, has had to go. Says she didn't mind the racket so much; but there will be a young family to bring up next spring, and she must think of them."

"Quite right too," said the Verandah. "Good old sparrow! But between ourselves, now, it was very funny sometimes, wasn't it? First of all *He* would slip in, in a modest and unassuming manner, as if he had called to tune the piano; then he —I mean Shea—would come and kick at the door; then she would open it for Sh—I mean him; and *He* would come sliding down our friend here, like a lamplighter. Then *He* would pick himself up and ring the visitors' bell; and Shea would open the door for *He*—I mean him; and all would be surprise, delight, and harmony. And the next night he'd give the Fire-escape a turn."

"He gave *me* a turn once or twice," said the Waterspout reflectively. "I've had a burglar down me, and a schoolboy or two, but never the idol of a nation's hopes and aspirations. The boat that carried Caesar and his fortunes will have to take a back seat now."

"By the by, old chap," said the Verandah, "what will the other old Waterspout say? The Grand one, you know—the head of your family." [This refers to Gladstone, who as a Liberal supported Parnell—but depended largely on the Nonconformist vote. The line of Liberal papers such as the *Manchester Guardian* and *Freeman's Journal* was that Parnell's private life had nothing to do with his politics.]

"Why," put in the Fire-escape, "he'll say that the subject is one of vast human interest, and he would like nothing better than to hear it fully and freely discussed. He fears, however, that at his time of life he must leave to younger and more vigorous—" The measured tread of the policeman approached down the quiet lane, and silence reigned once more in the peaceful little suburb.

This piece, ephemeral enough in itself, sheds a most interesting light on its author in the context of his subsequent development. It shows his first crude use of fable as a vehicle for satire, complete with the characteristic *non-human* viewpoint which always, in one form or another, gave edge and perspective to his criticisms. It also explodes that faint haze of otherworldliness, in the purely sentimental sense, which his more disastrous admirers are liable to attribute to him. Grahame, we should never forget, was one of the first English writers to pepper his essays with quotations from Rabelais:[18] this aspect of his nature was firmly suppressed by his wife and biographer after he died, and Sidney Ward's unfortunate disclosure remained in the obscurity of a private letter-file. There was a general air of French farce about the Parnell proceedings which must have caught Grahame's fancy; Parnell's horses were called Dictator, President, and Home Rule, while Mrs. O'Shea's maid declared under cross-examination that her mistress 'said there was a secret society about, and it was necessary to have the door locked'. Politically, too, he found irresistible the opportunity to poke fun at Gladstone and Parnell simultaneously.

This brings us back to Henley. In November 1888 one Fitzroy Bell, a rich business-man, was persuaded to sponsor a new literary weekly. 'It irked his northern pride,' as Kennedy Williamson put it, 'that the better half of Britain should be beholden to Sassenachs for a cultured survey of art and letters.'[19] The weekly was to be known as the *Scots Observer*: it was to resemble, more or less, the English *Saturday Review*. For the privilege of being associated with this venture Bell was willing to lose, and did lose, £4000 a year. He continued to cover the paper's deficits even after Henley, whom he had installed as editor, moved the editorial offices in 1890 to London, and rechristened the paper the *National Observer*.

The *National Observer* was from the first stamped with Henley's pugnacious and idiosyncratic prejudices on every page, whether political, artistic, or moral. He was violently anti-Socialist, so he lost Shaw as a contributor. He could reconcile—or even equate— Toryism with Radicalism, as 'a broad doctrine of individual freedom within the fabric of a firm but self-reformative social structure'. But he had no tolerance for the *practical* Radical,

> who would have had freedom without discipline, on the one hand, or authority without liberty, on the other. . . . It was Socialism that threatened to impose upon him the will of a Philistine mob. . . . As an antidote to Hyndman and the Fabians and the misguided aspirations of the rising Laborites, there remained the example of Disraeli in whose controlled democracy lay England's 'one defence against Socialism and the dominion of the Common Fool' [*Socialism in Excelsis*].[20]

Henley's somewhat ambiguous position gave his satirical guns a wide field of traverse. At one and the same time he was prepared to attack Gladstone (that 'Pantaloon'), Sir Wilfrid Lawson the tee-total M.P., General Booth of the Salvation Army, W. T. Stead

('Bed-Stead'), the famous journalist, and Richard Le Gallienne. His real enemy was Puritanism, which he instinctively associated in an unholy trio with Labour and Humbug. His comments on Stead are revealing: 'a good deal of Paul Pry, a good deal of Pecksniff, a touch of M. de Sade, and an infinite amount of Sunday School Teacher'.[21]

The *National Observer*, though its circulation was never high, had a dazzling gallery of contributors, ranging from Stevenson and Kipling to Yeats, and managed to blend literary virtuosity with slashing political indictments, such as Kipling's poem *Cleared*, on the Parnell Commission. It lasted for four years; and it finally failed because the intellectuals who should have supported its literary star were all progressives, politically speaking, while the Tories at whom it was aimed stuck to *The Times*, *Punch*, and the *Illustrated London News*.[22] Beerbohm, as so often, had the last word on it: 'The paper', he wrote, 'was rowdy, venomous, and insincere. There was libel in every line of it. It roared with the lambs and bleated with the lions. It was a disgrace to journalism and a glory to literature.'[23]

Henley's views all struck a responsive chord in Grahame. He had clearly been going through that tiresome initial process of finding a congenial editor. Nothing, in all probability, attracted him more than Henley's slashing assaults on Puritanism. In a letter to Coulson Kernahan, five years after the *National Observer*'s demise, he wrote: 'I liked your "Puritan" article immensely'— Kernahan had produced an 'onslaught on Puritanism', in Grahame's own words—'and it's so true—and the whole truth— that the *N.Obs.* left a hole, never yet filled up. They were good times, those; and I don't see the same output now.'[24] Elsewhere he admitted that Henley 'was the first Editor who gave me a full and a free and a frank show, who took all I had and asked me for more: I should be a pig if I ever forgot him'.[25]

It would be romantic—and indeed apposite—if Henley had, as Chalmers suggests, first made Grahame's acquaintance by way of that essay entitled 'The Rural Pan'. But the files tell a different story. Grahame's first known contribution to the *Scots Observer* was 'Of Smoking', which appeared on 18th October 1890. 'The Rural Pan' was not published by Henley till 25th April 1891; and by then five other contributions had preceded it, all submitted in that neat holograph which had so impressed a sub-editor on the *St. James's Gazette*, and given doubts to an old Scots ledger-clerk at the Bank of England ('It's no' the hand of a principal, young Grahame'.)[26] They had met, and taken a personal liking to each other; indeed, after a little, Henley first made Grahame a regular contributor, and then tried to argue him into giving up his career at the Bank and becoming a professional writer. But Grahame, who had strong views on the writer's amateur status, who 'held himself to be a spring and not a pump', for once held out against all Henley's persuasions and curses, and yet contrived —rare diplomacy—to remain his friend.

Henley, as Stevenson observed, was a man of tremendous energy and presence; and Grahame wrote, remembering him: 'My personal recollection of W. E. Henley is vivid enough still— perhaps because he was so very vivid himself. Sick or sorry—and he was often both—he was always vivid. The memory of this, and of his constant quality of stimulation and encouragement, brings him best to my mind.'[27] The lame, irascible, diehard poet, with his bawdy enthusiasms, his vitriolic satire,[28] and his nostalgia for the heroic simplicities of Homer's age, when 'men were not afraid of nor ashamed of death, and you could be heroic without a dread of clever editors',[29] made a deep impression on Grahame: there was something in Henley of Furnivall's tremendous yet always compulsive unorthodoxy. Grahame became a regular guest both at the Friday dinners held in Verrey's Restaurant for contributors, and at those more select gatherings on Sunday evenings in Henley's house.

These Sunday 'At Homes' have been described by Yeats, who also attended them,[30] and who 'disagreed with Henley about

everything, but admired him beyond words'. 'We gathered . . .',
he wrote, 'in two rooms, with folding doors between, and hung,
I think, with photographs from Dutch masters, and in one room
there was always, I think, a table with cold meat . . . he made us
feel always our importance, and no man among us could do good
work, or show the promise of it, and lack his praise.' Guests
ranged from Barry Pain and Charles Whibley to George Wyndham, who was later to become a Cabinet Minister and Irish Chief
Secretary; and according to C. L. Hinds, who was a guest in
September 1891, it was easy to distinguish the literary amateurs
from the professional writers. 'They looked more comfortable;
they ate their food in a more leisurely way; they were readier to
praise than to blame, because literature was to them a delightful
relaxation, not an arduous business.'[31]

Among these 'leisure-hour gentlemen of the pen', Hinds
noticed, was

> a tall, well-knit, blonde[32] man, who moved slowly and with
> dignity, and who preserved, amid the violent discussions and
> altercations that enlivened the meetings of the group, a calm,
> comprehending demeanour accompanied by a ready smile that
> women would call 'sweet'. And yet this blonde, temperate,
> kindly-looking man had also a startled air, as a fawn might
> show who suddenly found himself on Boston Common, quite
> prepared to go through with the adventure, as a well-bred
> fawn should do under any circumstances, but unable to escape
> wholly from the memory of the glades and woods whence he
> had come. He seemed to be a man who had not yet become
> quite accustomed to the discovery that he was no longer a child,
> but grown-up and prosperous [this was not true at the time,
> though it was in 1921 when Hinds wrote his essay.] Success did
> not atone for the loss of the child outlook. Every one of us
> has his adjective. His adjective was—startled.

It is one of the clearest and most characteristic descriptions of
Grahame which have come down to us: modified, perhaps, by
Graham Robertson's slightly more robust appraisal:[33]

He was living in London where he looked all *wrong*—that is to say, as wrong as so magnificent a man could look anywhere. As he strode along the pavements one felt to him as towards a huge St. Bernard or Newfoundland dog, a longing to take him away into the open country where he could be let off the lead and allowed to range at will. He appeared happy enough and made the best of everything, as do the dogs, but he was too big for London and it hardly seemed kind of Fate to keep him there.

Fawn or St. Bernard—it is significant, yet not surprising, that each attempt to convey his personality has recourse to an animal image.

Between 1890 and 1896, the years which marked Grahame's most intensely creative period, everything he wrote that did not go into *The Yellow Book* first appeared in Henley's *National Observer*, or, after that failed, in its successor, the *New Review*. (This division of loyalties, between Decadence and Counter-Decadence, is a fairly accurate analogue of Grahame's literary temperament.) There can be no doubt that Henley's editorial influence on his young Scots essayist was profound, and by no means always beneficial. Like certain American editors today, he had a habit of 'subbing' and touching up his contributors' material till it carried the Henley stamp. Yeats recalled how Henley 'often revised my lyrics, crossing out a line or a stanza and writing in one of his own. . . . At first, indeed, I was ashamed of being rewritten and thought that others were not [*i.e.* not being rewritten] and only began investigation when the editorial characteristics—epigrams, archaisms and all—appeared in the article upon Paris fashions and in that upon opium by an Egyptian Pasha.'[34]

It is quite plain that Grahame's material underwent the same processing: his contributions to the *St. James's Gazette* are easily distinguishable from those in which Henley had a hand. As soon as Grahame begins to publish in the *Scots Observer* his archaisms and quaintness take a sudden leap skywards. It is not difficult to guess why. To do him justice, he protested against this tinkering with his text. In the corrected proofs of 'A Funeral' we can see the battle going on, with Grahame excising or modifying the more blatantly archaic conceits which Henley had presumably inserted before sending the MS. to the printer. But Grahame was still only on the threshold of the literary world, and cannot be blamed for not pressing his point more strongly.

There is, indeed, a good deal of evidence that he fell under Henley's hypnotic spell after a while. The older man certainly fired him with a portentous enthusiasm for Stevenson, his former star contributor. Much of *Pagan Papers*, both as regards style and theme, reads like a variant gloss on *Virginibus Puerisque*, where we also find essays on Pan, walking-tours, smoking, and the pleasures of idleness. A reviewer remarked that Grahame was 'only one in a whole generation who turns out a "Stevensonette" as easily and lightly as it rolls a cigarette';[35] but it did not occur to him to ask *why* such subjects should, like Greek myths, stimulate such persistent attention.

Today, when we go through these stock themes—food and drink, tobacco, sleep, travel, walking, nature-mysticism, and the rest of them—it becomes clear that they are all regarded as *drugs*, either stimulant or soporific, escape-routes from an intolerable everyday reality. Grahame knows this perfectly well. There is, as he says, 'a certain supernal, a deific state of mind' which can only be produced 'after severe and prolonged exertion in the open air', followed by an evening at some village inn:

> There, in its homely, comfortable strangeness, after unnumbered chops with country ale, the hard facts of life begin to swim in a golden mist. You are isled from accustomed cares and worries—you are set in a peculiar nook of rest. Then old failures seem partial successes, then old loves come back in their fairest form, but this time with never a shadow of regret, then old jokes renew their youth and flavour. You ask nothing of the gods above, nothing of men below—not even their com-

pany. Tomorrow you shall begin life again: shall write your book, make your fortune, do anything; meanwhile you sit, and the jolly world swings round, and you seem to hear it circle to the music of the spheres.[36]

It is the same with tobacco, which is 'the true Herb of Grace, and a joy and healing balm, and respite and nepenthe':[37] an opinion echoed by Calverley, Arthur Machen, and, most strikingly, Lionel Johnson, in an essay which for cultural allusiveness must be almost *sans pareil* (it contrives to quote or refer to Shelley, Catullus, Milton, Lucretius, Aristotle, St. Augustine, Propertius, Horace, Apuleius, Glanvil, Shakespeare, Izaak Walton, and Addison, all in ten pages):

> The blue smoke curls and glides away, with blue pagodas, and snowy almond bloom, and cherry flowers, circling and gleaming in it, *like a narcotic vision*. O magic of tobacco! Dreams are there, and superb images, and a somnolent paradise. . . . Perhaps the cigarette is southern and Latin, southern and Oriental, after all; and I am a dreamer, out of place in this northern grey antiquity.[38] [*Italics mine.*]

Again there is the contrast between the grey puritan North and the colourful, abandoned Mediterranean; between the exotic dream and the intolerable reality.

When one reads widely in the literature of the period there emerges a nightmare picture—and perhaps a not entirely false one—of writers and artists doping themselves silly on liquor and tobacco, walking themselves into a muscle-bound stupor every week-end, turning Nature into a kind of personalized God: and why? To produce bigger and better compensation-fantasies for the disgusting deadness of urban life; to blunt their senses enough to make existence bearable; to stimulate their imaginations into producing an inner lotus-land to which they could retreat at necessity. No wonder that so many of them took to drugs or, like John Davidson, eventually committed suicide. To adapt a phrase from Bentley,[39] Johnson's tobacco would be mescalin if it could.

The trouble is that all these aberrations were based on perfectly sound instincts; they had simply become obsessive because of intolerable external circumstances. In no case is this clearer than the habit of walking, which has collected a surprising number of literary devotees, ranging from Hazlitt to Sir Leslie Stephen.[40] It is quite true (and a truth which we are liable to forget) that, as Grahame says, 'annihilate time and space as you may, a man's stride remains the true standard of distance; an eternal and unalterable scale'.[41] From this point of view the walking-cult is something more than physical recreation: it becomes a philosophy of life. But when this philosophy comes into conflict with the progressive mechanism of an industrial society, it at once places its adherents in the position of odd men out, anachronisms. The result tends to be its conversion into a drug, with all the potential dangers which every drug implies. It is used to mitigate the unpleasantness of a way of life, which, for practical reasons, even the minority are forced to accept.

The tragedy of Pre-Raphaelism, the return to the Middle Ages or the land, the cult of the gentleman-craftsman working his own loom, the flirtation with paganism, was simply this: that all these practices only attracted a handful of people, who were trying to recapture a lost ethic to which the majority were totally indifferent. It was the *immutability* of things which drove the artists to aesthetic or actual drugs, and forced them to cultivate their 'countries of the mind' as a refuge from actuality; and there followed from this the predictable attempt to prove that reality lay in the imagination, not in the visible world. Since official or Puritan Christianity seemed to the aesthetes to be a weapon employed against them by society, they threw it over: but not, as might have been expected, for scientific evolution. Instead they constructed a kind of synthetic pantheism based on nature-worship, a defence of rural fulfilment and seasonal rhythms against the machine's inhuman sterility. They saw a deep split developing between man's working life and his recreation, between what he had to do and what he wanted to do: a dissociation of sensibilities similar to that which Mr. T. S. Eliot perceived in the seventeenth century. It is not a coincidence that the 'holiday cult' really began in earnest towards the end of the Victorian era.

The protests made by a minority are fatally easy to misinterpret; and what began as an ideal is always liable to corruption in practice. When Stevenson wrote his 'Apology for Idlers', or Grahame his essay on 'Loafing', they had a perfectly valid proposition in mind: that the exclusive emphasis on material progress, the acceleration of the tempo of living beyond man's natural capacity, were starving and stunting the human soul. Stevenson made it quite clear that he was challenging current 'business' morality as well as proposing a therapeutic. 'Idleness so called', he wrote 'which does not consist in doing nothing, but in doing a great deal not recognized in the dogmatic formularies of the ruling class, has as good a right to state its position as industry itself.'[42] Obviously this is both true and psychologically important; but like all similar tenets, it was only too easily debased into an excuse for mere *fainéant* hedonism—a position which Society was not slow to attribute to it from the start.

The essays which Grahame wrote in this period are a clear enough guide to his own preoccupations and interests, and present a surprisingly coherent picture. On the whole he avoided the extremes represented by rural fantasy on the one hand and Henley's muscular sword-waving on the other. His comments are shrewd and realistic, with occasional whiffs of fantasy or angry satire as the mood took him. Like the Homeric heroes he and Henley vicariously admired, he is disturbed profoundly by the thought of death; 'from no love of them, but rather with a shuddering fear, he must be busy with all the emblems of mortality'.[43]

This fear of death is a characteristic of neo-paganism, a trait Grahame shares with Pater and many others. Their sensuous pantheism had no place for an eschatology. In Grahame's early work death is either feared openly, or its terrors exorcised by a jolly gallows'-humour, where people are shot, beheaded, chopped to pieces, and turned into burnt sacrifices as if it were a daily occurrence and the greatest fun in the world.[44] (This was also a reaction against what Henley called Grocerdom: the near-Fascist *Song of the Sword* explains, partially at least, the motives which drove Brooke to write his war-sonnets in 1914, the feeling that the Heroic Age had come again to sweep the money-lenders from the Temple.) It is a grim joke—and one which I suspect Grahame did not intend—that the wistful phrase, '*et in Arcadia ego*', was in fact originally an inscription on a tomb, and meant that even in Arcadia Death (who spoke the words) could not be avoided.[45]

The obvious central theme in these essays is what may be loosely described as Bohemianism, the kind of individualistic rural anarchy that can trace its descent from Arnold's Scholar Gipsy to Stevenson and even Buchan, who wrote in an early essay: [46] 'All immoment philosophies, nugatory and unsatisfying endowments born of the dreams of dyspeptic townsfolk are banished from his [the Bohemian wanderer's] brain; and he goes on his way with a healthy clarity of mind. . . . This is the true Bohemia; all others reek of foul air and bad tobacco, but this is filled with the very breath of Athena.' The lure of the open road, the call of the simple life, away from hammering modern ugliness and competition and smoke and complexity: that is what draws Grahame again and again, perhaps nowhere more effectively than in 'A Bohemian in Exile', the story of Fothergill, the modern scholar-gipsy, who had had the courage to break loose and contract out of society.[47] Fothergill at one point is lured back to property and respectability, but soon begins to mope in his cage, and vanishes once more.

The most interesting thing about Grahame's approach in this essay is its practicality. The whole thing is treated as a possible plan of action, not as fantasy; when Fothergill meets the narrator on the Berkshire Downs, and tells him of his experiences, he seems to be opening a gate into a tangible and realizable paradise:

> The old road-life still lingered on in places, it seemed, once one got well away from the railway; there were two Englands existing together, the one fringing the great iron highways wherever they might go—the England under the eyes of most of us. The other, unguessed at by many, in whatever places were still vacant of shriek and rattle, drowsed on as of old: the England of heath and common and windy sheep down, of by-lanes and village-greens—the England of Parson Adams and Lavengro.[48]

It is the last glimpse of the past, the death-throes of real country life; and Grahame was young enough to have caught its authentic flavour before it was lost for ever. Yet, as we know, he never emulated Fothergill; and Mr. David Daiches' verdict on Stevenson may well be applied to his disciple also: 'He poses all the more fiercely as a bohemian because he has renounced the ultimate implications of Bohemianism, and he plays his part as moralist all the more readily in order to cover up what is perhaps a secret feeling that when the real choice came he had neither the courage nor the selfishness to act on his own principles'.[49]

The two essays, however, which have most permanent value (and most clearly illustrate Grahame's awareness of the psychological dangers inherent in industrial civilization) are 'The Lost Centaur' and 'Orion'. They both state, very clearly, the same thesis: that man has fatally neglected the instinctive, animal side of his nature through spiritual pride, puritan repression, and material greed; and that this neglect will take its toll in outbursts of neurotic irresponsibility. In the first the symbol of unity is Cheiron, the wise Centaur, half man, half beast, and the emphasis is laid on the follies of unilateral development, the atrophy of the senses produced by over-emphasis on cold and rational logic. Here are the words which Grahame attributes to 'the mute and stunted human embryo' in the animal, and which are addressed to Homo Sapiens:[50]

> Was it really necessary, after all, that we two should part company so early? May you not have taken a wrong turning somewhere, in your long race after your so-called progress, after the perfection of this belauded species of yours? A turning whose due avoidance might perhaps have resulted in no such lamentable change as is here, but in some perfect embodiment of the dual nature . . .?

Let soul inform and irradiate body as it may, Grahame declares, the threads are utterly shorn asunder never: nor is man, the complete, the self-contained, permitted to cut himself wholly adrift from these his poor relations.

'Orion' extends the metaphor: the celestial Hunter, the primitive element in mankind, is contrasted with the Children of the Plough, the miserable half-men produced by centuries of civilization. Bitterly Grahame attacks 'the chains that are forged of peace, the irking fetters of plenty' that have turned mankind into 'a great chain-gang, the convicts of peace and order and law', and adds to this a venomous side-swipe at Original Sin. We can sense Henley's influence here, the lame crusader ferociously carving up grocers and Presbyterian ministers; but the theme has been given a cosmic significance which Henley never envisaged. The Hunter, Grahame emphasizes, is still very much alive in every human soul, and it is a dangerous fallacy to suppose that 'this drop of primal quicksilver in the blood' can safely be ignored or suppressed. Children preserve it in all its pristine fullness: 'in later years it is stifled and gagged—buried deep, a green turf at the head of it and on its heart a stone; but it lives, it breathes, it lurks, it will up and out when it is looked for least'.[51]

Safe in Victorian England, Grahame probably did not recognize what a powder-mine he had stumbled on. If in old age he had been told that this essay in ways anticipated both Freud and D. H. Lawrence he would have been frankly incredulous. Yet the truth is there: and at some point Grahame swerved away from its implications, retreated to a safe compromise, refused the challenge. This great central theme is never treated openly again, though its presence can be felt lurking behind much that he wrote later, and provided the satirist in him with endless ammunition. But if he had followed the argument to its logical conclusions, he would have needed to act as Lawrence did; and that would have been essentially repugnant to his nature. The political, sexual, and psychological implications of his thesis terrified him: perhaps that was why he concluded 'Orion' with a *Götterdämmerung* paragraph which must have seemed considerably more fantastic to him than it does to us:

> But for the Hunter—there he rises—couchant no more Nay, flung full stretch on the blue, he blazes, he dominates, he appals! Will his turn, then, really come at last? After some Armageddon of cataclysmal ruin, all levelling, whelming the County Councillor with the Music hall artiste, obliterating the very furrows of the Plough, shall the skin-clad nomad string his bow once more, and once more loose the whistling shaft? Wildly incredible it seems. And yet—look up! Look up and behold him confident, erect, majestic—there on the threshold of the sky.

It is easy to forget that both 'The Lost Centaur' and 'Orion' were written as early as 1892. Later, in 1914, the Hunter must have seemed an infinitely inspiring figure; and not even the atomic age has entirely robbed him of his archetypal power over men's minds.

The remaining essays illuminate various aspects of these major themes, but never reach the unifying height of perception which 'Orion' displays. They also tell us, incidentally, a good deal about Grahame himself: his passion for fine bindings and first editions, with exquisite typography and well-spaced margins; his hatred of London railway stations, those 'sulphurous houses of damnation',[52] of Thames steam-launches, of pseudo-Scotsmen, tall-story merchants, 'fadmongers, teetotallers, missionaries of divers isms'[53]—a list which reminds us that Gilbert and Sullivan had produced *The Mikado* in 1885. Ko-Ko's song was exactly the kind of thing that would have stuck in Grahame's mind: and there are other echoes of Gilbert scattered throughout his work. 'The White Poppy' illustrates the soporific, as opposed to the stimulant drug: it is the 'magic juice of oblivion'[54] that Grahame is after, like Keats, forgetfulness of the past, of the whole wretched human condition. Perhaps the oddest piece is a swingeing diatribe against Free Libraries—once again probably inspired by Henley— which deplores 'the cloyed and congested mind resulting from the free run of these grocers' shops to omnivorous appetites', on the curiously Calvinistic premiss that what is easy cannot be any good to one. Besides, 'the grocer's boy of letters is sure to prove a prodigious bore'.[55]

Another point which Grahame brings out with some clarity is the general conviction of his age that the mystery and higher reality of life had been destroyed by the advance of scientific discovery:

> Truly this age is born, like Falstaff, with a white head and something a round belly: and will none of your jigs and fantasies. The golden era of princesses is past. For your really virtuous 'prentices there still remain a merchant's daughter or two, and a bottle of port o' Sundays on the Clapham mahogany. For the rest of us, one or two decent clubs and plenty of nice roomy lunatic asylums.[56]

Science might open up new avenues of research, and offer mankind undreamed-of power; yet, paradoxically, mankind grew less and less satisfied. Sir Robert Ensor has put his finger exactly on the causes of this growing sense of limitation and constriction:

> The rapid rise of populations helped it; the individual felt dwarfed by their mass; the vast urban cemeteries with their labyrinths of tombstones seemed fit end for a life as crowded, blurred, and impersonal as that of the old villages had been detached and distinct. It was the same thing with the world's

geography; the map was getting filled up. Nearly everything worth exploring had been explored.[57]

Farewell, rewards and fairies: everything is known and measurable, there is no longer an incalculable dimension to life. Time has proved that the optimistic scientists were wrong; but to Grahame's generation the outlook must have seemed flat, grey, dismal, and hopeless. There was no salvation in God, for God was on the side of big business and the Puritans; there was no hope from science, for science ate like an acid into the mystery of life; there was no future in political radicalism, because the one aim of the radicals was to destroy the foundations on which English tradition rested. It is surprising, really, that thinking people remained as cheerful as they did.

Grahame's life, indeed, moved on tranquilly enough during these years. In 1888 he was transferred to the Chief Cashier's office: the Chief Cashier was Frank May, who five years later resigned under something of a cloud, having been in the habit, *inter alia*, of advancing high overdrafts on his own authority without consulting the Governor.[58] Here Grahame made friends with Gordon Nairne, who was in later years to be Chief Cashier himself when Grahame was Secretary. Nairne, in his reminiscences about Grahame, hints that he allowed more interpenetration between imagination and business than has generally been supposed. On one occasion Grahame 'had to write a very brief memorandum concerning the affairs of a pensioner of the Bank who had been under me. He asked whether I thought the facts were clearly stated and I remember being much struck by the touch of romance with which he had invested the official life of a very ordinary man.'[59] And, conversely, there was romance to be culled from the Bank in his writings: the magic evocativeness of words like *bullion* or *ingots*, the perennial thrill of a place 'where gold was thought so little of that it was dealt about in shovels'.[60]

Grahame did not remain in the Chief Cashier's office long; the following year he was transferred to the Secretary's office, and here he remained. At first he was occupied with the cataloguing of books in the Directors' Library; and, in Nairne's words, 'as these were mainly on dry-as-dust subjects, I doubt if the task proved very interesting to him'. However, it was here that he first met Sidney Ward. Perhaps because of Ward's delicacy and respect for Grahame's solitude, the two of them were soon intimate enough to go for long week-ends together on the Berkshire Downs. Ward recalls an occasion on which Grahame had borrowed a fourteenth-century cottage in the main street of Streatley, and they walked twenty miles along the Ridgeway before returning to 'chops, great chunks of cheese, new bread, great swills of beer, pipes, bed, and heavenly sleep'.[61]

This week-end, and others like it, supplied the material for several essays.[62] We can sketch in something of what Grahame did and felt on these occasions from his own record: the comfortable breakfast in shirt-sleeves, the stroll through the village street, punctuated by exchange of courtesies with various dogs; the irritation of a bicycle-bell, shattering the rural calm with its metal reminder of cities, speed, and progress. This is his cue to climb a gate and make his way towards solitude and the breezy downs, following the age-old Ridgeway:

> At once it strikes you out and away from the habitable world in a splendid, purposeful manner, running along the highest ridge of the Downs, a broad green ribbon of turf, with but a shade of difference from the neighbouring grass, yet distinct for all that. No villages nor homesteads tempt it aside or modify its course for a yard. . . . Where a railway crosses it, it disappears indeed—hiding, Alpheus-like, from the ignominy of rubble and brick-work; but a little way on it takes up the running again with the same quiet persistence.

Then comes the characteristic touch of animism, the anthropomorphic image: 'Out on that almost trackless expanse of billowy

Downs such a track is in some sort humanly companionable: it really seems to lead you by the hand'.[63]

After a while exercise accomplishes its task, and the moment for contemplation has come. This mild yet intense communion with nature is characteristic not only of Grahame but many of his contemporaries; none perhaps more than Richard Jefferies, whose spiritual autobiography, *The Story of my Heart*, was first published in 1883 and appeared in a second edition about the time Grahame's two 'Ridgeway' essays were written. Jefferies practised a passionate communion with earth and sun and sky; 'I was sensitive to all things,' he wrote, 'to the earth under, and the star-hollow round about; to the least blade of grass, to the largest oak. They seemed like exterior nerves and veins for the conveyance of feeling to me.' He attacked puritanism and the ascetic cult, and made what he called 'pilgrimages' from London into the country, 'to get away from the endless and nameless circumstances of everyday existence, which by degrees build a wall about the mind so that it travels in a constantly narrowing circle'.[64]

It was the direct reaction to life that Wordsworth, Arnold, Jefferies, or Grahame strained their whole art to recover: the recognition, as has well been suggested,[56] of a world in solution ready to be precipitated into who knows what miracle of loveliness, or excitement, or achievement. Yet by Grahame's time the drug-factor had begun to operate; and his description of his sensations on the Berkshire Downs contains the spirit not only of Jefferies but of De Quincey's Opium-Eater, of Coleridge making his laudanum-sodden approach to Xanadu:

Up here all vestiges of a sordid humanity disappear. The loafer is alone with the south-west wind and the blue sky. Only a carolling of larks and a tinkling from distant flocks break the brooding noonday stillness; above, the wind-hover hangs motionless, a black dot on the blue. Prone on his back on the springy turf, gazing up into the sky, his fleshy integument seems to drop away, and the spirit ranges at will among the tranquil clouds. This way Nirvana nearest lies. Earth no longer obtrudes herself; possibly somewhere a thousand miles or so below him the thing still spins like a fretful midge.

The loafer knows not nor cares. His is now an astral body, and through golden spaces of imagination his soul is winging her untrammelled flight[66] only to be recalled, a little later (with deliberate bathos to lower the emotional temperature) by the delights of tobacco, and food, and above all beer.

About 1890 Grahame visited Venice for the first time. Here he met mastiffs that—incredible to relate—flourished on a diet of *oar-blades*: they lived in a garden separated from the canal by an ilex-hedge, and passing boatmen, knowing their habits, would push old oars through the hedge for them: 'whereupon the great dogs, seizing the blades, would crunch them up as though they did but eat biscuit'.[67] And one September day, barefoot and paddling (supreme pleasure!) in the crinkled, sandy shallows of the Lido, his mind full of Ulysses, Grahame encountered an expatriate Englishman who gave him the material for one of his oddest and most revealing stories.[68]

> He was barelegged also, this elderly man of sixty or there-abouts; and he had just found a *cavallo del mare*, and exhibited it with all the delight of a boy; and as we wandered together, cool-footed, eastwards, I learnt by degrees how such a man as this, with the mark of Cheapside still evident on him, came to be pacing the sands of the Lido that evening with me. . . .

Just how much of the subsequent narrative was prompted by the actual, historical meeting, and how much added by Grahame's personal obsessions and fears, we cannot exactly determine. The old man is presented as a former Secretary of a City company dating from Henry VII; and one of his particular duties was 'ticking off, with a blue pencil, the members of his governing body, as they made their appearance at their weekly meeting'.

This function gave the old man a very sizable neurosis. First he lost all sense of time, which seemed to speed up into a nightmare gallop: some members dropped out of the Board, new ones appeared, 'the whole business was a great humming zoetrope', life was slipping through his hands like water spilt in the desert. Then he had a full-scale visual illusion: he saw Death personified, while on an Underground train, and Death was ticking the Secretaries themselves off with a blue pencil; and he knew that when his own name was reached he would die. He jumped out at St. James's Park with one name between him and destruction, and made his way to the Park itself; and there on the bridge over the water he halted, mopped his brow, and gradually recovered his peace of mind:

> Beneath his feet a whole family of ducks circled aimlessly, with content written on every feature; or else, reversing themselves in a position denoting supreme contempt for all humanity above the surface, explored a new cool underworld a few inches below. It was then (he said) that a true sense of his situation began to steal over him; and it was then that he awoke to the fact of another life open to him should he choose to grasp it. . . . The very next Board day he sent in his resignation, and with comfortable pension . . . crossed the Channel and worked South till he came to Venice, where the last trace of blue-pencil nightmare finally faded away.[69]

How far does this passage reflect Grahame's own predicament? To begin with, it is uncannily prophetic. It was written in 1895, when Grahame was not yet Secretary of the Bank—that came several years later—and thirteen years before he resigned and began travelling round the Mediterranean. What it may well indicate is the last kick of his imprisoned *alter ego* against the claims of respectability. Grahame was not yet Secretary: *but he must have known he soon would be.* The future stretched ahead, mapped out, predictable. Time raced dizzily, the blue pencil wagged like a metronome. Thoroughly scared, Grahame took a holiday in

Venice: but, unlike the old man on the Lido, he came back.[70] We cannot be certain how far 'Long Odds' is an accurate description of Grahame's state of mind: but much of it rings unpleasantly true. Once again he had driven his instincts down, deep below the surface: and this time they remained there, alive but invisible. The period of open conflict was over.

THE RURAL PAN
1893-1894

> Yet half a beast is the great god Pan,
>   To laugh as he sits by the river,
> Making a poet out of a man:
> The true gods sigh for the cost and pain,—
> For the reed which grows nevermore again
>   As a reed with the reeds in the river.
>
> ELIZABETH BARRETT BROWNING
> *The Great God Pan*

On 19th January 1893 Kenneth Grahame wrote to John Lane & Elkin Mathews, offering them a selection of his essays for publication in book form. It was a nervous, awkward, tentative letter: another Rubicon to be crossed, and always the chance of rebuff and failure:

Dear Sirs [Grahame wrote] I wonder whether you would care to publish a quite small selection of articles that I have had in the *National Observer* and *St. James's Gazette* during the past few years?

They are, I think, just sufficiently individual and original to stand it.

Mr. Henley suggested to me once, that a 'blend' of these short articles with verse would perhaps make a 'feature' that might take. But that is a detail I have no particular feeling about, one way or the other.

The two journals mentioned would, I think, give friendly reviews.

I can, of course, leave the things with you anyway, to look over.

Your attractive 'format'—which you maintain so well—has mainly prompted my suggestion.[1]

John Lane must have been amused by the naïve blend of flattery, self-advertisement, and shyness—not to mention the heavily underlined hint of friends at court. (It is hard to remember that the author of this letter was soon to be Secretary of the Bank of England.) But Lane perceived the quality of the essays themselves, and agreed to publish them in his autumn list.

Now it is not generally known that the first edition of *Pagan Papers* (as the collection was entitled) contained, in addition to the early essays, six stories which were afterwards to be incorporated in *The Golden Age*: these, in fact, were what many of the critics at once fastened on. But Lane could not have foreseen this when he accepted Grahame's MS., for the simple reason that at the time only one of them, 'The Olympians', had been written. (It had appeared anonymously in the *National Observer* on 19th September 1891, and was an instantaneous success with the literary world.[2]) The remaining five[3] were composed in a kind of creative frenzy between February and September 1893, and incorporated in *Pagan Papers* in time for its publication at the end of October. This was Grahame's first real appearance under his own name before a critical public: all his work hitherto (with the exception of one or two poems) had been unsigned. Henceforward, however, an anonymous essay by him was to be an exception rather than the rule: the three known to us were probably so presented at the author's request, since they all contain suggestive autobiographical material.[4]

What was it that suddenly released this new flow of inspiration in Grahame, and channelled it away from the 'Stevensonette', the method of direct presentation, to the more subtle medium offered by the short story? Why did he, at this moment, abandon the attempt to work out his motifs at surface level, and instead turn to the child's world as a vehicle for his satire and a satisfaction for his aching nostalgia? It seems more than coincidence that the tube-train fantasy—if I have argued the facts correctly—should have immediately preceded this new creative period, and that *The Golden Age* should have appeared, chapter by chapter, at a time when Grahame had once and for all driven his anarchic self underground. The change in style and approach fits exactly with the watershed that such an emotional crisis might be expected to produce. But something was needed to give Grahame the final impetus towards his creative revolution: and it was Henley, the born editor, who both sensed the change and took appropriate action. His intuitive mind at once saw that in 'The Olympians' lay the kernel of something entirely new, the blueprint on which a whole magic structure could be erected; and he used all his powers of persuasion to guide Grahame along the path he should take.

To begin with, he realized that Grahame's need for a mask, a *persona*, could be made to yield literary profits. Hitherto the statement direct had sheltered behind simple anonymity: Henley changed all that. He made Grahame cast his children's world in the form of fiction—characters, dialogue and all: this at once provided a *persona* of a far more subtle kind. Grahame could, without anxiety, now come out into the open, safe in the knowledge that his 'real self' was not addressing an audience direct. Precisely because of this, his imagination—and the only too well buried instincts on which it fed—could work far more freely. In *The Golden Age* the process was only half-complete; later, in *The Wind in the Willows*, it reached its full, logical conclusion.

Why Grahame expressed such gratitude to Henley in after years was because he knew—perhaps not consciously—that the lame editor had turned the one psychological key, at the one possible time, which released his full inner creativity. Henley knew Grahame's limitations no less than his talents: he guessed at once that here was a supreme miniaturist, who would destroy his own unique vision if he attempted to inflate himself into a fashionable 'major' writer, or continued to elaborate his ideas too consciously. Like every born editor, Henley's first concern was to realize his contributors' potential *on their own terms*, not his. When he cut Yeats's verses about it was, paradoxically, in the belief that he was making them more Yeatsian. He may have been wrong; but his intention was wholly innocent. Sometimes the process failed; sometimes—and *The Golden Age* is a shining example—he succeeded to perfection.

It was generally believed by the literary *cognoscenti* at the time that Henley's part in *The Golden Age* had been both more direct and less subtle. An anonymous critic of the *Academy*, summing up Grahame's achievement in 1897, hinted at this fairly broadly: [5]

> It may be that when the history of the *Scots* and *National Observer* is written—and it would make, with selections, a most agreeable and invigorating book—we shall be told to what extent Mr. Henley supplied not only a haven for young writers, but also an impulse and momentum. We shall then know whether Mr. Grahame wrote his stirring essay on Orion —the Hunter—from within or without, whether it was his own idea to continue the diverting narrative of the childhood of Harold and Edward, Charlotte and Selina. As the cause of wit in others Mr. Henley holds a very high position.

But such a critic had only to compare the *style* of *The Golden Age* with that imposed by Henley on the general run of his contributors to see that this was no case of literary hypnosis. Grahame at one stroke came back to something very near the vernacular; and Henley left his copy untouched. There was, indeed, the occasional artifice; but on the whole the stylistic metamorphosis was as remarkable and complete as the psychological one had been. (Any one who doubts this need only open *The Golden Age* and compare 'The Olympians' with any subsequent chapter.) For once Henley, perhaps pleased at his own percipience, was content to let well alone; and for both qualities he deserves—in this instance at least—our heartfelt gratitude.

Between acceptance and publication of *Pagan Papers* Grahame had a full and busy year. In Threadneedle Street there was a sizable flutter over the Chief Cashier's resignation, and another, of astronomical dimensions, over the decision to employ women for clerical and sorting work: this caused violent conservative disapproval, and a spate of tiresome jokes.[6] (It also was probably responsible in part for Grahame's one 'adult' short story, *The Headswoman*, which he was completing about this time, and which has sometimes been taken as an allegorical skit on the feminist movement.[7]) He was acting as a secretarial go-between for Sidney Lee and Furnivall over the latter's newly projected critical edition of Shakespeare—Lee was writing introductions for about five plays—and handing out surprisingly shrewd advice to the new editor of the *D.N.B.* on landlords and mortgages.[8] He returned towards the beginning of autumn from an Alpine holiday by the Rhône, cheerful and tanned, and ready for whatever the critics might say.[9] He wrote to Lane in September that 'Henley asks me to let him see a set of sheets of the book before it appears. He is anxious to see how it turns out.' His royalty agreement was an unusually good one for John Lane in those days: on a limited edition of 450 copies he got 10 per cent. for the first 200, and 20 per cent. thereafter. 'I don't call this a grasping proposal', he claimed '—especially from a Scotchman.' Lane's comments have not survived. If only a quarter of the chiselling tactics attributed to him by Baron Corvo are true, Grahame must have beaten him hands down at his own game.[10]

Pagan Papers was a pleasantly printed and produced little volume, which flaunted an arresting frontispiece by Aubrey Beardsley. Beardsley's elegant and Satanic Pan made a piquant contrast with the rural essay to which it mainly referred: the incongruity is significant. To judge by a passage in *The Golden Age*,[11] Grahame was as excited by his advance copies as any schoolboy. Edward, you will remember, when about to depart to school for the first time, acquired a trunk and play-box with his name painted on them in large letters:

> After their arrival the owner used to disappear mysteriously, and be found eventually wandering round his luggage, murmuring to himself, 'Edward ——', in a rapt remote sort of way. It was a weakness, of course, and pointed to a soft spot in his character; but those who can remember the sensation of first seeing their names in print will not think hardly of him.

And soon the reviews began to come in.

'There was no dissenting voice in the chorus of praise', Chalmers claims.[12] This is simply untrue. *Pagan Papers* got a very mixed reception indeed. The oddest assumption, shared by Grant Richards in *Great Thoughts* and the anonymous critic of the *Literary Echo*, is that the essays are not, in fact, pagan—'for', says Richards (can he be joking?) 'it was in the pages of Mr. Henley's ever-English organ that [their] contents made their first appeal'. Those who enjoyed the book praised its vitality, gusto, and colour; but others were not slow to attack its derivativeness, preciosity, and affectations, while the *Scotsman* declared, with Calvinistic rectitude, that the essays 'do not manifestly appear to be the work of a Christian'. 'Certain jewels', observed the *Pall Mall Gazette*, 'are endurable only under certain lights; but Mr. Grahame loves to display all his jewellery by every light that fills his sky or his chamber.'[13]

What strikes one most about these notices is their essential triviality. The only periodical that came remotely near the heart of the matter was the short-lived *Critic*, in a review written six years after publication—surely a record delay?—which at least touches on one main theme implicit in the book's title:

> Mr. Grahame [observes this leisurely reviewer] shows that the old gods, for so long slaves of the ink-pot, have yet some work left in them, and, if harnessed all together and touched up with the whip of invention, may be made to drag a conceit

through the ruts and bog-holes of a dozen paragraphs. Being capable of so much, he is surely capable of better. Let him turn the gods out to grass, and go, himself, in the shafts. Then we shall see what we shall see.

It was easy to be wise after the event—by 1899 not only *The Golden Age* but also *Dream Days* had been published—but there was a good deal of truth in this criticism, nevertheless. The aesthetic movement had converted the natural impulses of anti-industrialists into a convention of 'literary paganism', which was no less remote from reality than the profiteering Philistines it opposed. Grahame only succeeded inasmuch as he preserved his paganism from urban faking and coterie art.

He was quite explicit as to the main impulse behind this concept of life: it was an antidote to 'the shadow of Scotch-Calvinist-devil-worship' on which he had been brought up.[14] But, as in politics, he was forced to share his creed with a large number of people whose ideas and ethics differed radically from his. Arnold's gentlemanly rural pantheism was one thing: the aberrations of Decadents and Satanists and the rest of the queer crew who populate Mario Praz's *The Romantic Agony* were quite another.

What Grahame failed to see was that neo-Paganism implied something more than a relaxation of puritan taboos and the sensuous appreciation of nature's bounty. It had almost nothing in common with the pre-Christian ethic on which it was supposedly modelled. It was not, as Huxley suggested, Catholicism with the Christianity taken out, but a conscious *anti*-Christianity that made the antics of Aleister Crowley and the rest of the Black Magic brigade logically only too admissible. It was in vain that Arthur Machen pointed out the fallacy of supposing that 'whereas good Christians are obliged to lead very strict lives, good pagans could do exactly as they pleased', and reminded his readers that the stark elements of ancient morality 'make up a picture of old Greece that is strangely different from the Rosy Lubberland of our Neo-pagans'.[15] License was precisely what the rebels wanted, and they found it easy enough to manufacture an extenuating myth in support of their activities.

Today their daring naughtinesses, so hedged about with an ingrained aptitude for respectable public behaviour, strike us as comic and a little sad—sad, because they reveal so clearly the desperate underlying need for a charitable and nourishing faith. Browning's Mr. Sludge, the fake medium, is only a symbol of the mushrooming esoteric cults that sprang up to satisfy this inarticulate need, which got scant comfort from the Metaphysical Society or Bradley's *Appearance and Reality*. There was indeed Auguste Comte, with his 'deification of Humanity itself as the Great Being or Goddess',[16] but this was too vast an abstraction for easy emotional comprehension. Clough's acid *New Decalogue* had knocked the last nail in the coffin of the Victorian Established Church. What then was left but to go by opposites and turn the Established Church inside out, reverse all its values? An immense *Angst* and weariness were abroad: as Arthur Symons wrote,

> Trouble has come upon us like a sudden cloud,
> A sudden summer cloud with thunder in its wings.
> There is an end for us of old familiar things
> Now that this desolating voice has spoken aloud.

The sillier manifestations of this revolt are epitomized in the single number of William Sharp's *Pagan Review*, which appeared in 1892. It bears the epigraph '*Sic transit gloria Grundi*', and consists in the main of sultry melodramatic stories bearing titles like 'The Rape of the Sabine Women' or 'Dionysos in India'. These were all written by Sharp himself under various pseudonyms. Some are unintentionally funny in the extreme; the prize goes to 'The Oread', in which we are treated to the entrancing spectacle of a young man in full shooting rig, Norfolk jacket and all, chasing a naked classical nymph over a Scottish grouse-moor. 'The Black Madonna', an extraordinary play stuffed with mother-goddesses, blood-sacrifice, crucifixion, sex, sadism, and pseudo-primitivism, reads like a *New Statesman* parody of *The Plumed Serpent*—though it does contain one immortal scrap of dialogue:[17]

> *The Black Madonna* (trembling and strangely troubled): What would'st thou?
> *Bihr*: Thou!

In 1891 W. F. Barry published an extremely sensible article on neo-paganism in the *Quarterly Review*.[18] This traced its literary genesis (from the moral viewpoint) in Hume, Rousseau, Voltaire, Goethe, and Lessing; and, though overtly hostile to the core of natural passion which informed it, hit with deadly accuracy on the weaknesses inherent in its excesses. Of the retreat to mediaevalism Barry wrote: 'Despite its gorgeous tones we are conscious of an unreality. The masked figures, who are so well made up, cannot take off their visors without the enchantment vanishing . . . They could not raise the dead, but they found huge delight in imitating their grave-clothes.'

Barry deplored the usurpation of reason by 'the thrills and spasms of a nerve, or complications of intense and faint feelings'. He attacked the effeminacy and hedonism which characterized neo-pagan behaviour, attributing it (and here he had Henley, of all people, on his side) to sixty years of peace, idleness, and over-education. But his shrewdest thrust was when he compared the new recidivists with their spiritual ancestor Julian the Apostate. All that Libanius and the philosophers could do for Julian was to vote addresses of condolence to the gods of the *ancien régime*: Apollo and Jove could not be revived by the whim of an Imperial *littérateur*. 'From a mere literature', asks Barry, 'when has religion gone down into the popular imagination?' Great Pan was dead; and not the combined ministrations of rebels, aesthetes, pastoralists, and Satanists could ever wish him into life again, though they tried every trick they knew for more than thirty years.

'Pan', in fact, was a convenient short-hand term for their own anarchic emotional urges: he had become a literary symbol, without any highest common factor except a vague full-blooded animalism. The frequency of references to him in the literature, the recurrent representations of him in the art of the period offer an interesting side-light on that pantheistic nature-worship of which, over the years, he had become the convenient and accepted deity. The tradition ran unbroken from Coleridge and Wordsworth (on both of whom Hazlitt had some shrewd remarks to make in this connection [19]) through Keats, Shelley, Arnold, the Brownings, Swinburne, and Stevenson—who regarded Pan as the emblem of Anti-Science as well as Anti-Calvin. [20] The Goat-foot peeped out in Brooke and 'Saki' and E. M. Forster's early short stories. He inspired countless poems, including a volume by Miss Eleanor Farjeon. Maurice Hewlett and Richard Le Gallienne flirted with him. John Buchan had a personal experience of Panic terror while climbing in the Bavarian Alps: 'Sebastian the guide had seen the goat-foot god, or something of the kind—he was forest born, and Bavarian peasants are very near primeval things —and he had made me feel his terror'. [21]

The drawings and paintings told a similar story. Osbert Burdett said of Beardsley's 'The Mysterious Rose-Garden' that 'it is conventional art listening to the whisper of creative imagination in the familiar and formal garden of Victorian times: it is *the return of Pan, the repudiation of authority*'. (Italics mine.) This was the period that could find no room for the grotesque, that held Dickens in some suspicion and distrusted *Punch* till it had been thoroughly institutionalized. [22] Sometimes, as in Beardsley, Pan's healthy phallicism was subtly converted into urban pornography. Sometimes—and C. H. Shannon's woodcuts in *The Dial* are the most striking examples—he was portrayed as a dark, cruel, towering, monolithic figure: 'Pan Mountain' shows him crouched, merging with the rocky hillside, his pipes turning to pendent rock pinnacles, his half-crossed legs to wild foothills. The Earth-symbolism is obvious. [23]

There is equal variety in the literary treatment. What *was* he doing, the Great God Pan, down in the reeds by the river? What springs of the imagination, long choked with rational rubble, broke loose now to swell the stream where he dabbed his cloven hooves? To each, it seemed, he wore a different appearance. For some he incarnated terror and cruelty, the rejected forces of nature taking their revenge. In one of Machen's novels, for instance, a girl who sees Pan goes insane; and 'Saki', in 'The Music on the Hill', brings to a very nasty end a sophisticated London woman who is foolish enough to doubt his existence.[24] More often his sexual attributes are emphasized, the fierce unrestrained lechery free of all human conventions: Browning gives an excellent example of this:

> So lay this Maid-Moon clasped around and caught
> By rough red Pan, the god of all that tract . . .
> Bruised to the breast of Pan, half-god half-brute,
> Raked by his bristly boar-sword while he lapped
> —Never say, kissed her! that were to pollute
> Love's language . . . &c.[25]

This concept, which appealed strongly to the Decadents for several fairly obvious reasons, was occasionally watered down to suit more delicate and conventional tastes. T. Sturge Moore, for instance, in *Pan's Prophecy*, turns the demi-god into a confidant for the love-lorn, a kind of primitive Miss Lonelyhearts:

> . . . ofttimes nymph or faun
> To tell of their heart-breaking disappointments
> Seeketh me in the lone mid-forest lawn;
> Or with torn flesh, sprained joints requiring ointments,
> Fainting, will reach my hill-crest cave at dawn.

The last two lines I have quoted from Moore—lines which Grahame was to echo in *The Wind in the Willows*—bring us to a third aspect of Pan which the neo-pagans emphasized: his rôle as protector and healer of herds and country folk. This is the Pan

whom Keats drew in *Endymion*, the 'breather round our farms/
To keep off mildew and all weather harms'; [26] and this is the Pan
on whom Grahame largely founds his own variant. The basic
concept was admirably expressed by Maurice Hewlett in a letter
to Milton Browner, an American journalist: [27]

> The whole thing is really a myth. The root idea, I suppose, is
> the oneness of creation—man as a natural force, differing in no
> essential way from plants and animals. Then God is reduced to
> the same expression, and He and Man, and the Wind and
> Weather, Trees, Sheep, Love, Life, Death, Fear, all play their
> parts out and meet and merge, and mate and mingle. . . .

Richard Le Gallienne, too, had a word for Pan as a symbol of
revolt against hypocritical conventions:

> Pan is unmistakably the father of poets, and Pan, it is to be
> feared, is a god who is not always to be found in full evening
> dress and in perfect taste. . . . He is often found lacking in
> 'refinement', as understood in drawingrooms and seminaries.
> His exquisite products are usually brought about by processes
> quite coarse and shocking to refined individuals.[28]

Obviously the same fallacy is latent in the Pan cult as practised
by the neo-pagans, and in Morris's Pre-Raphaelism: a sophisticated, predominantly urban *élite* cannot recapture the instincts of
genuine primitivism, only self-consciously imitate its external
manifestations. These have a compulsive attraction for any jaded
intellectual: they contain something of which he has been totally
starved. At the same time he can only consider them through the
polarized lens of his own highly self-conscious preconceptions.
This becomes at once apparent when we consider Pan's history
in the ancient world. He was a primitive mountain daemon, half-
beast, half-man: ithyphallic, sender of epilepsy and bad dreams,
protector of herds, saviour from plague, an ambivalent demigod,
whose image was whipped magically with squills in time of
dearth. Nowhere did his cult touch the higher life of the society

or the higher religion of the state; but this did not stop urban philosophers from dabbling in its existing earthiness. As Farnell mildly observed,[29] 'there is no Greek cult so primitive and rustic but what some tolerant philosopher could infuse ethical thought into it'. Grahame would have approved of Socrates, on the banks of the Ilissus, praying to Pan—of all deities—for 'inner beauty of soul'.[30]

The neo-paganism of the Nineties had its exact analogue in Greece and Alexandria during the late Hellenistic period—after Alexander's conquest had spread urban cosmopolitanism, but before the supremacy of Rome was achieved. The scholar poets in their great cities sought the same synthetic replacements for the natural roots they had lost. They cultivated a conventional pastoralism, they wrote pseudo-epics in their studies (but never drew a sword) and they had a passion for primitive cults, preferably with a strong phallic ritual: not realizing that, now fertility was no longer a matter of life and death every year, the ritual had lost much of its true significance, and merely served as an excuse for sophisticated self-indulgence. These pallid Syracusans and Alexandrians envied the uncomplicated life that still went on in the 'Arcadian' countryside, but they could not live it themselves; they did their best by writing bucolic elegies.[31]

Grahame was thus in a curious position when dealing with Pan. Parts of the legend he must have found frightening and repellent; but the rest struck an answering chord in his own nature, and served as the basis for his own private mythology. It does not seem to have occurred to him that the subtle emasculation he performed invalidated the entire concept, or made it at the best a psychological prop for his own emotional instability. He picked out the attributes he needed, rejected those that did not suit him, invented others when necessary, and in general found himself walking an uneasy path between quagmires of sex on one side and terror on the other.

I will discuss the Pan of *The Wind in the Willows* later, in his proper place; here I am more concerned with his first manifestation in *Pagan Papers* and several of the other early essays. Pan is associated by Grahame with the spring,[32] but not in any crudely regenerative sense; and in 'The Lost Centaur' he is treated as a demigod

> in whom the submerged human system peeps out but fitfully, at exalted moments. He, the peevish and irascible, shy of trodden ways and pretty domesticities, is linked to us by little but his love of melody; but for which saving grace, the hair would soon creep up from thigh to horn of him. At times he will still do us a friendly turn: will lend a helping hand to poor little Psyche, wilfully seeking her own salvation; will stand shoulder to shoulder with us on Marathon plain. But in the main his sympathies are first for the beast: to which his horns are never horrific, but, with his hairy pelt, ever natural and familiar, and his voice (with its talk of help and healing) not harsh or dissonant, but voice of very brother as well as very god.[33]

Pan pipes at Mapledurham or in Hurley backwater;[34] he is, to quote the title of the essay which most concerns him, the Rural Pan, inimical both to fashionable dandy and plebeian pleasure-seeker, to be sought neither in Piccadilly, nor at Ascot or the Guards' Club in Maidenhead. No, his place is by the quiet river-bank, or

> under the great shadow of Streatley Hill . . . or better yet, pushing an explorer's prow up the remote untravelled Thame, till Dorchester's stately roof broods over the quiet fields. In solitudes such as this Pan sits and dabbles, and all the air is full of the music of his piping. . . . Out of hearing of all the clamour, the rural Pan may be found stretched on Ranmore Common, loitering under Abinger pines, or prone by the secluded stream of the sinuous Mole, abounding in friendly greetings for his foster-brothers the dab-chick and the water-rat.[35]

Pan avoids high roads and railways, preferring sheep-tracks, and the animal company they afford. He is not unsocial, but 'shy of the company of his more showy brother-deities'; his pleasure is more to go among unpretentious country folk, labourers and shepherds, 'simple cheery sinners'. He is, after all, only half a god, and there is a strong earthy element in him. Like the Scholar Gipsy, he turns up occasionally in remote inns, disguised as a hedger-and-ditcher, and 'strange lore and quaint fancy he will then impart, in the musical Wessex or Mercian he has learned to speak so naturally'—but it is only after he has gone that his identity is discovered. Commercialism, jerry-building, railways are reducing his domain: but there are still commons and sheep-downs where he can hide, though not for many years to come.[36]

I said earlier in this chapter that 'Pan' was a convenient symbol into which writers could pour their own anarchic urges: a receptacle for the id, so to speak. It is clear that this applies to Grahame with some exactness: his version of Pan provides a justification for his personal habits by giving them the sanction of a semi-divine myth. But when we examine his portrait more closely, we get the unescapable impression that this Pan was painted with one eye at least on the mirror: that Grahame has not only trimmed his god to suit his fancy, but undergone a considerable degree of self-identification with him. A change of names, and every passage would be accepted, with minor adjustments, as autobiographical: the distrust of Society, the country pottering, the love of animals, the fear of industrial development. The demigod who talks 'musical Wessex' in a country pub and is accepted by the locals as one of themselves at once recalls Grahame's peculiar delight at being mistaken for a Cornish fisherman.

He is, we may guess, all the more pleased because—in Grahame's myth—though *in* the country, he is not *of* it. This is a fact of some importance. Grahame's mythical ruralist—and indeed Grahame himself—never *does* anything in the country; he may be 'addicted to the kindly soil' but not 'to the working thereof'. When ploughing is being done, he is meditating by the furrow. At harvest-time he is gliding past in a canoe or skiff. He is perpetually

on holiday; and this is the weakest aspect of his myth. It is a week-
end myth: his real work, never acknowledged, lies elsewhere, in
the City. Even Rat, we remember, was in the way in a harvest
field.

If Pan is an aspect of Grahame's personality—or, to be more
precise, a *persona* into which he could put himself at a heightened
level—we are forced to consider the elimination of the demi-god's
sexual aspect from this presentation in more personal terms.
There is no evidence to suggest that Grahame was sexually
abnormal; but a good deal—his own not least—which indicates
that he preserved (perhaps as one element only in a dual nature)
what may be described as a pre-pubertal outlook: the child's
clear vision, with its characteristic selections and omissions. In
1897 we find him writing to Helen Dunham: 'I too have always
kept a scrap-book . . . of places where I'm going to live "when
I'm grown up". . . . I trust he will be more fortunate than I, and
really *attain*, some day—only that would entail growing up,
wouldn't it? Perhaps things are better as they are. . . .' And Miss
Dunham recalled him saying on another occasion in 1896 (she
had expressed herself 'afraid that he might grow up'): 'No—I
don't think I shall—I've just been writing about a circus and I
found I didn't feel a bit grown up'.[37] At the very end of his life he
wrote in a letter to the father of a childish admirer that 'she
mustn't grow any older, or she will get away from Mole and
Rat'.[38] He would, I suspect, have willingly numbered himself
amongst the rare souls whom C. E. Maud described as 'those who
have kept fresh in their hearts "the everlasting child", whose
eyes look out still with wonder on a wondrous world, who . . .
hear the pipes of Pan among the rushes, and the flowers talking in
the forest'.[39]

It is certainly true that many of Grahame's values and insights
were almost uncannily similar to those of children or primitive
savages: his curious indifference, amounting at times to callousness, over adult relationships; his intense self-liberating imagina-

'The High Street of the Golden City'

The River-Bankers

From drawings by E. H. Shepard

tion; his timelessness, his natural animistic sense, which endowed even lifeless objects with a personality of their own; his tendency to confuse matter and thought, internal and external, dream and reality. All these phenomena can be readily encountered in a book such as Jean Piaget's *The Child's Conception of the World*:[40] Grahame would have at once understood the child who, when asked why bears had four feet, replied: 'Because they've been naughty and God has punished them'.[41] It was half a shrewd and ambitious business-man, half an innocent child who was introduced by Lane to Henry Harland after the publication of *Pagan Papers*, and who became perhaps the most improbable contributor that the newly founded *Yellow Book* ever acquired.

THE GOLDEN YEARS
1894-1898

He thought he saw a Banker's Clerk
Descending from the bus:
He looked again, and found it was
A Hippopotamus:
'If this should stay to dine,' he said,
'There won't be much for us.'
LEWIS CARROLL: *Sylvie and Bruno*

Men look for retreats for themselves, the country, the seashore, the hills; and you yourself, too, are peculiarly accustomed to feel the same want. Yet all this is very unlike a philosopher, when you may at any hour you please retreat into yourself. For nowhere does a man retreat into more quiet or more privacy than into his own mind, especially one who has within such things that he has only to look into, and become at once in perfect ease.
MARCUS AURELIUS: *The Meditations*

The Yellow Book was first conceived by the expatriate American novelist Henry Harland, on a wet afternoon at his house in the Cromwell Road. Enthusiastically he held forth to the company in the drawing-room about starting a magazine which should represent—ominously familiar phrase—the 'New Movement'. 'New', in fact, was the operative word; everything acquired it as a prefix in the Yellow Decade. There was the 'New Woman', the 'New Morality', and, of course, the 'New Paganism'. Wilde wrote of the 'New Remorse'; H. D. Traill, in an article on the New Fiction, declared that 'not to be *new* is, in these days, to be nothing'. A penny weekly 'with a humanitarian and radical objective' was called *The New Age*. The world of art and literature was in a conscious ferment of re-orientation, and what Harland did was simply to crystallize this new feeling by providing an appropriate vehicle for its expression.[1]

In February 1894, at a riotously tipsy dinner-party in the Devonshire Club, John Lane gave the seal of his approval to the new project. Harland was appointed editor, on the grounds that he was more 'elevated' than anyone else present; Aubrey Beardsley became art editor, and Lane undertook to publish the *Yellow Book* quarterly from the Bodley Head.[2] Unlike many such wine-inspired fancies, this one became reality. The first number appeared two months later, in April, with a list of contributors that included Henry James, Richard Le Gallienne, Saintsbury, Gosse, Richard Garnett, George Moore, Arthur Symons, and A. C. Benson. Max Beerbohm supplied an undergraduate essay called 'A Defence of Cosmetics', while Harland himself reminisced about the white mice he had kept in childhood. Mr. Evelyn Waugh's father went so far along the path of respectability as to criticize lady novelists for describing childbirth—'this freedom of speech', he wrote, 'is degenerating into a license which some of us cannot but view with regret and apprehension'.[3] Could anything have been more modest and respectable?

Yet as soon as *The Yellow Book* appeared it was greeted with a howl of anger and derision by conservative critics, who were particularly upset by Beardsley's satirical drawings and Beerbohm's light-hearted irony, which they took (or affected to take) *au pied de la lettre*. This must have alarmed Harland, who for all his desperate attempts at unconventionality—the goatee beard, the unkempt hair, the stories composed in dressing-gown and pyjamas—was at heart a conventional bourgeois, shocked to the core by the least suggestion of irregularity or real vice. (There is a malicious portrait of him in Baron Corvo's novel *Nicholas Crabbe*, where his feverishness, shrill voice, and physical tics are described in merciless detail.[4]) Nevertheless, he persisted in his plan; the second number appeared towards the end of July, while the critical rumpus was still going on. It contained, *inter alia*, Grahame's first contribution, 'The Roman Road', perhaps the best of all the stories which compose *The Golden Age*.

Harland must have got in touch with Grahame, probably at Lane's suggestion, as soon as the first number had appeared. At all events, Grahame had the galley-proofs of 'The Roman Road' in May, when Mary Richardson came to visit him in the top-floor flat in Chelsea Gardens; he read the story aloud to her from corrected slips after tea (he had a beautiful reading voice) while she gazed out from his high window over the Thames to the sunlit greenery of Battersea Park.[5] Its moral—that only the artist and the child have a true vision of ultimate reality—agreed very well with the ideals expressed by Harland and his associates. It is not surprising that 'The Roman Road' was a considerable *succès d'estime*, or that Grahame was promptly invited to submit further stories to the new quarterly. He was, perhaps, all the more ready to comply when the *National Observer*, after a particularly virulent row between Henley and Fitzroy Bell, finally ceased publication in August. (It was not till 1895 that Henley found himself in an editorial chair again, in charge of another fresh venture which he called—almost inevitably—*The New Review*.)

Grahame, as a contributor, was inevitably drawn into the social set which revolved round the Harlands and the Beardsleys. He never felt really at home in this kind of *milieu*: there was a wide gap between his 'new paganism' and theirs, a gap symbolized by the contrasting tone of *Pagan Papers* and the Beardsley sketch which formed its frontispiece. On Saturday evenings he would turn up regularly at Henry and Aline Harland's flat in the Cromwell Road, but always seemed anxious to get into a corner and escape notice if possible.[6] The Harlands, truth to tell, were a little disconcerting. They were liable to invite people to dinner and then forget all about it, so that guests turned up in evening dress to find Henry and Aline sitting down in the kitchen over a pair of chops; they sulked and quarrelled in public; they never bothered to introduce people, or conceal their moods. In general they resembled a pair of completely spoilt children: once, when they failed to agree on a restaurant, Henry turned on Aline with: 'All right, we won't go anywhere at all'—and three guests lost their dinner.[7] But worse than their tantrums was the air of conscious 'decadence' cultivated by the *Yellow Book* circle as a whole, the faint flavour of epicenity which Grahame found highly disagreeable. It was certainly a change from the robust atmosphere of Henley's literary imperialism.*

Netta Syrett, a fellow-contributor, commented specifically on the solid masculinity, the humour, sanity, and normality which distinguished Grahame from the 'Beardsley group', and in particular 'his complete freedom from the affectations which so puzzled me in the other men of the set'.[8] Evelyn Sharp, in her autobiography, recalled his resentment at the famous *Punch* epigram, 'Uncleanliness is next to Bodliness'. Apparently he was so put out that he wanted Lane to take some kind of legal action against *Punch*; but Lane sensibly chose to treat the whole thing as a vast joke.[9] All the evidence suggests that while Grahame had a keen sense of humour, he could not and would not tolerate malice in any form. This led him to cross swords occasionally with Harland, who was nothing if not waspish: Grahame stopped him teasing Evelyn Sharp for her sexual innocence,[10] and refused to endorse his mockery of John Davidson's 'Ballad of a Nun', which Harland afterwards published.[11] He was wont to observe, as if for his own self-assurance: 'In the *Yellow Book* itself there is not enough impropriety to cover a sixpence, and there is no

---

* Anyone who wishes to get a malicious (but by no means inaccurate) picture of the seamier side of these literary aesthetes—their money-squabbles, squalor, sex-life, and jockeying for advancement—cannot do better than read Baron Corvo's novel *Nicholas Crabbe*: all the major characters are instantly recognizable.

indecency at all'.[12] They were really very respectable socially, these neo-pagans, for all their verbal sensuality and anarchic sentiments.

Evelyn Sharp has left us this picture of Grahame at the Harlands':[13]

He was, perhaps, shy among strangers, always looked away hastily if he caught you looking at him, simply hated being lionized but liked to talk about his work if he knew you were sympathetic and not likely to gush about it. . . . He was very kind and courteous, but had not an ounce of humbug in him. Very sensitive but would die sooner than let you think so if he could help it, and in many ways reminded one of the nicest kind of schoolboy except that he had a fine taste in literature instead of a passion for sport. He had a charming sense of humour and was a great tease. In the *Yellow Book* set we all admired him tremendously, and the appearance of one of his sketches in the Y.B. would be hailed as an event and discussed at length the next Saturday evening. . . . He never spoke much, only when he had something to say; he never said anything unkind about anybody, or to anybody, except through inability to say something sincere.

Though Kenneth may have felt distaste for the Decadents' morals, he shared their love of conviviality. He was always to the fore in the Harlands' kitchen, helping over supper; and it was probably after a particularly heavy *Yellow Book* dinner that the incident of the vegetable cart occurred. Kenneth wandered into Piccadilly late one night, in full evening dress and happy (to say the least) on the Harlands' claret. Here he saw a vegetable cart moving eastwards towards Covent Garden. He ran after it, swung himself aboard among the cabbages, and promptly fell asleep. When he woke it was broad daylight. He was still in the cart; but now it was empty, and moving down Piccadilly in the opposite direction. As Alan Lidderdale, who tells the story, observed, 'it was one of the regrets of Kenneth's life that he never knew what happened in the interval'.[14]

I have always thought this episode an apt symbol of Grahame's uneasy flirtation with the Beardsley group. He joined them in a fit of literary intoxication and woke up to a childhood morning without being quite sure how he had got there; he only knew he had a moral hangover. There were some things better forgotten, and he forgot them as quickly as he could. But the two years before Oscar Wilde's trial went deeper into his emotional make-up than he suspected, and left a queer literary legacy behind.

The ethical dilemma in which Grahame found himself was largely, of course, due to his education. One of the perennial problems which the monastic humanists of the Middle Ages were forced to face was the reconciliation of the Christian faith with a non-Christian tradition of literature and scholarship. By the nineteenth century this paradox had lost its sting: classics, cricket, and Christianity formed a holy trinity sanctified by upper-class usage. Thus when the post-Arnold aesthetic rebellion took place, the rebels found ready-made symbols waiting for them, symbols which they had learnt at school. Sixth-Form ushers who had sharpened young minds on the glories of Greece suddenly found their lessons being turned against themselves. So must the educationalists in India have felt when a prolonged diet of Burke and Mill gave their Hindu pupils practical notions about liberty.

One result of this common symbolism drawn from the classical world was to give a superficial appearance of unanimity to what was in fact a most diverse opposition. Henley, Morris, Beardsley, and Grahame (to take a random cross-section) were united by one thing only: anti-authoritarianism. In every other way they were deeply divided among themselves. The label of 'neo-pagan' covered a multitude of virtues as well as sins.

Grahame learnt fairly quickly that the ethics of the Decadents did not represent the pagan spirit as he understood it. He, more openly than Harland, was shocked by the cult of perversity and drugs, by Dowson's hashish, by the self-indulgence and self-destruction of James Thomson and Francis Thompson, by the dreadful gutter-fate of the painter Simeon Solomon.[15] The *nostalgie de la boue* propounded by Rimbaud and Baudelaire, the sedulous cultivation of vice as a gesture of defiance and despair merely disgusted and repelled him. He chose (as we can now see) the only path open to him: the cult of innocence. Everywhere corruption stared him in the face: industrial corruption, social corruption, corruption of the soul among those who should have been his allies in opposition. Only childhood, ever more golden in retrospect, remained untouched, and he fastened hungrily upon it. Between December 1893 and January 1895 the remaining eleven stories in *The Golden Age* were written: and in February 1895 it was published as a book.

Meanwhile Grahame had changed his address once more, and this time in a more radical sense. The days of 'digs' and flats were over. In the autumn of 1894 he and a barrister named Tom Greg took the joint lease of a house: No. 5 Kensington Crescent. Greg brought with him his own former housekeeper, Sarah Bath, an outspoken and strait-laced Somerset martinet who specialized in bachelors.[16] As a magic gesture of ownership Grahame fixed on the front of the house, between the drawing-room windows, the della Robbia plaque he had acquired during his visit to Florence. This, as Annie Grahame observed, 'formed a kind of landmark enabling one to find the house at once; it also served as a shrine for the Italian organ-grinders, who, Kenneth said, used to come and perform their devotions in front of it and then go down into the area and demand alms from Miss Bath, who, however (having travelled in Italy herself), was quite equal to them and sternly refused to give them anything, whereupon they departed muttering curses and shaking their fists at her....'[17] The Madonna and Child symbolized many things for Kenneth: simple and sincere faith; the whole atmosphere of the South; perhaps, too, the mother he had lost so early himself.

Why did he choose this particular time to set up house? Partly, in all probability, because he was for a short period appointed Acting Secretary at the Bank, though not yet thirty-five.[18] The great Hammond Chubb, after drafting his epoch-making Report on the reorganizing of Bank administration, had retired:[19] his tenure had lasted fifteen years, and no successor was immediately elected. Grahame filled the post for a few months, till G. F. Glennie's appointment was ratified; and it may well have been intimated to him that an Acting Secretary of the Bank of England could hardly entertain distinguished business guests in a top-floor Chelsea attic. But there was possibly another, rather more subtle, motive. In April 1894 Kenneth's cousin, one A. H. Hawkins, barrister-at-law, who had been a fellow-contributor to the *St. James's Gazette*, suddenly woke up to find himself famous. Using his first two names, Anthony Hope, as a pseudonym, he had published a romance entitled *The Prisoner of Zenda*. It made his fortune, and added a new word, Ruritania, to the English language. But its immediate result was that in July Anthony abandoned the Bar and set up as a full-time writer.

The effect of this decision on Kenneth can be only too easily imagined. For nearly fifteen years he had dreamed of just such a release, yet always shrank away from it at the crucial moment, despite the exhortations of Henley and his other friends. The thing remained deliciously impossible, a mirage tempting him with the unattainable; and now Anthony, in very similar circumstances, had actually taken the plunge. Kenneth was both envious and, we may suspect, somewhat irritated: irritated, because his own reactions to Anthony's success forced him to realize consciously that, given the chance of emulating his cousin, he would still refuse. The City owned at least half his soul by now: he needed his cage.

Corruption takes many subtle forms, and in Grahame's case it disguised itself as the security and public esteem conferred by material success. He had had a foretaste of power as Acting Secretary: in five years at the most, since Glennie was already an elderly man, the position would pass to him and be confirmed as a permanency. It was easier to confine one's anarchic whims to paper, and, indeeed, this gave them an extra force. Yet some gesture of individualism had to be made to still that small nagging voice of conscience; and the launching out into house-ownership was just sufficient for the purpose.

The bachelor establishment seems to have had a fair measure of success. Under Sarah Bath's sardonic eye Grahame and Greg settled down together amicably enough. Greg was a man of Grahame's own age and, like him, an amateur writer, who contributed occasional pieces to the *Pall Mall Gazette* and *National Observer*. He was a great-nephew of W. R. Greg, the author of the once-famous *Enigmas of Life*, and was for three years Art Critic to the *Manchester Guardian* and *Birmingham Daily Post*, during which time he wrote on practically every exhibition of importance in London. He was a connoisseur of wines, on which he wrote rather whimsical little essays, and sponsored a magnificent edition of the works of Sir Richard Burton. As an undergraduate at Oriel he first developed a mania for collecting pottery, and later wrote a monograph on the subject.[20]

It is plain that he influenced Grahame a good deal during the year they spent together at the house in Kensington Crescent before Greg's marriage. Over some things they disagreed; Walter Grahame noted Grahame's 'annoyance at Mr. Greg's insistence on hanging the pictures in their house in obedience to the dictates of what Kenneth called the Manchester School',[21] for instance. But in general they were temperamental congenial to a degree, as can be seen not only from Greg's interests but also from the essays he wrote, which occasionally give us a glimpse into that bachelor household, so snug and well-ordered, so pleasantly littered with *objets d'art* and collector's treasure-trove.

'As a bachelor with the freedom which is the attribute of celibacy,' he observes, 'by a copious use of stickphast and *The Times* newspaper, and by a liberal purchase from peripatetic ruffians of brilliant red sand-worms', the intrusive draughts were summarily removed.[22] He rhapsodizes over the special treasures he can display to visiting friends: the Grès de Flandres tankards, the salt glaze teapot, the two-volume first edition of Grimm's *Fairy Tales* 'with Cruikshank's plates, bound in their resplendent morocco, handiwork of Zahnsdorf, that Poole of book-clothiers'.[23] It was an atmosphere that Grahame was quick to share and absorb; for the rest of his life there were always first editions and Continental pottery somewhere in the background.

While *The Golden Age* stories were accumulating, Grahame found time to complete a somewhat different work, first roughed out in MS. as early as 1890. This was *The Headswoman*, the only story he wrote which dealt entirely with adult characters, and much less well known than it deserves to be. It may therefore be worthwhile to give a brief outline of the plot. The setting is the little French town of St. Radegonde; the time, early in the sixteenth century—though Grahame makes it clear that his moral is intended to be timeless.[24] The official executioner has died, and the Mayor and Council meet to appoint his successor. The office is hereditary, but the only direct claimant is Jeanne, the executioner's daughter. The Council want to pass Jeanne over in favour of her cousin Enguerrand, a lawyer ('there is no reason why a bad lawyer should not make an excellent executioner'); but Jeanne surprises them all by pressing her own candidature in no uncertain terms:

'My motive, gentlemen, in demanding what is my due, is a simple and (I trust) an honest one, and I desire that there should be no misunderstanding. It is my wish to be dependent on no one. I am both willing and able to work, and I only ask for what is the common right of humanity—admission to the labour market. . . . Shall I, from any false deference to that conventional voice which proclaims this thing as "nice", and that thing as "not nice", reject a handicraft which promises me both artistic satisfaction and a competence? No, gentlemen; my claim is a small one—only a fair day's wage for a fair day's work. But I can accept nothing less, nor consent to forgo my rights, even for any contingent remainder of possible cousinly favour!'[25]

The Council protest that such a thing has never been heard of before; but the Mayor makes some feeble remarks about 'the march of intellect', and Jeanne has clinched the deal and is out of the room before they can protest more effectively. As an executioner she turns out a great success, perhaps too much so; for her cousin, not thinking such an occupation fit for a lady, begins to transfer his affections elsewhere. This split between femininity and professionalism worries her, and some cheerful banter with an attractive young stranger does little to cheer her up. Then, by a series of accidents, she finds herself called upon to execute this young man (who of course is heir to a near-by château); he is rescued at the last minute by his Seneschal; and Jeanne, protesting to the last with remorseless logic that the whole thing is highly irregular, finally succumbs and marries him, leaving the office of executioner vacant for her cousin.

In one sense, of course, *The Headswoman* is, as the *Star*'s reviewer pointed out, a squib on feminism.[26] Jeanne trots out all the popular arguments for Women's Rights, and the young nobleman is an intellectual Radical who talks airily about 'the way of the bloated capitalist'. The satire is delicate and well-aimed, but Jeanne is by no means the victim of it: it is the Mayor, the pettifogging lawyer, the local bureaucracy who are really made to look foolish. Jeanne herself is drawn with great sympathy; and we remember that many of Grahame's friends at the time shared her aims—women such as Evelyn Sharp, Beatrice Harraden, and, later, Constance Smedley. What Grahame is really attacking is entrenched masculine prejudice: the feminist's weakness for being *plus royale que le roi* comes off very lightly by comparison. Mr. Roger Lancelyn Green further suggests that Grahame may have been parodying the historical novels of the period—'romance triumphing ingloriously over history in the works of such a man as S. R. Crockett',[27] and this seems very likely.

But what strikes a modern reader most forcibly is the prolonged joke about execution as such. It is somewhat morbid gallows'-humour at its best, and only Grahame's feather-light touch prevents it from being downright unpleasant. There were times when fantasy and reality got their wires a little crossed, and this was one of them: most of us would agree with the Radegondian Councillor who observed sourly that 'playing at mummers is one thing, and being executed is another, and people ought to keep 'em separate'. At times one almost suspects a touch of that supposedly modern phenomenon the death-wish, which was extremely prevalent in *fin de siècle* literature; at others an attempt to remove the horror from the fact of sudden dying:

> 'Instead of objecting, as they used to do, and wanting to argue the point and kick up a row, the fellows as is told off for execution come skipping along in the morning, like a lot of lambs in May-time. And then the fun there is on the scaffold! The jokes, the back answers, the repartees! And never a word to shock a baby! Why, my little girl, as goes through the market-place every morning—on her way to school, you know—she says to me only yesterday, she says, "Why, father," she says, "it's as good as the play-actors," she says.'[28]

It is easy enough to dismiss all this by a casual reference to *The Mikado* or the *Bab Ballads*,[29] where the same kind of thing occurs; but Gilbert simply provides extra evidence for gallows'-humour, he does not explain it. No; *The Headswoman* hints at the line Grahame might have taken if the world of childhood had not claimed him: satirical fantasy not unlike that practised by Voltaire. But this would have meant coming to grips more or less directly with all those vast unpleasant problems confronting Victorian society towards the turn of the century. It was useless for Grahame to call his story a fantasy and set it in the sixteenth century: his satirical eye was too acute, and the contemporary world would keep breaking in. If he had been a romantic fantasist (in the strict sense of the words) he could have happily turned out novels which bore no relation to reality, as so many of his contemporaries in fact did. Unfortunately he was a realist by natural endowment: once he chose a subject he treated it with exhaustive honesty.

This may go far to explain why *The Headswoman* remains his nearest approach to 'adult' fiction. Direct engagement stimulated his satirical sense, but put too great a strain on his delicate sensibilities. If today *The Headswoman* reminds us of anything, it is of a play by an author who in many ways resembles Grahame: Christopher Fry. In *The Lady's not for Burning* the treatment of the death motif and the ambivalent humour enshrouding it directly recall Grahame's story: there are further similarities of plot, setting, and character. It is fascinating to speculate just what would have become of Grahame's talent if he had continued to explore this field instead of abandoning it after a single experiment.

The Headswoman was published in October 1894,[30] in a number of *The Yellow Book* which also included John Davidson's 'Ballad of a Nun' and Beardsley's two famous satirical drawings, 'Lady Gold's Escort' and 'The Wagnerites', not to mention an authentic whiff of the Celtic Fringe from Nora Hopper.[31] (It is difficult to guess whether the presence of Beardsley or Miss Hopper embarrassed Grahame more.) By now America was interesting itself in the author of *Pagan Papers*; one Golden Age story, 'The Blue Room', first appeared in *Phil May's Illustrated Winter Annual*, another, 'The Secret Drawer', in the *Chicago Chapbook*.[32] By now, too, Henley's *New Review* had begun publication, and Grahame, loyal as ever to his old editor, let him print 'A Harvesting' and 'Lusisti Satis' in the March 1895 number, about the same time as *The Golden Age* appeared in book form.

This time Grahame (and Lane) had no cause to complain of the reviewers. Swinburne set the tone with a two-column eulogy in the *Daily Chronicle*, where he described the book as 'well-nigh too praiseworthy for praise', and in accordance with his own dictum spent the bulk of his space in lavish quotations.[33] He was supported by Richard Le Gallienne in the *Star*; Israel

Zangwill in the *Pall Mall Gazette*; and a host of women's magazines, which declared, in varying terms, that the work should become compulsory reading for English parents—'they will understand their own children the better for doing so'. The reservations, when they came, were all in the intellectual periodicals, the *Bookman*, the *Fortnightly Review*, the *Spectator*; and what they objected to, with some unanimity, was the ambiguous status of the narrator, fluctuating in viewpoint between child and adult. Here is Professor Sully, of the *Fortnightly Review*: [34]

> He is child enough, at any rate, to enjoy strumming, to take a toy-snake to bed with him, and to be addressed by strangers as a water-baby. Yet this small person not only gives himself now and again an air of superiority to the others' play, wandering forth into the fields alone to indulge in precocious poetic raptures, but shows himself capable of reading into a scene in which figure his little sister and her two dolls, a significance which could only have occurred to an experienced adult. . . .

Shortly after this point the professor loses control of himself completely, and begins snarling about 'a dishonour done to the sacred cause of childhood . . . merely the exaggeration of a tone of cynical superiority which runs through the volume'. Here we recognize the voice of a sentimental Olympian hit at his most vulnerable point. The child-cult of the later nineteenth century was not based on a sympathy for, or consideration of, children as they really were, on their own terms. It had far more selfish motives: relief of guilt, gratification of the ego. Children became the ideal symbol of their elders' glutinous yearning for purity. There was no question of communication or understanding: the traffic of sentiment all went one way. Children were regarded as *objects*—dolls, pets, almost mythic symbols, which reflected nothing but the magnanimity and tenderness of their elders.

Now Grahame, with his incurable realism, had stripped off this fulsome façade and drawn the relationship between upper-middle-class adult and child as it really was. The complacent

Professor Sully, author of a monstrously patronizing book called
Children's Ways,[35] was disconcerted for two obvious reasons. The
unflattering and only too accurate portrait of the Olympians
shattered his self-esteem; but worse, the thought of children
summing up their elders with such cool and precocious contempt
struck at the very heart of the Victorian child-myth. Children
were supposed to be innocent, unthinking, all-adoring, uncritical;
grateful acolytes sunning themselves in the benevolence of an
omniscient father-figure. Grahame destroyed the whole myth at
one stroke. He scaled adult pretensions and sentimentalities down
to life-size; he showed that children not only possessed a private
life of their own (which was romantic) but a mordant eye for the
weaknesses of their elders (which was highly embarrassing.)

The very word 'Olympians' was diabolically well-chosen. It
suggested simultaneously pompous self-elevation, arbitrary thun-
derbolts, and faintly ridiculous claims to divine infallibility.
Those who knew their Homer as Grahame did would also
remember that, for all their dignity, the original Olympians
behaved in a singularly ungodlike way, quarrelling, scheming,
full of jealousy and petty spite, activated by the lowest human
motives. Most 'Olympian' reviewers had received the benefits
of a Victorian grounding in the classics; they would not be slow
to take the hint. Broadminded people sometimes enjoy being
attacked; but few are tolerant enough to survive the puncturing
of their personal myths. Hence Professor Sully's incoherent
rage.

But the majority of readers found the delicate satire very much
to their taste: they too had suffered under Olympian tutelage. As
the critic of the *Academy* remarked of *The Golden Age* children:[36]
'So typical are their thoughts and actions, misgivings and ambitions, that *The Golden Age* is to some extent every reader's
biography'. A copy found its way to Miss Bradley's uncle, the
Dean of St. Paul's, who was laid up at the time with an attack of
bronchitis. His taste in secular literature was rather for Blue Books

'Dulce Domum'
From the drawing by Arthur Rackham

than pure romance; but he was found absorbed in the pages of *The Golden Age*, and even a little tearful. When asked the reason for such unwonted emotion and told that the book was only meant to amuse him, the octogenarian shook his head sadly and said: 'You see, I also was brought up by an Aunt. . . .'[37]

The Golden Age was published in February, and Grahame found himself famous overnight. The first edition quickly sold out, and Lane, with his usual acumen, reprinted at once. Invitations began to pour in to Kensington Crescent, not only now from literary friends but Society hostesses as well. The satirist of childhood was taken up as a literary lion—a process which he endured with mixed delight and embarrassment. But despite a constant round of dinner-parties, and his duties at the Bank, he continued to write. The creative impulse which had produced *The Golden Age* was by no means yet exhausted: about half the stories later collected as *Dream Days* were composed during 1895.

In the spring, however, fortified by steadily accumulating royalties, Grahame was able to gratify his annual migratory urge. Southward he went, following the swallows, till he fetched up at Alassio on the Italian Riviera—a place to which he was to return at least twice during the next three years, and which made a lasting impression on him.[38]

At that time Alassio had not yet become the fashionable resort it is today. It was still a picturesque, undisturbed fishing-port, and Grahame stayed, not in a smart hotel but with a private family, in their old-fashioned Ligurian home. Idiosyncratic features such as box-bunks and bowling-alley caught his fancy so strongly that later he transferred most of them to Mole End:

> On the walls hung wire baskets with ferns in them, alternating with brackets carrying plaster statuary—Garibaldi and the infant Samuel, and Queen Victoria, and other heroes of modern Italy. Down one side of the fore-court ran a skittle-alley, with benches along it and little wooden tables marked with rings that hinted at beer-mugs.[39]

Grahame has made only the most perfunctory attempt to integrate these memories into an English setting. Wine, indeed, has been nationalized into beer, and *bocciè* into our more familiar skittles; but what on earth is Garibaldi doing in Mole End? Yet such is Grahame's skill at creating a *mise en scène* depending solely on its own private logic and imagery, that these oddly-flavoured incongruities strengthen rather than destroy the illusion. In the same way we never notice the physical difficulties presented by Mole End—an open-air residence if ever there was one—existing at the bottom of a tunnel.

We catch a glimpse of Grahame's life at Alassio in 'Wayfarers All', where he puts some of his own experiences into the mouth of the Seafaring Rat:

> Then the crew took to the boats and rowed shorewards, singing as they went, and drawing after them the long bobbing procession of casks, like a mile of porpoises. On the sands they had horses waiting, which dragged the casks up the steep street of the little town with a fine rush and clatter and scramble. When the last cask was in, we went and refreshed and rested, and sat late into the night, drinking with our friends; and the next morning I was off to the great olive-woods for a spell and a rest. . . . I led a lazy life among the peasants, lying and watching them work, or stretched high on the hill-side with the blue Mediterranean far below me.[40]

From the same passage (and a reference in his correspondence) it seems probable that Grahame made his way home by way of Marseilles, where he characteristically developed an inordinate passion for the local cuisine.

Back in England life seemed stable, assured, and tranquil. There was £40,000,000 worth of bullion in the Bank—the highest figure yet recorded—and the wholesale price of English gold showing a steady upward trend.[41] Against this solid background the literary aesthetes—and *The Yellow Book*—continued to flourish; Grahame contributed essays to the April, July, and

October numbers.[42] But there was an undercurrent of depression, boredom, and disillusionment in the air. This was the year in which Max Nordau published *Degeneration*:

> The prevalent feeling [Nordau wrote] is that of imminent perdition and extinction. *Fin de siècle* is at once a confession and a complaint. The old northern faith contained the fearsome doctrine of the Dusk of the Gods. In our days there have arisen in more highly developed minds vague qualms of the Dusk of the Nations, in which all suns and all stars are gradually waning, and mankind with all its institutions and creations is perishing in the midst of a dying world.[43]

The symptoms are characteristic of a post-industrial society that has staggered through its religious crisis; and it was in an effort to stem the consequent tide of materialism that the aesthetic movement had developed. But in the autumn of 1895 this movement—fragile and artificial enough at the best of times—received its death-blow.

Oscar Wilde, though in point of fact he never contributed to *The Yellow Book*, had come to typify, in the public mind, the ethics for which *The Yellow Book* stood. His trial and condemnation for homosexual practices came as a horrible revelation to English society, and effectively prevented the aesthetic myth from taking general root. Those who had dabbled innocently in these fashionable literary waters extricated themselves with some speed; it is interesting to note that Grahame's only contribution to *The Yellow Book* after this date (apart from 'Dies Irae', which was almost certainly commissioned before the débâcle) is a short and indifferent poem. Evelyn Sharp, in her autobiography,[44] recorded that

> the Oscar Wilde trial shocked society into an extreme of prudishness never exceeded in the earliest days of the good Queen, and one London daily started a shilling cricket fund to which panic-stricken citizens hastened to contribute lest their sexual normality should be doubted—the connection was subtle, but felt at the time to be real.

It seems highly improbable that any of the mud flung was aimed at, let alone stuck to, Grahame. His subtle withdrawal from the extremes of aesthetic social intercourse was often remarked upon, and the subject-matter of his stories alone more or less guaranteed his immunity. But he cannot in any case have failed to be deeply struck by this classic instance of *Ate* overtaking *Hubris*—the gifted, brilliant, flamboyant playwright and after-dinner wit subjected to cruel public ignominy, and consigned to a common gaol. Wilde's fate sank deep into his impressionable mind; and twelve years were to pass before the core of that terrible episode re-emerged, transmuted and scaled down to animal fantasy in the misfortunes of Mr. Toad.

Grahame spent the Christmas of 1895 in Brussels, together with Evelyn Sharp and the Harlands, who were probably glad to be abroad during the worst period of scandal. As Editor of *The Yellow Book* Harland had naturally come in for a fair share of public abuse. Grahame, apparently, enjoyed himself in his own idiosyncratic way:

> On holiday he out-Harlanded Harland. One of his peculiarities was a curious conviction that he was a typical Englishman, though anyone less outwardly British could never have been invented. . . . There was never any doubt about K. G. being taken for an Englishman abroad because he was so very Scottish. . . . He was, as a matter of fact, like nobody but himself, though it is possible that he was somebody quite different in his official capacity at the Bank of England.[45]

He returned to work, unperturbed, in the New Year. 'Dies Irae' appeared in January; 'Saturnia Regna' in March, as a contribution to Henley's *New Review*, which also printed 'Mutabile Semper' a month later. Then there followed a break till December, when 'The Magic Ring' was published in *Scribner's Magazine*.

During the summer Grahame was once more drawn into the social round. We find him dining on 5th July with Gosse in a company that included the Harlands, Yeats, Lionel Johnson, Hardy, Ernest Rhys, George Moore, and Andrew Lang. There were Saturday evenings in the Cromwell Road, and luncheon parties such as that at which he first met Helen Dunham, 'at Mrs. Crawshay's—where there were also Ethel Arnold and Lady Horner, and Professor Butcher, and Mr. Goschen—and much good talk'.[46] The combination of scholarship, high finance, and high society tells its own tale.

The aftermath of the Wilde scandal brought an atmosphere of exhausted futility, which is clearly reflected in *The Yellow Book*. The grand concept of protest had ended in public ignominy: the forces of bourgeois convention were stronger than ever. 'Castle Ennui', Harland wrote in July, 'is the Bastille of modern life. . . . You can only escape from it at the risk of breaking your social neck, or remaining a fugitive from social justice to the end of your days.'[47] Less than a year later *The Yellow Book* itself had succumbed: the last issue appeared in January 1897. William Morris died in October, after completing the Kelmscott Chaucer; Stevenson was already dead, far away in Samoa. The New Age had failed and the old order was breaking up.

A new plutocracy, enriched by the South African diamond mines, had established itself in Park Lane. These *nouveaux riches* had their own ideas about progress and culture. 1896 saw the foundation of something revolutionary in the history of journalism—the *Daily Mail*. It also saw the appearance of that strange, noisy, lethal object, the Horseless Carriage. Nothing, perhaps, better symbolized the rising dominance of the Industrial Age: and motoring enthusiasts had to struggle against violent, almost hysterical, opposition. Till 14th November 1896 there was a ban on the monsters in England; and even after this ban was lifted, a 12 m.p.h. speed limit was imposed. It was generally held that the motor-car was noisy, dangerous, ridiculous, and a source of terror to horses. Even more than the railways, motor-cars, it was clear, would disrupt the peace of the countryside: trains at least stuck to their rails, but the 'petrol-piddling monster' (as Kipling called it) could reach the most remote village.[48]

It is not hard to imagine how Grahame reacted to this invasion: he still felt strongly on the subject in 1907, though by then the novelty had been more or less assimilated, if not accepted, as far as the general public were concerned. *Punch*, always fairly reliable as a weather-gauge in matters of this sort, suggests that at first opinion was contemptuous of the new device, and only later came to fear it. An 1896 cartoon has this caption: 'Decidedly Uncomfortable: Awkward position of Mr. Newfangle, who, when halfway up a steep hill, discovers by the sudden retrograde movement of the Autocar that the Motor has become exhausted'. By 1904 the tone has changed:

> *Motorist* (cheerfully—to fellow-guest in house-party): 'What luck? Killed anything?'
> *Angler* (bitterly): 'No. Have you?'

It is this later, more bitter, mood which is enshrined in Chapter II of *The Wind in the Willows*.

By the end of 1898 Kenneth Grahame was an established success both in his profession and in the world of letters.[49] He succeeded G. F. Glennie as Secretary of the Bank at the age of thirty-nine—one of the youngest Secretaries on record. At this period the Secretary, whose office dated back to 1694, was at one and the same time the Secretary to the Company [The Governor and Company of the Bank of England] and Secretary to the Governor. In the former capacity he was largely concerned with the constitutional side of the Bank's administration: he was present at meetings of the Court of Directors to take minutes, and it was his duty to see that the decisions made were subsequently carried out. He dealt also with all those duties which did not fall within the scope of the two other senior officials, the Chief Cashier and the Chief Accountant: he dealt with visitors and he organized Staff. As Secretary to the Governor his position was rather more vaguely defined: he was not primarily concerned with implementing banking policy but was, ideally, not so much a banker as a lay adviser: the Governor's conscience, so to speak.[50]

His elevation does not seem to have gone to Kenneth's head. When Evelyn Sharp wrote to congratulate him,

and supposed flippantly that he would now dress in red and gold and ride in the Lord Mayor's Show, he wrote back to say that he should do nothing of the kind, not because he hadn't a right to, if he liked, but because he couldn't ride. He was at the same time, he added, having gold braid put on the collar of his frock-coat and round his silk hat. I feel sure that this was not the Kenneth Grahame known to his colleagues at the Bank of England.[51]

Nevertheless he could not keep his literary *alter ego* a complete secret, even from the moguls of Threadneedle Street. His fame had spread too far. Old Dr. Kingdon, the Consultant Physician to the Bank, who had sympathized with Kenneth in his relationship to Uncle John the Parliamentary Agent, was now somewhat more down-to-earth:

Kenneth's a dear boy, a *very* dear boy, but he doesn't think half enough of his position in the Bank and in the City. They tell me that he *writes tales*. So did Charles Lamb—but what of that? Maybe Charles Lamb didn't think much of his position at East India House, but what after all *was* his position in the City to Kenneth's? Kenneth should think *less* of books and *more* of being what he has come to be in the City.[52]

But if the new Secretary was a little odd by Dr. Kingdon's standards, he had in his own terms reached a most effective compromise. The nightmare terror of galley-slave and hireling, the bureaucratic blue pencil chasing death down the centuries—these had receded into what Grahame described as the back-kitchen of his consciousness.

The literary world, too, had given him its accolade. He was a household name, and his royalties mounted steadily. In its issue of 4th December 1897 the *Academy*[53] included him among those selected for literary profiling and assessment under the heading 'Some Younger Reputations'. Others so honoured were Yeats, Gissing, Quiller-Couch, Wells, Beerbohm ('the world lies like a ball at his feet—and he kicks it'), W. W. Jacobs, Robert Hichens, and Anthony Hope. The article on Grahame is extremely enthusiastic; it ends with these uncompromising words: 'It matters very little whether or not Mr. Grahame writes any more. In *The Golden Age* he has given us a book, a four-square piece of literature complete in itself. Many a literary man writes hard all his life, and never a book—in the best sense of the word—is forthcoming. Mr. Grahame made one the first time.'

Perhaps as a result of this encomium Grahame was given the task, in the next issue but one, of reviewing Evelyn Sharp's *All the Way to Fairyland*,[54] an early example of the tendency to associate him with 'children's stories' in the ordinary sense. He produced an interesting and idiosyncratic piece (though what Miss Sharp made of it as a review we can only surmise) which was mainly concerned with emphasizing the conservatism of fairy-tale convention, and the supra-zoological behaviour demanded of fairy animals. There is a faint but unmistakable feeling throughout that Grahame is doing his best in the sentimental world of his supporters, and not particularly enjoying himself in the process. Perhaps the most valuable part from our point of view is the scrap of schoolroom autobiography with which he closes: another reference to the beloved paint-box. Mrs. Percy Dearmer's illustrations remind him of how 'the obstinate lid . . . jams and slides a little, and jams again in its old way—again the crimson lake sticks to the Prussian blue, and the gamboge persists in "rucking up" when the lid has to be pushed back—and the potent old smell asserts itself once more'. It is delightful to think that those words were written by the Secretary of the Bank of England.

In March 1898 Kenneth went down with one of his recurrent

bouts of influenza. On the 10th he wrote to Grace Dunham, Helen Dunham's sister, enclosing a specially bound copy of Blake's *Songs of Innocence* as a wedding present, and adding at the end: 'I am shaking with influenza myself, and feel like Shem or Japhet out of the Ark—left by a careless child on the carpet—trodden on by a heavy-footed housemaid—and badly mended with very inferior glue'.[55] However, he was well enough in April to lunch his visiting American publisher, Charles Scribner, at the Hyde Park Club. Perhaps as a result of this meeting, 'A Saga of the Seas' was published in the August issue of *Scribner's Magazine*. By now six of the stories that were to appear in *Dream Days* had been composed and published: the rate of production was noticeably slower than for *The Golden Age*. Two more—'A Departure' and 'The Reluctant Dragon'—were written during that summer, but never issued in any periodical; and at the same time Grahame found leisure to produce a long preface for Eugene Field's *Lullaby-Land*. *Dream Days*, the long-awaited sequel to *The Golden Age*, was published in December 1898.

The reviews were, if anything, more enthusiastic even than those Grahame had already received; but behind the chorus of praise we can once again discern the irritated complaints of a few Olympian reviewers. 'As a rule', observed the *Bookman*'s critic, 'children are in half their being enthusiastic admirers of the grown-up world, and in the other half supremely indifferent to it. The critical, scornful attitude of Mr. Grahame's children is quite exceptional.' The *Athenaeum*, with rather more truth, decided that *Dream Days* was not so much a children's book as a collection of stories about children for grown-up people.[56] But by now Grahame had reached the point where he could afford to ignore minority critics. The book became, first a best-seller, then a classic.

Grahame spent the Christmas of 1898 in Essex with Roland and his wife. Roland, like Kenneth, had been a frequent visitor on week-ends to the Feilings at Amwell Bury. In 1895 Joan Feiling was left a widow with two small sons, Tony and Keith, who had already unwittingly contributed material to *The Golden Age*, as we have seen. In 1897 she and Roland were married; and it is possible that the happy atmosphere of that family Christmas made Kenneth reconsider his ambition to be 'the felowe that goes alone'. After all, in a month or two he would be forty: middle-aged bachelorhood was a by no means unmixed blessing. Still, things were turning out excellently for him. He had reached the top of his profession (whatever his private feelings about it) with uncommon speed and no great exertion. He had—what undoubtedly pleased him more—made a considerable name for himself as a writer. Best of all, perhaps for the first time in his life, he knew real financial security. He looked forward to the New Year with cheerful confidence.

VIII

AUNTS, ARTISTS, AND OTHERS

> I, writing thus, am still what men call young:
> I have not so far left the coasts of life
> To travel inland, that I cannot hear
> That murmur of the water infinite
> Which unwearied babies smile at in their sleep,
> When wonder'd at for smiling.
>
> ELIZABETH BARRETT BROWNING

All minds, even the dullest, remember the days of their childhood; but all cannot bring back the indescribable brightness of that blessed season. . . . To imagine what he then saw and heard, [the writer] must imagine his own nature. He must collect from many vanished hours the power of his untam'd heart; and he must, perhaps, transfuse also something of his maturer mind into those dreams of his former being, thus linking the past with the present by a continuous chain, which, though often invisible, is never broken.

> WASHINGTON IRVING

One chief pursuit of the immature animal, human or other, is to prepare itself for the dangers of real life, while its elders are protecting it from them, by making believe to face them.

> R. G. COLLINGWOOD: *The New Leviathan*

The originality, if not the creative achievement, of Kenneth Grahame's short stories about children is often under-rated today. A post-Freudian epoch has accustomed us to the child's-eye view of things; we are prepared to accept the unpalatable truth that children of a certain age dislike and despise adult concepts. We are no longer either so complacent or so psychologically naïve as to saddle our offspring with our own sentimental yearnings, and call them 'the pure vision of childhood'. In Grahame's day the situation was radically different. There were plenty of books both for and about children; indeed, the market was swamped with them. But their picture of the childish mind remained alarmingly unreal.

It is true that the old-style moral tracts, heavy with morbid Sabbatarianism, were by 1870 on the decline. As Mr. Harvey Darton tells us,[1] 'fiction was now by a long way predominant over fact, magic was not rebuked but at large, nonsense was free. Children could go back to the enchantments of the Middle Ages without being told that they were really the work of the Devil . . . to folk-lore . . . without any warnings about superstition or ignorance or unreality; to fun, without being told not to be silly.' This revolution was due in great measure to the two *Alice* books; yet, despite their imaginative freedom and volcanic subconscious imagery, Alice herself remained a copybook child, a two-dimensional moral prig. That was one side of the Victorian child in literature; the other was represented by the sugary lispings and monstrous sentimentality of *Sylvie and Bruno*.

Carroll, nevertheless, as Mr. Empson persuasively demonstrated in *Some Versions of Pastoral*, shows us another use to which fantasy or children's literature could be turned in a morally repressive age. It served as an unconscious safety-valve for desires and feelings which the writer would not care to admit even to himself. Late Victorian England supplied ideal conditions for the growth of such symbolism: genuine religious feelings and scruples in conflict with harshly dogmatic materialism which yet represented Authority. If we then postulate psychological innocence, the thing is done. Nonsense-fantasy and animal fable become both an escape and a covert form of satire; it is no accident that they flourished in the second half of the nineteenth century as never before or since.

One example must suffice to show this 'concealed opposition' at work. Edward Lear not only symbolized in his longer poems the personal emotional truths which he could not face directly, but also used his famous Limericks to make a savage attack on the bourgeois society of his time. Angus Davidson, in his biography of Lear, has analysed this covert satire with some perception:[2]

> What a world of implication there is in Lear's 'they'! 'They' are the force of public opinion, the dreary voice of human mediocrity: 'they' are perpetually interfering with the liberty of the individual: 'they' gossip, 'they' condemn, 'they' are inquisitive and conventional and almost always uncharitable. The only people 'they' really approve of are people like the *Old Man of Hong-Kong/Who never did anything Wrong . . .*

The problem presented by the unseen 'they' was more agonizing than we can imagine today, when social and family ties have lost their immutable moral compulsion. There was, indeed, a well-organized opposition; but it was a minority of vocal and literary gentlemen, who seldom applied in practice what they preached in print. A glance at the life of Arnold or even Swinburne is enough to demonstrate this. Compromise was of the essence; though few creative writers extracted such a material success from their honest doubt as Tennyson, who contrived to make the best of both worlds, and ruined his poetry in the process. There were only two other attitudes which the rebel could adopt, and they are summed up neatly by two of Lear's Limericks.

The first, and rarest, is direct retaliation:

> There was an Old Man with a poker
> Who painted his face with red ochre;
> When they said, 'You're a Guy!'
> He made no reply
> But knocked them all down with his poker.

The more common and simple is retreat, in one form or another:

> There was an Old Person of Basing
> Whose presence of mind was amazing;
> He purchased a steed
> Which he rode at full speed,
> And escaped from the people of Basing.

That horse was popular during the nineteenth century; and since pursuit was involved, it assumed a Protean variety of disguises—including the Limerick and the Adventures of Toad. And Lear, no less than Grahame, knew very well the penalty of open non-conformity: he published it in one of the most sinister of all his verses:

> There was an Old Man with a gong,
> Who bumped at it all the day long;
> But they called out, 'O lor!
> You're a horrid old bore!'
> So they smashed that Old Man with a gong.

It is by no means the only occasion on which They indulge in the simple sport of 'smashing'.

A student of *The Golden Age* will at once recognize here a clinically exact description, not only of Them, but of Grahame's Olympians. The satire, if more specific and detailed in Grahame's case, is directed at the same target. Both use a disguise—though not, in all probability, with conscious awareness of what they are doing. Grahame's retreat to the world of childhood is especially adroit. Hitherto this had largely been a sentimental stamping-ground for the Olympians themselves, where they could indulge their mawkish imaginations with myths about Unspotted Innocence and Adoring Little Girls. Even Carroll was not exempt from this weakness. What Grahame did was to sneak a Trojan Horse inside the citadel; his children could get away with the kind of ferocious outspokenness that would not be tolerated from an adult. The Olympians were hoist with their own myth.

This, of course, largely accounts for the intrusion of adult opinions and behaviour in the children of *The Golden Age*: in one sense they are being used as stalking-horses, to put across their creator's satirical message in such a way that he himself remained unscathed. But quite apart from this, the effect on the Victorian child-myth was revolutionary.

After *The Golden Age* and *Dream Days* Kenneth Grahame might well have said, with Molière's physician, 'Nous avons changé tout cela'. He had indeed: the fictional child was never quite the same again. In all probability Grahame had no clear idea in his conscious mind of what he was doing. Half his imagination, throughout his adult life, remained that of a child: he simply wrote, as an artist, what he remembered and felt, moving effortlessly between the 'divided and distinguished worlds' of mature awareness and innocent vision. That the results (however familiar in essence and technique they may be to us) puzzled Grahame's contemporaries it is easy to deduce from his reviewers. The two things they all stuck on with virtual unanimity were, first, the scornful attitude to the adult world of Grahame's children; and second, the way in which Grahame himself shifted with fluid ease from the rôle of grown-up commentator to childish narrator, and even on occasion maintained both rôles simultaneously. Such tricks of psychological and stylistic technique do not bother us in the least; we have had half a century and more in which to absorb them. But to Grahame's early critics they were, obviously, startling innovations.

The anonymous critic of the *Spectator*[3] is typical. It does not occur to him that the double angle of vision produces a focused, stereoscopic picture; that the child's-eye view is given fresh depth and solidity by the adult commentator. Instead we get this:

> Other people are apt to look at childhood through the reverse end of the telescope, and to lose the sense of proportion when they try to understand the small figures and the limited horizons that they see. . . . Mr. Grahame looks through both ends of the telescope, and writes as a small boy with the knowledge and experience of a man, and this causes a sense of

artificiality and incongruity about some of the sketches, such as
'Sawdust and Sin' and 'The Roman Road'.

Today, since we have absorbed the double-level technique so
thoroughly that we are hardly aware of it, we would probably
claim precisely those two stories as the most brilliant in the book.
In no other way could the gaps between adult and childish
imagination have been so dramatically high-lighted; in no other
way could Grahame have explored each situation at all its contrasting levels, or analysed the *internal* changes which his narrator
underwent between boyhood action and mature recollection.

'Sawdust and Sin' multiplies these levels of awareness in a most
extraordinary way: it resembles a nest of psychological Chinese
boxes. Here, through the narrator's eyes, is presented an account
of Charlotte's dealings with her dolls over a tea-party. In addition
to Grahame's own two *personae* there is also Charlotte's; and, to
cap all, the dolls themselves (through a combination of Charlotte's
imagination and the narrator's) behave, or seem to behave, in
a quasi-human manner which parodies adult as well as nursery
behaviour.

To bring this juggling act off so brilliantly required a technical
tour de force of the first order: a fact recognized by Mr. Alan Pryce-
Jones, who described the story as

> one of the most exquisitely subtle records of the commonplace
> in modern literature. We know exactly how they (Rosa and
> Jerry, the two dolls) almost came to life, how in her mind they
> existed on two planes at once, human with half her mind and
> dolls with the other. And all the time the imperceptible grown-
> up, the reader himself, is watching, half-convinced when the
> dolls tumble together that they do it from malice, and simul-
> taneously contemptuous of the existence of dolls.[4]

Psychologically, the effortless skill with which this sort of thing
is done probably hints at Grahame's own emphatic duality of outlook; but the result in literary terms is almost unique. Throughout
the book his best effects are due to some variant on the same

double approach: the two halves counterpoint each other perfectly.

In 'The Finding of the Princess', for example, the narrator goes
exploring, and finds himself in the grounds of a country house.
He has been reading about the Sleeping Beauty, so it seems
natural enough to find her there. Obviously that gold-topped
pavilion is where she lies concealed; and sure enough, there she
is: 'in no tranced repose, however, but laughingly struggling to
disengage her hand from the grasp of a grown-up man who
occupied the marble bench with her'. The narrator is asked to
stay to lunch: and afterwards, his mind still running on fairy-tale
protocol, tells the couple that of course they ought to get married
—'meaning only that a man who discovered a Princess, living in
the right sort of Palace like this, and didn't marry her there and
then, was false to all recognized tradition'. The man, not un-
naturally, tips him two half-crowns for this; the girl kisses him;
and he goes on his way rejoicing.

This is not so simple as it looks. At first it appears to be an
elementary exercise in appearance-and-reality, with adult narrator
and adult characters sharing the same superior knowledge, smiling
tolerantly at the child for whom the footman behind his chair is
a taciturn lord and the whole house a fairy palace. Then we
realize that for the adults—though in a different sense—the fairy-
tale is true too; *they* see the world, and the child, through the
enchanted eyes of love. Each of them understands the other, but
each in his own way: it is a situation worthy of Pirandello.

Here, for once, the adult world and the child's fantasy meet
without disillusion. The words they use may carry completely
different connotations to speaker and hearer; yet each has seen
an aspect of the same universal truth, caught something of that
imaginative wonder which for Grahame is man's supreme
experience. A similar effect is produced by the scene between
the boy-narrator and the aged, scholarly, gentle clergyman of
'A Harvesting': superficially they are at cross-purposes, but at a

deeper level they have an intuitive knowledge of their common temperament.[5]

Normally Grahame uses the double-level technique in order to gloss his narrator's attitude to the adult world with the satirical voice of experience. The Prologue to *The Golden Age* is written throughout from the adult viewpoint in retrospect; after that the satirical *persona* only intrudes intermittently in a direct way. More often it is half-concealed in an ambiguity, and its tone ranges from the comic to the macabre. 'The Argonauts' offers a fine example. To the children landing from their punt the girl in the garden is both Medea and an English pseudo-Medea, who enters into their fantasy for the fun of the thing: '"Oh you boys!" cried Medea, throwing wide her arms with abandonment. "Where have you dropped from? . . . I've been shut up here for a thousand years, and all that time I've never seen anyone under a hundred and fifty!"' But a page or two later it becomes clear that 'Medea' *is* in fact shut up there, after a blighted love-affair which has slightly turned her mind. The boys cannot see this, but Grahame can, and we can: once again the dialogue is at cross-purposes, but this time the misinterpretation of the girl's mildly manic-depressive dottiness as part of a children's game is quietly horrific.

In the other story singled out by the *Spectator* for censure, 'The Roman Road', this method acquires additional depth and power from the fact that both the protagonists, boy and artist alike, represent different aspects of Grahame's own personality. This fictional diffusion of the ego is a common phenomenon: in Grahame's case, however, it has especial interest. The 'I' of 'The Roman Road' is Grahame as a child, still undisillusioned by experience, always mentally pacing 'down a delectable street of cloud-built palaces'. The Artist is Grahame the adult, who has actually been to magic places like Piccadilly, who has followed the road to Rome—and in a subtle way, has lost some part of his vision by so doing. The interaction of these two selves gives the story its peculiar power.

The whole point of 'The Roman Road' is that it is the child who, all unknowing, offers salvation to the older man. The Artist can quote Marcus Aurelius and Aristophanes, but somewhere he has lost a dream. When the child-narrator outlines his Golden City, and those who qualify for it, the Artist breaks in:

> "And the men who never come off," he said, "who try like the rest, but get knocked out, or somehow miss—or break down or get bowled over in the mêlée—and get no Princess, nor even a second-class kingdom—some of them'll be there, I hope?"
>
> "Yes, if you like," I replied, not quite understanding him; "if they're friends of yours, we'll ask 'em, of course."
>
> "What a time we shall have!" said the Artist reflectively; "and how shocked old Marcus Aurelius will be!" [6]

This sense of failure and disillusion runs deeper in *The Golden Age* than it did in *Pagan Papers*; but it is no less real for being driven underground. 'The Roman Road' symbolizes the solution which Grahame adopted. It was the child in him that rescued the artist from that worst of all disappointments—experience. The glamour of being grown-up, independent, a free agent, of travelling to all those Chimborazos and Cotopaxis of one's dreams, had proved largely illusory. The real Rome could never hope to match the Golden City of Grahame's young imagination: that gleaming mirage which both his childish and his adult self needed so desperately. 'About the only place I never got to', the Artist observes revealingly, 'was the Fortunate Island.' On the Golden City itself Grahame's last ironic comment is: 'Meantime, there only remained the finding it. An easy matter.'

This crystallization of Grahame's split desires into opposed fictional characters repeats itself throughout his work, and greatly heightens its dramatic tension. He is both Rat and Seafaring Rat in 'Wayfarers All', both Rat and Mole in 'Dulce Domum'. At other times his two protagonists share a basic identity of purpose; especially is this so in *The Golden Age* and *Dream Days*, where the innocent 'I' is a childish analogue to scholarly Rector or Bohemian artist, and only differs from them in clarity of vision.

The most complex example of ego-diffusion is to be found in that enchanting tale 'The Reluctant Dragon'. This, it should be noted, does not really belong in the Edward-Harold-Selina canon at all: Grahame seems to have felt this himself, since he adopts the transparent device of turning it into a story-within-a-story to bring *The Golden Age* children in somehow. Yet even so he contrives, by so doing, to add to its subtlety, since he is not only all three major characters in the tale itself, but also audience and story-teller.

Taken at its face-value, 'The Reluctant Dragon' is, of course, a satirical fable, rather in the gently debunking manner of *Don Quixote*. The dragon is a peaceable creature that only wants a quiet life; St. George is only anxious to do the decent thing, and quite happy to come to a private arrangement with his opponent; between them moves the innocent Boy, as a kind of go-between, oscillating from fantasy to disillusion and back again. The real villains are the villagers: and their basic crime is ingrained convention and habit. Dragons are pestilential scourges, everyone knows that; therefore this specimen *is* a pestilential scourge, whatever their senses tell them to the contrary. If St. George turns up, there *has* to be a battle. And so on. In the end, of course, they are defeated: St. George, the Boy, and the Dragon all walk off amiably arm-in-arm. The whole thing is beautifully done; the construction tight and economical, the humour delicately tinged with irony, the point made unmistakably yet without fuss, and a perfect balance struck between fantasy and farce.

Yet it is almost impossible to avoid reading it, at a deeper level, as the reconciliation (for the time being, at any rate) of Grahame's conflicting selves: it is no coincidence that the story was written in the year of his appointment as Secretary. St. George is the side of Grahame concerned with Honour and Duty: the public servant, the national figure, the representative of what we have come to know as the Establishment, the champion of convention. The Boy, of course, is the recurrent 'I'-figure of far-sighted childhood, 'wonderful knowing about book-beasts, as everyone allows', transferred for the occasion to a more exotic setting. But it is the Dragon whose character is drawn in greatest detail, for whom Grahame obviously felt most affection and sympathy; and the Dragon, beyond any reasonable doubt, is a living portrait of Grahame's anarchic, artistic, anti-social, irresponsible, indolent self.

It is an interesting Dragon who—at this juncture in Grahame's life—remarks that 'one must look about and reflect and consider before settling down. It's rather a serious thing, settling down.' The obliging beast continues with his self-revelation. He is bone-lazy by nature, he says, while 'all the other fellows were so active and *earnest* and all that sort of thing'. But then there was an earth-shaking catastrophe:

'I suppose . . . the bottom dropped out of something. Anyhow there was a shake and a roar and a general stramash, and I found myself miles away underground and wedged in as tight as tight. Well, thank goodness, my wants are few, and at any rate I had peace and quietness and wasn't always being asked to come along and *do* something. And I've got such an active mind—always occupied, I assure you! But time went on, and there was a certain sameness about the life, and at last I began to think it would be fun to work my way upstairs and see what you other fellows were doing. So I scratched and burrowed, and worked this way and that way and at last I came out through this cave here.'[7]

The symbolism could hardly be plainer: Grahame's creative mind, driven inward by the drudging, conventional duty required of him, has at last, with great effort, broken free. (The same symbolism, of course, was to be repeated in the first chapter of *The Wind in the Willows*.) His dilemma is plain: can he risk driving it back underground by going over to the forces of convention, *i.e.* by accepting the office of Secretary? The Dragon doesn't mean Them any harm; he only wants to read Them his poems; but They (as the Boy reminds him) regard *him* as an enemy of the human race. There he sits, a 'happy Bohemian', in Grahame's give-away phrase, enjoying the sunsets, telling stories, and polishing up his gorgeous blue scales (Grahame was a tremendous dandy), while all the time St. George is preparing for a battle royal. He can't be bothered to face the problem; he leaves the Boy to fix it. And fixed it is, as we might expect, with a great show of fighting; and ends with the Dragon painlessly transfixed, by arrangement, through an insensitive part of his neck, while all the villagers cheer. Then St. George (carefully side-stepping requests to finish the job properly) ends up, after the inevitable banquet, by helping the tipsy Dragon home, with the Boy in attendance. A compromise has been reached; the public decencies have been observed.

The results of this compromise were not immediately beneficial: Grahame wrote hardly anything for nine years, and then achieved his masterpiece almost by accident.

In *The Golden Age* and *Dream Days*, of course, 'They', Authority, public convention are represented by the Olympians. Now 'Olympians' and 'grown-ups' are not, as is sometimes supposed, interchangeable terms. When it comes to the point, 'Olympians' are middle-class relatives and their middle-class friends; Aunts, and, less often, Uncles, who impose their deadening will on the imaginative young according to some inscrutable canon of behaviour:

> On the whole, the existence of these Olympians seemed to be entirely void of interests, even as their movements were confined and slow, and their habits stereotyped and senseless. To anything but appearances they were blind. . . . Perhaps, indeed, it was one of their best qualities that they spent the greater part of their time stuffily indoors. . . . These strange folk had visitors sometimes—stiff and colourless Olympians like

themselves, equally without vital interests and intelligent pursuits. . . . It was perennial matter for amazement how these Olympians would talk over our heads—during meals, for instance—of this or the other social or political inanity, under the delusion that these pale phantasms of reality were among the importances of life.[8]

The Olympians, then, stood for bourgeois society at its most materialistic, mean-spirited, and (worst of all) unimaginative. Incapable of enjoying life themselves, they were determined to deprive those who could of the chance to do so. They took their holidays, not in Rome, but Brighton: they were stupidly blind as well as repressive. With them ritual had ousted belief: they hauled their children off to church on Sundays, though they had not the least inclination to go themselves. They were the great-grandparents of the Hollow Men.

Grahame hits off their foibles with deft economy of characterization and an acute psychological eye for the significant trait. Perhaps Uncle Thomas is his most devastating portrait. Detail is added to detail in each successive story: the senseless adult jokes at the children's expense, the fear of being left alone for a single minute, the superficial omniscience, the petulant outbursts of anger, the ridiculous self-importance. Yet, and this is of the essence, Uncle Thomas is not a two-dimensional monster, but, reading between the lines, a pathetic and unhappy human being, the victim of his own Olympian condition. In one story he is laboriously mocking psychical research; but soon enough, as we might expect, he is dabbling in it himself. His other fads, taken up and abandoned one after the other, include Rosicrucianism and hospital charities. 'The matching a ribbon, the running down to the stores, the interviewing a cook—these and similar duties lent constant colour and variety to his vacant life in London, and helped to keep down his figure.' We end by becoming rather sorry for Uncle Thomas: he is so utterly lacking in beliefs or purpose. Spiritually null, he suggests a premature victim of social *Angst*.

Governesses and tutors (as Grahame delicately suggests) do not really count as Olympians: they exist in a curious ambivalent limbo. As the source of dull, unimaginative, compulsory lessons they are heartily cursed by the children, yet without the emotional violence reserved for relatives. Perhaps their social status, teetering uneasily between kitchen and drawing-room, has something to do with this. By and large, the tutors, being more pretentious, come off worst: they believe in ghosts, or try to be hearty, or bring a wonderful whiff of greenery-yallery into the Berkshire countryside.[9]

But Miss Smedley is another matter. She belongs in the Great Tradition of governesses, with Maria Edgeworth's Madame de Rosier or Conrad's Flora Fyne.[10] She is wonderfully priggish, a rational killjoy of the first order with a brisk modernist line about fairies:

> "Do you mean to say it's all lies?" asked Charlotte bluntly. Miss Smedley deprecated the use of any such unladylike words in any connection at all. "These stories had their origin, my dear," she explained, "in a mistaken anthropomorphism in the interpretation of nature. But though we are now too well informed to fall into similar errors, there are still many beautiful lessons to be learnt from these myths—"
>
> "But how can you learn anything," persisted Charlotte, "from what doesn't exist?" And she left the table defiant, howbeit depressed.[11]

When the day comes for Miss Smedley to leave, however, the children's feelings are not quite what they expected. 'Exit Tyrannus' is one of Grahame's most flawless stories, both in technique and conception. The slow evaporation of pumped-up pleasure, the general seeping in of unadmitted misery; the recollection—too late—of gifts and kindnesses taken for granted at the time; the almost physical sense of loss and break-up, the children's semi-inarticulate exchanges—these are superbly done. We only learn by our losses: it is a theme that recurs again and again in Grahame's work.[12]

Miss Smedley, like Farmer Larkin, is betwixt and between in the children's hierarchy, a source of perplexity and doubt. 'It began to dawn upon me', Grahame wrote of the latter, 'that these Olympians must have certain good points, far down in them, and that I should have to leave off abusing them some day.'[13]

There remain the adults for whom Grahame expresses unreserved admiration: the curate who was ready to turn into a band of marauding Indians; the old country doctor; the Artist; the scholar-Rector; the Funny Man; and the family servants, Martha in particular. What are the common qualities they possess which endear them to the child-narrator?

Tolerance, respect, kindliness, imaginative sympathy: these most immediately spring to mind. The Artist and the Rector take the boy as they find him, and have an instinctive ability to enter the children's world: they do not flatten it with hearty, jeering laughter or self-assertive obtuseness. The servants are free from the shibboleths of upper-middle-class behaviour: they are invariably depicted as warm-hearted, spontaneous, given to demonstrations of affection. Harold's special friend was the cook; we could hardly imagine him flinging himself on Aunt Eliza's bosom in a moment of crisis. Martha lends the children money in an emergency ('only you mustn't tell your aunt') and is the narrator's idea of a 'real lady'. John Buchan, then a fellow-reader with Grahame for the Bodley Head, wrote in 1896: 'It is surprising with how equal a vision a child looks forth on life. He has no unreasoning prejudices—these are the heritage of later days—and few things are common in his eyes.'[14]

The central key to this ideal of sympathy, tolerance, and imaginative understanding is to be found towards the end of 'A Harvesting', in a speech of the Rector's:

'See . . . how this strange thing, this love of ours, lives and shines out in the unlikeliest of places! You have been in the fields in early morning? Barren acres all! But only stoop—catch the light thwartwise—and all is a silver network of gossamer! So the fairy filaments of this strange thing underrun and link together the whole world. Yet it is not the old imperious god of the fatal bow—ἔρως ἀνίκατε μάχαν—not that—nor even the placid respectable στοργή—but something still unnamed, perhaps more mysterious, more divine! Only one must stoop to see it, old fellow, one must stoop!' [15]

There is an unbroken line running back from this passage to the charity and humility of Sir Thomas Browne's *Religio Medici*. Grahame knew and loved Browne better than any other English author: it is not hard to see why. The rich idiosyncrasy of his style appealed to Grahame's feeling for words; but Browne's basic philosophy of life went home at a deeper level.

Like Grahame, Browne found himself out of sympathy with the Puritan sectarianism of his times, and longed for a faith that embraced gentleness, charity, and love. Like Grahame, again, he had a deep-rooted love of all created things, and was especially drawn to the intricate minuscule life of pond or hedgerow, Grahame was, we cannot doubt, *anima naturaliter Christiana*; and in Browne's example he found both comfort and guidance. What he abhorred was the inner emptiness of the merely social gesture: his cruellest gibes were reserved for vacuous curates or intolerant bourgeois puritanism. But there was, too, a more positive side to the matter. Grahame, no less than Browne, was drawn by the ritual beauty and spiritual power of the Roman Catholic Church. In *Dream Days* he speaks of 'the white gladness of the acolyte who, greatly privileged, has been permitted to swing a censer at the sacring of the very Mass'; and later describes, with sympathy and longing, the spiritually complete life of a monastic community:

> I had wandered up there one day, searching (as usual) for something I never found, and had been taken in by them and treated as friend and comrade. They had made me free of their ideal little rooms, full of books and pictures, and clean of the

antimacassar taint; they had shown me their chapel, high, hushed, and faintly scented, beautiful with a strange new beauty born both of what it had and what it had not—that too familiar dowdiness of common places of worship. . . . I thought of a certain look in their faces, as if they had a common purpose and a business, and were acting under orders thoroughly recognised and understood.[16]

'Friend and comrade'; 'the antimacassar taint'; 'that too familiar dowdiness'; 'a common purpose'—the contrast between these dedicated, purposeful, yet utterly charitable men and the tired materialism of the Olympians could hardly be more firmly underlined.

What was it that crystallized Grahame's complex childhood memories into the creative pattern they finally formed? It seems almost certain that the primary impulse—as so much else in Grahame—derived from Stevenson: more precisely, from the essay 'Child's Play' in *Virginibus Puerisque*, of which the second edition had appeared in 1887.[17] The coincidences are numerous and striking:

> Surely they [children] dwell in a mythological epoch, and are not the contemporaries of their parents. What can they think of them? What can they make of these bearded or petticoated giants who look down upon their games? who *move upon a cloudy Olympus, following unknown designs apart from rational enjoyment?* [Italics mine.]

In Stevenson we also find the child's indifference to adult activities, his brutal contempt for grown-ups in general, and his arrogant disregard for emotional calamities outside his own sphere:

> Once, when I was groaning aloud with physical pain, a young gentleman came into the room and enquired if I had seen his bow and arrow. He made no account of my groans, which he accepted, as he had to accept so much else, as a piece of the inexplicable conduct of his elders; and like a wise young gentleman, he would waste no wonder on the subject.

Compare with this Grahame's passage in 'Dies Irae' about the death of the housemaid's brother:[18]

> There had never been anyone like Billy in his own particular sphere; and now he was drowned, they said, and Martha was miserable, and—and I couldn't get a new bootlace. They told me that Billy would never come back any more, and I stared out of the window at the sun which came back, right enough, every day, and their news conveyed nothing whatever to me.

This callousness or indifference to death struck Stevenson with particular force; he returns to it again later in his essay. 'Not Théophile Gautier, not Flaubert,' he writes, 'can look more callously upon life, or rate the reproduction more highly over the reality; and they will parody an execution, a deathbed, or the funeral of the young man of Nain, with all the cheerfulness in the world'—a thesis which *The Golden Age* amply supports. It was Stevenson, too, who wrote of his own childhood: 'That was my golden age; *et ego in Arcadia vixi*'.

Perhaps a still earlier influence, with a sharper social edge to it, had been Anstey's famous *Vice Versa*, published in 1882. By employing the fairy-tale device of reversed identities, and playing steadily for laughs throughout, Anstey got away with what was, in fact, a bitter satire on contemporary society. In the person of Paul Bultitude he pilloried not only the stupidity and unthinking insensitiveness of middle-class parents, but the whole bourgeois way of life—emotionally no less than financially centred on Mincing Lane; while in Dr. Grimstone he held up puritan pedagogy to the most deadly ridicule. Grahame cannot have failed to read *Vice Versa*: its moral lay too close to his own beliefs. (He may well have known Anstey at this period, though there is no proof of their having met till after Grahame's marriage: Anstey was an old friend of Elspeth Grahame's family.) It is very likely that the 'Lesson for Fathers'—as Anstey sub-titled his book—contributed much to Grahame's indictment of the Olympians.

This is not to lessen the originality or value of Grahame's

creative achievement: it merely hints at the materials he may have found ready to his hand. There is all the difference in the world between Stevenson flatly asserting that children despise their elders, and Grahame dramatizing the fact in a series of memorable short stories. The critics took Stevenson's essay calmly enough: only the rational surface of their intelligence was engaged by it. But Grahame's stories got past their emotional guard and pinked their Olympian self-esteem, with what results we know. This implied great creative skill and artistic originality. Grahame's highest gift was for characterization; and in *The Golden Age* he made children live as they were, not as their elders would wish them to be. This was a completely new achievement; and it soon caught on. The year after *Dream Days* was published Kipling did for the adolescent schoolboy what Grahame had done for his younger brother: and the result was *Stalky and Co.*

We have already seen something of Grahame's skill in characterizing adults: but his two volumes of short stories must stand or fall, in the last resort, by the childish family quartet round whom they are built: Charlotte, Harold, Edward, Selina, with the personality of the narrator omnipresent in the background. His success may be gauged from the fact that these prototypes have left their mark on almost every subsequent fictional family of the kind, from E. Nesbit's *The Railway Children* to Arthur Ransome's *Swallows and Amazons*. This is all the odder since we know practically nothing about them in the way of external detail: they are never physically described, and their background is of the sketchiest. Our visual impression of them is almost entirely derived from E. H. Shepard's evocative drawings and silhouettes.

This was clever of Grahame. He saw very clearly that any writer who wishes to give his characters permanency must work from inner, rather than external, characteristics; and in seizing on those perennial traits which embody the whole essence of childhood, he created a minor classic. The social evils he attacked have long since passed away: it does not matter. Grahame's children are timeless: yet each remains a sharply differentiated individual.

The two girls, Charlotte and Selina, are divided by temperament no less than age. Charlotte is not only younger, and therefore free from the turmoils of impending adolescence which affect her sister: she is also endowed with a dreamy, imaginative, introspective nature, radically different from Selina's fierce, nervous energy. She is a chronic day-dreamer, with infinite capacity for solitary pleasures. It is for her that dolls come to life, and she moves into the timeless, enchanted landscape of a picture-book as easily as Alice passed through the looking-glass. She is artless (though stubbornly persistent in the defence of her beliefs), easily moved to tears, and endowed with a fascinating streak of morbid piety: 'I hope he'll die tonight,' she remarks of Uncle William, 'for then he'll go straight to heaven'.

Selina is older and more complex: she has 'just reached that disagreeable age when one begins to develop a conscience', and her confused chrysalis state, half child, half adolescent, is observed with uncommon fidelity. She is not too old to kick shins or be scared of a thunderstorm; but she is, nevertheless, beginning to turn towards Olympian Society. She subscribes to the *Young Ladies' Journal* and has a sneaking fondness for feminine gossip and paying calls. On the other hand, she is still an expert on the British Navy: and this is responsible for her curious behaviour one Trafalgar Day, when in a burst of patriotism she breaks all the domestic rules and lights a huge illicit bonfire in honour of the occasion. She is described—and portrayed—in this story as 'Maenad-like', 'possessed'; reference is made to her 'weird seizure'. Once again the reader sees a little further than the narrator: what Selina is experiencing is one of the passing storms that so often seize a girl in that awkward transitional period between childhood and adolescence.[19]

Harold and Edward form an almost exact male analogue to Charlotte and Selina. Harold, like Charlotte, lives in a private world of his own devising, untroubled by the later, inevitable, inroads of maturity; muffin-man or clubman at will, playing conspirators by himself, or obliviously window-gazing, he is both the eternal innocent and the eternal victim. If anyone is caught or wrongfully accused, it is bound to be Harold; but despite this— and in sharp contra-distinction to the narrator—he

> never brooded, moped, nor ate his heart out over any dis-appointment. One wild outburst—one dissolution of a minute into his original elements of air and water, of tears and outcry— so much insulted nature claimed. Then he would pull himself together, iron out his countenance with a smile, and adjust himself to the new condition of things.[20]

He is generous and naïve: easily taken in, quickly consoled; and still has a touching faith in the omniscience of his elders. Not un-naturally, he has always been the favourite with critics, from Swinburne to Mr. Alan Pryce-Jones:[21] he is Grahame's nearest approach to the popular sentimental ideal.

Edward is a vastly different creature: dogmatic, extrovert, practical, aggressive, and very conscious of his rights as the eldest child. (The quartet's lives are governed by immutable nursery ritual. Birthdays always produce holidays; at various ages comes promotion to knives or toothbrushes, or slates: and precedence goes rigidly by age.) But Edward, too, is approaching the difficult age: his emotional compass veers wildly. At one moment he is attacking girls, the next he is hopelessly in love; his bombast hides chronic uncertainty. When the fatal day comes, and he is faced with the prospect of departure 'out of our placid backwater, out into the busy world of rubs and knocks and competition, out into the New Life',[22] his courage momentarily fails him, and he becomes a little boy again.

Lusisti satis: you have played enough; the moment of respite is over, and irrevocable change must follow—this is the climax to which Grahame moves in both *The Golden Age* and *Dream Days*, and which gives the first, especially, a clear organic structure. It seems not to have been remarked hitherto that the stories in *The*

Golden Age are printed in a very different order from that of their actual composition. 'A Holiday', for example, which immediately follows the Prologue, was one of the last pieces to be written: it appeared in March 1895, simultaneously with the book's endpiece, 'Lusisti Satis'. We may assume, then, that Grahame rearranged the stories to form some kind of pattern; and a consecutive reading at once reveals what this pattern is. From page to page we trace the slow vanishing of childhood, the advance of age and scepticism, the destruction of a vision, the inexorable process of growing up.

In *The Golden Age* we begin with the children's minuscule world unbreached by disillusion: but story by story reality breaks in a little further, the magic pictures begin to fade, the sandcastle to crumble before the advancing tide, till 'finally we found ourselves sitting silent on an upturned wheelbarrow, our chins on our fists, staring haggardly into the raw new conditions of our changed life, the ruins of a past behind our backs'.[23]

With *Dream Days* the development of the pattern is not so clear; but this is hardly surprising. It is a sequel only in the most superficial sense: the stories it contains are later additions to an already complete creative pattern. (It is tempting to fit them into *The Golden Age*—the thing can be done [24]—to form one single coherent volume.) The danger of disillusion here lurks throughout, and the fantasy in consequence becomes more strained. But the final story, 'A Departure', forms a logical conclusion to the whole sequence. It was, in point of fact, the last thing of its kind which Grahame ever wrote, and seems designed as a conscious valediction to his dream-children.

In this story, you will remember, the Olympians—always open, as Grahame remarks, to sentiment of a treacly, woodcut order— have, without warning, parcelled up the children's toys 'for dispatch to London, to gladden the lives and bring light into the eyes of London waifs and Poplar Annies'. The children—growing too old for toys, yet still inarticulately resentful of this outrage to their private, familiar world—steal the parcel before it goes, and bury the toys by moonlight. (They are being neither selfish nor snobbish—no more snobbish, at least, than all children—but they do instinctively condemn the gesture of their elders as not only arbitrary but false.) We leave the dolls in the care of the Man in the Moon:

> He was going to see after them, it was evident; for he was always there, more or less, and it was no trouble to him at all, and he would tell them how things were still going, up here, and throw in a story or two of his own whenever they seemed a trifle dull.

It is, of course, not only the dolls—symbol of childishness— that are being buried; it is Harold, Edward, Selina, and Charlotte themselves. Time moves inexorably on, and these dream-children pass into the keeping of the Man in the Moon, the artist, the story-teller. For him they never change or grow old; and only he—'a good fellow too, cheery, comforting, with a fund of anecdote; a man in whom one had every confidence'—can by his magic preserve them unchanged for ever.

MR. GRAHAME AND
MISS THOMSON
1899

If the root of the matter be in him, and if he has the requisite chords to set in vibration, a young man may occasionally enter, with the key of art, into that land of Beulah which is upon the borders of Heaven, and within sight of the City of Love. There let him sit awhile to hatch delightful hopes and perilous illusions.

R. L. STEVENSON: *Virginibus Puerisque*

I have met with women whom I really think would like to be married to a Poem, and to be given away by a Novel.

JOHN KEATS: *Letters to Fanny Brawne*

I was at Hazlitt's marriage, and had like to have been turned out several times during the ceremony. Anything awful makes me laugh. I misbehaved once at a funeral.

CHARLES LAMB: *Letter to Southey, 9th August, 1815*

To judge from the evidence offered by his published work, Kenneth Grahame was not, any more than Benedick, a marrying man. The particular pre-adolescent age-group with which he felt most sympathy was precisely the one that most despised 'this flaw that so often declared itself in enviable natures of fullest endowment', the process of romantic passion and its consequences. *Amo* is the dreariest of verbs; women are irrational creatures;

196

marriage is a deadly and soul-destroying institution. Girls are by definition an inferior breed who kick shins, gossip about trivialities, and use their feminine armoury in order to dominate, tease, and devour. The most sheerly happy moments in Grahame's work come when he—or his *alter ego* the narrator—is utterly alone, savouring the subtle magic of solitude, 'the world forgetting, by the world forgot'.

On the other hand, it is plain that behind this rejection lies (as in the parallel case of Stevenson) not basic aversion but immature romantic idealism. It is not the *concept* of love which fails to touch Grahame's sympathies: the fairy-tale convention of Finding the Princess, the *amour courtois* absorbed from Malory and the Troubadours, these he prized above almost anything else. What he hated and feared were the all-too-imperfect manifestations of love's power as observed in the adult world. The Olympians married, not for an intangible ideal, but for money, or dull social reasons, or driven by the blind impulses of the sexual urge. Sex, of course, and more particularly the onset of puberty, is one of the great enemies in Grahame's world. It disrupts the timelessness, wreaks appalling metamorphoses in hitherto right-minded children, breaks up the entire ideal pattern. One of Grahame's deliberate motives in writing *The Wind in the Willows* was 'by simply using the animal, to get away . . . from weary sex-problems'; in the blurb he wrote for his publishers the book is described as 'clean of the clash of sex'.[1]

This kind of emotional make-up, especially when combined with normal, healthy, physical instincts, can have peculiarly disastrous effects. The 'I' of Grahame's early books loses his heart three times; and the three objects of his affections might have been selected as text-book illustrations of delayed adolescence. There is the baker's wife, symbolizing maternal affection; the star-spangled circus equestrienne, who is the Unattainable Ideal in her magic ring; and the all-too-human, pert, teasing girl of 'Mutabile Semper', whose qualities Grahame had already outlined in 1892:[2]

In later life it is to her sex that the wee (but very wise) folk sometimes delegate their power of torment. Such understudies are found to play the part exceeding well; and many a time the infatuated youth believes he sees in the depth of one sole pair of eyes . . . the authentic fairy wicket standing ajar; many a time must he hear the quaint old formula, 'I'm sure, if I've ever done anything to lead you to think', etc. (runs it not so?), ere he shall realize that here is the gate upon no magic pleasance but on a cheap suburban villa, banging behind the wrathful rate-collector or hurled open to speed the pallid householder to the Registrar's Office.

The implication could hardly be clearer. Grahame, in his own way, was extremely susceptible; but every time he tried to incorporate the object of his affections into that charmed, illusory, childish, sexless world of ideals, trouble was sure to follow. In most cases, luckily, once the girl got some inkling of what she was up against, that would be that. The real danger would be a woman who, superficially at any rate, shared Grahame's dream-world herself.

Since Grahame's diary has not survived, and any intimate letters connected with his early life have long since vanished, it is almost impossible to reconstruct this side of his life during the years before his marriage. Yet there are tantalizing hints of an earlier affair. Poems, I know, are dubious evidence; but Grahame had the autobiographical habit well ingrained in his creative impulse, and besides, bad poems tend to be more accurate in these matters than good ones. They are often written for primarily non-literary reasons. Here is the most important from the biographical point of view: it was published in the *National Observer* on 27th February 1892: [3]

> Cupid sounds the call to arms!
> And at once the Loves, upspringing,
> Hither running, hither winging,
> Snatching bow and catching quiver,
> Come a chattering, sparkling river,
> Like the hiving bee in swarms,
> At the merry call to arms!

See the stately foe advance
Where the small immortals brave her,—
But the troops of Eros waver,
See the ranks begin to shake!
Then the little cowards break,
Routed ere the touch of lance
By her terrible advance.

Was I wise in my defiance?
With but half a mind to fight,
Scorning compromise or flight,
What remains for me to do
But to kneel and humbly sue
Pardon, peace—perhaps alliance?
Any way, no more defiance.

This, at first sight, is simple enough, and its conventional form
tempts the mind to slide quickly over it without really taking in
its full meaning. Grahame has fallen in love; his advances have
been in some way discouraged; he has made some act of non-
co-operation or defiance that requires an apology; he is contemplating marriage. So far so good; the fallacy (when we re-read
the poem carefully) lies in the assumption that this describes the
rebuffing of an importunate suitor. In fact, the case is exactly the
other way round.

Why, if Grahame is so pressing, is his passion—in a revealing
metaphor—'Routed ere the touch of lance/By her terrible
advance'? It seems a strange word until we accept the fact that what
Grahame really means is that he has been scared off by a girl not
only emotionally but sexually more mature than himself. This
also explains that odd word 'defiance'. What is Grahame defying?
Why, if routed, should he apologize? If he is angling for 'alliance',
i.e. marriage, why should he only have 'half a mind to fight' if
the phrase is to be taken in its usual sense of 'engage in Love's
warfare'?

His 'defiance', then, is actually his refusal to commit himself sexually—though the thought of so doing is by no means un-attractive to him at one level of his nature. *That* is why he only has half a mind to fight—against his own inclinations. He is not perverse; merely immature and scared, with too great a share of childish idealism in him to make the step easily from boyhood to manhood. He will not 'compromise', *i.e.* let the situation straggle on unresolved; nor will he take refuge in his usual stand-by on such occasions, a frantic rush to escape from the whole thing. What he has to apologize for is not impetuousness but the exact opposite: the girl has, quite naturally, taken offence at his rejection of *her* advances, which presumably went rather beyond what his childish moral ideal permitted. In certain circumstances it is a far worse insult not to make love than to persist in doing so. But this time Grahame wants to make it up; and he closes with the idea of marriage, which, one supposes, would solve all his scruples.

This poem appeared a week after 'The Fairy Wicket', with its references, quoted above, to teasing, materialistic women. It is tempting to correlate the two; we can picture this curious relation-ship only too clearly. Grahame has put Miss X into a dream-world, a cocoon of his imagination; and the cocoon is constantly being torn by her natural passion and urge for ultimate domes-ticity, *his* natural passion and childlike emotions in conflict. The quarrel was, apparently, patched up, and Grahame moved towards a more adult acceptance of human relationships. Perhaps the thought of marriage was still in the air: at any rate in October 1892 he published a *Cradle Song*, which is so far from his normal territory that it seems to indicate a strong external influence.[4]

But, as we know, the affair—if indeed it existed—never reached the altar. The only hint as to its conclusion is contained in another scrap of verse, preserved by Chalmers from Grahame's lost ledger-diary:[5]

Let bygones be bygones? Very well, dear, e'en have it so,
The more that we cannot help it; the hurrying years that go
Make bygones only too quickly and I can't, if I would, say no.

But indeed, could I bid old Time turn round and halt the flying
    minute,
I would have it all back, each quarrel of old (never mind who was
    first to begin it!)
And you with your tempers and tears and sulks—for the sake of
    the good that was in it!

This fragment is undated and without ascription; but it seems a
fair presumption to connect it with the mysterious relationship
that was ended long before Grahame's marriage.

    One last point remains. Can we guess at the identity of Miss X?
I think we can, with a fair degree of certainty. Who would it be
but the girl whom he first met at Drayton Gardens, and holidayed
with at Pitlochry and in Italy; the girl who joined the New
Shakespere Society with him and shared all his private literary
devotions: his cousin, Annie Grahame? 'I had been reared on old
Scotch ballads and stories and folk-lore', she wrote, 'which
appealed to Kenneth also and *later on at any rate formed a bond of
union between us*'; and of the holiday at the Villino Landau:

> We made some very pleasant expeditions—notably one to
> the Madonna del Sarso—a little church on a hillside some miles
> at the back of Fiesole where on the second Sunday in May a
> festival is held annually. . . . We got back at about 7 p.m., none
> the worse for the long day, which Kenneth had beguiled with
> delightful fairy tales. . . .

Poor Annie: she never married, and Elspeth Grahame, though using
her information to supply background material for Chalmers'
labours, carefully saw to it that he should not mention her once
in his finished book. Arguments *ex silentio* are notoriously un-
reliable; but this one seems more suggestive than most.

    It is plain from the whole episode that Grahame failed to
achieve, and probably did not desire, a normal adult relationship.
After all, most men taking their girl-friend for a long walk in the
Florentine hills do not beguile the time with fairy tales, delightful or otherwise, whatever else they may talk about. Grahame's

confession to Helen Dunham, in 1896, that he did not feel in the least grown up, and did not anticipate any immediate change in that direction, simply confirms the diagnosis. In all probability he would have gone to his grave a gentle, fantastic bachelor (like Lear, Carroll, and Hans Andersen) if fate, having a taste for irony, had not thrown Elspeth Thomson in his path.

Elspeth, like her future husband, was born in Edinburgh, on 3rd January 1862. She was the second child in a family of four, the youngest of whom was later to become Lord Courtauld-Thomson, the owner of Dorneywood. Her father, Robert William Thomson, was a remarkable inventor, who took out patents on, *inter alia*, the pneumatic tyre, and a special type of fountain pen with a glass nib: he also produced a steam-driven road vehicle, and designed the first floating dock.[6] Her mother, Clara, whose maiden name was Hertz, was of a literary and artistic bent, and a constant stream of distinguished visitors frequented the house in Moray Place. From her earliest years Elspeth was accustomed to such company. When Mark Twain arrived, to find her parents out and only the children at home, in the nursery,

> Elspeth received the visitor and offered him tea. He replied that he drank only whisky. Undaunted, and with rare social sense, the little girl ran down with a teapot and persuaded the butler to fill it with whisky, which the guest drank neat.[7]

And at the age of ten—shortly after her father's death from locomotor ataxia—Elspeth, on holiday at Pontresina with the rest of the family, struck up a precocious friendship with Tennyson. All her life she was to feed on the personalities of artistic celebrities, and use their genius as a prop for her own lack of creative talent.

Furthermore, she not only cultivated a particularly sentimental brand of fairy-tale fantasy (which contrasts sharply with Grahame's own private world), but had a strong enough personality to impose her own terms on many of her distinguished correspondents. In 1890 Justin McCarthy, the leader of the Irish Party, was writing lyrically to the twenty-eight-year-old Elspeth about his love for 'Rivers—and poets who love Rivers and painters who give us pictures of them'. Old Sir John Tenniel bombarded her till the end of his life with coyly gallant Valentines and sub-Carrollian fantasies, such as his invention of a flying machine called the Furious Flycycle.[8]

In 1875, three years after Robert Thomson's death, and when Elspeth was thirteen, her mother married again. Her second husband was a penniless barrister named John Fletcher Moulton, who, sustained by Clara's income, rose rapidly in his profession, and finally became a Lord of Appeal. The family moved from Edinburgh to London, and set up house at 57 Onslow Square. Here they lost no time in establishing themselves:

> They were both keenly interested in literature, science, and art, and their circle included practically all the mid-Victorian leaders in these subjects, notably Swinburne, Browning, Oscar Wilde, Lord Kelvin, Spottiswoode, Lord Leighton, Frank Dicksee and Tenniel, as well as many visitors of great interest from continental countries, since Mrs. Fletcher Moulton as well as her husband spoke French and German perfectly.[9]

Their elder daughter was given a cosmopolitan education as it was then understood: her sister Winnie, too, was an excellent amateur musician and artist. Elspeth spent some time as a pupil in a French convent: here she exercised her undoubted talent for languages (she spoke fluent Flemish as well as French), and acquired a superficially 'Continental' outlook on life to offset those gloomy Calvinist Sundays remembered from Moray Place.[10]

Later she was to set down her recollections of this convent; and it is immediately clear that one thing she shared with Grahame was an anti-Puritan religious romanticism:

> There was a strange glamour about the garden and indeed about the whole place. The silences, the clamour—the brilliant

youth and high spirits, the calm and self-abnegation. The cold stone stairs with the faint warmth of incense, the chapel with the white veiled scholars, and the black shrouded teachers the tall misty candles the formal altar flowers the lovely chanting voices, then the garden, especially in an autumn haze was magical. Frosted wheels of spider web, dew glittering on the Christmas roses, a strange hint of incense blended with flower breaths.

There is a curious similarity between this and the young narrator's reactions to 'the Settlement' in *Dream Days*: yet even here one can distinguish the blurring sentimentality wholly lacking from Grahame's make-up.

By the time Elspeth Thomson met Kenneth Grahame she was nearly thirty-seven, and had reached a critical period in her life. For almost twenty years she had lived in the house at Onslow Square, first as Fletcher Moulton's stepdaughter, and after 1888 (the year of her mother's death) as his hostess and housekeeper also. She entertained the world of literature and art, filled her days with luncheons, tea-parties, soirées. When Fletcher Moulton went into politics, Elspeth was there to support him. His was a stormy passage; elected for Clapham in 1885 as a Liberal, he lost his seat the following year, and did not regain it till 1894. 1895 saw him back in the wilderness, and it was not till August 1898 that he found a safe constituency at Launceston in Cornwall.[11] All this time Elspeth was at hand to discuss his campaigns, often in letters to him in his constituency, and give him unfailing support.

The trouble was that Elspeth had achieved little in her own right—unless we count a curious little penny novelette about a virtuous working-class girl, issued in 1888 over the pseudonym of 'Clarence Onslow', and entitled *Amelia Jane's Ambition*. Bachelors perhaps fought shy of this strong-minded, strong-featured girl, with intellectual pretensions and an inexhaustible fund of conversational gambits. She was both a blue-stocking and an aesthete, simultaneously clever and fey: not particularly pretty, and verging on middle age. In later life acquaintances remembered her as 'a superficial and twilight woman' [12] who 'talked stridently and interminably, laying down the law about her preferences in literature and art, and never taking much heed of what anybody else had to say'.[13] She bears an unhappy resemblance to Thurber's monolithic *ingénue*, who bursts into a drawing-room announcing that she comes from haunts of coot and hern: an impression hardly lessened by Miss Bradley, who remarked that Elspeth 'had a happy indifference to the lesser conventions of the social world'.

There cannot be any doubt that she regarded Kenneth Grahame as an ideal potential catch. He was Secretary of the Bank of England, and therefore both respectable and a man of substance; he was also the author of *The Golden Age*, a factor which appealed to the sentimental child-fantasist in her. The two attractions in combination proved irresistible; and Elspeth set about playing her fish with dogged ruthlessness.

How, or exactly when, the two of them first met we cannot be certain. There is a story of Kenneth's having gone to see Fletcher Moulton on banking business, finding him out, and being entertained instead by his elder stepdaughter: [14] it sounds probable enough, though the hostess of 57 Onslow Square would have had no difficulty in making his acquaintance by more orthodox means.

It seems likely that their acquaintance dates from some time in the second half of 1897. There is a certain amount of circumstantial evidence which supports this view. The announcement of the engagement caused considerable surprise; and from 1898 onwards a curious change of tone is observable in much of Grahame's writing. A soft, false, dreamy sentimentality begins to intrude, utterly out of key with the tough, satirical note struck in *The Golden Age*. Grahame begins to behave as though he were an ordinary romantic children's writer, and seems to find the rôle uncomfortable. We have already observed this embarrassment in his review of Evelyn Sharp's *All the Way to Fairyland*. It lurks behind his 1898 preface to Eugene Field's *Lullaby-Land*, though leavened with stronger matter from Swift and Sir Thomas Browne. His piece on *The Fabric of the Fairy Tale*, which appeared in the *Daily Mail* some six months after his marriage,[15] is so sugary that it might almost have been dictated by Elspeth. But the Introduction to Billinghurst's *A Hundred Fables of Aesop* is another matter. Here we can see Grahame's satirical ego in the process of being driven underground again, and its incipient re-emergence in symbolical animal disguise. We shall return to this later.

Elspeth (as is abundantly clear from her later activities) had a remarkable talent for imposing her own beliefs, habits and wish-fulfilments on other people. She was a woman of dominant, almost obsessional personality, which could absorb even so canny a politician as Justin McCarthy: there is no reason to suppose that Kenneth Grahame was any more immune from her hypnotic self-projection.

Elspeth firmly convinced herself in a very short time that here was a man who shared her own private world of childish senti-mentalism: more disastrously, she convinced Grahame as well. He was not only a potential husband but an ideal romantic fairy-tale soul-mate; she saw herself playing Georgette Leblanc to his Maurice Maeterlinck. Once she got an idea of this sort into her head, the facts were simply made to fit in. After a while Grahame slipped into his allotted rôle. He fell in with her whimsies con-scientiously. He attempted to incorporate her as a childish dream-princess in his story 'A Saga of the Seas', and the result was a page or two of frightful mawkishness.[16] He even took to writing her coyly mis-spelt little *billets-doux* which outdo Swift's *Journal to Stella*. Then, in the early spring of 1899, he played right into her hands by falling seriously ill.

As usual, it was his chest that proved his undoing. At first he seemed to be suffering from nothing worse than a tiresome, debilitating cold and cough. On Easter Sunday he wrote to

Elspeth, who was similarly laid up, the first of a series of baby-talk letters: [17]

> Darlin Minkie Ope youre makin steddy progress & beginnin ter think of oppin outer your nest & avin a short fly round. I ad nuther good nite & avnt ardly corfd torl terday—but it aint so nice a day, & doesnt tempt one out. . . . Feel orfle slack still but am wearin down the cold grajjly. Wish the sun wood cum out fer a bit. Im very dull & bored ere. Spose youre a bit dull'n bored were *you* are, aint you? But you've got a maid, & a poodle, (tho they're bicyclin most of the time) & your friends do drop in sumtimes. Easter is always detestable. Your whale-books a rippin good book, [almost certainly this refers to Melville's *Moby Dick*] wif lots o reedin in it, & it sor me froo Good Friday triumphantly. Spose youve got a sort o mudie box spred out on *your* quilt.
>
> This aint much uv a letter my deer but aint got no spirits & dont take no interest nor no *notice* just yet. But Im wishing you elth & appiness my deer & a speedy recuvry & peece & quiet. Goodbye darlin from your own luvin Dino

Grahame got up the same afternoon, and returned to work in the City the next day, Monday 3rd April. In the evening he attended a dinner of the Court of Directors, which he mentioned to Elspeth in a letter on Tuesday afternoon. At this point the correspondence ceases abruptly for some time. Grahame's confident diagnosis of recovery had been sadly mistaken. A bad relapse set in, with pneumonia and empyema. Grahame underwent an operation involving section of the ribs and returned to Kensington Crescent to be nursed by his sister Helen and his devoted housekeeper, Sarah Bath. His convalescence was difficult and prolonged.

This situation suited Elspeth very well. She was a constant visitor, with carnations and grapes: [18] she persuaded her stepfather—who was still in ignorance of her precise relationship to Grahame—to send the young Secretary gifts from his ample cellar. The necessary degree of intimacy had been achieved, clearly, before Grahame fell ill ('wot a alibi terday if we ony cood use it', he wrote on 3rd April); now matters had to be stabilized. Elspeth—who presumably read Grahame's works—must have seen that to rouse his romantic instincts was one thing, but to get him as far as matrimony was quite another. From both *Pagan Papers* and *The Golden Age* it was only too obvious that Grahame made the same distinction as Stevenson between romance and marriage, very much to the latter's disadvantage. 'In marriage', Stevenson wrote, 'a man becomes slack and selfish, and undergoes a fatty degeneration of his moral being.' There was also to be reckoned with Grahame's obsessional, almost mystic passion for solitude.

I am not suggesting that Elspeth, like any coolly scheming middle-aged woman, deliberately set out to compromise Grahame: there is no doubt that she was genuinely in love with him at this point. But she was adept at concealing her own motives from herself, and the fact remains that she used by far the most effective weapon available to her: a playing on Grahame's sense of honour and social propriety. Elspeth had by now convinced herself that Grahame exactly fitted her own dream ideal: all that remained was the mechanical process of making the dream come true. Relentlessly Elspeth took the initiative; and such were her persuasive powers that for just long enough she convinced Grahame as well. By the time he began to have doubts it was too late.

By 21st May Grahame was fit enough to 'crawl about with a stick', and to write a short note to Fletcher Moulton thanking him for 'your *second* most kind consignment of ancient Port'. On the 25th he wrote to Elspeth as follows:

> Darling Minkie This is just a *smuggled* line—for I'm not supposed to sit up writing letters yet—to say I've begun coming down in the afternoon and *seeing* my *friends*. I did not even know you had not gone away for the holiday, till this morning [19] —and indeed while I was in *quod* I was told nothing about anybody. The surgeon has done with me—says I've made a

famous recovery as far as *his* share of the thing goes—but says
I must go away the moment I can—in a very few days if
possible—& for a *long* time, so as to get through the winter
without a breakdown. My dearest I mustn't write any more—
but I wonder if I shall see you? It's been a bad two months.
        Your loving   Dino

On the same day he wrote to Miss Bradley that 'I've been having
a desperately bad time of it, but am going to be stronger than
ever some day'. Apparently there had been some abortive attempt
to enlist Helen's support for the idea of marriage, because he adds:
'No object in talking things over with my sister *now*. *Irresponsive*
is not the word. . . .'

Four days later another consignment of wine arrived from
Fletcher Moulton, together with the offer of a carriage. Grahame
was still very shaky, and declined the carriage (he had only been
out once yet), but seems to have done justice to the port:

> Like Lord Rosebery I am regretting the possession of only
> one stomach—and one head; and I think of the historic Scotch-
> man who never could sleep a wink as long as there was a drop
> of whisky in the house. It will be hard indeed for me to go back
> to the humble 'four ale'—which more properly belongs to my
> lot in life.

But by Sunday 4th June, since Fletcher Moulton still persisted
(and as Grahame was due to move to the Cornish Riviera on the
Monday), his offer was accepted, and Grahame went for a drive
in the afternoon. His position *vis-à-vis* Elspeth was still a
secret: Fletcher Moulton might have raised his eyebrows at the
note which Grahame had sent her on May 26th: 'Darling—come
when you can, tomorrow afternoon—I rather think my sister's
going out about 3.30 or so, for the rest of the afternoon—anyhow
come. Your lovin own   Dino.' By now he was deeply compromised; and Elspeth, while perhaps uneasy about her stepfather's possible reactions, knew that Kenneth himself was sure.
The etiquette governing a relationship of this kind was far stricter

in 1899 than it is now, and any infringement of the rules (such as unchaperoned visits) provoked much more stringent social reprisals. And even if this had not been so, Grahame's sense of decency was only too easy to work on.

Kenneth and Helen travelled down to the west country together. The first ten days of Kenneth's convalescence were spent at Torquay; and from the moment of their arrival Kenneth wrote to Elspeth at least once a day. His letters—but not Elspeth's replies—have all survived. Unlike any of his other surviving correspondence, they are all scribbled in pencil, and use the curious baby-spelling which he had first adopted while an invalid in London:

Wensdy artnoon [June 7th] My Dearie Fanx fr mornin letter wich I redd *insted* o gettin up & ketchin a bote wot wos goin to Exmouf it wasn't tickler erly but Id ad a rarver wakefle nite so ventchly I sor the bote steem orf (and very cool and nice she looked) & then I was sorry I adn't ardned my art & cort er cos settin on a bote & smokin is a good way of flatin a lung & the place is rarver shut in & I wants the open sea & the roll of the billers. My room as a balkiny & a stript ornin & looks over the arber so I sees the botes I orter ketch goin orf wich is next bes ter ketchin of em.

I've bin settin on the peer this mornin in a cool breeze reedin bout Kitchner. Torkin o Kitchner, 'digestible' aint got no hay in it. [Spelling was never Elspeth's strong point.]

Dont bovver to let loose enny muvverly large people on me I dont want to be muvvered just now if I do theres a chamber-made wot'll take it on. There aint no 'bar' ere torl wich seems a rotten rangement.

Dont care much bout the otel. Legs is gettin orfle strong, & the place is airy & sunny & not too ot orl same shall move on nex week unless sumfin ideal in chambermades turns up. I wanter get down to the shore & paddle & this place is too Tory orltogevver for that.

Goodbye darlin pet & I wish you were here we wood go crors the bay in the little steem ferry bote & *not cum back*— there is poppies t'other side. Your lovin Dino.

Kenneth Grahame, *c.* 1895
Elspeth Thomson as a girl
From the painting by Sir Frank Dicksee, P.R.A.

This letter is a fair sample of Grahame's mood at the time. Under the undoubted affection the caged Bohemian is chafing a little: he dislikes the idea of being looked after and organized; his mind is straying wistfully towards beer and—characteristically— chambermaids. The following day his tone becomes somewhat shorter. Elspeth was bombarding him with umbrellas, mufflers, and food parcels. One of the latter provoked this outburst:

> There *was* musturd in the pasties so it needn't lay on yr conshunce—& I'll eet it orl if you want me to, but dont jor me no more bout diet cos you are mixin me up so fritefly. I eets wot I chooses & wot I dont want I dont & I dont care a dam wot they does in Berlin thank gord I'm British. [There follows a good deal about chambermaids again.]

On 11th June the correspondence took yet another turn—and more than ever one wishes we had Elspeth's side of it:

> This eesterly wind bliges me to spend a good deel o time on the leeside of the cliff. . . . You wd like it my deer . . . & I could play at frowin you over—over the cliff I mean, but I woodn't do it reely—and you cood play at bandonin me art- lessly for nuther—but you wouldn't do that neither. . . . Chambermaid don't share your views—ses she aint paid to old ands orl nite—& she'd lose er karacter besides—She ad on a nice wite gown wif pink spots this mornin, wot 'stood out' wif starch & virtue. Praps if you starcht your gowns you woodnt tork so lightly bout spendin orl nite wif dinos—but praps you'd better not starch 'em!

Elspeth was apparently already beginning to find Grahame's emotional elusiveness a little trying. On 13th June she sent him a long letter on the subject, which evoked this singularly ambi- valent response:

> It sums it up, wot you say bout 'abit o not bein interested' speshly wen its cuppled wif much natral 'gaucherie' wot as never been strove gainst. Your remark bout wastes in lanes is simply indecint & never will I trust myself alone in the same lane wif you—at least not in my presint week state.

The following day Grahame and his sister moved to Fowey, the little Cornish fishing port later to be incorporated in *The Wind in the Willows*. 'As the river mouth came in view larst nite with the boats & the little grey town I felt summow 'sif I was coming '*ome*', Grahame wrote, 'from boardin-school at Torquay.' He found the Fowey Hotel a charming place, '& bed a nice *narrer* sorft one insted of a broard ard one that leadeth to destruckshin'— which seems to suggest which way his mind was subconsciously turning about the future.

But his side was healing well, and the exercises to inflate his damaged lung were proceeding successfully, and there were the harbour and the valerian-smothered lanes to explore. The only drawback seems to have been Helen, who was always urging him, unsuccessfully, into more 'social' activities. She seems, too, to have been curiously devoid of a sense of humour:

> My sister went along the cliffs & climed down to a little cove & as she sat there a big rat cum out & sat bside er & ett winkles! I sed did ee buy them orf of a barrer & drop em in is at but she looked puzzled & seriouse & sed no ee only scraped in the seaweed wif is little pors & fetcht em out. Then I began agin was it a *black* pin—but by this time she evdently thort I was *ravin* so I dropt the subjick.

Presents continued to arrive: not only toilet water, bundles of magazines, and good advice from Elspeth ('Dont *you* get sittin up too late & doin too much neither my deer cos it weekins the fect of your preechin to me') but also the *Contes drolatiques* from Fletcher Moulton, who still, apparently, thought of Grahame as no more than a close friend.

Clearly this situation was an impossible one; and for once Elspeth's nerve seems to have failed her. At any rate, it was Grahame now who took the initiative. He had been showing some concern at the endless calling, dinner-parties and good works with which her life was filled; and on 22nd June he wrote: 'My darlin, this is orlso to say that I'm ritin to your farver today cos

I think it wos time you was "brort to your bearins" & got a chance of actin for your own future & not rampagin bout for uvver peeple'. Helen had decided to move on to friends at the Lizard, and Grahame was hoping, among other things, to get Elspeth down to Fowey, which probably sharpened his resolve.

The effect on Fletcher Moulton seems to have been, at first, disastrous. He was a strong-willed, egotistic man, and had got used to Elspeth running the Onslow Square house for him. All the evidence suggests that he put up the most violent opposition to her proposed marriage. On 24th June Grahame is thanking Elspeth for a long letter 'ritten midst the shouts & the crash o battle soterspeak'. After the engagement was officially announced Miss Bradley wrote to Elspeth that 'Papa [the Dean of Westminster] is quite distressed that there should have been so much anxiety and trouble connected with it, and wishes he could have helped you . . . he is of course very sorry for Mr. Moulton but will probably not know how to say so'. Though Fletcher Moulton was persuaded to give his consent, it is unlikely that he viewed the affair with any great favour—especially since it had been conducted behind his back. But the essentially practical nature of his objection is suggested by the fact that hardly was Elspeth off his hands before he himself married again.[20]

Nor was Elspeth's attitude, once her stepfather knew how things lay, calculated to sooth Grahame's strained nerves. Now the position was clear to all concerned, she seems to have changed her tack and become infuriatingly casual and unpractical. While the row at Onslow Square was still raging, Grahame wrote:

My deer it is so eesy, I know, to misunderstand letters . . . but the drift of your larst simply seemed ter be 'Oh do for goodness sake leave me be, wif my notes & invitashuns & sum day wen the coste's cleer I'll send you a wire & run down & settle up your little affair' wich is orl very well but—if I may insult you by common detales—unless you're bound for a registrars, & even then, some notice & lapse of time is legally required, & in our case a speshle license wd ave ter be obtained, wich probbly carnt be done by wire.

By the 25th Grahame himself was talking about a possible elopement; he had had no reply from Fletcher Moulton, and was in a highly nervous state. But on the 26th Fletcher Moulton wrote a stiff and grudging letter of capitulation, and the tension eased a little. The marriage was fixed for 22nd July in Fowey.

There can be little doubt that what helped Grahame through this crisis more than any other single factor was his incipient friendship with Quiller-Couch. Q had settled permanently in Fowey eight years previously, at a pleasant house called The Haven, looking out over the harbour; and he soon developed an interest in the convalescent writer whose tastes for literature and sailing were so identical with his own. He took Grahame out on yachting-parties, introduced him to Fowey society, and lent him a little skiff, the *Richard and Emily*, to go exploring in on his own up the creeks and backwaters. Q went out of his way to charm Helen Grahame with expeditions and river-picnics: as a result Grahame wrote, 'sister as bin distinckly more amiable & reely I fink it is ony er sort o' "awkwardness"'. She went off to the Lizard on the 27th, but firmly announced, to Grahame's dismay, that she was coming back.

Meanwhile arrangements for the wedding got, rather creakily, under way:

> I see you wos thinkin orl the time bout close [clothes] wile poor me was ony angshus to fulfil the requirements of the lor! Fowey'd be orl rite, for a wemmick-marriage [Wemmick was the lawyer's clerk in *Great Expectations* who suddenly got married one morning [21] on the spur of the moment: see ch. 55] —but I wish you'd tell me *ow much* of a wemmick-marriage its got ter be. [June 29th]

The following day Grahame and Q ran down a 'tame curate' in the billiard-room and got him to put up the banns; and Grahame contemplated wearing 'a blue serge soot & a soft at, & ee [Courtauld Thomson, Elspeth's brother] mite liketer do same'—an improbable hope. From internal hints it looks as though Elspeth's friends and relations took much the same line about the whole thing as Fletcher Moulton.

Helen returned to Fowey sooner than Grahame expected; and the first knowledge she had of the official engagement was the announcement in the *Morning Post* on Saturday 1st July. 'She's just sed she'd seen it, & that was abslootly orl. There must be sumfin at the bottom of er sullen sort o silence wot I ain't got at yet.' There was: she detested Elspeth, of whom she had seen quite enough while looking after Kenneth in Kensington Crescent. There is a by no means improbable tradition that she asked Grahame, after reading the news in the *Morning Post*, whether he was *really* going to marry Elspeth; whereat he replied, in an infinitely despondent voice: 'I suppose so; I suppose so'.[22] At this Helen 'sed she was goin ome on Toosday wereat I bowed my edd in silence, saying nuffin'. But there was always Q to cheer Kenneth up with 'messing about in boats'; as Kenneth himself admitted to his fiancée, she was a martyr to tides ('but mustnt complane its the moon wot dus it'), and letters had to wait.

As July drew on more and more practical details pressed in on Grahame. There was accommodation to be arranged (he left his room in the hotel and stayed with Quiller-Couch), the honeymoon site to be chosen, invitations to be agreed on. Elspeth shocked conventional opinion by refusing to wear an engagement ring; so Grahame sent one to Miss Bradley instead. 'I respect unconventionality of any kind too much to even protest', he wrote. 'But I do feel strongly that there ought to be a ring in the business *somewhere*—to appease the gods.' (Elspeth's attitude to jewellery of any kind was a little odd: Grahame described it, accurately, as 'nonconformist', and the nearest they came to an open row was when he sent her a pendant.) The machinery of society had taken over, and the private fantasy was being dragged to its public, conventional, irrevocable conclusion.

Something of this conflict is reflected in an odd note Grahame sent Elspeth on 7th July, in the course of which he wrote:

> Mrs. Q ses larst nite wy dont we jus go way ter Newquay 'from the Satty till the Mundy' wich I fort a most immoril sjeschin—Wensdy to Friday wd a bin orlrite not bein a 'week-end'. Darlin, ow'd you like ter go on livin at Ons: Sq: & cum away wif me fer week-ends? Then [several words illegible] and you needn't rite no notes & it wood be so nice & immoril & yet nobody coodnt find no forlt not even arnts.

Nice and immoral—yet safe from aunts: nothing could so vividly have summed up Grahame's simultaneous desire, fear, and emotional childishness. The tempo of his letters, stimulated by improving health and mental anticipation, quickens considerably towards the end. He is worked up into an unmistakable state of passion which he can hardly understand, let alone keep in proportion. His last letter of all, posted on Thursday 13th July, ends: 'Goodbye sweetie & dont sorst yourself cos its a long journey down & I want ter do the sorstin of you wen you gets ere—so you've goter save up fer your luver my pretty oos awatin of you ere & is your lovin own Dino'. This enforced separation, filled by constant letters, was perhaps the worst thing that could have happened to both of them. It projected the actuality of their relationship—and emotional capacities—on an inflated, imaginary scale. It excited Grahame to a tension he could not sustain, and led Elspeth to believe all the more firmly that he was the passionate lover of her dreams. They were both to be cruelly disappointed.

All the time congratulatory notes poured in to off-set what Grahame described as the 'shock-and-blow' letters. There was old Sir John Tenniel ('I am bold to offer you the very respect-fully *affectionate* congratulations of a venerable *fossil*'); Sir Frank Dicksee, who had painted Elspeth; the Lidderdales; and many others. To Elspeth, Beatrice Roberts wrote: 'If Mr. Grahame is as nice as his books, you are very much to be congratulated', a compliment which sets the general tone, and nicely balances Sir

Martin Conway's remarks to Kenneth: 'You are going to marry a very charming and very clever lady, and you will never be bored again as long as you live'. In his reply Kenneth declared (presumably with Onslow Square week-ends still at the back of his mind): 'My beastly virtue has been my enemy through life, but once married I will try & be frankly depraved, and then all will go well'.

The wedding finally took place on Saturday 22nd July 1899, at St. Fimbarrus's Church, Fowey. Fletcher Moulton, together with Elspeth herself and Courtauld, Harold and Winnie Thomson had arrived before the week-end. Elspeth had thrown Grahame into a last-minute panic by turning up (as we might expect) in very un-Wemmicky finery, complete with poodle and lady's maid. Anthony Hope Hawkins, the novelist, who was also Grahame's cousin ('When I mention it to his admirers it is always received with a sort of incredulity') had agreed to be best man, and took his duties in a spirited way: he hired a hurdy-gurdy man to grind his organ outside The Haven at crack of dawn, and make sure the household woke up in time. At the Fowey Hotel Elspeth (in one of her more exhibitionistic back-to-nature moods) went out before breakfast to admire the view from the Castle, and broke into the dining-room when the meal was nearly over, still in her old muslin, and with a daisy-chain strung round her neck. Wemmick won after all: Elspeth decided to get married as she was, and the expensive wedding-dress remained unpacked.[23]

Elspeth Thomson, that *habituée* of dinner-table and salon, was no more; Mrs. Kenneth Grahame had made her first characteristic gesture, before the ring was even on her finger.

X

THE WILD WOOD AND THE
WIDE WORLD

1900-1907

'Beyond the Wild Wood comes the Wide World,' said the Rat.
'And that's something that doesn't matter, either to you or me.
I've never been there, and I'm never going, nor you either, if
you've got any sense at all. Don't ever refer to it again, please.'

The Wind in the Willows, Ch. I

Because of some inadequacy in themselves—poverty or physical
weakness in men, poverty or ugliness in women—those with the
gift of creation built for themselves a rich interior world; and
when the inadequacy disappeared and the real world was spread
before them with all its wealth and beauty, they could not give
their whole heart to it. Uncertain of their choice, they wavered
between goals; were lonely in crowds, dissatisfied amid noise and
laughter, unhappy even with those they loved best. The interior
world called them back, and for some it was a case of having to
return there or die.

FRANK O'CONNOR: *Domestic Relations*

Elspeth did not have her husband to herself for long. Three days
of the honeymoon were spent at St. Ives; but when the coast was
clear of relatives the Grahames soon returned to Fowey, and the
congenial company of the Quiller-Couches. Once again Elspeth
became a martyr to tides, but this time in a more physical sense.
Nothing—not even marriage—could keep Grahame for long

from his beloved boats, or the uninvolved male companionship, free of emotional stress, which he came more and more to rely upon. Q was a great yachtsman, and the rest of July was spent afloat, in yawl or dinghy. It was not, we may surmise, Elspeth's kind of world; Fowey and Onslow Square had little in common, and the London hostess probably felt somewhat out of things in this bracing atmosphere.

From the start she and Q failed to hit it off: each saw the other as a dangerous influence, and Q, one suspects, made short work of her literary pretentiousness. Nor did she feel any natural sympathy with Grahame's other great Fowey friend, Edward Atkinson. 'Atky', as he was universally known, represented the extreme of all those characteristics which Elspeth learnt to distrust in her husband. He was a sixty-two-year-old bachelor of private means,[1] who owned thirty boats and—though an indifferent sailor—was Commodore of the Fowey Yacht Club. He was also an obsessional collector of *objets d'art*, and his beautiful riverside house up the Fowey estuary was filled to overflowing with knick-knacks of every description: the surplus went into forming a Fowey art gallery. He had drawerfuls of mechanical toys (which delighted Grahame) and a rope-ladder in lieu of a staircase. His neat grey beard and aquiline features were a familiar sight in the Fowey streets—generally crowned by an exquisite and idiosyncratic hat ordered specially from Paris. He lived alone with his devoted housekeeper, Miss Marsden, but occasionally took undergraduate friends on canoeing trips in the South of France.[2] Grahame found him highly congenial; Elspeth saw him as a subtle menace to her marriage. It probably never occurred to her, then or later, that Atky's influence would play a large part in the crystallization of *The Wind in the Willows*.

Grahame had been away from the Bank for nearly four months now, and it was essential that he should get settled back into his duties before September. The honeymoon was cut short (by Grahame's standards of leisure, at any rate) and the Grahames returned to London. Sarah Bath, Grahame's old housekeeper at Kensington Crescent, had declined to continue in office after his marriage—she had probably formed her own opinion of Elspeth during the carnations-and-grapes period—and Kenneth shows some embarrassment in his letter to Elspeth on the subject:

> Bout *Sarah*, I aint conshuns-stricken, & ony rote er a sivvil note sayin if she cared ter stay wif me I shd be very glad, *cos* you arst me to, afore I left, sayin it wd save so much trubble. But in many respex she aint kwite the person for us, and she *as* got 'erself' on the brane—those peeple of the *pessant* clars orfin ave. Aint erd from er gain.[3]

One of Sarah's predominant characteristics, we know, was a certain blunt outspokenness;[4] it is likely that she gave Master Kenneth her unvarnished opinion of his prospective wife. Poor Grahame: in this episode perhaps most of all we sense the embarrassed falseness of his relationship with Elspeth—the artificial baby-talk; the nervous self-justification; the incompatibility of her world and his, however ignored or disguised; the pathetic effort at compromise.

Worst of all, after months of exacerbated anticipation, their physical relationship proved a bitter disappointment—to Elspeth at any rate. She was hardly married before she sent a desperate *cri de cœur* to Mrs. Thomas Hardy at Max Gate, which elicited, *inter alia*, the following remarks:[5]

> It is really too early days with you to be benefited by advice from one who has just come to the twenty-fifth year of matrimony. . . . I can scarcely think that love proper, and enduring, is in the nature of men—as a rule—perhaps there is no woman 'whom custom will not stale'. There is ever a desire to give but little in return for our devotion, and affection—theirs being akin to children's, a sort of easy affectionateness. . . . Keeping separate a good deal is a wise plan in crises—and being both free—and expecting little, neither gratitude, nor attentions, love, nor *justice*, nor anything you may set your heart on—Love interest,—adoration, and all that kind of thing is usually a

failure—complete—someone comes by and upsets your pail of milk in the end—If he belongs to the public in any way, years of devotion count for nothing—Influence can seldom be retained as years go by, and *hundreds* of wives go through a phase of disillusion—it is really a pity to have any ideals in the first place.

After which Mrs. Hardy (remembering the politenesses due to a bride, however distraught) congratulates Elspeth in due form, and invites them both to look in if they are ever in the neighbourhood of Dorchester.

Elspeth's reactions were only what we might expect in the circumstances. Both she and Grahame were living in a dreamworld, but it was not the same dream-world. As in the case of the Golden City, imagination was vastly more romantic than physical reality. Besides, neither of them was young; both were totally inexperienced; and Grahame was still convalescing from a very serious operation. If they had possessed the wisdom of maturity they would have been patient; but all they could understand was that life had failed to measure up to their private fantasies.

Mrs. Hardy's letter, taken in combination both with what we know of Grahame's temperament, and some very odd poems written by Elspeth after her marriage, suggests an additional difficulty. Elspeth was clearly by nature a passionate woman: it is she who makes all the real running in the engagement correspondence, and talks of nocturnal delights. She had been discreetly chaste for thirty-seven years; and Grahame's initial burst of ardour must have roused all her dormant instincts. But it seems all too clear that this ardour—as far as Grahame was concerned—had been artificially stimulated, and vanished almost at once, leaving Elspeth bitter and frustrated. 'My first touch of the earth', declared Keats' Endymion, 'came nigh to kill': and so it was, in all probability, with Grahame. Shattered and repelled by this adult relationship, he retreated even further than before into his safe, private world—a world, this time, not of children but of animals. *The Wind in the Willows*, you will remember, was, in Grahame's thrice-emphasized words, clean of the clash of sex.

It is at this point that Elspeth most clearly earns our sympathy. Pretentious, shallow, and domineering she may have been; but she was also desperately unhappy. She had pursued a dream, and it had shattered in her hands. Soured by disappointment, she let herself go; and as though in some horrible fairy-tale, each of her virtues gradually turned into the corresponding weakness. Her cleverness became glib arrogance, her conversational powers degenerated into opinionated loquaciousness, her gift for household management into close-fisted thrift. From a smart hostess she turned, within a very few years, into something very little short of a slattern; and her unconventional tricks ripened equally fast into plain eccentricity. Both she and Grahame are equally to be pitied; perhaps hers was the harder lot of the two. He had preserved his dream-world inviolate: hers was irreparably destroyed, for love was its cornerstone—sentimental, romantic, ideal love —and love she had found wanting.

The same theme, of dejection and disillusion, runs through poem after poem in her private collection:[6]

> Ah love, I dare ask but the slenderest boon
> For I know thou art cold as the half risen moon
> Yet thou surely wilt grant me so trivial a part
> Of the bliss I once dreamt might illumine my heart
> [From a poem entitled *Rejected*]

> But now, alas! that I have grasped him [Love]
> I would I ne'er had caught and clasped him,
> The cruel rogue has sent a dart
> Right through my fondly trusting heart;
> Love *is* not fair, Love *is* not kind,
> To let him loose I have a mind.

Misery very frequently gives way to gusts of irritation and anger: it is plain that Grahame withdrew further and further into himself, living his own life with evident satisfaction, and giving Elspeth little emotional warmth in the way that she so desperately needed:

> Ah happy eyes that smile and sleep
> But never watch and never weep
> Ah lovely eyes that glance and gleam
> But never muse and never dream.
>
> Ah cruel eyes whose radiant light
> Has cast a shadow as of night
> Over my heart, yet all the while
> Have no remorse but sleep and smile.

And Grahame's deliberate self-removal, in every sense, provoked this vigorous rebuke:

> When I go out, you stay at home,
> No sooner am I in,
> Than you desire at once to roam,
> I vow it is a sin!
>
> Oh! It really is unbearable
> And would provoke a saint!
> By all oaths that are swearable,
> There's reason for complaint!

Human kind, as Mr. Eliot reminds us, cannot stand very much reality.

Nevertheless, Elspeth had one consolation. As if subconsciously sensing that her first opportunity would also be her last, she became pregnant immediately after her marriage.

Grahame had taken a long lease of a house in Campden Hill— 16 Durham Villas—which was to be their home for the next six years. He was at once plunged back into City life, to the exclusion of more literary pursuits[7]—though his uncreativity during those early years of marriage must be attributed in part at least to more personal causes. He had suffered a severe shock, and it would be some time before his mechanism readjusted itself. Nor were his duties as Secretary especially arduous: and Kenneth, as he himself confesses, was indolent by nature.

'An accomplished, but, it would appear, not an assertive Secretary': that is Sir John Clapham's opinion,[8] and one that commands general agreement. Mr. H. A. Siepmann, a distinguished banker himself, is somewhat more severe: 'The tradition is that he was a very dilatory and lackadaisical Secretary. Perhaps that is the reason why so little has been said about his activities in the City. I rather think that, in quite a few ways, he fell short of the Bank's standards—such as they were.'[9] After Grahame's death his brother-in-law Courtauld Thomson (that astute businessman) wrote to the then Governor of the Bank, with wry irony: 'Though possibly these books were not all written during banking hours, his duties as Secretary may have suggested the titles *Golden Age* and *Dream Days*'. No; it seems fairly certain that Grahame's abrupt creative stoppage (which lasted for nearly seven years) was not due to professional overwork so much as emotional and psychological difficulties.

Furthermore, there is evidence of a rather exotic sort that Grahame continued after his marriage as a reader and adviser for John Lane. During the latter half of 1900 he was conducting a curious correspondence with Frederick Rolfe—Baron Corvo himself—and from Corvo's letters it is clear that Grahame exerted considerable influence in the publishing world of his day. The first is dated 16th August:

> Dear Sir: I believe you read the MS of Toto Maidalchini's Folk Lore which I am publishing with Lane and calling A Sensational Atomist; and have earned my gratitude by generous praise.
>
> Will you allow me to ask whether you have influence to use to get for me permanent and regular literary work, so that I may be delivered from desperate and restless circumstances, and also freed to realize some literary plans which I have made. To prevent misconception, may I sternly state that what I have

said here is a 'necessary proposition', unsuggested by another, *entirely confidential*, and a liberty for which I apologise.
    Yours faithfully, Frederick Baron Corvo.

Grahame must have replied encouragingly; almost by return of post Corvo sent him a vast list of projected works, somewhat akin to the experiments performed by the Laputan scientists in *Gulliver's Travels*. (The most arresting is a history of the Houses of Poplicola di Santacroce, who, Corvo asserts, 'descend from Publius Valerius Publicola, who descends from Perseus, the original St. George and the Pterodactyl'—a touch that must have appealed to Grahame.) Finally Grahame obtained Corvo an introduction to Smith, Elder & Co., and the correspondence lapsed. There is no evidence that the two men ever met. In his novel *Nicholas Crabbe* (till recently suppressed for fear of libel actions) Corvo revealed that Grahame, whom he referred to as 'Kenneth O' Lympos', had also reported favourably on *In His Own Image*. It says something for Grahame's character that, alone among *The Yellow Book* circle, he escaped Corvo's castigation in this bitter, paranoiac, and malevolent satire, which reads in places like a parody of Wyndham Lewis's *The Apes of God*.[10]

At the beginning of her married life—till the birth of her child at least—Elspeth attempted to reproduce in Durham Villas the atmosphere of Onslow Square. There were dinner-parties and soirées; but Kenneth (like Badger) was awkward in her sort of 'society'. Miss Bradley, a frequent guest, later wrote that 'the easy informal hospitality at the Grahames' house on Campden Hill will be remembered with peculiar pleasure by many of their intimate circle', but she added:

Kenneth's mind was not ruled by the ordinary conventions. He made little attempt at small-talk but his silences were curiously companionable; & presently the thought would flow. . . . He was a good—sympathetic—conversationalist because he was as genuinely interested in the person he was talking to & in the latter's views as in his own—he was entirely without pretensions or affectations of any description. Never a great talker in a mixed company, he would sometimes give utterance to his least conventional sentiments with genial but unhesitating conviction.[11]

Kenneth was far more at ease in the company of Graham Robertson, the artist and playwright, who (besides writing *Pinkie and the Fairies*) designed the original frontispiece for *The Wind in the Willows*. Robertson at this period lived just round the corner in Argyll Road, and the two became close friends.[12] Robertson was an Old Etonian bachelor, who believed in fairies and owned a houseful of dogs: whether he was also a close friend of Elspeth's we do not know. Certainly some of the details he has recorded about Grahame are more revealing and vivid than almost any other single source. In particular, he analyses the exact impression given by Grahame's withdrawn 'otherness':

> Oddly enough (for he was a most attractive man) Kenneth had few friends. He simply didn't want them. He would say rather wonderingly to his wife: 'You *like* people. They interest you. But I am interested in *places*!'[13]

And in his memoir of Grahame he wrote:[14]

> He had a marvellous gift of silence. . . . He would slowly become part of the landscape and a word from him would come as unexpectedly as a sudden remark from an oak or a beech.

One can understand Elspeth's irritation even when one sympathizes with it least.

Another fact on which Robertson sheds some light is Grahame's increasing passion for toys:[15]

> His special room in No. 16 was most characteristic; it looked like a nursery. Books there were certainly, but they were outnumbered by toys. Toys were everywhere—intriguing, fascinating toys which could hardly have been conducive to study.

Clearly the buried dolls were having a resurrection; it looks as though the result of marriage was to accelerate Grahame's childish

Kenneth Grahame, 1912
From the drawing by John S. Sargent

reversion. Yet already the subject had cropped up regularly in his letters to Elspeth from Fowey. While she wove coy little fantasies about a private Love-Post, he rummaged in playboxes. 'By the way,' he enquires disconcertingly, 'oos lookin arter my drorful o dolls at ome & givin em seed & water & grounsle?' [16] Later he recounts how Q took him up-river to 'Rosebank', Atky's house, where 'we found a drore full of toys wot wound up, and we ad a great race tween a fish, a snaik, a beetle wot flapped is wings, & a rabbit'. [17] The split between Grahame's public and private selves, apparently healed at the time of 'The Reluctant Dragon', now began to widen once more under the stress of an intolerable personal relationship.

The birth of a son to the Grahames clearly eased their domestic tension. But—as so often in such a case—the child did not solve its parents' problems: it merely enabled them to ignore what could not be undone. Each projected on to it the image of their disappointed dreams; and the result, inevitably, was tragic.

Alastair Grahame was born, prematurely, on 12th May 1900; and to his parents' intense distress, proved to have congenital cataract of the right eye, which was completely blind, together with a pronounced squint in the left—which was also 'over-sighted'. [18] He was to be their only child: the reasons for this we can only surmise. Kenneth's retreat from passion would not account for it entirely: we must remember that at the time of Alastair's birth Elspeth was thirty-eight, and that during the next few years she was to be constantly ill, or hypochondriacal, or both. It is possible that the Grahames refrained from increasing their family on medical advice, or even for fear of producing a second child with worse physical defects than the first: there are some indications that Alastair's semi-blindness may have been hereditary.

Whatever the reason, the inevitable result was that Alastair (or 'Mouse', as everyone called him) became the recipient of both his parents' thwarted emotions. To say that he was chronically spoilt (which of course he was) is to over-simplify the problem. Kenneth wrote *The Wind in the Willows* for him; Elspeth fed him with fantasy of another sort. He was a sickly, physically handicapped, sensitive but not over-bright child: and throughout his life he had to struggle with the image of himself which his mother created and steadfastly believed. Elspeth managed to convince herself—and did her best to convince everyone else—that Alastair was, in every respect, whether physical or mental, not only normal but brilliant. The boy's whole life became a struggle to live up to the impossible ideal she set him: and in the end the strain proved too great. But all this lay in the future. For the time being it was enough that Mouse's nursery had become the focus of life in 16 Durham Villas.

In other respects Kenneth, at least, was marking time during this period. He only came into the public eye once: but this was in a peculiarly bizarre way. On 24th November 1903,[19] at about eleven in the morning, a respectably dressed stranger presented himself at one of the offices in the Secretary's department, and asked to see 'the Governor, Sir Augustus Prevost'. Now Prevost was no longer Governor; but the messenger, finding nothing amiss, asked the stranger (who had given his name as George F. Robinson) if he would care to speak with the Secretary, as Sir Augustus was out of town. Mr. Robinson agreed, and was taken to a waiting-room, where Grahame presently arrived to interview him.

The visitor at once repeated his original question: were Sir Augustus Prevost, or Mr. Morley (the then Governor) at the Bank? No, Grahame said, somewhat puzzled, they were not. 'I suppose you're in charge, then', said Robinson, and thrust a large roll of manuscript towards him, tied with ribbon at each end. As Grahame hesitated, Robinson peremptorily ordered him to read it. Grahame, by now thoroughly annoyed, declined the privilege, and asked Robinson to state his business briefly. The answer was unexpected and startling. Remarking 'well, if you won't, then—' and something else which Grahame failed to hear, Robinson suddenly produced a large Service revolver. The Secretary retreated rapidly outside the door, just in time to stop one of the Directors who was about to come in. At the same time Robinson fired his first shot, and followed it up with two more.

Grahame quickly took charge of the situation. The police were fetched, and the Governor and the Directors warned of the danger. Robinson came out of the waiting-room and fired another shot at a messenger in the corridor; then, tiring of this sport, wandered into the Directors' Library, where the Head Door-keeper, with great presence of mind, turned the key on him. As he threatened to shoot anyone who came near, he was left alone until a powerful fire-hose could be brought to bear on him. This knocked him off his feet, and after a tremendous struggle he was carted away by the police, tied up in an ambulance.

At Cloak Lane police station he was charged with 'Wandering in Threadneedle Street: deemed to be a lunatic', and harangued the police in a way that is only chastely hinted at by the brief report in *The Times*: 'From statements made by him at the station he appears to hold Socialistic views'. The following day, at the Mansion House, Sir Alfred Newton, judging him unfit to plead, adjourned the case *sine die*, and he was committed to Broadmoor—but not before he had delivered himself of a remarkable pronouncement:

> The prisoner pleaded that his rolled documents had been tied at one end with a black ribbon, at the other with a white. These documents had been presented to Mr. Grahame length-wise. It had therefore been open to Mr. Grahame to grasp either one of the two ends. Instead of the innocuous white end Mr. Grahame had preferred to take the end bound by the black ribbon, thus proving that Fate demanded his immediate demise. Mr. Robinson looked upon himself as a mere instrument in the matter and quite without prejudice or guile.[20]

Letters of sympathy and congratulation poured in: not only from friends and relatives, but complete strangers as far afield as

Nova Scotia, panic-stricken at the thought of any danger befalling the author of *The Golden Age*. From Onslow Square Fletcher Moulton wrote to Elspeth:

We both send you our deepest sympathy in the shock and anxiety which you have had today. Nothing but the promptness and presence of mind of your husband could have avoided a terrible calamity and you must be very proud of his having shewn himself so cool and courageous. But don't let yourself brood over it—such an outrage cannot occur again. It was an accident that he was the one in danger & it is not possible that such carelessness will be allowed in future on the part of the Bank servants.

This touched on the really important significance of the affair. 'Mr. Kenneth Grahame', observed an anonymous wag in *Punch* the following week, 'is wondering what is the meaning of the expression, "As safe as the Bank of England".' And Edward Clodd, the Secretary of the London Joint Stock Bank (but better known as an amateur anthropologist and friend of Andrew Lang), wrote to him along the same lines: 'If one, outside Arcady, could have named an ideal spot, immune from risks, even were the whole world running amok, it would have been such a sanctum as yours!'

Clodd spoke more shrewdly than perhaps he realized. Over the years—and especially since his appointment as Secretary—Grahame's attitude to the Bank had been slowly changing. From a prison it had changed insensibly into something of an ivory tower. It represented tradition, continuity, solid values, a firm structure of society. Outside, cads and Radicals might snarl: it made no difference. But now, in an hour, the whole fabric had been torn from top to bottom. A lunatic—and not only a lunatic, but a *Socialist* lunatic, the equivalent of those dreadful bomb-throwing anarchists—had wandered into the sacred precincts and assaulted the person of the Old Lady. The whole episode, for all his fortitude at the time, must have shocked Grahame in a deep and indefinable way. He was not to forget it.

Equally odd, though on a different level, was the lawsuit brought by Elspeth and Winnie against their own stepfather, Fletcher Moulton.[21] When Clara Thomson died in 1888, she left her income in trust to Fletcher Moulton, to be divided in equal shares among her four children by her marriage to Robert Thomson. Each share came to something over £600 a year. In 1902 Courtauld, the youngest child but the shrewdest business head among the four, discovered that no written arrangement existed as to how the trusteeship was to be administered; and that in fact Fletcher Moulton was sole trustee. He asked his stepfather for an account of the monies paid or due to his sisters; Fletcher Moulton refused; and Courtauld—in Elspeth's and Winnie's names—brought a civil action against him, which was heard in April 1905.

Fletcher Moulton's case was that no question of accounts arose, since the permanent arrangement with his stepdaughters had been that their income should go towards their household expenses—'including clothes, journeys, cures, pocket money etc. etc.' Elspeth and Winnie denied any such arrangements; and a professional accountant, after making all possible allowance for necessary expenditure, calculated that Fletcher Moulton owed them something in the neighbourhood of £10,000. In the witness-box Elspeth gave fascinating side-glimpses on life in Onslow Square—the bazaar-opening, constituency-nursing, perhaps best of all 'the method employed by both ladies to supply themselves with petty cash. They did this by having accounts with the butler, the cook, and one of the maids, who advanced them money "when in funds". Elspeth sometimes drew as much as £3 : 10s. a week through these unofficial sources'.

The judge summed up, on balance, in favour of Fletcher Moulton, and laid down that he was 'to have credit for all monies provided by him that were received or expended by the children for their own benefit'. Elspeth and Winnie appealed against this maintenance order; and while the appeal was pending Fletcher

Moulton was appointed a Judge of the Court of Appeal, which cannot have made matters easier for anyone. The appeal was finally allowed; and Fletcher Moulton, after dallying with the notion of taking the case to the House of Lords, in the end settled out of court for £8,250, and resigned his trusteeship. He may have sailed near the wind; he was certainly autocratic in his domestic affairs, as well as being a reckless speculator; but there is no suggestion that he actually tried to defraud his stepchildren.

What Kenneth thought of all these family revelations—in particular that his wife had been considered too unbusinesslike by Courtauld and Winnie to handle the household accounts—we can but surmise. He put in one brief appearance only during the hearing: and that was to deny, emphatically, any responsibility for any part of the claim against Fletcher Moulton. He probably found the whole affair intensely distasteful and embarrassing—especially as it was none of his doing in the first place.

Otherwise his existence remained unruffled. Peter Pan had arrived in Kensington Gardens; Anthony Hope was married at St. Bride's; Henley died—another link with the old days gone—and Grahame was a mourner at his funeral. The Wright Brothers made their famous flight, and the speed limit for motor-cars—poop! poop!—was raised to 20 m.p.h.

Elspeth's health had been deteriorating in a way that hints at nervous origins—she spent nearly all day on a sofa, sipping hot water—and in May 1904 she left London, alone, for a long cure at Woodhall Spa in Lincolnshire. In a letter to Mrs. Ward, a day or two before Elspeth's departure, Grahame wrote: 'He [Mouse] had a bad crying fit on the night of his birthday, and I had to tell him stories about moles, giraffes & water-rats (he selected these as subjects) till after 12'.[22] In the same month the Grahames' maid, a Wiltshire girl named Louise, being asked by Elspeth why the master was late (they were going out to dinner, and Kenneth was supposed to be changing) replied: 'He's with Master Mouse, Madam, he's telling him some ditty [story] or other about a

Toad'.[23] So, three years before Grahame set pen to paper again, the first germ of *The Wind in the Willows* was being evolved in bed-time stories for a small child. The major characters were all assembled (perhaps it is just as well that the giraffe dropped out along the road); now they only needed a background and shaping motif. Grahame's spring of creative imagination, all the more powerful for its long confinement underground, was once more slowly forcing its way towards the surface: and this time it brought with it an unprecedentedly well-stocked sub-conscious mind.

Meanwhile occasional reminders of Grahame's past literary activities continued to reach him. In October 1904 a young lady in San Francisco, having been tickled by the essay 'Marginalia' in *Pagan Papers*, decided on a highly original *réplique*. 'When', Grahame had asked rhetorically, 'shall that true poet arise who, disdaining the trivialities of text, shall give the world a book of verse consisting entirely of margin?' Miss Josephine Hoveed obligingly supplied it. *Margin*, which she sent to Grahame with her letter of appreciation, was, like the Bellman's Chart, a perfect and absolute blank.

Two months later (for reasons which will be apparent in a moment) Grahame replied as follows:[24]

Dear Madam: Please accept my sincere thanks for the beautiful copy wh. has reached me of your new work 'Margin' —a copy which I understand exhausts the Edition & baffles the clamorous Public. Nothing cd be more charming, or more acceptable, than the binding, lettering, and general bodily format of

But the format must give place to the pleasure the contents have given me. For your verse has a limpid spaciousness, a clarity, & a breadth, wh. soothes while it satisfies, and throughout there is a haunting suggestion of broad heaths, moonlight, wind-swept spaces & the Open Road. To these positive virtues one must add the negative qualities—an absence of all that frets or jars—the superior English of the Printer's Reader—the

Celtic Twilight or the Split Infinitive. Such verse as yours must it seems to me go far—it must arrive. Indeed it has done both. Hence this line.

It is an amusing letter; and it has an added interest from the incidental light it sheds on Grahame's preoccupations at the time —including the (capitalized) Open Road.

In September Kenneth decided to go abroad alone, to Spain. Mouse, who had been playing up his German governess (he used to lie dreamily in the middle of the road when motor-cars were approaching), was sent off to Broadstairs to stay with Nancy and Enid Mitchell, distant cousins of Elspeth's on her mother's side. At the time, despite his eye-trouble, he seemed in good general health. Elspeth was still taking her cure; there is no evidence that Kenneth suggested her accompanying him to Spain, and much which inclines one to believe he was glad of the chance to get away. It may well have been on this occasion that Elspeth wrote:

> I wonder when you said good-bye
> So lightly—almost with a smile—
> If you remembered, Love, how I
> Should miss you all the weary while.
>
> .   .   .   .   .   .
>
> For days to you like hours seem
> The hours as moments only
> And so you neither think nor dream
> Of me so sad and lonely.
>
> I wonder when we meet again
> If you'll come gaily with a smile
> As if forgetful of the pain
> I've suffered all the weary while?

On this occasion he certainly did not. He had only got as far as the Pyrenees ('Do you remember an Inn, Miranda? Do you remember an Inn?') when a telegram reached him—rather miraculously for the Spain of 1904—summoning him home at once. Mouse had gone down with a sudden attack of peritonitis; and Elspeth, galvanized out of her sickly lassitude, had at once left Woodhall and joined him in Broadstairs. Here she stayed during the operation and subsequent crisis; and here Kenneth found her.

It is a bad set-back for her [he wrote to a friend in December]. She had to cut short her cure just when she was getting most benefit from it, and the anxiety and strain have been very great. [Elspeth was unwell enough to be forbidden letter-writing at this date.] . . . I stayed at Broadstairs till the worst danger was over, and then came back to work. The poor little fellow has suffered a great deal of acute pain, but his pluck and cheerfulness have been wonderful. It is a pathetic thing that little children are not *resentful* about undeserved pain thrust upon them, but rather apologetic than otherwise! [25]

By the end of the year Alastair was on the mend, though still not well enough to be moved from Broadstairs. Miss Bradley, with a rather misplaced sense of occasion, sent the child a copy of her father's Addresses; and Kenneth tactfully replied, 'It shall be put by for him beside his Horace; & later on it shall be read to him, but before the Horace I hope'. On 3rd January 1905 he was able to write to Q as follows: [26]

Very many thanks for the beautiful Christmas book you have sent to poor Mouse. He is devoted to picture-books, and they are most useful now that he is mentally active again & has such long hours to get through each day. I am glad to say that since the wound healed entirely, he has forgotten his pains and terrors, and 'rots' everybody all round as before. The other day when the doctor arrived he cocked his eye at his nurses whom he knew to be modest and shamefaced women beyond the ordinary, & began cheerily: 'Hullo doctor! Are your bowels open to-day?' One of the women stupidly begged him not to refer to such things—'it wasn't *nice*'. This gave him the opening he wished for. 'Not *nice*?' he said furiously, 'then what does he say it to me for? I didn't begin it, he said it first!'

And thenceforth he chanted the enquiry in plainsong, till the doctor was hustled out of the room.

    E. is still down there, & I don't know when she will return. All regards & good wishes to all four of you.

Elspeth was certainly back in London by April, for that was the period when the Fletcher Moulton case was heard; and Alastair appears to have been completely recovered by his fifth birthday, in May, which 'included a visit to the Zoo—a Maypole—and a gipsy caravan with brushes and baskets which he has been selling ever since, at somewhat inflated prices'.[27]

In August the whole family went to Scotland for a summer holiday, and stayed at what Elspeth described as 'a famous old Scottish castle', though she does not name it: it *may* have been Inveraray. Kenneth does not appear to have enjoyed himself; it was a stupid idea, he told Q, and Scotland 'had gone down-hill considerably since I was there last—anyhow I didn't care about it'. But this distaste for his surroundings did not stop the nightly development of his bed-time stories for Alastair. A guest who arrived late for tea one day and wanted to meet Kenneth, was directed upstairs to the night-nursery, where she eavesdropped, fascinated, outside the door. Kenneth was telling his story, and Alastair interrupting from time to time—'sometimes asking for an explanation, sometimes arguing a point, at others laughing'. When asked what the story had been *about*, the guest replied: 'I know there was a Badger in it, a Mole, a Toad, and a Water-rat, and the places they lived in and were surrounded by'.[28] Badger had now arrived; the pattern was developing.

In the autumn of 1905 it was decided that Alastair's nurse should be replaced by a governess. Already he was showing those unmistakable symptoms peculiar to a spoilt only child of educated parents: pertness, precociousness, a trick of mimicking his elders' aphorisms without understanding them. Elspeth kept him largely segregated from other children, and dressed him in girlish or *outré* clothes: she played Elizabeth Barrett Browning to his Pen.

She was, moreover, only too ready to encourage his premature signs of 'brilliance' or sophistication: nothing is more pathetic than the way in which she preserves his childish sayings. For her they obviously enhance his nature; the unprejudiced reader will find them irksome at first, and, finally, tragic. Elspeth was a tremendous snob, among other things: so Alastair's childish desire to have the sweep in for tea (what child is ever conscious of social distinctions?) she magnifies into a 'complete understanding of, and sympathy with, human beings of every class in life, from the highest to the lowest'.[29]

Miss Naomi Stott, the governess, clearly did her best to counterbalance the fantasy and pseudo-sophistication which Elspeth injected daily into her son; in the memoir she wrote of him for Chalmers she emphasizes other, more likeable, qualities—his fearlessness, hatred of suffering, charming manners, sensitivity. But even she tells some unconsciously devastating anecdotes about Alastair:

> I am told that, at the age of three and on a railway journey he was continually urged by his nurse to 'see the pretty lambs' or other objects of the flying landscape. Presently the travellers caught sight of the sea and Nannie made haste to call attention to the 'pretty ships'. Alastair said, 'Oh, Nannie, do leave the boats in the water, they look very well there'.

At four he was complaining primly of 'vulgar eating and arms on the table'. (His precocious vocabulary caused an older girl to say, with more truth than perhaps she knew, 'You are only a baby who has swallowed a dictionary'.[30]) One thinks of Macaulay's famous *réplique* at the same age—'Thank you, Madam, the agony has abated'—but Alastair never showed any degree of Macaulay's stamina: even though Kenneth could write to Q that winter saying Mouse had 'become most bookish'.[31] In that household it would have been surprising if he had not.

The Christmas of 1905 was remarkable for a double visit— from Anstey Guthrie (better known as F. Anstey, the author of

Vice Versa) and old Sir John Tenniel, who still kept up a playful correspondence with Elspeth, and sent her a verse Valentine every year. Guthrie, too, was an old friend—he first met Elspeth in 1889—and she occasionally told him off to 'chaperon' Kenneth at City dinners. On this occasion he chased Alastair up to bed, growling like a wolf; but later, under Elspeth's prodding, and after several revisions, sent her a stiff little memoir for publication in which he said that meeting Alastair 'was rather like being presented to a young prince'.

In May 1906 Kenneth Grahame and his family moved house: after thirty years and more of London life he returned to the country at last. The change may have been partly dictated by medical considerations: neither Elspeth, Alastair, nor Grahame himself were in anything like good health. What is interesting and infinitely revealing is the place they chose. With the whole of the Home Counties to pick from, Grahame went back to the very centre of his childhood: Cookham Dene. As he wrote a year or two later of Mole, 'the wafts from his old home pleaded, whispered, conjured, and finally claimed him imperiously'. The pattern was now nearly complete. Lingering on a summer evening by the same chalk-pit which had obsessed and fascinated him so as a child, which symbolized for him the burial-ground of all his youthful dreams and ambitions, Grahame may well have recalled what he wrote on the subject so long before, in 'A Funeral':

> The sun is low by this time and strikes athwart: a cool wind wanders up the valley; the rabbits are dotting the neighbour field, intent on their evening meal; and—did somebody mention beer? or did I only dream it with the rest? It is time to have done with fancies and get back to the world of facts. If only one could! But that cry of the Portuguese Nun wails ever in the mind's ear: 'I defy you to forget me utterly'.[32]

How—in that place of all places—could he ever forget?

THE ROAD TO XANADU
1907-1908

Part 1: Background, Structure, Symbol

The notion that the creative imagination, especially in its highest exercise, has little or nothing to do with facts is one of the *pseudo-doxia epidemica* which die hard. For the imagination never operates in a vacuum. Its stuff is always a fact of some order, somehow experienced; its product is that fact transmuted.

JOHN LIVINGSTON LOWES: *The Road to Xanadu*

You must please remember that a theme, a thesis, a subject, is in most cases little more than a sort of clothes-line, on which one pegs a string of ideas, quotations, allusions, and so on, one's mental undergarments, of all shapes and sizes, some possibly fairly new, but most rather old and patched; and they dance and sway in the breeze, and flap and flutter, or hang limp and lifeless; and some are ordinary enough, and some are of a rather private and intimate shape, and rather give the owner away, and show up his or her peculiarities. And owing to the invisible clothes-line they seem to have some connexion and continuity.

KENNETH GRAHAME: *Miscellanea*

Just as the characters which populate *The Wind in the Willows* are (as we shall later see) composite portraits drawn partly from life and partly from literature, so the general background and thematic material of the book has similar antecedents. It will perhaps be easier to discuss the background first. In both cases

Grahame adds to the core of reality he employs: the final product differs essentially from its models. His inner purpose throughout was threefold: to satirize contemporary society, to sublimate his personal fears, and to construct an ideal model of the Good Life. His treatment of the River Bank offers a good example of the process at work.

The core of reality, in this case, is that stretch of the Thames which runs, roughly, from Marlow to Pangbourne; and in particular the area round Cookham Dene. This had the most powerful and emotive associations for him. He had known it during his most impressionable period as a child; he had returned to it in middle age, drawn by compulsive and no longer to be neglected memories. Here he had spent—and still spent—long hours in backwater or eyot, watching water-rats, moles, otters, and toads go about their private business. This was the still centre about which the book evolved.

But—as we have come to recognize—Grahame never drew straight from life, but borrowed piecemeal. His various models were absorbed like those snips of coloured paper which combine to form a pattern under the kaleidoscope. For this reason it is a task as pointless as it is fascinating to press any topographical identifications too closely. Toad Hall, for example, contains elements from Harleyford Manor, Mapledurham House, and Cliveden—each supplied part of its *mise en scène*. Elements from a dozen river-islands, weirs, and backwaters have been blended in 'The Piper at the Gates'; elsewhere Cookham merges into Cornwall, and the Thames (as we shall see in the next chapter) flows seaward to Fowey.

The River is perhaps the most all-persuasive symbol running through the book; and it is interesting to measure the degree of idealization which Grahame imposed on his Thames-side setting in order to achieve that timeless, drowsy beatitude. The River acts as a boundary, to begin with; beyond it lie the Wild Wood and the Wide World, with which it is several times contrasted.

It is a symbol of rural traditionalism, faithful, steady-going, reliable; and though the railways may have killed out the pleasant life of the road, still (as Grahame had observed as early as 1892[1]) 'many of its best conditions still linger round these old toll-gates, free from dust and clatter, on the silent liquid Highway to the West'. Water stands for purity, natural life, lushness, the slow, peaceful, primitive tempo of existence; the river-god's rhythm, as Mr. T. S. Eliot aptly reminds us, was present in the nursery bedroom. There is a hint of mysticism in its whispering reeds, so closely connected with the pipes of Pan. It is the perfect background for a reaffirmation of all Grahame's values.

The actual river, of course, whether at Cookham or Fowey, was not like that at all, and Grahame, as a keenly observant naturalist, knew it perfectly well. His symbolism demanded that animals should show themselves as more natural, more peaceable, and (oddest of all) less concerned with sex than humankind; and therefore the whole Nature-red-in-the-tooth-and-claw concept, not to mention the mating season, had to be rejected.* Furthermore, since the River Bank was to stand for idyllic peacefulness, another very material element had to be suppressed. Richard Jefferies was complaining bitterly in the eighties that the Thames otter, the water-rat, the moorhen, and indeed the whole river-bank population, were in danger of being exterminated by sheer senseless slaughter:

> The result is [he wrote] that the osier-beds on the eyots and by the backwaters—the copses of the rivers—are almost devoid of life. A few moorhens creep under the aquatic grasses and conceal themselves beneath the bushes, water-voles hide among the flags, but the once extensive host of water-fowl and

---

* It is interesting to compare, in this connection, Grahame's Mr. Badger with Beatrix Potter's Tommy Brock: the latter is considerably more realistic. See *The Tale of Mr. Tod*, pp. 9-10: 'He was not nice in his habits. He ate wasp nests and frogs and worms; [also baby rabbits] and he waddled about by moonlight, digging things up'. Stinking, cunning, and evil tempered, he is far more accurately observed than the benevolent father-figure in his earthy womb under the Wild Wood.

river life has been reduced to the smallest limits. . . . The shameless way in which every otter that dares to show itself is shot, trapped, beaten to death, and literally battered out of existence, should arouse the indignation of every sportsman and every lover of nature.[2]

Nothing of this appears in *The Wind in the Willows*: the terrors lie elsewhere, and this is Arcadia. Grahame was no longer willing to see—as Jefferies always saw—the skeleton exposed in the stream among the buttercups, and tall grasses, and flowers, and summer happiness.[3] There was a time when his attitude to nature had been more realistic; when he had accepted the decaying hedgehog or murdered chaffinch with cheerful aplomb.[4] But now Death had been ousted from his summer idyll altogether; sex was not the only exile.

Yet Jefferies' books had a considerable influence on the shaping of *The Wind in the Willows*. There is a striking similarity between his and Grahame's descriptions of the 'pageant of summer' and the whole variegated picture of river life.[5] In *Bevis* and *Wood Magic* the resemblances become more specific still. Here we find whispering reeds and river-talk which recall the final paragraphs of 'The Piper at the Gates;'[6] there are also, for good measure, a talking Weasel, Mouse, and Rat who may well have been at the back of Grahame's mind when he wrote his own fable.

This idealization of the River Bank had very deep roots in Grahame's past. All his life, as we know, he had fought with nostalgic doggedness to preserve his faith in a pre-industrial, agricultural, essentially aristocratic society. But as early as 1890 it was becoming uncomfortably clear that the rural squirearchy was collapsing (or at least being profoundly modified) under economic pressure from the Machine Age and slowly increasing political infiltration by Radicals. In 1906, with the Liberal landslide, fifty-three Labour M.P.s were carried into Parliament; and the same year saw the first public appearance of that hearty, flamboyant, gabby vulgarian, Horatio Bottomley, who 'perceived that the moment had come for the exploitation of . . . a

Alastair Grahame
as an undergraduate

Alastair at Blewbury
c. 1912

sort of jolly-good-fellowship all round'.[7] He also, without being aware of it, supplied a good deal of colour to the character of Mr. Toad.

The result of this social upheaval was a violent, often unformulated nostalgic urge for 'escape', which—oddly enough—cut across political denominations: even the early Radicals yearned for lost rural innocence, as a glance into William Morris or Blatchford's *Merrie England* at once makes plain. It took many forms, from the 'simple life' to a preoccupation with childhood,[8] but all of them were basically a protest against urbanism; and many identified urbanism with political anarchy of a vaguely proletarian sort. This produced an impalpable but widely diffused atmosphere of unease:

> No one, surely, who remembers that time, can have forgotten, unless he is abnormally insensitive, the apprehension, never very far below the threshold, of some approaching peril —it might be German, it might be Red or even Yellow, but in any case destined to break the continuity of the safe and prosperous life of those who could afford to live it.[9]

There is no reason to suppose that Grahame was immune from this infectious emotional apprehensiveness; and a good deal which indicates that *The Wind in the Willows* was, *inter alia*, a subconscious defence against it, a fantasy in which country gentlemen finally triumphed over the unprincipled radical *canaille*. This general terror had, in Grahame's case, been made extremely personal and specific by the attack on him by Mr. Robinson, the Socialist lunatic, some four or five years before. The episode reappears in the exchange between Toad and the trigger-happy ferret sentry; but its effects went much deeper. The lurking lawless terror of the Wild Wood, the open anarchy when Toad Hall is usurped by stoats and weasels—all this is Grahame's minuscule projection of his own social fears.

Grahame's attitude to Socialism was very much that of Henley —who must have influenced him considerably—or of Cobbett before him. He was all for individual freedom to the point of eccentricity as long as it was contained 'within the fabric of a firm but self-reformative social structure' [10]—as long, that is, as the rural *status quo* was preserved, complete with its attendant class-structure. Anything that threatened this he regarded as destructive Philistinism. His attitude, like Cobbett's, was semi-patriarchal; he had the same characteristic distaste for the education of the lower orders, [11] which he 'regarded much as a modern man would receive a suggestion that his old nurse was useless without a course of Pelmanism'.

This static rural traditionalism which Grahame idealized was, of course, in many ways a product of ardent wish-fulfilment. We have already seen how actual village life was visibly breaking up, [12] and no one was more acutely aware of the changes going on—especially in his early essays—than Grahame himself. Nor, indeed, did he have any illusions about the crimes, brutality, violence, and poverty, which characterized the earlier England of Fielding. [13] The social picture which *The Wind in the Willows* presents is not life as Grahame thought it was, or once had been: it is his ideal vision of what it *should* be, his dream of the true Golden Age. It is precisely because he knew at heart that the dream was lost beyond any hope of realization that his imaginary world acquired such compulsive fascination for him. The contrast is brought out sharply when Grahame's attitude is compared with that of the actual villagers in Cookham Dene, who 'were ever child-like admirers of Progressive Stunts—and not given to nostalgia'. [14] Again, of course, something of this local addiction to the new-fangled has been gently satirized in the character of Toad.

Throughout the whole book there runs the *leitmotif* which may be roughly described as the conflict between Us and Them—or more specifically, the attempts made by Grahame's ideal rural society to defend itself against encroachment. (The curious thing is that though Grahame set out to create a trouble-free Arcadia he could not stifle his private anxieties: the Wild Wood loomed menacingly across the River, stoats and weasels lurked ready to invade Toad's ancestral home.) This society is specifically identified with the River-Bankers: Rat, Mole, Badger, Otter, and their friends form a close-knit community of leisured landowners who observe an extremely strict code of responsible behaviour.

The paramount virtue in this code, emphasized over and over again, is loyalty to one's own caste: and in this, of course, the animals come very close to their human counterparts. The whole moral and ethical point about Toad's behaviour is that he has *let the side down*. He has been corrupted by modern gadgets; he has made a public fool of himself; he is conceited and irresponsible and a spendthrift; he has disgraced his friends by being imprisoned. The stoats and weasels are enabled to gain possession of Toad Hall precisely because Toad has neglected his property and gone gallivanting on unbecoming picaresque adventures. The one thing that can bring Badger out of his cosy retirement is this threat to River-Bank society: he and Rat lecture Toad with the inflexible moral fervour of Alcoholics Anonymous:

'You knew it must come to this, sooner or later, Toad,' the Badger explained severely. 'You've disregarded all the warnings we've given you, you've gone on squandering the money your father left you, and you're getting us animals a bad name in the district by your furious driving and your smashes and your rows with the police. Independence is all very well, but we animals never allow our friends to make fools of themselves beyond a certain limit; and that limit you've reached.'[15]

Toad, of course, stands for a figure who was becoming increasingly prevalent after the turn of the century: the landed *rentier* squandering his capital on riotous pleasures. This kind of irresponsibility provided the best possible propaganda for radicals who wanted to bring the whole system of inherited wealth and traditional class-values crashing down. In this sense the Adventures of Toad constitute a social object-lesson. If you neglect your responsibilities, Grahame proclaims in effect, you are letting in the enemy and betraying your own friends. And what happens as a result? You are 'handcuffed, imprisoned, starved, chased, terrified out of your life, insulted, jeered at, and ignominiously flung into the water—by a woman too!' You return home to find your country house occupied by insolent riff-raff. Only the loyalty of your friends finally contrives to restore the traditional *status quo*.

Examined from this point of view, the whole business of the Wild Wood and Toad Hall's capture takes on an unmistakable social symbolism. The Wild Wooders, stoats, weasels, and the rest, are clearly identified in Grahame's mind with the stunted, malevolent proletariat of contemporary upper-middle-class caricature. They have 'little evil wedge-shaped faces . . . all fixing on him [Mole] glances of malice and hatred: all hard-eyed and evil and sharp'.[16] They are carefully contrasted with the rural community; and their main delight is to crow over a member of the privileged classes who has infringed his own social code. Toad's imprisonment gives them peculiar pleasure.

Again, like the urban mob-anarchist of every Edwardian upper-middle-class nightmare, they have no notion of how to behave: they are lazy, messy, and ill-organized:

> 'And the Wild Wooders have been living in Toad Hall ever since', continued the Rat; 'and going on simply anyhow! Lying in bed half the day, and breakfast at all hours, and the place in such a mess (I'm told) it's not fit to be seen. . . . And they're telling the tradespeople and everybody *that they've come to stay for good.'* [17] [Italics mine.]

Nothing could be more evocative of that nervous mood, half-contemptuous, half-terrified, which ran through the English bourgeoisie with increasing insistence from about the turn of the century. Toad Hall, its dignity destroyed, the prey of ignorant *sans-culottes*, typifies the entire myth; and one's mind travels forward, with a certain ironical relish, to contemplate those other Stately Homes which today house Civil Servants or delinquent adolescents.

It is a characteristic touch of Grahame's that when the invaders are finally ousted, the first thing they are made to do is sweep under the beds, change the sheets, and supply each room with 'a can of hot water, and clean towels, and fresh cakes of soap'.[18] What could better symbolize the triumph of the *ancien régime* over the upstart Unwashed (who of course kept coal in their baths)? And that triumph itself is in accordance with the stock caricature, according to which the proletariat always show themselves vicious but spineless, miserable cowards when confronted with a tough and united front. (Weasels, ferrets, and stoats are admirably chosen creatures to support such a picture.) Their mistaken aggressiveness is soon dissipated by a little gentlemanly strong-arm work, and they revert to forelock-pulling obsequiousness with comforting rapidity. Pathetically eager to be of service to the gentry, they fulfil the last detail of the legend by blaming their leaders for leading them astray.

Thus the nagging terror of the mob—as Grahame had known it, for example, in the Pall Mall riots—has been exorcized by the most time-honoured reactionary's recipe of them all—physical violence. The paternal squirearchy is restored in triumph, and Wild Wooders gaze in respectful admiration as the Old Order, safely restored to its traditional authority and privilege, goes swaggering by on the last page. In this sense *The Wind in the Willows* was provoked by Grahame's need to combat his ever-increasing fear (shared by many of his class and period) that the structure of society might be destroyed through social revolution.

This also, of course, suggests one reason why *The Wind in the Willows* had no sequel. In 1908 the rural myth, though tottering, could still be maintained with some plausibility. There was yet hope that the squirearchy might triumph if it managed to curb its more irresponsible members. A few years later—even before 1914—it was plain that the old order was irretrievably doomed, and no amount of wishful thinking could ever bring it back. The Motor-car no less than Labour had come to stay: the power of the Unions grew steadily; gentlemen of private means, far from going back to the land, took up speed-boats and aeroplanes; and urban industrialism finally got a stranglehold over the entire country. It is appropriate that Grahame, asked what became of Toad's good resolutions for the future, replied: 'Of course Toad never really reformed; he was by nature incapable of it. But the subject is a painful one to pursue.'[19] It was indeed.

This hint of things to come, the ultimate triumph of mechanical progress over rural traditionalism, is sounded very early in *The Wind in the Willows*—'The Open Road' deals with it in unmistakable terms. The destruction of the caravan—which Grahame associated symbolically with untrammelled country Bohemianism —by the inhuman and somehow monstrous motor-car: this is the core of the matter. Into that chapter Grahame packed a whole social revolution, focused and scaled down into an episode at once fabulous and beguilingly familiar.

The most interesting thing about Grahame's Arcadian animal society is that it has more in common with the rich bourgeoisie than the aristocracy. All the River-Bankers are of apparently independent means; their life seems to be one unending holiday, boating, tramping round the countryside, eating enormous meals, and getting caught up in occasional adventures. They don't run farms or administer big estates; Toad is blamed, not for neglecting his duties as a landlord, but for behaving badly. What Grahame has done, of course, is to project his own private dream on to a social pattern which he admired, but to which he did not belong.

Nothing brings this home so sharply as Grahame's attitude to money. At first one suspects that, like so many rural Utopians, he wants to dispense with it altogether, or has left it out for the benefit of his childish audience. Then comes a revealing little episode which aligns Grahame more nearly to his middle-class banking forebears than to the aristocratic ideal he so admired. Toad at the booking-office in his washerwoman's disguise, without a penny to his name, is a bourgeois anxiety-dream incarnate:

To his horror he recollected that he had left both coat and waistcoat behind him in his cell, and with them his pocket-book, money, keys, watch, matches—pencil-case—all that makes life worth living, all that distinguishes the many-pocketed animal, the lord of creation, from the inferior one-pocketed or no-pocketed productions that hop or trip about permissively, unequipped for the real contest.[20]

Miserably he tries to carry the thing off with upper-class panache, and fails in the most ludicrous fashion. Toad's father may have been an admirable animal, as Badger says; but he almost certainly made his pile in copper-mines or tea-broking.

This incident suggests what one of the underlying emotional driving-forces of *The Wind in the Willows* may have been. For all his Scottish pedigree, Grahame, like Mr. Salteena, felt 'rather mere' about his lack of inherited wealth. When Fletcher Moulton sent him presents of port, he made embarrassed references to 'the humble "four-ale"'—which more properly belongs to my lot in life'. By 1900 wealth rather than breeding had become the criterion of acceptance; Sir Gorgius Midas had come into his own. A lifetime spent in banking can only have added to Grahame's self-consciousness on the subject.

To this self-consciousness was added a deep self-distrust, what Grahame described to Elspeth as 'much natral "gaucherie" wot as never been strove gainst'.[21] Grahame seems to have been constantly afraid that his colleagues and employers, and Society at large in the authoritarian sense, were sneering at him, condemning him, ready to pursue and punish him for his shortcomings. This anxiety-state is confirmed only too accurately by the dream which Grahame (with pre-Freudian candour) incorporated in 'Bertie's Escapade':[22]

Mr. Grahame's night was a very disturbed one, owing to agitating dreams. He dreamt that the house was broken into by burglars, and he wanted to get up and go down and catch them, but he could not move hand or foot. He heard them ransacking his pantry, stealing his cold chicken and things [? 'trifles'], and plundering his wine-cellar, and still he could not move a muscle. Then he dreamt that he was at one of the great City Banquets that he used to go to, and he heard the Chairman propose the health of 'The King' and there was great cheering. And he thought of a most excellent speech to make in reply—a really clever speech. And he tried to make it, but they held him down in his chair and wouldn't let him. And then he dreamt that the Chairman actually proposed his own health—the health of Mr. Grahame! and he got up to reply, and he couldn't think of anything to say! And he stood there, for hours and hours it seemed, in a dead silence, the glittering eyes of the guests—there were hundreds and hundreds of guests—all fixed on him, and still he couldn't think of anything to say! Till at last the Chairman rose, 'He can't think of anything to say! *Turn him out!*' Then the waiters fell on him and dragged him from the room, and threw him into the street, and flung his hat and coat after him; and as he was shot out he heard the whole company singing wildly 'For he's a jolly good fellow. . . !'

This dream suggests several compulsive fears. First, there is the terror of losing property, which reminds us of that scene in the booking office. This again brings us back to the bourgeois nightmare of revolution and expropriation. (Significantly, what Grahame most fears to lose is food—that well-known substitute for emotional satisfaction.) Next we find the generalized fear of impotence—not specifically in a sexual sense. Grahame can't move, can't speak, can't think of anything. Lastly there is the terror of disgrace or ridicule as a result of this or some other shortcoming, and in particular of *public* disgrace. Some of this anxiety may stem from Grahame's indifferent capacity as Secretary of the Bank; but the dream also provides a link between the repressed Bohemian of his earlier work and Toad's curious behaviour in *The Wind in the Willows*.

We have seen how Grahame compounded more and more with respectability as he grew older: but the public figure, though it might overshadow the anarchic Id, could not wholly destroy it. What provided the tension, I suspect, was the new *persona*'s terror that at any moment the old Adam might disgrace it. There was a time when Grahame had wanted nothing so much as to contract out of Society into Epicurean idleness: and deep down this was what he still wanted. But he had learnt—from Wilde's example above all—how mercilessly Society dealt with any infringement of the unwritten laws. Taken in this context Toad's adventures make considerably more sense; they represent Society's ruthless pursuit of the nonconformist, the heterodox, the *déclassé*.

Grahame's attitude to Toad is extremely ambivalent. He is ostensibly on the side of the angels, yet shows very little sympathy for Authority as such. While condemning Toad's excesses, he has, one suspects, a sneaking urge to behave in exactly the same way: Toad, in fact, is a sublimation of all his own unrecognized desires, and is harried by all the forces which Grahame himself found particularly terrifying. There is no one so congenitally scared of a magistrate as your thoroughgoing romantic Bohemian: he has nightmares about prisons, pursuit, disgrace, the ineluctable hand of the law.

This kind of compulsive terror permeates all Toad's adventures. The pursuit-motif is repeated again and again: most strikingly, perhaps, in the railway chase:

> 'They are gaining on us fast!' cried the engine-driver. 'And the engine is crowded with the queerest lot of people! Men like ancient warders, waving halberds; policemen in their helmets, waving truncheons; and shabbily dressed men in pot-hats, obvious and unmistakable plain-clothes detectives even at this distance, waving revolvers and walking-sticks; all waving, and all shouting the same thing—"Stop, stop, stop!"' [23]

These authoritarian pursuers can be linked not only with the Olympians, and the villagers in 'The Reluctant Dragon' and the *They* of Lear's Limericks; but, beyond these, with the whole ugly apparatus which in 1895 represented England's condemnation of Wilde and everything his decade stood for. Grahame still felt the urge towards Bohemianism; but now he was haunted by those fearful Furies which outraged Orthodoxy had let loose when the arch-Bohemian went one degree too far.

We have now traced the main motifs behind *The Wind in the Willows* against their personal and historical impulses in Grahame's mind. There is the idealized river-landscape with its peaceful Epicurean inhabitants; the menace, finally destroyed, of the Wild Wood; the conflict between a paternalist society and the hubristic, Bohemian individual, as exemplified by Toad; and the stabilization of the traditional *status quo* by the realization of a completely self-contained and self-sufficient myth. We have seen how this myth was constructed from diverse elements in Grahame's life and background, and enriched by constant associative allusions. There remain for consideration the two most personal and idiosyncratic chapters, both of which lie outside the book's overall structure: 'The Piper at the Gates' and 'Wayfarers All'.

What these chapters have in common is an overwhelmingly violent emotional experience, which in both cases can be related with some confidence to Grahame's own life. If, at one level, *The Wind in the Willows* subsumes the totality of its author's life —his fears, passions, pleasures, disappointments and beliefs—into a timeless myth, 'The Piper at the Gates' and 'Wayfarers All' crystallize, mythically, the most intimate and intensely felt experiences that Grahame ever sustained. The first forms a mystical testament to his *fin de siècle* faith in the beneficent, personalized powers of Nature; the second enshrines what he felt— and had felt for many years—to be his betrayal of that gleaming sunlit dream, and hints fairly clearly at the compromise he finally settled on.

The vision of Pan may perhaps stand as the supreme example of nineteenth-century neo-pagan mysticism: intensely felt, flawlessly written, with an exquisite, balance between chaste simplicity of style and the rich, colourful, almost sensuous atmosphere which the words themselves evoke. Yet this said, it must be admitted that Grahame's achievement here succeeded only by a hair's-breadth, and could never be repeated. As Mr. MacNeice remarked, apostrophizing his hypothetical Communist, 'this poise is perfect, but maintained for one day only'. The 'kindly demigod' whom Grahame presents has been transformed: desexualized, paternalized, the Friend and Helper of Victorian iconography, a cross between Aesculapius and the Good Shepherd.[24] He contains in his pagan body something of those Christian traits which Grahame sought for so long and never found—or dated to accept. This Pan is an extraordinary syncretic compromise, a projection of Edwardian ruralism, post-Beardsley social opposition, wistful yearning for conformity, an urge towards some replacement for Arnold's God as a comforting Father Figure. It is significant that this Pan's last and most welcome gift (which he never had in antiquity, and which seems to be a creation of Grahame's own) is forgetfulness. The awe of that ultimate revelation was too much for the small creatures who inhabited Grahame's fantasy-world: it may have been too much for Grahame himself—or he may have shrunk from the recognition of its transience.

But there were other things, too, that he wished to forget: all his lost aspirations, the life he might (or dreamed he had) have led if things had turned out differently. Years before, in 'The White Poppy', he had written:[25]

Let black, then, rather stand for hideous memory: white for blessed blank oblivion, happiest gift of the gods! For who indeed can say that the record of his life is not crowded with failure and mistake, stained with its petty cruelties of youth, its meannesses and follies of later years, all which storm and clamour incessantly at the gates of memory, refusing to be shut out? Leave us alone, O gods, to remember our felicities, our successes: only aid us, ye who recall no gifts, aptly and discreetly to forget.

'The Piper at the Gates' celebrates a vision; but in the very O
altitudo of participation Grahame is already begging for the release
which oblivion brings. What he cannot bear to remember is his
own denial of the light. Like Edmund, he had the white vision in
the meadow, but he compromised and was lost. And for that he
never quite forgave himself.

'Wayfarers All' deals with the same essential problem in
slightly different terms. This time the symbol is the Southern
mystique of sun and wine and warm Mediterranean shores, the
anti-Puritan Good Life; the call to adventure:

> Restlessly the Rat . . . lay looking out towards the great ring
> of Downs that barred his vision further southwards—his
> simple horizon hitherto, his Mountains of the Moon, his limit
> behind which lay nothing he had cared to see or to know.
> Today, to him gazing south with a new-born need stirring in
> his heart, the clear sky over their long, low outline seemed to
> pulsate with promise; today, the unseen was everything, the
> unknown the only real fact of life. On this side of the hills was
> now the real blank, on the other lay the crowded and coloured
> panorama that his inner eye was seeing so clearly.[26]

At this critical moment comes the seductive propaganda of the
Sea Rat; in a hypnotic trance Rat prepares to go South with the
rest of them; but at the door he runs into Mole. Mole stops
him (as they had both earlier restrained Toad) by sheer physical
violence—'grappling with him strongly he dragged him inside,
threw him down, and held him'—and sits by him till the hysteria
has worn off. Then slyly, he slips him a pencil and some sheets of
paper, and suggests poetry as a therapeutic. The Rat swallows this
elementary bait:

> The Rat pushed the paper away from him wearily, but the
> discreet Mole took occasion to leave the room, and when he
> peeped in again some time later, the Rat was absorbed and deaf
> to the world; alternately scribbling and sucking the top of his
> pencil. It is true that he sucked a good deal more than he

scribbled; but it was joy to the Mole to know that the cure had at least begun.

Clearly, in this private drama, all three participants represent aspects of Grahame's own personality. Rat is the repressed Bohemian Ulysses, fretting in London and at Cookham Dene, feeling an unformulated migrant urge in the blood. The Sea Rat speaks with the inner voice of the self-tempter: every voyage, each landfall from Corsica to Alassio and Marseilles was one Grahame had already made himself. Mole here is the respectable, conformist side of Grahame: conscientious, practical and loyal, he stands for all the domestic and public virtues.

It almost looks as though in 1907 Grahame was on the edge of leaving Elspeth. We remember the long period of separation: and had not Grahame's father, forty years earlier, vanished in precisely the same footloose way? The Sea Rat's motives for emigration are interesting: 'Family troubles, as usual, began it. The domestic storm-cone was hoisted, and I shipped myself on board a small trading-vessel bound for Constantinople....' The voice that lured Grahame to the untrammelled life of an Italian beachcomber was persuasively insistent: 'Take the Adventure, heed the call, now ere the irrevocable moment passes! 'Tis but a banging of the door behind you, a blithesome step forward, and you are out of the old life and into the new!' [27]

But, as we know, the step was never taken. The struggle may have been an internal one: its reality and agonizing force cannot be in doubt. The entranced, spellbound Rat was defeated: once again, and for the last time, Grahame compromised. The dream of the solitary traveller was abandoned for ever. There would be no escape now, no enchanted and lonely pursuit of the warm, elusive Southern mirage, no miraculous new life. It was over and finished. And yet not quite finished: for one outlet still remained through which Grahame could obtain the emotional release he so desperately needed. Like Rat, he took a pencil and a few sheets of paper; he sucked and he scribbled; and out of his despair and yearning a classic was born.

The Wind in the Willows was finally published in October 1908, with a jacket and frontispiece by Graham Robertson that delighted the author. 'It's as windy and willowy as they make 'em,' he wrote, 'and we are critics of willows down here, and of wind too.'[28] Neither publishers nor critics, however, at first realized the windfall that had landed in their laps. The Bodley Head turned *The Wind in the Reeds* (as it was then entitled) down flat, and it was eventually taken on, with some misgivings, by Methuen. Elspeth, nervous of the reception the book might get, wrote to Anstey Guthrie begging him to review it. A long time had elapsed since *Dream Days*; and there was the danger that the public might be disappointed at not getting something along the same lines. Guthrie replied rather guardedly.[29] 'At present', he wrote, 'I am, as you see, away from town, but even if I were not, I could do very little, as I do not review for any paper, and though I belong to a literary and artistic club, never go to it, and am not on intimate terms with any reviewer.' Having administered this ancient bromide, he then relented slightly: 'If by any chance the book should not have been noticed by the time I return, I will certainly find an opportunity of mentioning it to someone on the *Punch* staff'.

Elspeth's fears were only too well justified in the event. Anstey Guthrie apparently failed to put in a word with *Punch*; their anonymous reviewer described the book as 'a sort of irresponsible holiday story in which the chief characters are woodland animals, who are represented as enjoying most of the advantages of civilisation'. 'His rat, toad and mole', declared the *Saturday Review of Literature*, 'are very human in their behaviour, and remind us of undergraduates of sporting proclivities.' H. W. Nevinson in the *Nation* took a similar line: 'All the animals had a very stirring time, and but for their peculiar shapes they would well pass for first-rate human boys'. This reviewer ran the book eleventh in a mixed bag of thirteen. And *The Times* made the inevitable comment: 'For ourselves we lay *The Wind in the Willows* reverently aside and again, for the hundredth time, take up *The Golden Age*'.

It was *The Times*, too, which (together with *T.P.'s Weekly*) levelled a criticism at Grahame's method which strikes most oddly on modern ears. 'As a contribution to natural history,' proclaimed the anonymous pundit in Printing House Square, 'the work is negligible.' And *T.P.'s Weekly* referred to numerous incidents 'which (I am sorry to say) will win no credence from the very best authorities on biology'.[30] The Olympian critics were having a field-day.

One of the longest and most thoughtful notices was that composed by Mr. Arthur Ransome for *The Bookman*.[31] Having analysed, with some penetration, the 'horrible chasm between dream and reality' which characterized Grahame's earlier works, he went on:

> *The Wind in the Willows* is an attempt to write for children instead of about them. But Mr. Grahame's past has been too strong for him. Instead of writing about children for grown-up people, he has written about animals for children. The difference is only in the names. He writes of the animals with the same wistfulness with which he wrote of children, and, in his attitude towards his audience, he is quite unable to resist that appeal from dreamland to a knowledge of the world that makes the charm of all his books, and separates them from children's literature. The poems in the book are the only things really written for the nursery, and the poems are very bad.
>
> If we judge the book by its aim, it is a failure, like a speech to Hottentots made in Chinese. And yet, for the Chinese, if by any accident there should happen to be one or two of them among the audience, the speech might be quite a success.

Now this review has a good deal of cogency. Mr. Ransome only goes badly wrong over two points: the assumption that Grahame was aiming at the nursery, and its corollary that children would not understand the result. Like so many adult critics, Mr. Ransome was worried by Grahame's shifting planes of reality; but here his author knew rather better than he did the psychology of the child's mind. As Grahame wrote, years later, to a friendly schoolmaster: 'It is the special charm of the child's point of view that the dual nature of these characters does not present the slightest difficulty to them. It is only the old fogies who are apt to begin "Well, but . . ." and so on. To the child it is all entirely natural and as it should be.'[32]

Several reviewers at once suspected, as Graham Robertson had feared,* that the book was some kind of allegory or satire. 'Some grown-up readers', *Punch* declared, 'may find in the story a satirical purpose which its author would probably disclaim.' 'Grown-up readers', *The Times* pronounced uneasily, 'will find it monstrous and elusive'—a queer pair of epithets—and went on: 'Beneath the allegory ordinary life is depicted more or less closely.' But it was Arnold Bennett—one of the few serious writers and critics who thought the book worth their attention—who went straight to the heart of the matter:[33]

> The book is fairly certain to be misunderstood of the people. The publishers' own announcement describes it as 'perhaps chiefly for youth', a description with which I disagree. [It is interesting to recall that Grahame had written this blurb himself.] The obtuse are capable of seeing in it nothing save a bread-and-butter imitation of *The Jungle Book*.[34] . . . The author may call his chief characters the Rat, the Mole, the Toad,—they are human beings, and they are meant to be nothing but human beings. . . . The book is an urbane exercise in irony at the expense of the English character and of mankind. It is entirely successful.

Bennett, of course, only penetrated to one level of *The Wind in the Willows*; but among so much jejune and wrong-headed criticism, we may well be grateful that he achieved so much.

The most broadly based and perceptive notice, however, was beyond doubt that written by Richard Middleton in *Vanity Fair*.

* See below, p. 274.

'Ducks are a-dabbling'
The Wild Wood (Quarry Wood, Cookham Dene)

He accepted the allegory in the spirit (conscious or unconscious) which had directed the author's creative processes:

> The book for me is notable for its intimate sympathy with Nature and for its delicate expression of emotions which I, probably in common with most people, had previously believed to be my exclusive property. When all is said the boastful, unstable Toad, the hospitable Water Rat, the shy, wise, childlike Badger, and the Mole with his pleasant habit of brave boyish impulse, are neither animals nor men, but are types of that deeper humanity which sways us all. To be wise, an allegory must admit of a wide application, and the man has read his *Pilgrim's Progress* in vain who does not realise that not merely Christian but Ignorance, Talkative and Justice Hategood himself, are crying for mastery in the heart of us all. And if I may venture to describe as an allegory a work which, critics, who ought to have known better, have dismissed as a fairy-story, it is certain that *The Wind in the Willows* is a wise book.

Grahame himself, we may well suppose, approved this generous and far-sighted appraisal; at any rate Elspeth allowed Chalmers to quote it in full—an act which tells its own story.

The critics would, perhaps, have been better employed even on their own terms if they had used some of their space to point out Grahame's literary influences, and the strange way he contrived to transmute them for his own purposes. It is true that direct allusions were far less frequent in *The Wind in the Willows* than in Grahame's earlier books (I shall deal with this point more fully in the next chapter); but even so no one seems to have noticed that Toad's dealings with the gypsy are a hilarious parody of *Lavengro*, while the Sea Rat's historical musings on Constantinople are lifted direct from William Morris's *Sigurd the Volsung*.[35] Even more remarkable (and equally unnoticed) is Grahame's *penchant* for parodying Homer.

This amiable habit goes back to *The Golden Age* and *Dream Days*. We remember the toy snake that was taken to bed every night, 'till what time its spinal cord was loosed and it fell apart, and went the way of all mortal joys'. In 'The Twenty-First of October' we hear tell of 'the stout soul of a black Berkshire pig' that 'was already faring down the stony track to Hades'. The gardener's boy, engaged with the narrator in a clod-throwing contest, receives the full heroic treatment:

> He, the foolish one, witless on whose side the gods were fighting that day, discharged yet other missiles, wavering and wide of the mark; for his wind had been taken with the first clod, and he shot wildly, as one already desperate and in flight.

The trick is characteristic of all Grahame's literary borrowings: it simultaneously elevates the child's world to a Homeric level, and mocks self-assured adult dignity by reducing it, conversely, to the children's level.[36]

In *The Wind in the Willows* this Homeric motif is developed more fully. Most of Toad's adventures bear a certain ludicrous resemblance to Ulysses' exploits in the *Odyssey*; and the resemblance becomes detailed and explicit in the last chapter, which parodies the hero's return and the slaying of the suitors. (Its very title—'The Return of Ulysses'—offers the broadest of hints as to what Grahame had in mind.) There is an irreverent take-off of the stock Homeric arming ceremony:

> First, there was a belt to go round each animal, and then a sword to be stuck into each belt, and then a cutlass on the other side to balance it. Then a pair of pistols, a policeman's truncheon, several sets of handcuffs, some bandages and sticking-plaster, and a flask and a sandwich-case.

Yet Grahame is quite capable of turning a Homeric simile to striking and serious use when he chooses: there is an excellent example in 'The Piper at the Gates':[37]

> As one awakened suddenly from a beautiful dream, who struggles to recall it, and can recapture nothing but a dim sense of the beauty of it, the beauty! Till that, too, fades away in

its turn, and the dreamer bitterly accepts the hard cold waking and all its penalties; so Mole, after struggling with his memory for a brief space, shook his head sadly and followed the Rat.

It is interesting to speculate whether Grahame knew the famous ancient parody of Homer, the *Batrachomyomachia*, or 'Battle of Frogs and Mice', which is often included with texts of the *Iliad* and *Odyssey*.

Clearly, as always, Grahame derived Toad's adventures from many sources, not Homer only; Mlle Fyrth suggests, with some plausibility, that he may also have drawn on mediaeval romances and ballads,[38] to which we may add the early English picaresque novels by authors such as Fielding. But in any case this rich alluvial deposit of parody and imitation must have its effect on the reader, whose enjoyment is deepened—perhaps without his being consciously aware of it—by the associations such a technique evokes.

The general question of Grahame's reading in English literature is a complicated one, and bedevilled by his admitted habit of making up his own quotations when he could not find one to fit the occasion.[39] His favourite authors seem to have been Shakespeare, Malory, Sir Thomas Browne, Tennyson, Browning, Matthew Arnold, and (as we might expect) Lewis Carroll. But his allusions extend into a far wider field.[40]

A close examination of his work reveals one other major debt, on which we have already touched. Grahame never admits as much in so many words, but a host of references make it clear beyond any doubt that he was profoundly influenced by Ruskin and the whole Pre-Raphaelite movement. The first supplied both his passion for the Gothic Revival and his interest in the more external phenomena of Roman Catholicism: Mr. Graham Hough observes of Ruskin (but it might just as well have been of Grahame) that 'its effect on him was not to turn him to Catholicism, but to cause him to rely more and more on impressions derived from art and the imaginative life which were quite inconsistent with the Bible

Protestantism of his childhood'.[41] To Ruskin he also owed, beyond any doubt, his admiration of the Italian Primitives.[42]

The other member of the group who had a strong influence on Grahame's style and ideas was William Morris. This raises a point which Graham Robertson made as to what *The Wind in the Willows* was *not* about, and gives it a rather suggestive appearance.* It was *not*, Robertson said, 'a Socialist Programme'. In the sense in which Morris would have used the term, it could well be argued that it was. 'Socialist sentiment' (to quote Mr. Hough again [43]) 'has often owed a great deal to these political or poetical myths of a time of unfallen simplicity before the institution of civil society or private property.' Now Grahame would not go all the way with Morris over this; but he did share, very strongly, Morris's dream of a rural, non-industrial Earthly Paradise: the return of the lost Golden Age.

What is more, he knew the works of Morris very well: not only the beautifully illustrated mediaeval folios that issued from the Kelmscott Press (and which are clearly referred to in 'Its Walls were as of Jasper') but also such books as *The Earthly Paradise* or *News from Nowhere*, with their more specifically social content. He had made a personal pilgrimage to Kelmscott, and wrote detailed notes of the occasion; his obsession with the New Jerusalem, the Golden City that haunted all Utopians from Augustine to Cobbett and Morris himself, is amply documented in his own writings.[44] He would certainly have subscribed to Morris's declaration in *The Earthly Paradise*: [45]

> Dreamer of dreams, born out of my due time,
> Why should I strive to set the crooked straight?
> Let it suffice me that my murmuring rhyme
> Beats with light wing against the ivory gate,
> Telling a tale not too importunate
> To those who in the sleepy region stay,
> Lulled by the singer of an empty day.

* See p. 274.

And this leads us to the central reason for the perennial success which *The Wind in the Willows* has enjoyed, and continues to enjoy, with readers of all ages: the reason for its continued sale of about 80,000 copies every year. Its symbolism embodies some of mankind's deepest and most ineradicable yearnings: the pastoral dream, the Golden Age, the search for lost innocence. 'The book', Mr. Hough writes of *News From Nowhere*—but again he might have had Grahame in mind—'derives its strength from another source—it has the reality of a myth. Myths are after all fundamental to the psychic life: no demonstration of what is merely possible can fill the minds of men unless it can draw energy from these underground sources: and no merely personal or fashionable fantasy can do so, except for a limited time and class.' [46] If that is true in the present case, it will have been of some service to demonstrate the nature and antecedents of the myth which Grahame evolved.

It may also serve to answer those readers who will, doubtless, accuse me of having profaned a mystery by practising what has been neatly defined as 'a new kind of Puritanism, a sort of self-conscious post-analytical rectitude, a knowing superiority over non-Freudian self-deceivers'. [47] Such has been very far from my intention. It is true that I believe our appreciation of Grahame's work can be deepened and enriched by knowing the elements which went to compose it, personal no less than literary; Grahame himself was to declare—and he spoke truer than perhaps he knew —that his readers 'liked the subject-matter; they did not even notice the source of all the agony, and all the joy. A large amount of what Thoreau called life went into the making of many of those playful pages.' [48] It did indeed. But in the last resort it is the work which endures, on its own merits. The contemporary or ephemeral problems which agitated Grahame's mind so deeply are forgotten today: the vision, the intense personal experience, the myth—it is these that remain.

THE ROAD TO XANADU
1907-1908

Part 2: A Mosaic of Characters

Once inside this particular door—if one takes the pains—how one is possessed by the inhabitants, their surroundings, their ways, and their points of view! Emerging, one really expects to meet them at every corner, to be hailed by them, to put the natural question and get the appropriate answer. One forgets, for the moment, that the real four-legged or feathered fellows one encounters are sullen, rancorous, and aggrieved—have a book of their own, in fine, a version in which it is *we* who point the moral and adorn the tale!

KENNETH GRAHAME: *Introduction to A Hundred Fables of Æsop*

'Is the story about me?' asked the Water-rat. 'If so I will listen to it, for I am extremely fond of fiction.'

OSCAR WILDE: *The Happy Prince*

Two interesting curves, one rising, one falling, could be plotted on the graph of Kenneth Grahame's literary development, and their close influence on each other deduced with some certainty. The falling curve is that of self-conscious explicitness—the openly stated theme, the deliberate literary quotation or allusion, the carefully ornate style. *Pagan Papers* is packed with all these things; *The Golden Age* has less of them, *Dream Days* less still, and *The*

Wind in the Willows virtually none at all. The rising curve is that of unconscious, implicit symbolism, and allegory, which is practically non-existent in the early essays, begins to show itself in the children's stories, becomes obtrusive in 'The Reluctant Dragon' and all-pervasive in *The Wind in the Willows*. This double phenomenon squares very well with the facts of Grahame's life as we have traced them so far. He progressively stifled his conscious urge towards personal anarchy and artistic individualism; he came to terms with his successful career in the City; and close on top of this he made an emotionally disastrous marriage. The inevitable result was that—as in the cases of Lear and Carroll—his imaginative, creative impulses were driven down deep into his subconscious mind. His son Alastair provided the focal point for their transmutation and eventual release.

Elspeth always believed that she was the inspired fire behind *The Wind in the Willows*—which explains why she denigrated Grahame's earlier work by comparison—and in a tragic sense she was right. If Grahame had never married her it is extremely doubtful whether the book would ever have been written: it needed exactly the emotional shock she provided for the creative flash-point to be reached. Repressed, unhappy, driven in on himself, badly bruised by contact with adult passion, Grahame turned—without being aware for one moment of what he was about—to the world of symbol and myth. In so doing he released the full strength of his genius.

Three technical stages can be distinguished in the shaping of *The Wind in the Willows*. First, there were the nightly bedtime stories which Grahame told his son over a period of three years or more, probably beginning early in 1904. This stage we have already considered in Chapter XI. Next comes the famous series of letters written to Alastair from Fowey and London, which form a skeleton outline of Toad's Adventures. With this stage we may bracket certain elements in 'Bertie's Escapade', the *jeu d'esprit* which Grahame wrote for Alastair's nursery magazine,

The Merry Thought. Last comes the finished draft, substantially as it appears today.

These three stages in a single creative process form the expanding nucleus to which a multitude of associative motifs and fragmentary memories attached themselves. For a shorter or longer period they lay in what Professor Livingston Lowes so aptly termed the 'well of the sub-conscious'; then they re-emerged, transmuted by Grahame's idiosyncratic imagination into a new, coherent, completely self-sufficient pattern.

The genesis of the letters was as follows. In May 1907 Alastair went with his governess, Miss Stott, on a seven weeks' holiday to Littlehampton. At the same time his parents left for the West Country. They spent a few days in Falmouth, and then returned for a prolonged visit to their beloved Fowey. (Chalmers suggests that Grahame was tied to London by Bank duties:[1] the letters tell a different story.) Half-way through June Elspeth returned to Cookham Dene to be with Alastair, whose holiday was now over; but Kenneth, for reasons we can only surmise, went to London— the house in Durham Villas had been kept as a *pied-à-terre*—and remained there at least till September, occasionally coming down to Cookham Dene for week-ends. During this period—from spring to autumn of 1907—he wrote Alastair a series of letters, which Miss Stott, with considerable foresight, preserved. They contain, in embryo, the central narrative theme of *The Wind in the Willows*—Toad's adventures—from the theft of the motor-car to the final banquet.

Now this, as is at once apparent, covers rather less than half the matter in the final draft: it represents chapters vi, viii, and x-xii only. There is no trace of chapters i-v ('The River Bank', 'The Open Road', 'The Wild Wood', 'Mr. Badger', and 'Dulce Domum'); nor of chapters vii and ix ('The Piper at the Gates of Dawn' and 'Wayfarers All'). The latter two we know to have been written separately and later inserted in the draft;[2] and the same may possibly be true of the earlier chapters as well.

On this point, however, we cannot be certain. It may be that Miss Stott only came to realize the unique value of these letters after she had destroyed some of the earlier ones; and in support of this presumption may be mentioned the fact that Rat, Mole, and Badger suddenly appear in the later letters without explanation or introduction.[3] On the other hand, there are two suggestive pieces of evidence which tell a different story. The first is the earliest surviving letter, dated 10th May 1907, which contains this paragraph: [4]

> Have you heard about the Toad? He was never taken prisoner by brigands at all. It was all a horrid low trick of his. He wrote that letter himself—the letter saying that a hundred pounds must be put in the hollow tree. And he got out of the window early one morning, & went off to a town called Buggleton, & went to the Red Lion Hotel[5] & there he found a party that had just motored down from London, & while they were having breakfast he went into the stable-yard & found their motor-car & went off in it without even saying Poop-poop! And now he has vanished & everyone is looking for him, including the police. I fear he is a bad low animal.

The latter half of this passage is familiar; the opening is not. It suggests a different beginning to Toad's adventures, in which his friends probably did not feature at all.[6]

The second piece of circumstantial evidence concerns 'The River Bank'. While the Grahames were at Fowey in May and June of 1907, they made the acquaintance of an American family also on holiday there—Mr. and Mrs. Austin Purves of Philadelphia, and their five sons, Dale, Austin Jr., Pierre, Edmund, and John. Kenneth actually stood godfather to Pierre, the youngest, at his Fowey christening, which 'was unusual in that old Cornish customs were carried out, a procession to the Church and the presentation of the Kimbly cake to the first person encountered'.[7] Grahame and Austin Purves continued to correspond regularly until the latter's death in 1915; the two families met again at Fowey just before the First World War, and after it Grahame entertained the Purves boys on various occasions both in Oxford and in Rome.

All the brothers are happily alive today; and all agree in believing that the general setting of *The Wind in the Willows* is largely derived from Fowey and the Fowey River. This is suggestive and revealing. Hitherto it has generally been supposed that Fowey only contributed 'the little grey sea town' of the Sea Rat's tale, and that the rest was unadulterated Thames-side Berkshire. But it is entirely in key with his Coleridgean methods of composition that Grahame should have added elements from Fowey as well.

More specifically, the Purves brothers confirm that the opening chapter, 'The River Bank', was inspired by a boating trip up the Fowey River, undertaken by Grahame, 'Atky', and their father, 'to a little village called Golant, on the right bank, for tea. They probably hired someone else to row them.'[8] Similarly, the entire open-air sequence of 'Wayfarers All' is supposed to have been directly provoked by a walk Grahame and Austin Purves (or 'Atky') took in the near-by countryside;[9] perhaps 'towards the west on the Fowey side, past Ready Money Cove, to St. Catherine's Castle and the hills and sea-coast beyond that'.[10]

Now, as we have seen, any direct identifications in *The Wind in the Willows* must be handled with extreme caution: Grahame's creative processes were deep, complex, and associative. Nevertheless we have no reason to doubt that the conscious, immediate impulse for these two chapters came about in the way described—with ample corroborative evidence—by the Purves brothers. This means that they cannot have actually been composed before May or June at the earliest, and probably—if we leave time for subconscious digestion—at least three months later. We can now make a nearer guess at the order of composition. The Toad-narrative evolved first; the River Bank sequences came next; and the two set-pieces, 'Wayfarers All' and 'The Piper at the Gates', were composed last of all.

But the external impetus to crystallize the letters and bed-time stories into a book almost certainly came from that extraordinary woman Constance Smedley. Miss Smedley, an ardent feminist (she had written a work entitled *Woman: A Few Shrieks*) and co-founder of the International Lyceum Club, was in 1907 living at Bray, within convenient range of Cookham Dene. Among her other activities she was European representative of the American magazine *Everybody's*. The editor, John O'Hara Cosgrave, wrote asking her to try and persuade Grahame to produce a new book. Miss Smedley duly invaded the household at Cookham Dene, and endeared herself to Kenneth by declaring that she was a relation of that other Miss Smedley, the governess in *The Golden Age*. This linking of fantasy and life was a neat psychological stroke: Miss Smedley had sized up her quarry extremely well.

Despite her modernity, her feminism, and the fact that she travelled—unspeakable!—by motor-car, Constance Smedley made closer contact with Grahame than most people. He talked with surprising freedom to her, saying how the return to this scene of his childhood had stimulated his early memories: 'The queer thing is,' he said, 'I can remember everything I felt then, the part of my brain I used from four till about seven can never have altered. Coming back here wakens every recollection.' She approached him, tentatively, about the new book; he told her he hated writing, it was sheer physical torture. Miss Smedley kept her eyes open, observed Grahame's special relationship with Alastair, and saw her way clear:

He [Alastair] had about him something of his father's remoteness and was perpetually playing games with himself. . . . Every evening Mr. Grahame told Mouse an unending story, dealing with the adventures of the little animals whom they met in their river journeys. This story was known to him and Mouse alone and was related in a bed-time visit of extreme secrecy. . . . Mouse's own tendency to exult in his exploits was gently satirized in Mr. Toad, a favourite character who gave the juvenile audience occasion for some slightly self-conscious laughter.

It looks very much as though Miss Smedley managed to gain admission to these secret sessions; at all events she made Grahame talk about the story, and at once exerted all her influence to get him to write it down. No one since Henley had had such an instinctive editorial flair for pushing him in the right direction.

Their meeting took place about the middle of August. Her work accomplished, Miss Smedley extracted an introduction from the Grahames to Thomas Hardy, and drove off, popping and banging, in the direction of Dorchester and Max Gate. Elspeth—equally loath to let an opportunity slip—entrusted her with some personal poems for the great man's perusal. Hardy apparently liked both Miss Smedley and the poems: [11]

> She is most bright and interesting [he wrote], and we had a long talk. . . . Your verses are charming, and certainly remarkable for being made on the top of an omnibus, where my attention is always too distracted by the young women around me in fluffy blouses to be able to concentrate on inner things.

By now the Grahames had moved from their temporary furnished house, Hillyers, to a big sprawling building known as Mayfield—now a school—complete with large garden and paddock. Here they remained till the move to Blewbury in 1910; and here, before he drafted *The Wind in the Willows* in its final form, Grahame composed that curious little fragment, 'Bertie's Escapade'. This was a *jeu d'esprit* for domestic consumption, full of private allusions. It involved the Grahames' pig (Bertie himself) and Alastair's pet rabbits, Peter and Benjie, whose names remind us that Beatrix Potter's *Peter Rabbit* had been published in 1904. (There is a faint element of Potterism in Grahame's own book, especially where rabbits and hedgehogs are concerned.) The plot is simple. Bertie, Peter, and Benjie go carol-singing;

they set up such a fearful caterwauling that Mr. Stone (a neighbouring farmer) turns the dogs loose on them. Then they retreat
to 'Mayfield', where they raid the larder ('I know where Mr.
Grahame keeps his keys—very careless man, Mr. Grahame') and
have a tremendous feast.[12]

It is the incidental oddities which are most revealing in this
sketch. The first place the animals go to is that highly-charged
and recurrent symbol in Grahame's mythology—the chalk-pit.
They pull out a piece of chalk, and behold! a tunnel. At the end
of the tunnel is a lift operated by—inevitably—a mole, which
rapidly shoots them up and out into the moonlight. Later the mole
is brought back for the feasting, and returns home in the small
hours to find 'Mrs. Mole sitting up for him, in some uneasiness of
mind'. There follows immediately the long and detailed anxiety-
dream experienced, it is stated, by Grahame himself, which I have
discussed at length in the previous chapter. (See pp. 249-51.)

This dream has personal as well as social implications. To begin
with, the entire sequence—not merely the final fantasy—has every
appearance of being transcribed from a genuine nightmare. The
dream-symbolism is both classic and transparent. The chalk-pit
stands for the creative, sub-conscious self, where—as we see from
'A Funeral'—not only the imagination but also all emblems of
despair, nostalgia, failure, and resignation have their home. The
tunnel, as we know from 'The Reluctant Dragon' no less than
'The River Bank', is the outlet for the creative force; and the
Mole—another symbol for the subterranean, upthrusting, blind
imagination—is, of course, an aspect of Grahame himself. In fact,
the two merge here almost explicitly. The Mole stays out late
after an enjoyable feast (a habit which his creator occasionally
shared) and the uneasy Mrs. Mole waits up for him. But it is
Grahame himself who thereupon (with the abruptest of transi-
tions) suffers the kind of nightmare generally induced by over-
eating and mixing one's wines.

When Grahame came to write The Wind in the Willows, as we

know, Mrs. Mole had been quietly jettisoned altogether, and Mole was a comfortable bachelor once more. The change is at least suggestive.

Now, at last, the long incubation of Grahame's masterpiece was nearly complete. From all directions and every year of the half-century memories, images, fears, regrets, friends, books, vivid scenes, half-forgotten incidents converged on the single focal point, at last achieved, 'the real, the unmistakable thing, simple, passionate—perfect'. Some of these influences Grahame used consciously and deliberately; others worked themselves in below the threshold of his awareness. Summers of casual Mediterranean wandering; the childhood pattern set by Berkshire meadows and the lazy Thames, the eternal solitary lure of the Ridgeway; paganism, Pan, and *The Yellow Book*; the odd near-eccentric friends who were or had been especially close to him—Furnivall, Henley, Q, 'Atky'; years of political unrest, the collapse of the country squirearchy; the anarchic, proletarian, urban Radicalism which meant strikes and riots; the London Scottish Territorials; the winding creeks and quiet backwaters of Fowey; books by the hundred, known and re-read time and time again—the *Odyssey*, Grimm, Andersen, Æsop, William Morris, Jefferies, Anstey, Wilde, Matthew Arnold; his own life, with its chequered pattern of repressions, disappointments, and compromises; above all, the small child for whom, night after night, he wove the beginnings of the fabric—all these met, mingled, were transformed in the light alembic of that delicate mind.

Why did Grahame choose, at this stage in his career, to write a book in which the main characters were animals? This question was asked by a number of disappointed reviewers who, with the dogged singlemindedness of their kind, had been expecting yet another *Golden Age*; and it is fatally easy to brush it off with a superficial answer. It may be said—and generally is—that the conventions of the bedtime story demanded animals, and that Grahame had plentiful models in the fairy-tales and folklore he knew so well. Both these statements are quite true; but they only scrape the surface of the problem.

It seems probable (though he almost certainly did not recognize it himself) that Grahame's general attitude towards the animal kingdom was directly derived from popularized notions of scientific evolution. In reaction against the theological concept of man 'set above the brutes' there developed an emphasis on our kinship with all four-footed creatures; and this in its turn set a fresh premium on the 'animal' qualities of passion and instinct. Stevenson summarized this trend admirably:[13]

> A new doctrine, received with screams a little while ago by canting moralists, and still not properly worked into the body of our thoughts, lights us a step further into the heart of this rough but noble universe. For nowadays the pride of man denies in vain his kinship with the original dust. He stands no longer like a thing apart. . . . The browsers, the biters, the barkers, the hairy coats of field and forest, the squirrel in the oak, the thousand-footed creeper in the dust, as they share with us the gift of life, share with us the love of an ideal. . . .

The final words show what curious inconsistencies and exaggerations such a theory could produce. Grahame and those who thought as he did both claimed the animal as a brother—thus vindicating Darwin—and at the same time execrated science for taking all the mystery out of life. The traditional English love of animals, which certainly does not pre-date the Romantic Movement, may well stem from the same muddled source, a mixture of evolutionary theory and natural pantheism.

But there are several deeper reasons for the use of animal characters; and they are hinted at, as usual, in Grahame's own work. To begin with, the trend we have observed in his development away from the explicit to the implicit, from statement to symbol, would very much encourage it. He was ripe for unconscious allegory. Secondly, there was his long-dormant satirical *persona*, which needed a mask more effective than that supplied by childhood. Thirdly, there was his growing aversion to humanity as such, which almost certainly had an intimate connection with his unhappy marriage. At this level he turned to the animal world in much the same spirit as Swift, who drew such a telling comparison between Houyhnhnms and Yahoos in *Gulliver's Travels*. He wished both to show the animal's moral superiority to the human species, and at the same time, by an anthropomorphizing trick, to satirize his society in the persons of half-human animals.

It is important to remember, at this point, that Grahame himself had, or professed, no such ulterior motives in writing the book. This is exactly what we should expect. Conscious allegorizing is almost invariably disastrous; and in Grahame's case, as we have seen, extremely powerful motives existed for driving down unpleasant truths into the subconscious mind. In a letter to Theodore Roosevelt [14] Grahame declared: 'Its [WW's] qualities, if any, are mostly negative—*i.e.*—no problems, no sex, no second meaning—it is only an expression of the very simplest joys of life as lived by the simplest beings of a class that you are specially familiar with and will not misunderstand'.

Even on the internal evidence of the book itself this is so flagrantly untrue that one's curiosity is at once aroused. The discrepancy suggests an unconscious covering-up action, which is always accompanied by categorical and emphatic denials. (Obviously this phenomenon must be handled with care; denial does not invariably—to reverse the process—imply a hidden motive.) A letter of Graham Robertson's [15] to Grahame confirms one's suspicions in a most singular way. 'Don't you think', he writes, 'that Methuen himself, in his preliminary announcement of the book, should mention that it is not a political skit, or an Allegory of the Soul, or a Socialist Programme or a Social Satire? It would save critics a good deal of unnecessary trouble.'

The more one looks at this statement, the odder it is. What prompted Robertson to make it in the first place? And why should he pick on just these four things, all of which (with the possible exception of the third)★ undoubtedly *do* lurk below the immediate surface of *The Wind in the Willows*? There are several possibilities. Either friends had seen the MS. and had been struck by its various latent meanings (as reviewers such as Arnold Bennett and Richard Middleton were later[16]); or Grahame, still covering up, had compulsively told Robertson that these were the things the book was *not*, in much the same vein as he had written to Roosevelt; or Robertson himself had sensed the depths in the book as he read, and was hastening to bring his suspicions into the open and kill them out of hand. Perhaps the second supposition is the most likely.

Nevertheless—and this must be emphasized—we can never be dogmatic about interpretations of motive in such a context. We know that from the moment of its completion, theories circulated about the inner meanings of *The Wind in the Willows*; we know that Grahame explicitly denied any ulterior purpose in writing it; and that, in the direct sense, is all we know. Cumulative circumstantial evidence, however convincing, is not the same as proof. What follows should be considered in that light.

Grahame's special attitude to animals dates back at least as far as *Pagan Papers*, and is there expressed most explicitly in 'The Lost Centaur'. He contrasts the 'forked radish' with so-called lesser creatures, making it quite plain that for him the beasts of the field are morally equal, if not superior, to Man.[17] There was, indeed, something of this Franciscan attitude apparent in his own life: birds, as well as dogs or cats, took to him instinctively.[18] He crystallized his views on the animal fable most clearly, however, in the little-known introduction he composed in 1899 for P. J. Billinghurst's *A Hundred Fables of Æsop*. It is hard to believe that he did not profit by his own precepts eight years later.

After discussing the moral purpose of the *genre* ('the preacher fell upon the element of fiction, and the fable was born'), Grahame

★ But see p. 262.

remarks on the disinclination of society to swallow direct censure. What, then, was the satirist to do?

> The friendly, tactful, unobtrusive beasts around him—could they not be seized upon and utilized to point the requisite moral? True, it would be no good to hold up their real characteristics for the public admonishment. The moment they were really studied they were seen to be so modest, so mutually helpful, so entirely free from vanity, uncomplaining, and determined to make the best of everything; and, finally, such adepts in the art of minding their own business, that it was evident a self-respecting humanity would not stand the real truth for a moment. But one could deal out the more prominent of human failings among them. . . .

By easy stages Grahame achieves the Swiftian position of setting the animals up as judges of human behaviour, and clinches the point with a witty inverted fable of his own:

The Ape and the Child in the Leghorn Hat

A frolicsome ape, who in much careless ease inhabited a lordly mansion in Regent's Park, lounged up one afternoon to certain bars, on the other side of which selected specimens of humanity were compelled to promenade each day for the instruction and diversion of philosophic apes. A little maid in a Leghorn hat having timidly approached the bars, her large fat mother, shaking her imperiously by the shoulder, ordered her to observe the pitty ickle monkey, so mild and so gentle, and give it a piece of her bun at once, like a good, kind, charitable ickle girl. The small maiden, though herself extremely loth, proffered her bun to the ape, who possessed himself of it with a squeal of delight, and bit her finger to the bone as well: for he had bitten nothing more juicy and succulent than a neighbour's tail for a whole week past; and tails are but gristly things at the best. But the large, fat mother, falling upon the already shrieking little girl, shook and cuffed her unmercifully, protesting that of all the naughty, tiresome, self-willed little trollops, and that never, never, never would she take her a-pleasuring again.

Moral

Parents of the human species have an altogether singular and unaccountable method of rearing their young. Yet they grow up somehow, nevertheless, and often become quite good and useful citizens: so there may be something in it, and it's a lesson to us not to be proud and think we know everything.

This acid little sketch not only demonstrates Grahame's close and merciless observation of adult behaviour (which we knew already from *The Golden Age*) but reveals that he could also deal in fables with a purpose when he chose. The pattern, whether employed consciously or not, existed in his mind.

The animals of *The Wind in the Willows* are composed from several distinct and separate sources. At one level they are normal creatures of riverside and woodland: moles, water-rats (more accurately water-voles, but Grahame probably wanted to avoid a clash of names), badgers, otters, stoats, and weasels—all are common in the neighbourhood of the Thames round Cookham. We know, too, that Grahame took a keen and direct interest in such creatures. Charis Fairbanks, who stayed at 'Mayfield' about this period, wrote:[19]

> I recall one day, wandering round Cookham and Marlow, his stopping on a wee bridge and endeavouring to call the attention of someone, or something, by a most alluring whistle, as sweet and imperative as any pipe of Pan. I know I'd have gone anywhere it called! But there was no response. After several calls he gave it up, remarking: 'There's a Water Rat down there, at least, it's his home; he's quite a friend of mine. Evidently he's gone on some excursion—I shall hear about it one day.'

This recalls a remark in 'A Funeral': 'the rabbits—I have it from one of themselves—have all gone to an At Home today'. Grahame's affectation to understand animal-talk crops up in several other places (notably his introduction to Billinghurst, where the Badger puts in a first brief appearance): perhaps he even half-believed it himself.

A similar incident lay behind the creation of Mole. One evening, when Grahame was dressing for dinner, he happened to glance out of his bedroom window (it was late summer, and still light) and saw 'some sort of flurry or disturbance going on' under the trees at the far end of the lawn. Quickly, he stole out in his stockinged feet, and found a robin and a mole fighting for possession of a worm. The robin flew off; but Grahame, with some dexterity, managed to capture the mole, and took it indoors with the intention of showing it to Alastair the following morning. He put it for the night in a small grass-lined hamper on the piano, with a heavy iron weight to hold the lid down. But in the morning the mole had inexplicably vanished—leaving both weight and lid intact. Mrs. Blunt, the housekeeper, admitted to having killed what she thought was a 'young rat', by the back door; but she was getting near-sighted in her old age. When Grahame told her what the mole had been for, she said: 'Oh, but, sir, couldn't you just make the mole into a story for Master Alastair?'[20]

The last part of this anecdote (like so much else in *First Whispers*) may well be apocryphal, since Mole had had his first tentative beginnings some time before; but the little creature's mysterious and somehow symbolic escape from prison would not have been lost on Grahame. It may well have triggered off other more personal and associative details. Grahame can be more nearly identified with Mole than any other of his characters: the patient, tunnelling, laborious Mole who suddenly bursts through into the sunlight and the leisurely life of the River. Like Grahame, he is tactful, wide-eyed, a little naïve, content to play Watson to Ratty's Holmes; like Grahame again, he develops a violent, aching nostalgia for his old home—and goes back to it. Mole's moments of self-analysis could be applied with equal justice to his creator:

The Mole saw clearly that he was an animal of tilled field and hedgerow, linked to the ploughed furrow, the frequented pasture, the lane of evening lingerings, the cultivated garden plot. For others the asperities, the stubborn endurance, or the clash of actual conflict, that went with Nature in the rough; he must be wise, must keep to the pleasant places in which his lines were laid and which held adventure enough, in their way, to last for a lifetime.[21]

Thus the Mole has evolved, a being in his own right, rather as crystals accumulate on a thread suspended in solution: he begins with a line in a poem of John Davidson's,[22] gathers up not only subterranean symbolism but also the behaviour of a real live mole in the garden, and is completed with oblique strokes of auto-biography and self-analysis. This is Grahame's normal method of composition: and Mole is a comparatively simple example. All the other animals reveal similar constituent elements—natural observation of the beast in question; literary associations; under-lying symbolism; a degree of self-portraiture. They also incor-porate features borrowed from Grahame's friends.

But—and this is the important point—their final realization is completely individual. They are not patchwork or *pointilliste* portraits: the material has been absorbed into a new entity. Just as in his children's stories Grahame experimented with fluid levels of awareness, so here he has contrived matters in such a way that animal, human, and symbolic traits co-exist, without any sense of incongruity, in the same character.

Rat is more complex altogether. He is a handyman, but also a dreamer; a man (or rat) of action and a poet; cool-headed in a crisis, yet liable to mystical seizures and symptoms indicative of hysteria. In the autobiographical sense he stands for Grahame's emotional extremes—at one end of the scale the practical business-man and freshwater sailor; at the other the volatile, highly imaginative, psychologically disturbed Celt. It may be Rat who supports Mole in his emotional crisis of longing for Mole End; but the rôles are reversed when Rat hears the call of the South and marches out, for all the world like a hypnotized zombie, his eyes no longer brown but a streaked and shifting grey. (Where did Grahame find this odd phenomenon? It sounds like a mild case of hysterical glaucoma.) And the 'seizure', we should note, is cured by—creative writing. There could hardly be a closer parallel.

But other, external, strands went into the Rat's making. There is a touch of Henley in his occasional bursts of blunt dogmatism; and his general habits and appearance derive in large measure from 'Atky', whose riverside bachelor home and passion for 'messing about in boats' struck an immediately responsive chord in Grahame. Further back still, his sculling expeditions and loaded luncheon-hampers recall an older, more eccentric, friend—Dr. Furnivall.[23] (Furnivall also provided one aspect of the appearance and *mise en scène* of Pan in 'The Piper at the Gates'. Professor Livingston Lowes describes 'an island in the Thames, where, of a Sunday afternoon, [Furnivall] used to recline against a tree, like a glorious old British river-god with white and curling beard'.[24]) The Downs are his natural horizon; it is that *alter ego* the Sea Rat who tempts him with stories of Sicily and Alassio. Even as early as *Pagan Papers* he appears, momentarily, as the foster-brother of Pan, the rural deity who may be found 'stretched on Ranmore Common, loitering under Abinger pines, or prone by the secluded stream of the sinuous Mole'[25]—an odd verbal coincidence.

There is one very striking literary source for Rat, and that is a story by Oscar Wilde called 'The Devoted Friend', which was published in *The Happy Prince* in 1888. The similarities are obvious and undeniable:

One morning the old Water-rat put his head out of his hole. He had bright beady eyes and stiff grey whiskers, and his tail was like a long bit of black indiarubber. The little ducks were swimming about in the pond . . . and their mother . . . was trying to teach them how to stand on their heads in the water. 'You will never be in the best society unless you can stand on your heads', she kept saying to them; and every now and then

she showed them how it was done. But the little ducks . . . were
so young that they did not know what an advantage it is to be
in society at all.[26]

Grahame must, too, have noted with sympathy how Wilde's
Water-rat described himself:

'Ah! I know nothing about the feelings of parents,' said the
Water-rat; 'I am not a family man. In fact I have never been
married, and I never intend to be. Love is all very well in its
way, but friendship is much higher. . . .'[27]

And that, of course, is one of the unspoken motifs running through
The Wind in the Willows, where nobody who matters is married,
or needs to work, and where the *summum bonum* is loyalty, with
creature comforts a close second: an apologia, in fact, for the
country bachelor's life.[28]

Badger, again, contains elements of Henley—in particular his
weakness for pontifical polysyllables off-set by vernacular slang,
and the gruffness which masked a vast benevolent paternalism.
He also bears an odd resemblance to old Mr. Iden in Richard
Jefferies' *Amaryllis at the Fair*: we have seen in the previous chapter
how extensively Jefferies influenced the whole background and
treatment of *The Wind in the Willows*.[29]

But, as in Mole's case, the greater part of Badger is autobiographical. It was Grahame—as we remember from those Campden
Hill soirées—who felt awkward and out of place in 'Society';
and it was certainly Grahame who turned 'rather low and despondent when he's wanting his victuals'.[30] Slip-shod but well-
equipped, indifferent to fashions but careful of comfort, Badger
represents Grahame's own conception of himself as the rural *ours
philanthropique*.[31]

The most attractive feature about him from his creator's point
of view, however, was undoubtedly his labyrinthine underground
home, safe from the storms and blizzards of the Wild Wood—
yet lying at the very heart of it. This grandiose, earthy catacomb,

partly based on Roman ruins (a neat symbolic touch) was a comforting, womb-like, protective concept. It may have been suggested in part by the eccentric activities of the fifth Duke of Portland, who 'had been given to disappearing for weeks; he had avoided the sight of his fellows, and built himself strange underground rooms and passages in his great park at Welbeck'.[32] These facts emerged during the hearing of the Druce case in 1907, about the time Mr. Badger's residence was being invented.

One of the most curious (and least commented-on) features of *The Wind in the Willows* is the frequency with which characters indulge in violent, eccentric, and near-pathological emotions or actions. This psychological ferment is in striking contrast to the rural tranquillity of the setting. We would expect Mole and Rat, at least, to behave with 'English self-restraint'; but not a bit of it. Mole goes into hysterical sobs at a whiff of his old home, while Rat (as we have seen) is hypnotized into a kind of hysterical trance by the Seafarer. But it is, of course, in Toad that such phenomena reach a peak of intensity; at times his behaviour almost suggests that he is, as it were, the Id personified.

If (as Miss Smedley affirmed)[33] Toad was partially intended to satirize Alastair himself, then some of his actions can be explained as mere childishness—his wailing and leg-kicking, and refusal to be comforted; the game he plays with chairs when locked up in his bedroom:

> He would arrange bedroom chairs in rude resemblance of a motor-car and would crouch on the foremost of them, bent forward and staring fixedly ahead, making uncouth and ghastly noises, till the climax was reached, when, turning a complete somersault, he would lie prostrate amidst the ruins of the chairs, apparently completely satisfied for the moment.[34]

But this can hardly be used as an over-all explanation; for the most part, indeed, Toad's behaviour is irresistibly suggestive of an adult manic-depressive. His entire life is a series of violent excesses matched by balancing moods of black and lachrymose despair; he shows the classic symptoms of irresponsibility, faddishness, bombastic fantasizing, tearful but impermanent repentance. Even A. A. Milne spotted something of this when he came to write *Toad of Toad Hall*: Alfred the horse remarks to Rat, after one of Toad's more curious outbursts: 'Psychological—that *was* the word he wanted. Not encyclopaedia. I thought it seemed funny somehow. Psychological.'[35]

Grahame himself hints at such a diagnosis by the language he uses to describe Toad's eccentricities. It is remarkably consistent and revealing. After the smashing of the caravan Toad is in 'a sort of trance', 'spell-bound, sleep-walking'; mention is made of his 'violent paroxysms', his 'painful seizures', his 'possession', in relation to motor-cars. This compulsive urge to steal cars is, on the evidence of the text, purely pathological. As Rat very sensibly asks, why *steal* them? Toad is rich enough to have bought —and to go on buying—cars by the dozen. But when he hears that familiar poop-poop! outside, he has to 'hold on to the leg of the table to conceal his overmastering emotion'. When, compulsively, he drives off in the car, 'as if in a dream, all sense of right and wrong, all fear of obvious consequences, seemed temporarily suspended'. And what goes on in his mind as he tears along the highway suggests the kind of compensation-fantasist for whom fast cars (now as then) symbolize unattained power, potency, or pure irresponsible authority:

> He was only conscious that he was Toad once more, Toad at his best and highest, Toad the terror, the traffic-queller, the Lord of the lone trail, before whom all must give way or be smitten into nothingness and everlasting night. He chanted as he flew, and the car responded with sonorous drone; the miles were eaten up under him as he sped he knew not whither, fulfilling his instincts, living his hour, reckless of what might come to him.[36]

What was it gave Grahame the impulse to introduce all these pathological traits of behaviour into *The Wind in the Willows*? In particular, where did he find the model for Toad's extraordinary, and very well-observed, symptoms—the specialized kleptomania, the complex manic-depressive behaviour? This problem remains something of a mystery. Up to a point there can be little doubt that he was describing his own unfulfilled and—in the normal way—firmly repressed urges: letting his anarchic Id out for a fictional romp. In this respect Toad has something in common with the Reluctant Dragon. But there remains the fact that the *external* symptoms are delineated with uncommon fidelity, as though taken directly from life. The only pathological character we know Grahame to have been on close terms with was old Dr. Furnivall, a compulsive but harmless exhibitionist: and while Furnivall may have supplied Toad's hearty insistence on making his friends share his own pleasures, there is no suggestion that he ever indulged in car-stealing.

Other elements are more easily traced. Toad's faddishness probably owed something to the unknown relative who inspired Uncle Thomas of *The Golden Age*; while (as I have already suggested) his flamboyant egotism, his *penchant* for after-dinner speaking, his scandalous downfall and imprisonment—these must surely reflect something of Oscar Wilde's tragedy.[37] Cookham Dene was almost in sight of Reading Gaol. Some psychologists might trace a sinister connection between Wilde's offence, the Wild Wood, Toad's behaviour with cars and Grahame's repressed emotions: but these are depths of speculation beyond the proper scope of any biographer, and in the present case more improbable than otherwise. It would be more accurate, perhaps, to see Toad as the symbol of Grahame's urge towards swashbuckling action and Romantic heterodoxy. But that queer pathological streak still remains to tantalize us.

Just as in his earlier books Grahame had achieved a convincing fluidity of viewpoint, which shifted without effort from child to adult, so with *The Wind in the Willows* he takes the process one step further. All the animal characters veer constantly between human and non-human behaviour. Rat lives in a river-bank hole, and also writes poetry. Mole burrows underground, but is capable of rounding up a horse from the paddock. As Mr. Guy Pocock intelligently observed,[38] the book is neither a pure animal book, nor 'a fairy tale like *Puss in Boots* in which an animal is simply a human being dressed up; for every now and then, for all its frank anthropomorphism, the story shows an extraordinary insight into the feelings and doings of little wild animals. . . . Rat is always a rat, though armed to the teeth; and Mole is always a mole even when he wears goloshes.' Perhaps the oddest instance of this duality is the moment when Toad is recognized for what he is by the bargewoman: instantly he ceases to be a humanized animal capable of driving cars or combing its hair in the middle, and becomes a mere toad, small t, to be thrown overboard in disgust.[39]

This fluidity explains why it has always been so difficult to illustrate *The Wind in the Willows* convincingly. Like Harold or Selina, the animals are not conceived in visual terms—or rather, they are never the same for two minutes running: both their size and their nature are constantly changing. Grahame himself was well aware of this problem, and dealt very prettily with queries about it. When asked specifically (apropos the escape on the railway train) whether Toad was life-size or train-size, he answered that he was both and neither: the Toad was train-size, the train was Toad-size, and therefore there could be no illustrations.[40] He later capitulated, and Mr. E. H. Shepard came as near as possible to capturing the essence of Rat, Mole, and Toad; but the point remains that the inner eye sees no incongruity in these metamorphoses (and in fact hardly notices them), while visual representation at once pins down Grahame's imagination to a single static concept.

An examination of the illustrated editions[41] confirms this point only too well. Again and again Grahame can suggest with words something which visual art, in the programmatic sense, not only fails to capture but renders fatally banal. The classic example is the mystical climax of 'The Piper at the Gates'. Every single attempt to illustrate the scene on Pan's Island is—must be— a disastrous failure. Maxfield Parrish, the American artist and illustrator of *The Golden Age*, writes of this chapter: 'Music might go with it, but nothing else'.[42] Graham Robertson, too, saw the impossibility of such an illustration: 'In the "appropriately pictured" edition [he begged Elspeth] we won't have a picture of Pan, will we? Perhaps a little bit of his shadow, but no more.'[43]

Pan is a special case, but Grahame's whole imaginative process in *The Wind in the Willows* lies beyond those fixed dimensions which every artist is compelled to impose by the very nature of his medium. There is no *stability* in Grahame's dream-world, and no incongruity. Human magistrates of a highly contemporary nature try and condemn toads to imprisonment in mediaeval dungeons guarded by halberdiers. The same toad can bargain with a gypsy for a horse, and ride off on it. Most curious of all, a humanized Rat and Mole can walk through a village on a winter's night, and still consider its inhabitants somehow alien—including their dogs and cats.* [44] This interchangeability of essential nature is Grahame's hall-mark; and the oddest thing about it is that it still leaves every character sharply defined and psychologically consistent. Perhaps only a writer who combined a satirist's talent with the imperturbable vision of a child could have managed it.[45]

* I am grateful to Mr. David Daiches for pointing out how this scene in 'Dulce Domum', with its observation of human domesticity through the window, from the outside, also derives from a favourite motif of R. L. Stevenson's.

XIII

THE VANISHING DREAM
1908-1913

Is there anything in life so disenchanting as attainment?
R. L. STEVENSON: *The Suicide Club*

> Thou shalt make castels than in Spayne,
> And dreme of joye, al but in vayne.
> GEOFFREY CHAUCER: *Romaunt of the Rose*

The road must needs follow each contour moulded
By that fire in its losing fight with earth:
We march over our past, we may behold it
Dreaming a slave's dream on our bivouac hearth.
Lost the archaic dawn wherein we started,
The appetite for wholeness: now we prize
Half-loaves, half-truths—enough for the half-hearted,
The gleam snatched from corruption satisfies.
C. DAY-LEWIS: *O Dreams, O Destinations*

> O suitably-attired-in-leather-boots,
> Head of a traveller, wherefore seeking whom
> Whence by what way how purposed art thou come
> To this well-nightingaled vicinity?
> A. E. HOUSMAN: *Fragment of a Greek Tragedy*

While *The Wind in the Willows* was slowly coming to fruition, Grahame continued to perform his not very onerous duties at the Bank of England: in much the same spirit, it seems, as Charles

Lamb at the East India House. He entertained King George V's children to tea, showed them round the vaults, and let them each sign a £1000 bank-note: this visit took place on 23rd April 1907.[1] He was popular with junior officials, and seems to have been at some pains, as one of them later wrote, 'to adapt the Queen's English to the purposes of official letters. . . . I listened carefully to some advice he once gave me on the subject of punctuation and the construction of sentences.'[2] But, as the same witness remarked of him, he did not fit in with one's preconceived notions of a Bank official; and the literary aura which by now hung round him probably made his colleagues a little uneasy.

From the point of view of the Governor and the Court of Directors, we may surmise, Grahame had certain disabilities as a Secretary. Chief among these, without any doubt, was his frequent absence through illness. He had never been a wholly well man since his dangerous attack of empyema in 1899, and the mental stress under which he had been living thenceforward must have pulled him down physically as well. Consequently he tended to work short hours and take long holidays. A young member of his staff recently wrote:

> I was too much of a junior to have any personal contact with him in the Bank. My only recollection is of a tall figure striding through the Secretary's outer office shortly before four o'clock, bound for Paddington and Cookham Dene. Even in those more leisurely days it seemed an unconscionably early hour for such an important figure to be leaving for home, but I think the explanation lay in the fact that he had already been warned by his doctors of a decline in health, and he did, in fact, retire very soon afterwards.[3]

Was Grahame's premature retirement exclusively to do with the state of his health? We cannot be certain. Chalmers, indeed, has no doubts on the matter. He speaks of 'an intermittent and virulent form of influenza', and a Harley Street opinion that Grahame must give up his sedentary City life. He further claims that the Court of Directors begged Grahame, instead of retiring, to take a year's holiday with full pay. Though other documents relative to Grahame's resignation were carefully preserved by Elspeth, this one does not appear among them. There is something improbable about the whole story, and one or two hints from external sources suggest an alternative version. To begin with, there is a persistent tradition in banking circles that Grahame did not get on well with William Campbell Middleton, the new Governor appointed in 1907. There is also that curious anxiety-dream which Grahame at this time incorporated into 'Bertie's Escapade'. Some of it, considered in a professional context, is highly interesting: 'At last the Chairman rose, and said "He can't think of anything to say! *Turn him out!*"'[4] (When he *has* been flung out, as tends to happen with forced resignations in real life, everyone sings 'For he's a jolly good fellow!')

It certainly looks as though Grahame may have been under some kind of official pressure: and if the dream he recorded is any guide at all, this pressure must have been connected with his conduct as Secretary. Inability to speak in a dream generally implies some real or imputed incapacity connected with one's daily life. Grahame could very easily have got off on the wrong foot with Middleton, who had the reputation of being a tough, efficient, go-ahead Governor: a new broom very ready to sweep clean. There is the further point that Grahame resigned in June 1908, four months before *The Wind in the Willows* was published. He was not seriously ill at the time: would it not have been more prudent and more practical to wait till the end of the year, when fresh royalties might well be pouring in? Lastly, the pension granted him by the Court of Directors was no more than £400 p.a.—a surprisingly low figure for a retiring Secretary, even one forced to abdicate early through illness, and hardly consistent with their supposed generous offer of a year's holiday on full pay. The decision, communicated to him on 2nd July, is couched in the coldest of official language; and no personal letters of sympathy or farewell from his colleagues at the Bank survive among his private papers.

Obviously there can be no final proof in this matter. But if there *was* official disagreement between Grahame and the new Governor, it would suggest yet one more contributory cause to the sense of terror and the motifs of pursuit by Authority which run through *The Wind in the Willows*. It might, too, have had another and at first sight more beneficent effect. Whatever the reason, Grahame's long stint aboard the galley was over. Now, at last, he could see the Good Life within reach: and that prospect may well have spurred him on to capture in words what was shortly to become reality.

Yet here again we sense impending tragedy. He had waited too long and compromised too often; above all he was no longer the 'felowe that goes alone'. Perhaps (with all the experience of his childhood behind him) he guessed that the Good Life, when it came, would fall hopelessly short of the long-cherished dream: if so, what he did—as in *The Golden Age*—was to make the dream immortal before it was destroyed. And he succeeded. Despite its disturbing landscape and deep-rooted symbolism—indeed, Grahame celebrated his release from bondage on the very first page—the book *does* succeed somehow in giving an over-all impression of still, warm peace and tranquillity. The occasional anachronisms that 'date' it—early motor-cars, references to Kitchener or Garibaldi—fail to make any real impression on our minds: its atmosphere is outside history. It embodies in miniature the whole essence of pre-1914 England—the smooth lawns, the river-picnics, the long, sun-drenched days of idleness, the holidays in Italy, the self-assurance and the stable values. The currents of change and revolution do little more than ruffle the surface of this summer stream: they eddy deep below among the sinuous weeds, unseen, biding their time.

What Grahame did, by creating this self-sufficient world, was to stop the clock. In *The Wind in the Willows* there is no sense

Kenneth Grahame, aged about 60

of time: only, against the repetitive seasonal cycle, an Arcadian Nirvana. Nothing changes: Pan sits for ever with the pipes close to his lips, and the whole scene holds the dynamic immobility of Keats' Grecian Urn. This is what gives the book its mythic, perennial quality to the conscious mind; its other stimuli operate more subtly.

One of Grahame's staunchest admirers was—of all people—Theodore Roosevelt, who wrote asking for autographed copies of *The Golden Age* and *Dream Days*, and invited their author several times, in vain, to come over and stay at the White House.[5] (Another even more improbable fan was Kaiser Wilhelm, who only had two books in his cabin on the royal yacht *Hohenzollern*: the Bible and *The Golden Age*.[6]) In due course Grahame sent Roosevelt a copy of *The Wind in the Willows*; and after the usual initial disappointment at the absence of children, the President became a staunch convert—partly through the prodding of his family.

This turned out very much to Grahame's advantage. Curtis Brown, his literary agent, had experienced (as he tells us in his memoirs) great difficulty in marketing the new book:

> I tried it with magazine editors all over England and America. They thought it too fantastic and wouldn't have it. Then it went to Charles Scribner, father of the present Charles. He said it wouldn't go; but just then he got a letter from Theodore Roosevelt . . . saying . . . that it was such a beautiful thing that Scribner *must* publish it.

He did. In England Methuen proved equally sceptical at first; he did not even have sufficient faith in the book to pay a guaranteed advance on it. Nevertheless, convinced that he had nothing to lose, he 'agreed to excellent rising royalties, just in case the book *should* fulfil my dreams'.[7] The University of Oxford (to which foundation Grahame's copyright eventually reverted), and in particular the Bodleian Library, have cause to be grateful for Curtis Brown's optimistic contract.

Grahame was too busy with the completion and publication of *The Wind in the Willows* to celebrate his new-found independence by going abroad at once: perhaps he was even anxious to postpone the moment of discovery. He spent much time with Alastair in the woods and lanes round Cookham, teaching him country lore, recapturing something of his own youthful spirit through the child's wonder.[8] Constance Smedley was a regular visitor, and has left us a vivid description of the domestic *mise en scène* at Mayfield:

> I remember [she wrote] the sloe gin poured into tiny cordial glasses . . . the ceremony of the salad, served in a great basket with herbs and flasks of condiments and solemnly prepared by Mr. Grahame; the rows of tear-bottles of Bristol glass, the peasant toys from all countries, the wonderful collections of old glass and china used, not only looked at. One night I remember being greatly intrigued. Some very tall glasses with a curious convoluted edge were before us through which one saw everything as through the wrong end of an opera glass. They were most fascinating to drink out of: Mr. and Mrs. Grahame appeared like animated toys miles away across a miniature dining-table. When I left, the housekeeper was waiting in the hall with one of these glasses most beautifully packed up and tied. 'It is the custom', said Mr. Grahame, 'to give your guest the cup he has drunk from.'[9]

Miss Smedley had a tremendously fey side to her which perhaps appealed to Elspeth rather more than to Kenneth. One of the odder examples of this was a Fairy-tale Dinner which she organized that autumn at the Women's Lyceum Club in Piccadilly, and for which she enlisted the Grahames' support. Her idea was to re-create, for an evening, the magic world of Grimm and Andersen: 'the world', as she inimitably described it, 'of William Morris without its cruelty, savage passions and fighting and its somewhat heavy sexuality. The princes and princesses, the goose-girls and swineherds love and mate [*sic*] in simple kindliness. It did not seem inappropriate to bring the atmosphere for one evening into the Lyceum Club.'[10]

The actual dinner was less startling than this might suggest, but by no means less bizarre. Miss Smedley herself was the Fairy Princess, complete with a 'bower of autumn foliage'; the guests were presented with the Order of the Golden Rabbit, and Grahame was told to produce a menu, which included goldfish, cream tarts, and (of course) gingerbread. The high-light of the evening seems to have been 'the arrival of Grimm and Andersen who supped in an adjoining room and sent in constant messages for Soup from a Sausage Peg, Buns and other delicacies'. The evening was rounded off with toasts in rowan wine and exchanges of fairy stories. 'On such occasions', Miss Smedley recorded, 'I felt thoroughly at home.' How Grahame felt we can only guess.

On 3rd November he wrote the first surviving letter in a long correspondence with his American friend Austin Purves:[11]

> The fact is [he told Purves blandly] when one has written letters for many years for one's daily bread, and suddenly finds oneself free of them, a revulsion sets in which must be allowed to work itself off.

After thanking Purves for reviewing *The Wind in the Willows* for an American magazine, and discussing the holiday activities of the Purves boys, he went on to talk of his and Elspeth's plans for future travels:

> I am hoping to manage it after the New Year—in Switzerland to begin with, and then perhaps a drop into the northern part of Italy, for colour and anemones and Chianti and so on. If I can get E. sufficiently patched up for the journey. By the way, about her photo. She has not been done for many years, and now absolutely refuses to undergo the process until she is less of a Living Skellington. . . .
> We have had a beautiful summer here, and now we are having an equally beautiful autumn—still and misty and mild and full of colour. I had a jolly day at Oxford a short time ago.

Everything in full swing and the river covered with men doing 'tubbing' practice. The old place was just as beautiful as ever, and I bought some youthful ties and some 'Oxford sausages' in the delightful market—they are a small species without any skins on their poor little persons—and took a walk down Mesopotamia, and explored many old corners.

We can't extract any Fowey news from Q, who is probably mighty busy, and neither Atky nor Miss Marsden have given any sign of life for a long time. I wish we could get down there for a bit before the year closes. Perhaps it may yet be possible.

For some reason, however, he and Elspeth went to Devonshire instead, where he caught influenza yet again. It left him weak and groggy; by mid-December he could still 'only walk a mile or two, and then an armchair and slumber until dinner-time'. The mummers turned up at Mayfield, and disappointed him sadly: 'Hardly any of the good old "St. George and the Dragon" play left', he informed Purves. 'Instead, cheap comic songs from the London music halls. But Mouse liked it.' He added drily: 'E. is Christmassing for all she's worth and is not precisely sane at the present season'. There was still no news from Fowey.[12] On the other hand there was a begging-letter from Trant Chambers, who had edited the *St. Edward's Chronicle* with Grahame, and was now a hopeless down-and-out, 'friendless, hungry, penniless, shelterless and without immediate prospect of any kind'.[13] Once again time had shattered the precious yet illusory memories of youth. Grahame sent him a cheque by return, and tried to forget the incident. But he was not to be so easily rid of his former school-fellow; throughout the years this pathetic and destitute drunkard continued to send appeals to Grahame at irregular intervals, turning the knife in old memories, emphasizing the gap between recollection and reality.[14]

By the beginning of 1909 Grahame seems to have withdrawn himself still further into his private world of fantasy. Retirement probably accelerated the process, though it can hardly account for the whimsical tinge which now began to creep into his corre-spondence. When Constance Smedley announced her engagement, in January, Grahame congratulated her on choosing Gloucester-shire for a home—'at least there is only one more possible county, and that is Double-Gloucestershire—if you can find the way there'. This provoked him to a catalogue of 'astral' counties ('Lie-in-bedfordshire is warm and sheltered, an excellent county for a prolonged stay'); but the letter closes with a flash of his old sardonic wit: 'E. will be writing to you herself, and as for Mouse, I dare not tell him, for he cannot keep a secret [cf. Toad and the secret passage] and would run out tomorrow to tell all the pigs and cows. And as you say, it will be time for all the pigs and cows to know on or about the 20th.'[15]

In February Kenneth and Elspeth left England on their pro-jected trip to Switzerland and Italy, from which they returned in the spring. This long-awaited return to the South raises some interesting problems. Chalmers states categorically[16] that every year after his retirement from the Bank Grahame spent from February to May following the sun northward from Sicily. Documentary evidence tells a different story. The compulsive Mediterranean travelling which Chalmers mentions took place either before Grahame's marriage or (for reasons which will be apparent later) after 1920. During the war, of course, such holidays were impossible; but between 1908 and 1914 the Grahames only went abroad once after this first venture: and that was not to Italy but Brittany.

There is no conceivable reason why Chalmers should deliber-ately present a false picture of events, and indeed, with Elspeth closely supervising every stage of his work, he would have had little opportunity to do so. We must assume that (as in the parallel case of the dating of Grahame's essays[17]) he accepted Elspeth's own version. But why should Elspeth have wanted to suggest Mediterranean journeys that did not in fact take place?

The odd thing is that if she had left well alone, no suspicions would have been aroused. In January 1910 Grahame was writing to Purves: 'We are both somewhat stale and rusty and I want to smell foreign smells again and drink wine in the country where it grows; but we feel it would be wiser to get our troubles [house-moving] over first'. This seems reasonable enough till we notice the significant switch from 'we' to 'I'; and again, as if to emphasize the point, Grahame says, '*I* want to go on *my* travels with a light heart'.

Here we are in the realm of conjecture; but a plausible hypothesis may, I think, be advanced to explain Elspeth's treatment of this period. Surprisingly but suggestively, there is no evidence that Elspeth had ever been abroad with Grahame since their marriage. (His trip to Spain in 1904, for instance, was made independently.) It is very likely that he would wish to keep his Southern dream-landscape, with all its memories, private and inviolate. The trips he made to Italy were solitary emotional pilgrimages: and it seems infinitely probable that the joint visit with Elspeth was an inner, if not an acknowledged, disaster. (It is only too easy to imagine Elspeth rhapsodizing over his cherished symbols, and thus for ever destroying them.) Brittany was a compromise; it offered neutral territory, uncharged with associative memories.

But Elspeth could not admit defeat, or, indeed, anything less than perfection: and she had to convince the world—perhaps even herself—that she had shared in Kenneth's Southern expeditions from the moment of his release. Hence, in all probability, the picture she painted for Chalmers: she was, after all, only anticipating the truth by twelve years or so. It was an infinitely pathetic gesture, rather on a par with her efforts to prove that Kenneth was still working productively later than 1910.

There are other hints that some sort of emotional crisis may have taken place on that Italian trip. By July Grahame was deep in the grip of a paralysing indolence which henceforth never entirely left him. Apologizing to Austin Purves for his shortcomings as a correspondent, he reveals his state of mind with fascinating clarity.

> And yet, do you know, I do write you any quantity of magnificent letters. In my armchair of evenings, with closed eyes—strolling in the woods of afternoons—or with head on pillow very late on a thoroughly wet and disagreeable morning. I see my pen covering page after page of cream-laid parchment-wove extra antique. Such good stuff, too—witty, anecdotal, pensive, pathetic—I feel myself lick the envelope—I see myself running to the post—I hear the flop of the letter in the box. It's all so real to me—that I was quite surprised to find that you weren't asking me to limit them to, say, three a week. Please believe, that if they never reach you, *it's not my fault.*[18]

Both the indolence and the intensification of Grahame's fantasy life may have been the result of emotional shock, a self-protective defence set up against disappointing reality. The long-dreamed-of release had proved, in the event, a mirage.

This was by no means entirely Elspeth's fault, but was an essential condition of Grahame's character. Elspeth may well have been an irksome travelling companion on a journey to the Hesperides; but with her or without her, the Golden Apples (once they could be plucked whenever Grahame chose) turned out nothing more than common or garden oranges after all. Grahame himself revealed this idealistic attitude to life—and the disappointments it entailed—with great candour in his late essay, 'Ideals', first published in 1922. 'Do we not', he wrote, 'nearly always find in our past imaginings . . . just those two touchstones of the ideal —a fantastic unlikeness to the real thing, together with a special beauty nowhere else to be found?' The real Rome is a perilous disappointment when compared with our ideal image of it; life never measures up to the dream of what life might be; experience is a continual and deepening disappointment. It is the imaginative romantic idealist's classic *cri de cœur*. And so Grahame retreated deeper into his English, as opposed to his Mediterranean, myth:

the Cockayne of boating and food and rural seclusion. It was 'Wayfarers All' all over again; and once more Mole had defeated Rat.

Summer that year was miserable, wet and cold, and boating remained out of the question. Elspeth was suffering from inflammation of the optic nerve in one eye,[19] which debarred her from reading; Alastair, as Grahame wrote to Purves, was 'down at his favourite sea-side resort—Littlehampton, a rather horrid little place, which he adores'. Then, as though to anticipate comment, Grahame produces an oddly flimsy pair of excuses for Elspeth and himself not being with the boy: 'I wish our taste in places were similar, so that we could be together; but in any case E. can't take her bad eye to the sea yet, on account of the glare'. And a few lines earlier he had been complaining of July's rainy dismalness! We remember an exactly similar situation in the summer of 1907; it almost looks as though both Kenneth and Elspeth *avoided* having holidays with Alastair.

But there were consolations, for Kenneth at any rate: chief among them two surprise visits from 'Atky', who 'just dropped from the clouds, without notice, ate a hearty lunch, talked a great deal, and flitted away again into the outer darkness'. Kenneth also managed to get away for a flying visit to the Quiller-Couches at Fowey, where he met a young Oxford *littérateur* named Compton Mackenzie. Fan-mail continued to pour in from all over the world: Kenneth's grateful readers included Alfred Deakin, the Prime Minister of Australia; a charming Boston spinster who enquired, 'If you keep writing books that I have to read all the time, how am I ever going to read anything else?'; children of all ages, everywhere; and Margot Asquith, who decided that *The Golden Age* would be good for her German governess—and *en passant* made some shrewd comments on the book itself: 'The right to pursue one's own individuality without being constantly corrected can only be given by real mothers and fathers. The conscientious wish to do what you are paid for—

teach and correct—lies hard in the bosom of Authority.' Her final judgment was that *The Golden Age* 'is so horribly true and *innig* [heartfelt, intimate]'—with which we may well agree.

By autumn the lease of Mayfield was running out, and the area was becoming too thickly populated for the Grahames' taste.[20] They were busy house-hunting, with very little success, till the New Year. Meanwhile Lloyd George had introduced his radical People's Budget, which had repercussions all over the country, dividing friends and causing tremendous agitation: Lord Rosebery described it as 'Socialism, the end of all—the negation of Faith, of Family, of Monarchy, of Empire'. The stoats and weasels were indeed having a time of it, though today the proposals seem mild enough: a super-tax of 6d. in the £ over £3,000, slight additional duty on spirits and tobacco, and new land taxes.

This Budget was finally passed in November 1909 but thrown out by the Lords, and a General Election loomed ahead. Q, to Grahame's irritation, came out strongly in favour of Lloyd George: 'Q is frightfully busy over the election,' he wrote to Purves, 'propagating his pernicious doctrines throughout the west country'; and to Q himself he declared, perhaps only half-humorously: 'I must not wish you luck in your nefarious designs on our savings, our cellars, and our garden-plots; but I do hope you'll get some fun out of it'. Q did; and three years later he wrote a most entertaining account of his electioneering activities in *News from the Duchy*.

Alastair, too, expressed himself forcibly about the hated Budget. He was ten, and more precocious than ever; but his concern with politics went back a considerable way, and was almost certainly instilled into him by Elspeth, who had been a staunch Liberal campaigner for her stepfather. Two years before, his governess, Miss Stott, had written to Elspeth that Mouse liked 'to have discussions with Miss Passey. Their latest "bone" is a political sort. She upholds the Conservative Party, & he denounces that party and borrows the word "cursed" from Spenser to describe his foes and their doings. I heard her say "Liberals are not to be trusted any more than Chapel people, and Gladstone was a wicked old man". Mouse rolled up his sleeves and suggested a fight with fists. . . .' [21] But the Budget changed his attitude—which probably means that it had changed Elspeth's: 'You may be sorry to hear,' Grahame wrote to Q, 'that, after being a staunch Liberal all his life [Alastair] has lately crossed the floor of the House. "I had been having doubts for some time," he said: "and this Budget is the last straw." I tell him that there are many good points about the Budget; but he only replies that he has failed to detect any.' [22]

After Christmas Grahame at last found the house he had been looking for, in the village of Blewbury, near Didcot. (He still remained firmly attached to Berkshire.) 'Boham's' was a brick farm-house, with a thatched roof, which dated back to the Tudor period. There were two splendid farm-kitchens, a granary, an apple-loft, and a trout-stream. When eight coats of paint had been removed from the doors they turned out to be three-hundred-year-old linen-folded oak. [23] Grahame wrote loving descriptions of his new property to various friends about a fort-night after moving in. The best, as we should expect, was to Austin Purves:

Blewbury is perhaps the most beautiful of a string of very pretty and very primitive villages stretched along the northern edge of the Berkshire Downs. It is only about 54 miles from London, but 5400 years remote from it in every way. This is the heart of King Alfred's country, 'Alfred the Great' who beat the Danes close by here; about 860, and nothing has really happened since. True, a tiresome innovator called William the Conqueror came along some years later, and established a thing called the Curfew bell, which still rings here during the winter months, to the annoyance of the more conservative inhabitants, who say they used to get on very well before these new-fangled notions; but this is all that divides us from Saxon times. . . .

'A little way off,' he informed Constance Smedley with evident delight, 'there is a farmer whose family has been here for a thousand years. They are real Saxons. They live in a lovely old farm-house with a ghost in it. Indeed all the houses here are very old. They do not build the horrid little red houses that spring up round Cookham.' He was retreating further and further into the protection of the past: not only the pre-Industrial Revolution now, but pre-Conquest. A letter to Alan Lidderdale gives some of the more mundane details:[24]

> We moved into this little old farmhouse a fortnight ago, and have been slaving ever since to get it straight, with very little result—the trouble being that we have got too much stuff for so small a space. I was very sorry to leave Cookham Dean, [sic] but there was really nothing there that suited us at all. This is a very beautiful village, in quite a different way, and the Downs are at one's door. I hope for some fine walking when I have finished picture-hanging and falling over rolls of carpet.
>
> Mouse is down at the sea-side, to be out of all this stramash. E. hunts chickens—dead ones—through the village all day, & tries to persuade the farmers wives to part with provisions of any sort, which they refuse to do.

Before the end of May Theodore Roosevelt arrived in Oxford to give the Romanes Lecture. Warren of Magdalen, his host, enquired whether there were any people he particularly wished to meet, and Roosevelt listed Kipling, Andrew Lang, Grahame, Gilbert Murray, and Charles Oman, the historian. Grahame had a long talk with Roosevelt after the lecture, and Roosevelt himself later described Grahame in the *Saturday Evening Post* as 'simply charming'.[25] About the same time an American scholar named Clayton Hamilton, who was in London collecting material for a book on Stevenson, managed to get an invitation for a week-end at Boham's, and coaxed a good deal of interesting talk out of his host.[26]

'He was very tall and broad,' Professor Hamilton recollected, 'a massive figure, but with no spare flesh. At that time he was fifty years of age. His hair was white, but his face was almost beatifically young, and he had the clear and roseate complexion of a healthy child. He was dressed in knickerbockers, a soft shirt, and a baggy coat of tweeds.' Grahame seemed to his visitor uneasy indoors: he would lapse into silence for an hour or more. But as soon as the two of them got away for a solitary cross-country walk, Grahame 'would break into an easy current of cheery conversation'. Clearly he had certain inhibitions about letting himself go in Elspeth's presence; and in any case she had a weakness for monopolizing the conversation.

Professor Hamilton records several long disquisitions of Grahame's *verbatim*; and though these must obviously be treated with certain reservations (unless the Professor had a really phenomenal memory) they almost certainly represent the essence of Grahame's credo: [27]

> The most priceless possession of the human race is the wonder of the world. Yet, latterly, the utmost endeavours of mankind have been directed towards the dissipation of that wonder. . . . Science analyses everything to its component parts, and neglects to put them together again. . . . Nobody, any longer, may hope to entertain an angel unawares, or to meet Sir Launcelot in shining armour on a moonlit road. But what is the use of living in a world devoid of wonderment? . . . Granted that the average man may live for seventy years, it is a fallacy to assume that his life from sixty to seventy is more important than his life from five to fifteen. Children are not merely people: they are the only really living people that have been left to us in an over-weary world. . . .
>
> In my tales about children, I have tried to show that their simple acceptance of the mood of wonderment, their readiness to welcome a perfect miracle at any hour of the day or night, is a thing more precious than any of the laboured acquisitions of adult mankind . . .

This, undoubtedly, Grahame firmly believed, and it shows out in *The Golden Age* and *Dream Days*. But when it came to *The Wind in the Willows*, he once again flagrantly defied the evidence of his own text:

As for animals, I wrote about the most familiar and domestic in *The Wind in the Willows* because I felt a duty to them as a friend. Every animal, by instinct, lives according to his nature. Thereby he lives wisely, and betters the tradition of mankind. No animal is ever tempted to belie his nature. No animal, in other words, knows how to tell a lie. Every animal is honest. Every animal is straightforward. Every animal is true—and is, therefore, according to his nature, both beautiful and good.

It hardly needs pointing out that none of the animals in *The Wind in the Willows* is domestic, and that several of them (Toad in particular) know very well how to tell lies.

But the principle enunciated, of virtuous instinct, the 'natural' condition, is peculiarly interesting in itself. It goes back to Grahame's two essays, 'The Lost Centaur' and 'Orion': it looks directly forward to D. H. Lawrence's anti-urban cult of self-fulfilment through the blood. The odd thing is that Grahame never saw the logical consequences of his *credo*; he had managed to remove sex altogether somewhere along the line. Even towards the end of his life he never actually managed to read Lawrence (it would have been interesting to observe his reactions to *The Plumed Serpent*): apparently, according to Mr. Malcolm Elwin, 'he knew nothing of his work except the contemporary fuss over *Lady Chatterley's Lover*, of which he said that it was allowing realism to run riot if we were to print words which hooligans wrote upon the walls of public lavatories, and he could see no merit in describing a physical act which every adult person performed sooner or later'.

It is interesting to consider this personal attitude in the light of evidence thrown on the Grahame's domestic *ménage* by the Purveses. Mr. Purves and his wife (but not their children) came over to England in July 1910, and stayed with the Grahames. Grahame had suggested, rather desperately, that Purves might care to 'walk from here, by way of the Downs, to Fowey? Atky says six weeks would do it quite comfortably.' (Atky was now roaming between Corsica and Sardinia; each year, as Grahame put it, 'his St. Anthony's fever seems to agitate his lean limbs more violently'.) But Purves prudently declined: he and his wife spent their time photographing local beauty-spots, and keeping an astonished eye on their host and hostess:

> I remember clearly [writes Mr. Austin Purves, Jr.] my mother's amusement, or consternation, or both, at the fact that Mr. and Mrs. Grahame lived in separate parts of the house. My parents were very connubial and the Grahames simply expected their guests to enjoy the same household and sleeping arrangements as they themselves did. . . . Anyway, at breakfast after this nocturnal separation of the sexes there was tea and toast and one egg. Mrs. Grahame said: The egg is for Kenneth.[28]

There was no doubt that by now the Grahames were becoming mildly eccentric recluses. Andrew Lang and Edmund Gosse both lamented the fact that they never saw Kenneth any more, and that he only came to London once in a blue moon.[29] Guests were warned against bringing evening clothes; and Grahame seems to have spoken no less than the truth when he told R. E. Moody, the artist: 'We live here in a state of primitive simplicity which is almost shocking'.[30] Elspeth was determined that the whole village should revolve about her; she stumped round with a stick (and in clattering sabots after her Brittany expedition) laying down the law and getting laughed at behind her back. She seldom got up before eleven, often went to bed in her clothes, and kept rolls of silk and satin dresses upstairs which she never wore: she preferred an ancient navy-blue serge coat and skirt, with a frayed cardigan and hand-knitted stockings. Much of the time she spent on her divan, sipping hot water. She ate practically nothing, and mouse-nests proliferated in the larder; she put Kenneth into special underwear which was only changed once a year.[31] It is perhaps not surprising that he took a long solitary walk on the Ridgeway every day.

Publishers were still busy dangling baits for him, however. On 27th July he received a letter from Gordon Home of A. & C. Black, asking him to write a 40,000 word book called *Highways and Hedges*, which was to give the reader a breath of country life as seen from the hedgerow and suggest any ideas that such scenes conjure up. It could, said Home, warming to his theme, contain 'anecdotes, folk-lore, philosophy, political economy, botany, ornithology, and references to anything and everything that rambles in beautiful English country are likely to bring to mind'. Grahame found the idea attractive, and persuaded Home to grant him the right to publish in serial form; but the whole thing foundered when Home proposed a £50 fee for the whole rights in lieu of royalties. Not unnaturally, Grahame refused. We may regret Home's shortsightedness: this is a book which Grahame would have done superbly.[32]

Autumn and winter passed in a country round of sheep-fairs, circuses, and village gossip. At East Ilsley sheep-fair 'Mouse was soon in the thick of it, but when I sought him out and discovered him bidding at the auction for pedigree rams [Grahame wrote] I had to haul him out of action'. It was all very rural and back-to-nature; but there is a certain wistfulness in Grahame's complaint to Q, that Christmas, of missing all the chief events and pageants of life. But he was down with another attack of bronchitis at the time, which must have depressed him; and he was saddened by the premature death of Roland's wife, Joan, after an unexpected heart attack.

In February of 1911 the whole family, Alastair now included, began a prolonged holiday, first at the Lizard, then at Fowey, which continued till the end of April. 'I want Mouse to make the acquaintance of my Cornish haunts, and friends, before he goes to school', Grahame told Purves; and on the whole this holiday seems to have been a success. Alastair enjoyed himself in the wild scenery round the Lizard; at Fowey there were the Quiller-Couches, and Atky, who provided magnificent lunches ('mostly

fancy hors-d'œuvres and every sort of sausage') and let the boy
browse among his books and records.

But Alastair was now eleven; and it was high time for him to
be sent to school, whatever misgivings his parents may have had.
(Kenneth had supplemented the teaching of Miss Stott with his
own general knowledge papers: his idiosyncratic questions were
only matched by Alastair's pseudo-adult—and often highly
amusing—answers. Example: *What do you know about the Phoenix?*
'The Phenix is an inshurance co. There is only *one* at a time.
Before it dies it lights a bonfire and roosts on it and when it is
dead a new Phenix pops out of the ashes—but is it a new one?
peradventure it is the same old bird all the time?? tut-tut! a strange
bird it lives 100 years.') The school chosen was The Old Malthouse, at Langton Matravers, near Wareham, on the Dorset coast,
and Mouse went there soon after Easter, 1911. His departure is
faintly reminiscent of Edward's in *The Golden Age*:

> Since we got back from Cornwall we have been very busy
> fitting M. out for school and getting him off. The joy and pride
> of a complete new outfit of clothes—including even 'Eton'
> jacket and trousers for Sundays—no doubt mitigated the pangs.
> At any rate he made the great plunge last Monday, going off
> very manfully and composedly, and from what we hear he is
> falling into the ways of the new life very well. It is very quiet
> here now without him.[33]

The Old Malthouse, in fact, turned out to be the only school where
the boy was happy and relaxed: it seems to have been a cheerful,
friendly, permissive place, very far from the harsh discipline and
narrow ethics of the typical contemporary prep school.

Alastair's letters from The Old Malthouse shed as much incidental light on his parents as they do on his own activities. 'My
dear Madame,' he writes to Elspeth on 21st May, 'your humble
servant is glad to hear that improvements are coming up like
bulbs and that Inferiority is doing some work *at last*!' A pencilled
note in Elspeth's handwriting informs us that 'Inferiority was

Mayfield, Cookham Dene
Boham's, Blewbury

his whimsical [*sic*] name for his father at that time'. Comment would be superfluous. The 'improvements' were to Boham's: we do not know their exact nature. Nor do we know what Grahame was supposed to be working at; whatever it was came to nothing.

In September an unhappy tragedy occurred. 'Atky' was drowned while out yachting with Bevil Quiller-Couch, despite the younger man's gallant attempts to rescue him. Grahame wrote to Purves:

> Again and again in imagination I get into my boat at White-house Steps and scull up the river by the grey old sea-wall, under the screaming gulls, past the tall Russian and Norwegian ships at their moorings, and so into Mixton Pill, and ship my oars at the little stone pier, and find Atky waiting on the steps, thin, in blue serge, with his Elizabethan head; and stroll up the pathway you know, to the little house above it, and be talking all the time and always some fresh whimsicality. . . . I feel as if we had all suddenly grown much older. All, that is, except Atky. He couldn't do it; he didn't know how.[34]

The old familiar faces were going, the timeless myth slowly being destroyed; the creative spark was nearly dead. As Bardolph told Pistol, 'the fuel is gone that maintained that fire'. Only country solitude now remained for comfort.

Alastair was returned to school on 28th September, and Kenneth and Elspeth went for a few weeks to Pont-Aven in Southern Brittany, 'because', as Grahame put it to Curtis Brown, 'we want something fairly cheap—and not too far—and yet proper foreign. . . . It has been a beautiful summer here—but I want a change of diet and a change of smells—and I believe the smells of some of the Brittany ports are very rich and satisfying.'[35] Yet on his return he wrote to Purves: 'We had rather an interesting time in Brittany in the late autumn—saw a lot of new country and new things. But to me that is not the *South* and therefore— nothing. You've got to have the Alps to the north of you before the air begins to have the right feel in it.'[36] Then why, we may ask, did he not go South? The plea of poverty was absurd: by now he was affluent—though Elspeth watched every penny. It looks inescapably as though he was unwilling to cross the Alps at this period other than alone.

All the same, he had a pleasant enough time at Pont-Aven. He was addressed (appropriately enough, considering his semimilitary appearance) as 'Mon Colonel', and invited to take part in a full-dress Breton wedding. Elspeth recounts an interesting, if improbable, anecdote of his compulsive effect on small children: as soon as he arrived at his hotel, she says, he was surrounded by a group of Breton urchins, all demanding a story—in a language they could not understand. Those with experience of small Breton children outside hotels might surmise that they were offering to shine the English milord's shoes, or simply begging for coppers— Elspeth never missed an opportunity of making events square with her preconceptions.[37]

They returned to a vile winter of storms and high winds: 'I hardly get out at all now,' Grahame wrote to Q in December, 'as we are surrounded by a sea of mud. I never knew mud was so potent. And gale after gale comes battering down on us. I was explaining to E the other day that wind does not always move in a strict horizontal plane, backwards and forwards, which did not seem to have occurred to her; & later I found myself browsing, before the fire, on Milton, & reading, or trying to read, the *Epitaphium Damonis*; & I came to

> at malus Auster
> Miscet cuncta foris, et *desuper intonat ulmo*

& that struck me as rather jolly.'[38] In another letter to Curtis Brown he declared: 'When this sea of mud abates, I will go forth once more on the Downs, and give it prayerful consideration among my friends the hares and plovers'.

But about his writing he said nothing, for there was nothing to say. What he had produced was the fruit of a certain conflict in the mind: first, the tension between his banking career and his Hesperidean dreams; second, the struggle for mastery between the Felowe that Goes Alone and Mr. Grahame the family man. Both of these antitheses could be subsumed under the general head of Desire versus Duty. But his retirement had automatically destroyed the first; and *The Wind in the Willows* had largely resolved the second. He had a sufficient income; he had lost his dream; there was now no driving impulse for him to go on writing. Instead, he sat by the fire and read Milton, or tramped for hours (the old, well-tried anodyne) over the Berkshire Downs.

He had tried to recapture his own youth through Alastair; but Elspeth monopolized the boy. From the tone of Alastair's letters it even looks as though she encouraged him to disparage Kenneth: certainly there was a sense of rivalry between them for the boy's affections, and at this time Mouse himself obviously inclined towards his mother. 'I also enclose a warning to Inferiority,' he wrote to Elspeth on 10th December 1911: *could* he have coined that nickname himself? 'If he does not take me to the Pantomime, and to Monte Carlo, and give me three helpings of Christmas pudding, and mince-pies, and otherwise show his paternal afection, [*sic*] well—I'll let him know it.' Poor Inferiority!

In March 1912 Grahame made one of his rare visits to London to see a trial performance, in a small theatre, of a dramatized version of 'The Roman Road'. ('I find it difficult to think that so undramatic a bit of writing can possibly appeal from the boards', he wrote, and he was right; though perhaps for the wrong reasons.) The moving spirit behind this venture was an American entertainer and children's writer called Kitty Cheatham, who had already visited the Grahames at Blewbury. Grahame hated publicity of any kind, but felt it was only fair to attend: Miss Cheatham was rounding off the evening with other dramatic readings from *The Golden Age*. Curtis Brown was also there, and describes the scene backstage:

After it was over, we went around to the artist's reception-room. Kitty was surrounded by a congratulatory throng, but when she saw that beautiful head, she literally leaped through the crowd and landed with both arms round K. G's neck, exclaiming: 'You Angel Lamb!' Not even pistol shots could have been more startling to his grave dignity; but there was nothing in his attitude to indicate it.[39]

That year the notion of going abroad was not repeated. The Grahames spent a fortnight in Lyme Regis, and then moved on—inevitably—to Fowey, where Grahame was saddened by the bare and desolate state of Atky's magical house up the estuary. The wonderful collection of clocks and barometers, the curious, faded, damp-speckled water-colours had no attraction for the dealers. Atky was dead, and his Arabian Nights atmosphere dissipated: nothing remained but a houseful of old junk. 'The place is for sale,' Grahame told Purves unhappily, 'not to be let, and I don't think it will sell in a hurry—it's not everybody's house.' He hankered after buying it himself; but the various snags and drawbacks proved too great, and they returned to Boham's. Once again August brought cold and incessant rain: vague plans for a trip to Scotland had to be abandoned.

In January 1913 Quiller-Couch accepted a Professorship in English Literature at Cambridge (he had been knighted the previous June) and on Thursday 15th May of that year Grahame was his guest at the Rustat Audit Feast in Jesus. Q had a second guest, A. E. Housman: one would dearly like to know how Grahame and Housman reacted to each other. Sir Sydney Cockerell, to whose rooms the party afterwards moved on, remembered that they sat talking till midnight: but added (in a letter to Elspeth nearly twenty years later) 'alas that I cannot recall any word of what must certainly have been a very interesting conversation!'[40] Indeed it must: Housman, the scholar who had conquered poverty —and worse than poverty—to fight his way to the top of the academic ladder; Housman, the poet-fantasist with his dream of rural Shropshire—who could better have personified all that Grahame himself had desired and failed to achieve? There is only one hint of the effect that their meeting may have had on Grahame; and that is uncertain. Two months later he broke his long literary silence with 'The Felowe that Goes Alone'.[41] Was it possible that he had Housman's example in mind?

That summer the Purves family (despite Mr. Purves' ill-health) managed once more to holiday in Fowey for ten days or so, and also visited the Grahames at Blewbury (where Pierre's most vivid recollection was of a mechanical ship in a bottle). There is a significant little vignette by Austin Purves Jr. of their reception in Cornwall:

> We arrived on the evening train and Mr. Grahame was on the station platform. My brother Pierre, whose godfather was K. G., did not of course remember G., but nevertheless kissed him on arrival. G. said in effect, Pierre it is all right this once, but men don't kiss. Pierre, then aged six, received, for a child, something of a shock.[42]

The truth of the matter is that Grahame (like A. A. Milne, who admitted it) was uneasy with children except in very special circumstances, and tended to ignore them, through shyness or conventionality, in public. C. L. Hinds records a very similar meeting, also on a station, with Grahame again as host, 'watchful, a little fussy, bothering about wraps and a carriage, ignoring two children who were of the party, but studiously polite to their parents'.[43] His talent was for silent companionship: when Dale and Austin rowed him up the coast to Lantick Bay, not more than fifty words were exchanged during several hours. 'Nor', writes Dale, 'was there any need for words: communication was either needless or unrestrained—I don't know which. I think we all regarded it as time excellently spent.'

In August the long-projected trip to Scotland came off at last; and once again Alastair was included in the party. He seems to have enjoyed himself vastly: enough, at any rate, for Grahame to turn down an invitation from Purves to show the boy something of Holland that month. 'Of course,' he wrote to Graham Robertson, 'travelling in August is always infernal, and we had to couch like the beasts of the field in temperance inns and such. But the weather was magnificent, and we were in the most beautiful country, even for the Highlands. The boy was simply drunk with it all, and grieved sorely to leave it.' [44]

Alastair was now in his final year at prep school, and both Elspeth and Kenneth were determined that he should have a public school education. In 1912 Kenneth had approached Q with enquiries about Winchester and Rugby: finally they settled on the latter, and Alastair was provisionally promised a place if he passed the entrance examination. This he contrived to do—though very near the bottom of the list—on 5th July 1914. The time for fantasy was over: for the first time in his life Alastair was going to be confronted with harsh and unimaginative realism. He had had a governess till he was ten; he was still immersed in a world of pirates and fairies, mixed with much precocious and aphoristic chat picked up from his parents. He was gruff-voiced, spotty, appallingly shy, and much given to waving his arms about in moments of excitement. Worst of all, there was that frightful squint, with its accompanying semi-blindness. It was not an auspicious endowment for public school life. Alastair was what his parents had made him; he had always struggled desperately to live up to their myth. But the private myth of *The Wind in the Willows* and the public myth of the English gentleman were hard for a thirteen-year-old boy to reconcile. Q foresaw trouble, and events proved him right.

XIV

ILLUSION AND TRAGEDY
1914-1920

It was a theme
For reason, much too strong for fantasy.
JOHN DONNE: *The Dream*

Children begin by loving their parents. After
a time they judge them. Rarely, if ever, do
they forgive them.
OSCAR WILDE: *A Woman of No Importance*

Into my heart an air that kills
From yon far country blows.
A. E. HOUSMAN: *A Shropshire Lad*

Alastair Grahame entered School House, Rugby, in September
1914, and was desperately unhappy there. His father later declared:
'I took great pains and trouble to assure myself that that was
the best school he could go to'; perhaps he was unaware of
Rugby's robust tradition. He went down to the school after a
week or two, and saw Alastair's tutor, Roger Raven, who seems
to have been a charming and enlightened man. At all events he
sent the following note to his pupil:[1]

You know, your Father kindly came on Tuesday to see me
and had a long talk with me; so that I more or less understand
how things are. I said to him then what I repeat to you, now,

that whenever you want somewhere to sit by yourself I hope you will come round here,—mornings, afternoons, &, if you like, after lock-up. I do all my work upstairs in the study, so that the dining-room below is always at your disposal. I know that invitations to 'drop in any time' are difficult to accept in practice, but I hope you will test this one at once; and you will find that you will be welcome and undisturbed. If you feel any delicacy in appearing to make free of someone else's rooms, you have only to put your head round the study door and say 'me voici' when you arrive; or if you find me unoccupied, you shall come in and talk to me as long as you like. There are some books here if you haven't enough of your own.—I have written this because I thought that if I came to your study and did not find you alone, it would be difficult to *say*. But in all cases believe me

Your affec. tutor, R. A. Raven

Such delicacy and kindness might palliate Alastair's condition, but obviously could not cure it. 'So far as I could gather,' Grahame wrote to Austin Purves,[2] 'the pace and the pressure were altogether too much for him, and I fancy that the new boys, with whom he naturally had to spend his time, happened to be a roughish lot. Anyhow though he stuck it out for six weeks, he got no better, and in the end I thought it right to take him away.' He then wrote to Q for advice, and got it in no uncertain terms:[3]

I had my doubts all along and for two reasons. (a) The Public School business has become such a silly specialized system that only the *larger* preparatory school really prepares the poor chap for what he has to undergo. . . . The smaller private school (with better intentions) quite frequently doesn't. (b) Rugby is the place of all others where you get the system in full blast, with the least pity. Plenty of kindness on the part of X & Y but in the end no pity at all from the system. At Eton, Winchester, Wellington [!] a toad may dodge the harrow: they allow for 'eccentricities' (as they call 'em) and a certain understood adoration of the place often carries through a boy who is not of the run. He understands it (after a pathetic struggle often)

314

and it first allows for and finally gets a particular liking for him—or may. But Rugby is ruthless. And it's all system.

Q was very anxious indeed about the boy, and said so. He then went on, tactfully, to suggest two possible alternatives. First, there was Clifton, which had the advantage of accepting day-boys as well as boarders. 'But,' he adds revealingly, 'you will not only have to live there; Mrs. Grahame would have to make a vow to yield the boy over to the School while living under the same roof with him.' Perhaps sensing the improbability of Mrs. Grahame ever doing anything of the sort, he next suggests a private tutor— 'a thundering good fellow, massive, ex-Rugby Blue for Oxford'. Nevertheless, probably under pressure from Elspeth, Grahame got the boy into Eton, in January 1915. The war, it seems, made the usual long wait for a vacancy unnecessary.

Alastair lasted rather longer at Eton than he had at Rugby; over a year in fact. 'Scratch us,' he declared during this period, 'we are all barbarians but it happens that I prefer curios and they prefer cricket bats.'[4] This kind of remark would probably find more tolerance at Eton than at most other schools; but even so his Dame was moved to admonish Alastair for not talking to his neighbours at table, which produced the reply: 'How can I talk to people whose powers of conversation lie only in their elbows?'[5] This aloofness seems to have impressed the maid in his tutor's house, however: 'He was the only boy', she declared, 'that I ever even *thought* of cutting the bread-and-butter thin for'.[6] She also sent him a Christmas card signed 'Your faithful maid': this amused Grahame, who said it sounded like a pastoral poem.[7]

Alastair was promoted to the Remove in the Michaelmas Term, 1915; and on 11th December Elspeth and Kenneth went down to see him and two hundred other boys confirmed by the Bishop of Oxford. Kenneth gave him a bicycle, and Elspeth wrote to her brother that 'he seems to have won very good opinions in the short time he has been at Eton'. But despite Elspeth's incurable optimism, within two months another emotional crisis had occurred, and in the middle of the Lent Term, 1916, Alastair was removed from Eton also. On 28th March Elspeth wrote about the whole affair to Courtauld, who was now in the Middle East with the Red Cross:

> K. and I are very grateful to you for your kind letter and advice & what is more, agree with all you say as to Eton—but Mouse really was getting into a settled unhappiness there which was harming body and mind & the more he got used to the place the less he could endure it. Probably the very same reasons, or conditions, which made Rugby unbearable to him did so to a minor extent at Eton—and if we had fully understood that he could neither be well, work well—nor be happy in those conditions we should have avoided a year of misery for him at Eton—but everyone was so eager we should try Eton as affording the greatest *contrast* to Rugby or *any* of the first class schools that we did so—thinking it wrong to neglect *any* chance of his taking to a Public School.
>
> The result however was that while he found Eton less intolerable than Rugby he was very unhappy indeed there & more so as time went on. We do not profess *ourselves* to understand exactly why a Public School life is so uncongenial to him for he is by nature the most spartan & the most uncomplaining creature possible. . . . It is so great a disappointment to us that it makes me unhappy even to write about it. . . . K. was really splendid in trying to do everything in his power to buck him up with plenty of pocket & subscription money & good clothes & orders on the shops & *anything* that cd hearten & help him— & attach him to the place & life there—but we *cd* do no more than we have done & it was not of *any* avail as things are.
>
> We hope after the Easter holydays [*sic*] he will go to a very good Tutor in Surrey. . . . He had a younger son of Lord Methuen's for some time. . . & one of the Hon. A. W. de Moleyn's sons. He is they say really a gentleman & very particular whom he takes.

Up to that critical point both she and Kenneth appear to have believed that they could *bribe* the boy into accepting a system which, quite patently, drove him nearly insane. Yet Elspeth wrote this letter in the firm belief that they had done all they possibly could to make Alastair happy. That they should have sacrificed their own ambitions long before never seems to have occurred to her. Only physical collapse would force her to face the truth: Alastair must have had a really serious nervous break-down.

How far Kenneth was influenced by her wishes over Alastair's education we have no means of telling. But he must have been either weak or blind; there is no other alternative. Q had warned him in the strongest possible terms; and any man of Grahame's intelligence must have seen the danger of plunging a nervous, taciturn, precocious, and physically handicapped boy into the rough-and-tumble of Rugby or Eton. Perhaps he wanted to get him away from Elspeth's smothering and eccentric influence: if so, he acted too late. 'I don't think he [Alastair] will care about the young human boy in the raw', he prophesied before the Eton period, and added, 'Nor do I, for that matter'. It seems more likely that he was powerless to resist Elspeth's social demands for Alastair's career, and surrendered despite his own inner misgivings.

Q later blamed Elspeth bitterly for Alastair's sufferings: and it cannot be doubted that she tried to mould the boy into her own preconceived fantasy of what he ought to be. We can see this process of idealization at work in her letters, in Chalmers' account of Alastair, and most especially in her little book *First Whispers*. Till the age of ten she kept him in a world of sentimental fantasy; then, after an abrupt transition, she expected him to turn overnight into an athletic and social Apollo like Bevil Quiller-Couch. She had not the least notion of the havoc this kind of treatment would wreak on a boy of Alastair's nervous temperament, and was puzzled and hurt when, in later adolescence, he drifted away from her emotionally.

This kind of fantasy-behaviour is most often rooted in a need for compensation: and we do not have to look far to find it in

Elspeth's relationship with her son. The truth, I suspect, is that *au fond*, whether consciously or not, she was bitterly ashamed of Alastair; that she resented his squint, his semi-blindness, his acne, and his gaucheness; the fact that he was not particularly clever or good at games, that he had been born with a cataract and was distinctly odd in his behaviour. She stifled this resentment by over-lavish maternal attention, and by creating a mythical Alastair in whose actuality she firmly believed: brilliant, witty, accomplished, and, above all, *popular*. Over and over again she emphasizes how popular Alastair was: independent witnesses are considerably less enthusiastic. After Chalmers' book appeared the then Bishop of Oxford wrote, rather drily, to Elspeth, remarking that 'the account of Alastair is very different from my experience of him'. We may well believe it.

Meanwhile the war had come to Blewbury; seventy volunteered out of a total population of five hundred, among them the ex-sergeant of Marines who, with his wife, had been helping to run Boham's. 'For over six months', Grahame wrote to Purves, 'we have rubbed along somehow with casual help from the village, rough and untrained, and though at last we have secured a couple, they only came two days ago; and meantime the garden of course had gone to pot, and the house was dirty and disordered.' (Kenneth and Elspeth themselves appear to have lacked domestic enthusiasm, for all their passion for the simple life.) Kenneth was on the Derby Committee, and, as Elspeth told her brother, 'we've also been extremely busy with our war work—making crutches and splints, leg & back rests for base & shop hospitals—in the shed generally used for repairing agricultural machines'.

On top of all this Grahame found himself (as an ex-Territorial) more actively concerned with military matters:

> The 'veterans' of Blewbury have started a Volunteer Defence Corps, and we drill in the evenings in a beautiful great framed thatched barn—like my own, only three times as big. The rats run in and out of the thatch along the rafters, and the barn cat,

who ought to be attending to them, sits on wheatsacks and reviews us with great delight. He is having the time of his life, for he thinks that these drills are specially got up for him, to brighten the monotony of his long dull evenings. The Corps have elected me their Commanding Officer—the cat concurring —because they said I was the most martial looking of the crowd—and there I agree with them; they were careful to add, however, that it wasn't for any other reason whatever, and that also I can fully understand. [8]

Q was equally busy: he had been released from Cambridge for the term and was going round Cornwall on a recruiting drive ('with a visit now and then to fire off a lecture at the seat of learning'). It was all very new and strange and alien: yet Grahame, curiously, welcomed the change. To a correspondent in Washington he wrote: 'Yes, Latin is passing fast away, and many another thing with it; and a new world is being born, wherein they will tell other tales than those of tall Troy and Phaeacia. And one cannot grieve for the old, the new is all so wonderful.' [9]

Despite his many other preoccupations, however, Grahame found time to complete a project which he had begun several years earlier—the *Cambridge Book of Poetry for Children*. The anthology was well under way in 1913: 'I have got my two little vols about three-quarters done', he told Graham Robertson on 4th December of that year, 'but am rather stuck for a little more matter, which I can't find to my liking, so I have been rather letting the thing slide; but I shall have to make a push and send the stuff in to Cambridge, somehow'. In June 1914 he was still rounding up material; on the 22nd John Masefield wrote to him: 'All the poems you mention are at your service, but I would prefer them to remain anonymous if you do not mind. . . . [Grahame complied with these terms.] The boys will be lucky to be catered for by you.' [10]

The 'two little vols' finally appeared early in 1916, and, on the whole, reviewers echoed Masefield's tribute. 'If Mr. Grahame cannot compile a book of poetry for children,' the *Literary World* declared,[11] 'then Lord Kitchener could not compile a book on Army organization!' But certain criticisms were made. The *Scotsman* considered many of the poems too abstruse, the *Morning Post* decided that the American patriotic pieces were 'tosh'. (With this judgment Grahame was in private agreement: he only included them, he told Graham Robertson, 'for little boys to spout before their besotted parents on prize day'.) The *Athenaeum* thought more room might have been found for narrative poems, while to the *Aberdeen Daily Journal* 'the bibliomaniac in long clothes, however dear to a peace-loving father, is perhaps—to the thoughtful mother—more a source of carefully-suppressed suspicion than of undiluted joy'.[12]

It was certainly an idiosyncratic collection. Shakespeare headed the list, with seven entries; Blake, Herrick, Scott, and Tennyson had five apiece; Longfellow, Wordsworth, Browning, de la Mare, and W. B. Rands four. Single entries ranged from Coleridge to Jean Ingelow. Sections were divided under such headings as 'Seasons and Weather', 'Toys and Play', 'Fairyland', 'Green Seas and Sailor Men' or 'Arms and the Man'. In the section called 'Day Dreams' Grahame included (clearly for personal reasons) a poem no child would appreciate: Elizabeth Barrett Browning's 'The Lost Bower', which echoed his own nostalgia and spiritual loss. And though the selection contains much matter of battle and chivalry, there is no Kipling.

In his preface Grahame described his task as being 'to set up a wicket-gate giving attractive admission to that wide domain'. We have met that wicket-gate before, in *Pagan Papers*. The vision of the green fairy hill still lingered. Grahame also—following the principle he had established in *The Wind in the Willows*—explicitly ruled out one particular theme:

> In the output of those writers who have deliberately written for children, it is surprising how largely the subject of *death* is

found to bulk. Dead fathers and mothers, dead brothers and sisters [had he forgotten Harold's last will and testament—the famous 'death-letter?'] dead uncles and aunts [how many had his younger self wished to perdition?] dead puppies and kittens [had he not himself written a poem 'To Rollo, Untimely Taken?'] dead birds [cf. 'A Holiday' and 'Quis Desiderio?'] dead flowers, dead dolls [what about 'A Departure'—or even the end of 'Sawdust and Sin?']—a compiler of Obituary Verse for the delight of children could make a fine fat volume with little difficulty. I have turned off this mournful tap of tears as far as possible, preferring that children should read of the joy of life, rather than revel in sentimental thrills of imagined bereavement.[13]

Although one can sympathize with this attitude, the motives that produced it were not, perhaps, entirely healthy; and Katharine Tynan's objections in the *Observer* [14] have a good deal of force:

How could one give them heroic poetry without death? And in another mood of all normal children Death is the play-fellow, the funeral the favourite form of the pageant. When the two children I knew best first found themselves in leafy Sussex, escaped from the London suburbs, they had funerals for each flower as it faded when there was no dead beetle to be had. After all, there is beauty in such funerals. It is our love for the *pompa mortis* that makes human funerals grotesquely dreadful.

Grahame may well have been oppressed in spirit by the thought of the fearful slaughter at that moment proceeding in France; but his distaste for death was more deeply rooted than that, went back further. He had never come to terms with any religious faith, in the end: and one characteristic of neo-pagans bred in the Yellow Decade, who depended on sensation of one sort or another for their well-being, was a progressively increasing distaste as they got older to face the fact of mortality. Grahame was no more immune from this weakness than any of his contemporaries. His

ideals had rested on fragile and transient foundations: now everywhere the dream which had supported him was being attacked.
He was cut off—in more than one sense—from the South. He had
quarrelled with Roland over money matters in 1913, and now the
brothers were not on speaking terms. He had long been estranged
from Helen. His marriage was, at best, a compromise. Worst of
all, his only child was physically malformed—perhaps the sport
of hereditary disease—and desperately unhappy. He could no
longer find the heart to write: the mainspring of his creative mind
had failed. And day by day the hideous unromantic war ground
on its muddy course. Where were the Hesperides now? 'Perhaps
some day', he wrote wistfully to Cockerell, 'there will be Feasts
again, and these present things will seem far away.'

In the summer of 1917 he and Elspeth took Alastair for a holiday at Blue Anchor in West Somerset—'no church, post, nor
shops, in fact *nothing*'.[15] There was, however, excellent swimming,
which delighted Alastair: like many people handicapped for other
sports, he took naturally to the water. Perhaps for the same
reason he developed a passion for riding about this time, 'first
getting lessons from a Trainer on the Downs & then at his Tutor's
in Surrey. The Trainer told us', Elspeth characteristically adds
'that he "never saw anyone take so naturally to a horse".' Like
his father—and with more obvious reason—Alastair clearly had a
penchant for solitary pleasures.

At the same time, however, he joined the Volunteers, and,
again, according to Elspeth, 'is only afraid that the war might end
before he gets into the regular army'. But there was little doubt
that he would be rejected for service through his grave defects of
eyesight; and nothing more clearly shows up Elspeth's capacity
for self-delusion than her obvious fear that he might, in fact, see
active service. 'Of course,' she wrote defensively to Courtauld
that December, 'once a boy *is* overstrained or broken down he is
of no use to himself or his country either.'[16] There is no mention
of his bad eye as an excuse. It was true, though, that Alastair *had*

Elspeth Grahame, *c.* 1930

Selling Barnstaple Baskets at
Blewbury 'Church Feast'

Church Cottage, Pangbourne

outgrown his strength—he already stood six foot two in his stock-inged feet—and the Colonel of the O.T.C. and Cadet Corps at Oxford had advised Kenneth that the boy should train for a commission with them. He would not, the Colonel said in explanation, be fit for A Class at the age of eighteen. For this reason it was arranged that he should go up to Christ Church earlier than had been intended, in the Lent Term of 1918, instead of having another term with his tutor. 'This is all unexpected to us', Elspeth declared to her brother. It is difficult to see why until we remember the myth.

Alastair was no happier at Oxford than he had been at Eton: perhaps he found any kind of community life intolerable. Yet the University would not put the same kind of pressure on him; if he chose to remain solitary no one would stop him. It seems that his unhappiness had become endemic, and that his surroundings made little difference to him. Professor Sir Keith Feiling, who at the time was his tutor, recalls how he always seemed miserable during his time at Christ Church, sighing and groaning audibly. Apart from anything else his bad eyesight (which had apparently deteriorated) must have handicapped him considerably in his reading. He eventually took Mods (at the second attempt) by *viva voce* examination, and the Senior Examiner suggested that application be made for an amanuensis for future occasions, as was done in the case of blind candidates.[17]

Occasional well-meaning efforts were made to draw him out of his solitary gloom. Kenneth's agent, Curtis Brown, invited him up to London in 1918 for his daughter Beatrice's coming-out dance. Beatrice herself (now Mrs. Horton) recalls how Elspeth sent him off with a little American flag as an identification-mark for those expecting him at the London terminus. She found him very reserved and sardonic, and still suffering badly from acne. He made no attempt to dance, but spent all the time talking 'interminable dullness' to her father. The expedition seems to have pleased Kenneth, however; when it was over he wrote to · Curtis Brown:

It was most awfully good of you to give the boy such a splendid time. He seems to have enjoyed every minute of it. Owing to the War he has been simply starved on the social side of him and this visit was just what he wanted and what was best for him. For he is a 'social animal' really. I dare say you discovered what a passion he has for abstract discussion and first principles as opposed to anything concrete. He would, for instance, sit up all night discussing the principles that went to the drawing up of the American Constitution, while being languidly indifferent to personal details concerning any President.[18]

Was Grahame putting a brave social front on a hopeless case? It seems hard to believe. More probably he, no less than Elspeth, could not bring himself to face the bitter truth, and therefore managed to convince himself that the mythical Alastair represented his son's true condition. If this is so, he was to pay a bitter price for his unwillingness—or inability—to come to terms with reality.

The state of his mind in 1919 is curiously illuminated by a letter he wrote on 24th September to Professor G. T. Hill of London University, who had enquired (being a literal-minded man) how Mole's goldfish, and Mole End generally, had been looked after during the owner's prolonged absence. The letter is, obviously, a *jeu d'esprit*; but it is one that only a certain type of mind, adept at dodging unpleasant problems, could have thought up. After solving the question by producing a mythical 'char-mouse', Grahame goes on:

In support of his theory, I would ask you to observe that our author practises a sort of 'character economy' which has the appearance of being deliberate. The presence of certain characters may be indicated in or required by the story, but if the author has no immediate use for them, he simply ignores their existence. . . . Toad Hall . . . must have been simply crawling with idle servants eating their heads off. But the author doesn't happen to want them, so for him they simply don't exist. He doesn't say they are *not* there; he just leaves them alone.[19]

It is clear that Grahame extended this principle to his dealings with life in general; indeed, his whole career, and everything he wrote, demonstrate his refusal to face unpalatable realities. At the first hint of trouble he took refuge in an ideal fantasy-world, and from this vantage-point satirized what he had rejected. The satire itself was tough, astringent, and very much to the point: but the satirist's personal position was fatally vulnerable. Sooner or later his account with the world of facts would have to be squared.

In February 1919 Bevil Quiller-Couch, after surviving four years in action, died of Spanish influenza within a month or two of returning home. It was a bitter blow to Q, and a dark presage of what was to come.

From the beginning of 1920 Alastair was working desperately for the Mods examination, and at the same time grappling with a personal religious crisis. (How had the author of *Pagan Papers* and opponent of 'Scotch-Calvinist-devil-worship' dealt with his son's problems of faith? We do not know. During his time at Blewbury Grahame seems to have adopted the habit he pilloried in the Olympians: he made the social gesture of attendance at church on Sundays, and even read the lessons.) In February Alastair unburdened himself to his former tutor, A. W. Dall, who had little to offer in the way of spiritual comfort: 'Your letter interested me very much', he wrote briskly on 1st March. 'I am not surprised at your Agnosticism. A logical and strongly introspective mind which takes life seriously *always* passes through this phase. P.S. I think your writing has improved.'

We know very little about this side of Alastair's nature; but what evidence there is has a suggestive quality. Even as a young child he had been what his governess described as 'a bit of a mystic':

> On one of my early days with him [Miss Stott wrote in her memoir [20]] he saw a picture of Our Lord in a Holland Street shop. Mouse pointed it out to me. 'That is my Friend,' he said, 'the Carpenter. When I was ill [during his attack of peritonitis

in 1904] He came to see me and sometimes I go and talk to Him.' On another day he said to me, 'Death is promotion'.

Where did Alastair get such notions from? Did Kenneth's suppressed religious longings emerge during those long bed-time talks? It seems hardly likely; though he may have passed on some of the thoughts he had found in Sir Thomas Browne. ('This life is a prison', he once declared to a young friend:[21] one immediately thinks of the *Religio Medici*.) We cannot rule out the possibility of Alastair's having had some kind of genuine mystical experience: and that would have made his later agnosticism all the harder to bear.

Alastair got through Mods on 19th March 1920: on Palm Sunday a friend of his wrote: 'I hope you are enjoying a holiday, with the consciousness that the bogey of Pass Mods has been settled with for ever. Of course I was not surprised at the news, for we were both determined that nothing else should happen, were it only for the Toad's sake! But now you have satisfied yourself that "will" means "can" you will go on to success in the subject of your choice.'[22] Elspeth's attitude to this examination can be gauged from a letter she wrote at this time to a young acquaintance of Kenneth's still at school: 'Now your foot *is* on the ladder do not take it off again but mount it steadily rung by rung. . . . Your place in form should be just as zealously guarded and as keenly contested as any goal at footer. . . . There is no doubt if you can forge-ahead sufficiently to do all you can . . . *while* at school it gives you far more time to devote to getting an Honours-Degree the only aim of the true Scholar. . . .'[23] It is not hard to imagine the effect of such constant exhortations on a nervous, depressed, and purblind boy.

By 4th May it seems as though Kenneth had made an attempt of a sort to help Alastair's religious difficulties: on that date a clerical friend of the family wrote to the boy:[24]

By your parents' desire, I am sending you 'Cruden's Concordance' which I hope you will find useful. I trust you have

settled down comfortably in your new rooms and find everything as you wish. I am wondering what you have decided to
go in for. Whatever it is, I wish you all success. In any case,
you will have to work jolly hard. . . . As in a way you are
making a new start at Oxford, I hope you are arranging your
life there on practical lines. You have much to do and time is
short.

Time, indeed, was shorter than this well-meaning correspondent
could have foreseen.

On the night of Friday, 7th May 1920, Alastair Grahame dined
in Hall at Christ Church, and at the end of the meal asked for a
glass of port—'which', a fellow-undergraduate afterwards testified, 'I had not known him do before'. After Hall—it could not
yet have been dark—he went out for a solitary walk across Port
Meadow, where his father as a boy had played cricket for St.
Edward's. This was the last time he was seen alive. Early in the
morning some railway gangers found his body on the line at Port
Meadow, lying across the rails, at some little distance from the
level crossing. He had clearly been killed by a train; and in his
pockets were a large number of religious tracts.[25]

The inquest was held on Thursday 13th May and the Coroner's
jury contained among its members several Christ Church dons.
The Dean, Dr. T. B. Strong, testified that Alastair was 'a very
quiet and reserved man, and I never got to know him well'. The
boy's family relations were described as excellent, and he had, it
was stated, no financial difficulties. His blindness in one eye was
confirmed, and the jury quickly reached a verdict of Accidental
Death. It was assumed that he had crossed the tracks with his blind
eye towards an oncoming train, and perhaps abstracted in a brown
study; and had thus been struck down and killed.

Unhappily, there is considerable evidence which suggests that
another and grimmer verdict—though it might have served no
useful purpose—would have come nearer to the truth. Many
people, including Q, suspected that Alastair had committed

suicide.[26] Q went out of his way in his *Oxford Magazine* obituary notice to kill the rumour, which had already come to Grahame's notice. His own original suspicions are confirmed by the letter he wrote to Elspeth after hearing an account of the episode from her husband: 'K's reply and the convincing story lifted for ever a great weight off my heart, I read the evidence carefully; I know the place: it is all as clear as clear to me. I shall answer Kenneth's letter separately to this effect.' [27]

It was not a convincing story; nor, indeed, as we know from independent testimony,[28] was Q himself convinced by it. But he was chivalrously determined to spare his old friend the useless agony of mind which blunt honesty would have brought about. Alastair was dead, whatever the verdict; it was the living who needed comfort.

We do not have to rely on Alastair's personal or family history to support the case for suicide, though they corroborate it strongly; nor on the opinions of contemporary friends. We need, in fact, look very little further than the inquest itself. The body was found, not at the level-crossing, but some way further down. It was lying across the rails. Even taking Alastair's blind eye into account, are we to assume that he was also deaf? And if for some reason he had chosen to cross the lines away from the normal point, would he not have taken extra precautions? We cannot be sure at what time the accident occurred: but even in the dark a steam-driven locomotive is hard to miss.

But the most conclusive piece of evidence is that provided by the medical officer, Dr. W. D. Sturrock, who examined the body: [29]

> The cause of death was decapitation, and that was compatible with being run over by a train. The right arm was fractured below the shoulder, the left leg four inches above the ankle, and all the toes of the right foot. There were also numerous bruises on the body.
>
> *The Coroner*: Are these injuries compatible with being

knocked down by a train and then run over?—I could not answer the first part of the question as to being knocked down, but certainly they are compatible with being run over.

Nothing could be clearer or less ambiguous. The nature of the injuries makes it almost certain that Alastair lay down across the track, in a slightly diagonal position, his neck and one shoulder resting on one rail, his right foot and left leg on the other. It is impossible to conceive any other way in which those particular injuries could have been inflicted. The 'numerous bruises' would be due to abrasure by projecting parts of the engine and train as they passed over him. No intelligent person who 'read the evidence carefully'—least of all Q—could have reached any other conclusion: and whether Grahame himself, in his heart of hearts, ever believed the alternative verdict seems extremely improbable.

There remains the question of motive: and here we have ample choice. Alastair's visual deficiency, coupled with his nervous disabilities, would alone have provided a sufficient cause. He was intensely shy, and cut off from much of the social gregariousness of his class and age. He felt himself, there can be little doubt, marked, peculiar, different, a misfit, and an outcast. His extraordinary upbringing left him cruelly defenceless when he was suddenly exposed to a harsh, unfriendly world that had no patience with oddness or precocity. The myth that Elspeth wove round him—and expected him to live up to—must have strained him almost beyond belief: apart from anything else, he was forced to fight against a terrible physical handicap in struggling to attain even an average academic standard. Lastly, there was the religious crisis, the loss of faith, which he experienced shortly before his death: this may have deepened his depression to the point where he totally despaired of the future. All things considered, it is a miracle that he survived as long as he did: Elspeth was right when she described him as 'a real Stoic, who never would complain, or plead his own cause in any way'. He suffered silently; there was no one to whom he could turn.

The funeral took place in Oxford, from Keith Feiling's house in Holywell, and Kenneth scattered lilies of the valley over his son's coffin. Perhaps, as he made that last gesture, he remembered with bitter irony those other obsequies he had celebrated so many years before: 'Achievement ever includes defeat: at best I should only have found myself where I am now—with a narrowing strip of sun and sward between me and the vast inevitable pit agape for us each and all. And the grapes are sour; and the hopes are dead; and the funeral is nearing its end.'[30] As in Ibsen's *Wild Duck*, the Claims of the Ideal had, all unwittingly, destroyed a young human life: Alastair and Helga suffered the same tragic fate. The over-drawn account with reality was squared at last: but it had been a grievous and insupportable price to pay for a lifetime of wistful illusion.

THE REEDS BY THE RIVER

1920-1932

Everything he wrote was read,
After certain years he won
Sufficient money for his need,
Friends that have been friends indeed;
' *What then?* ' sang Plato's ghost. ' *What then?* '

W. B. YEATS: *What Then?*

Moving through the fields, or still at home,
Dwarfed by his shadow on the bright wall,
His face is lit always from without,
The sun by day, the red fire at night;
Within is dark and bare, the grey ash
Is cold now, blow on it as you will.

R. S. THOMAS: *The Last of the Peasantry*

Sweete *Themmes* runne softlie, till I end my Song.

EDMUND SPENSER: *Prothalamion*

In August 1920, three months after Alastair's death, the Purves brothers returned for yet another visit to England; and Kenneth, despite his bereavement, undertook to show them round Oxford. He booked them rooms, came up from Blewbury for four or five days, and devoted the entire time to their enlightenment and entertainment. Every college and many other of the University buildings were explored in turn. 'I am not aware', Austin

Purves writes, 'that Grahame liked or knew anything about music [1] but he made it possible for us to have very special seating at organ recitals in Christ Church College. Some of us drew and painted and Grahame suggested various spots such as Iffley where we could sketch some truly romantic English things.' He rhapsodized over wainscoting, and was mildly surprised to find that his young guests could not read the Latin inscriptions. These he obligingly translated, 'and was, I am sure, unaware of our lack of interest. This was not, I think,' Austin pleasantly comments, 'good manners on his part, or bad manners on ours.' [2]

Why did Grahame insist on discharging the duties of a cicerone at such a time? Partly, of course, out of respect for the memory of the boys' father, who had been his close friend; but, at bottom, his motives seem to have been more complex and personal. Mr. John C. Purves recalls him on this occasion as 'a sensitive, shy, broken man' with whom 'we could not establish an entente. Grahame was too reserved, and his suffering must have been intense.' Mr. Purves suggests, very convincingly, just what it was that drove him to swallow his private grief and overcome his natural urge for solitude. 'We boys had never seen Mouse,' he explains, 'but Grahame believed that it was Mouse's earnest wish to show Oxford to us. Back of this was Grahame's deep love for a University and town of which he had never been a part as a student and which he attended vicariously through his son.' [3]

This last sentence hints at a good deal more than its immediate context. Though neither of them would ever have admitted it, even to themselves, Alastair's death (once the initial shock was over, and a satisfactory 'accidental' cause established) must have lifted a great weight off his parents' shoulders. However they might have disguised the fact, their son had always been a standing reminder to them of much they would rather forget. He infected them with a permanent sense of guilt. Furthermore (as tends to happen even with normal only children), they had come more and more to live their lives, vicariously, as Mr. Purves says, through

Alastair. In Alastair, Grahame at last entered the long-denied gates of Oxford; in Alastair Elspeth re-created her long-abandoned myth of high society. Their guilt and unhappiness was all the greater because their son would not, could not, play the part they had chosen for him.

But with his death everything changed. A coroner's verdict had effectively stifled any lingering sense of personal responsibility they might have felt: Alastair's end was a tragic sport of Fate, fit theme for a Hardy novel. Now there was no longer any awkward living reality to confront the myth they had built up in their imagination. Alastair himself was forgotten: only his legendary *alter ego* remained, growing steadily more perfect and brilliant as the years went by. Furthermore, the guilt with which his parents had been forced to live during his brief existence was now lifted from them: unhappiness was smoothed away in blessed oblivion. Once again Kenneth and Elspeth could exist as themselves, and not merely through their child. They said nothing; but their actions were eloquent.

The first thing they did after the Oxford episode was to sell a large number of their personal effects from Boham's—Dutch and Sheraton cupboards, French mirrors, sets of Wedgwood china, all their Bohemian glass-ware, a Weber player-piano, various dolls' services, their Welsh dresser 'with Nelson's head and motto on the handles', and all Kenneth's 'Sailor's Farewell' glass rolling-pins. They were not short of money; it was as though they were consciously abandoning everything that reminded them of their old life.[4] Most significant of all, Elspeth disposed of all Alastair's clothes and possessions at a Blewbury jumble-sale: an action which, not surprisingly, disconcerted her neighbours,[5] but only serves to confirm one's suspicions as to her state of mind at the time.

A month later Boham's was let for eighteen months to a Mr. Davies. On Thursday, 28th October, Kenneth and Elspeth moved to London; and two days later they embarked on the S.S. *Orvieto* (with a personal introduction to the captain) and sailed from England. Their destination—at long last, and in a sense too late—was Kenneth's beloved Italy. In some curious way Alastair's death seemed to have reopened this door also. Kenneth and Elspeth were drawn closer by their loss—and the unconscious relief it brought them—than ever before in their marriage; and, for the first time perhaps, Kenneth was glad of companionship. He was never to travel alone again. In any case he was now over sixty; and though Ulysses at that age still nursed an incurable Hesperidean urge, Grahame was made of gentler stuff. He had returned to his Golden City; but now—supreme irony—it was as an ordinary cultured tourist, with the tourist's main preoccupations: architecture and food.

Of the two, architecture emphatically occupied the second place. It was the local cuisine that drew him irresistibly: cheeses, *mortadella* sausage, roast chicken or *porchetta*, fresh anchovies, and every other Italian delicacy, together with their accompanying wines. As Chalmers delicately puts it, 'again and again crops up throughout the records that I have of his Italian wanderings, an artistic love of the table and the bin'.[6] It was the major consolation he had left; and the cathedrals, as he said, knew how to wait. The Grahames spent most of 1921 in Rome, and during that time Kenneth got to know every restaurant and *trattoria* the city contained. He also developed an inordinate passion for Italian ice-cream, which Elspeth (believing it was bad for his health) tried in vain to curb.

But his explorations had their more serious and cultural side. He became an expert on Roman topography, and learnt all he could from the English and American archaeologists resident in the city. Among his closer friends were Frank and Charis Fairbanks, who were on the staff of the American Academy: Charis later wrote to Elspeth, after Kenneth's death:[7]

I remember so well the first trip I made with both of you to the little church of San Onofrio, 'Tasso's church' on the

Gianicolo, where the lovely Pinturicchio frescoes were just being uncovered, and his great pleasure in their beauty, and in showing them to me, that great glorious boyish joy he had in exploring, and showing off his discoveries! . . . Another time strolling over the Gianicolo, and sitting on a bench where he could see the cross on the obelisk in the Piazza of St. Peter's, he observed in his inimitable way, 'They say there used to be a ball on the top of the obelisk where the cross is now; that was said to contain the ashes of Julius Caesar. Probably did—anyhow we haven't any proof that it didn't!'

Water had always had a dreamy hypnotic effect on him; and now he would sit for long hours by any of the innumerable fountains which abound in Rome, lulled by its quiet music, eyes fixed on the glittering coins thrown for good luck into the broad, shallow basin beneath it.

Just as he had delighted, a year before, in showing off Oxford, so now he yearned to guide willing guests round this other city of his dreams. About Easter his ideal audience appeared once more. Dale and Edmund Purves, both now students of architecture, wrote from Naples asking if he could find them rooms in the capital: they had been touring through Southern France and the Riviera. Grahame obtained hospitality for them at the Fairbanks', who lived in a villa on the Academy grounds, and generally had a student or two about the house. (Their current guest was a young man named Thornton Wilder.)

> Mr. Grahame [Edmund Purves recalls[8]] took us under his wing immediately after our arrival in Rome and there seemed to be scarcely a day go by that he did not call for us or send for us and then he, Mrs. Grahame and ourselves would walk about Rome—generally stopping at some shop in the morning to buy some bread, cheese, sausage and a bottle of wine for our noontime meal, which we would eat wherever we happened to be when hunger struck us. It was a wonderful experience as Mr. Grahame knew every nook and cranny in Rome and seemingly every bit of its history. I do not know how any three American students could have had any more enlightening experience for

we saw Rome as few others, especially Americans, ever saw it. He was a wonderful and thoughtful companion—always cheerful and kind and gave no evidence of the tragedy that had recently occurred.

He also—when Elspeth was absent from these expeditions—made a habit of refreshing himself liberally and frequently in taverns along the route: a practice in which the Purves boys, who had been strictly brought up, did not join him.

Meanwhile an indignant letter had arrived from the Grahames' tenant, Mr. Davies, complaining—not altogether surprisingly—that 'a good deal of litter and disorder' had been left behind. There were also those mouse-nests in the larder. Grahame replied denying the charges with the kind of self-explanatory heat which is normally engendered by embarrassment. Every farm-house had mice, he declared; and then, changing his tack, added: 'Personally I have not myself seen a mouse inside Boham's for years, though, I am perfectly well aware that every time Mr. Lay thrashes out a rick, some non-paying guests of this sort seek admission to the house, and my cat's face begins to wear a strained and haggard appearance suggestive of the need for a rest-cure. But nothing more is seen of the mice!'[9] With this crumb of comfort poor Mr. Davies had to be content.

During the same year there was another interesting sign of Grahame's 'release': he began to write again. The American Ambassador, Mr. R. U. Johnson, asked him in February for a five-minute tribute to Keats, to celebrate the centenary of the poet's death on the 24th of that month. Grahame, surprisingly, agreed. The speech has not been preserved, but in it he remarked 'how easily John Keats might have heard his nightingales on the rural heights and twilit copses of the hamlet that, in those days, his native Hampstead remained'.[10] The occasion was a striking success; and Sir Rennell Rodd, the British Ambassador, who was also present, promptly invited Grahame to lecture to the Keats-Shelley Association.

Once again Grahame accepted; and the talk he gave, entitled 'Ideals', was later reprinted in the *Fortnightly Review*.[11] It forms an extended and revealing apologia for his main *credo*: and I have quoted from it extensively during the course of this book. It led up to a discussion of 'the dream-city, the City Celestial or the New Jerusalem'; and its climax may appropriately be reproduced at this point:

> What, then, is the conclusion of the whole matter? Is it not that we are all idealists, whether we would or no? And that we are all idealists, chiefly by virtue of our waking dreams, those very imaginings which we are so ashamed of, and so reluctant to speak about, which we sternly discourage in others, but which all the same we secretly cherish to the very end? For in these dreams we are always better than ourselves, and the world is always better than it is, and surely it is by seeing things as better than they are that one arrives at making them better.

It is the despairing claim of one of the last romantics, in a post-war age which laughed at such high ideals: and its concluding words supply an ironic gloss on the tragedy of the speaker's own life. He had indeed seen things as better than they were; but his optimistic self-delusion had brought only calamity.

In August the Grahames made a visit to Cortina d' Ampezzo in the Italian Dolomites, where Kenneth once again resumed his habit of long solitary walks in the mountains. Another holiday-maker there recalls that 'he was a remarkable-looking man, striding across hill and dale, his Inverness cape swirling around him, his hair all swept up by the wind. On and on he went, solitary, absorbed in his own thoughts, until he vanished in the distance. I think he was deeply grieved over the loss of his son and I hesitated to intrude on his self-imposed isolation.'[12]

That autumn Curtis Brown wrote to him suggesting excerpts or an abridgment of *The Wind in the Willows* for use in schools: this proposal Grahame turned down without hesitation. 'I can't abridge satisfactorily without loss of quality,' he told his agent, 'and that's the long and short of it. I know that School Committees will only have books on their own terms, more or less, but that's not my fault.'[13] But he raised no such objections when Q demanded two long extracts (including a large part of 'Wayfarers All') for the *Oxford Book of English Prose*. This settled, he and Elspeth left Rome and made their leisurely way north to Rapallo, which they reached in February 1922. They spent the spring on Lake Garda, and returned for a short visit to England in June. Mr. Davies' tenancy had expired, and on 1st September Grahame wrote to A. A. Milne offering to let Boham's to him as soon as they returned to the Continent. The deal seems to have fallen through: the Milnes were looking for a permanent house.

Kenneth and Elspeth got back to Italy in time to witness Mussolini's march on Rome. As Elspeth later wrote to her brother,[14] 'we used to hear the Fascists cracking the skulls of the Socialists at street corners, with cannons at both ends of the bridges and snipers shooting over the high wall surrounding the courtyard of the G.P.O.' This did not appear to disturb Kenneth; he had found a new restaurant run by an exiled Russian princess, who wore diamond earrings while cooking omelettes. When the meal was served by an Archduke, the danger of being shot at by revolutionaries when you stepped out into the street seemed unimportant by comparison. After Christmas they migrated to Capri, where they stayed in the Pensione Faraglioni. Here Kenneth had another attack of bronchitis; but this did not prevent him gossiping 'with old women porters who would "remember back", to please the Englishman, to the very times of Tiberius'.[15] If he met Axel Munthe or Norman Douglas, there is no record of it. Douglas he might have found highly uncongenial; but the master of San Michele was a man after his own heart.

By the spring of 1923, after a month or two in Sicily, they were back in Rome once more: as Elspeth put it, 'we wintered in Rome, and summered there, and Eastered, and Christmas'd

The Wind in the Willows

and knew every one of the 490 old churches'. On the whole they avoided Roman society: visiting cards piled up unanswered in their hotel. By now Elspeth had acquired the habit of dealing with much of Kenneth's fan-mail; it was she who answered the young enquirer who wanted to know what the Otter's story about Toad and the lock-keeper was. Kenneth merely signed it. 'I am afraid I must not tell you', she wrote. 'The fact is, they both lost their tempers, and said things they much regretted afterwards. They are now friends again, so we have all agreed to let the matter drop.'[16]

In August they moved on to Florence, and thence to Siena for the Palio, which took place on the 16th. Anstey Guthrie, who was with them on this occasion, has left a vivid description of the scene:

> Immense square; drapery in various tones of crimson and scarlet hanging from every window and balcony; stands black with people; crowd circulating along course. Clusters of air balloons, like bunches of yellow, blue and purple grapes, swaying over their heads. One balloon escapes, soars high into the cloudless blue sky, and disappears behind the Campanile, to intense delight of crowd. Maroons go off at intervals.

The Grahames were invited by a local priest to watch the proceedings from the window of his house, 'where we . . . were regaled on biscuits from china bowls and delicious golden wine in blue Venetian glasses'. That evening they drove back to Florence expecting their car to be shot at or at least held up, as the Socialists were in power in that area. And indeed they were held up by crowds, on several occasions; but all their captors wanted to know was which *contrada* had won the Palio.[17]

They spent the winter and early months of the New Year at Ospedaletti; and then, in the spring of 1924, they returned to England once more. Grahame had succeeded in selling Boham's: the house and village had disagreeable memories for them, and they were probably anxious to move somewhere where the details of their private tragedy were not so intimately known. Blewbury, after all, had been Alastair's home for ten years. And Kenneth was beginning to yearn for a Thames-side home once more: the River claimed him, as it had always done. Now he made his last home at Pangbourne, in a pleasant house called Church Cottage; it had the old village lock-up for a tool-shed, a big ship's bell at the front door, and a garden that ended in an enchanting high-banked grass amphitheatre. Kenneth once said (with his perennial passion for circuses) that 'there ought to be Shetland ponies galloping round, ridden by monkeys'.[18]

The new arrivals struck the inhabitants of Pangbourne as distinctly odd. Kenneth they found withdrawn but amiable: a tall, white-haired figure in black-and-white check scarf and consciously countrified red-brick Harris tweeds, who sat alone in his garden for hours on end and refused to have either servants or telephone permanently installed in the house. Elspeth was another matter. By now she was a pallid, haggard ghost, with an aureole of fuzzy grey hair and clothes that would have disgraced a jumble-sale. Her meanness, especially over food, was proverbial. The village would often be treated to the spectacle of Mr. and Mrs. Grahame taking lunch on the porch out of a paper bag; and Elspeth was quite capable of haggling like a fish-wife over two ounces of ham in the local butcher's—much to Kenneth's embarrassment.

Despite all this she had lost none of her lady-of-the-manor forthrightness: she stumped round Pangbourne, a dragon anything but reluctant, and her bemused neighbours found themselves doing her endless favours without knowing quite how they had been talked into it. As a last touch of eccentricity, it was quickly noticed that the Grahames might stint themselves on food (though Kenneth occasionally treated himself to a complicated curry of his own making) but that their consumption of champagne and port was remarkable.[19]

Yet Elspeth, in her own curious way, could still be charming and considerate when she chose. Her fund of anecdotes about the great literary figures of her youth was fascinating and inexhaustible. Her interest in people (as Kenneth had remarked years before) remained intense: and they did not need to be notabilities. She cultivated friendships with care; her memory for domestic minutiae was phenomenal; and till her sight failed she was an indefatigable letter-writer. She could even, on occasions, be a good listener. In her old age she seems infinitely pathetic: a lonely, disappointed woman, still clinging to the tatters of her past, still playing the *grande dame* to an indifferent audience.

Grahame was now virtually a recluse. 'I very rarely go up to town nowadays', he wrote to A. J. A. Symons in July 1925. However, he was lured out on occasion: sometimes to make a Prize Day speech at St. Edward's, sometimes to address the Pangbourne Literary, Dramatic and Musical Guild, for which he wrote 'A Dark Star', afterwards published in the *Cornhill*. This piece deals, characteristically, with the special *contemporary* appeal of any period in literature, and forms an illuminating résumé of his own literary tastes. Mr. Malcolm Elwin recalls him in the train to Paddington, talking City shop with an old friend, the late Sir Harold Hartley, 'sitting in his corner seat with his back to the engine, elegant in pepper-and-salt trousers, short black coat, and neat cuffs, a handsome and dignified figure of an elderly city man'. Mr. Elwin also met him and Elspeth twice at the Hartleys' house, and gives this telling portrait of them together:

> He was a biggish, broad-shouldered man, inclined to portliness as all of his generation over sixty tended to be, grey of hair and grey of face, his shoulders bent so that he stooped slightly, his general appearance giving the immediate impression that he suffered from ill-health. I suspect that he also suffered from the wearing personality of his wife, a chinny woman of leathery countenance, who wore well-cut tailor-made tweeds [this clashes with most evidence: perhaps Elspeth dressed up to go calling] and talked stridently and interminably, laying down the law about her preferences in literature and art, and never taking much heed of what anybody else had to say. I gathered that Mr.

Grahame had long since learned that it was a waste of time and energy to attempt to express any opinion in his wife's company.[20]

Nevertheless, Grahame continued to write a little. In 1925 he produced his most substantial piece since *The Wind in the Willows*: a long and vigorous Introduction to 'Lord' George Sanger's memoirs, *Seventy Years a Showman*. This is full of rich reminiscence of circus-life and the magic spell of caravans: nostalgic, witty, and wistful. On the other hand he reveals in it a new avenue of escape-fantasy he has recently discovered—the cinema. 'We like it', he wrote (and here he had the vast majority of the population on his side), 'because it is not exactly the sort of life we daily lead; and as we stroll homeward across the starlit common towards our farmhouse, vicarage, or simple thatched cottage, we think "I wish—oh, *how* I wish—I had married an Indian half-breed".' Perhaps that was no more than the truth.

And year after year the obsessional, restless travelling went on. It was as though Kenneth still nursed the dwindling hope of somewhere, some day, finding his New Jerusalem. *An easy matter*, he had written, long ago; but now the irony had a bitter flavour. Venice, Perugia, Genoa, Taormina; the Northern Lakes and the Dolomites, he saw them all. They never returned to any place more than once, with the exception of Rome, Florence, and Venice. They looked on at vintage festivals (like Rat in the harvest-field), struggled across the lava-fields of Etna, and in Palermo attended the re-trial of a notorious brigand who was appealing against a sentence of a hundred years' imprisonment. (The charges included thirteen proven murders.) In 1926 they reached Amalfi; and here they made friends with an American girl, June Mussey, who later sent Elspeth her recollections of the occasion:

> Mr. Grahame's white hair and moustache seemed to light up the room; and the first impression he made was always one of distinction. . . . It was not long before he was guiding us round

Amalfi. Although he walked leaning on a cane, he took us up and down through the labyrinth of passages and stairs that pass for streets there; he seemed to know every odd corner of the ancient town. His knowledge of the history of Amalfi, and of almost everything else, was encyclopedic. I remember his saying, 'The strongest human instinct is the desire to impart information, and the second strongest the desire to resist such teaching'; I have often since thought how true it is generally, but it was not true of him. . . . Mr. Grahame always seemed interested in any new fact or idea, even from somebody like me, who had few of either. His modesty was such that he had to be drawn out before one found out how much he knew, or, indeed, who he was. . . . It all wound up in a grand party to which we invited everyone in town, native or foreign. Mr. Grahame sat in a corner, as he had when we first saw him, and enjoyed it all in silence.

In 1926, too, Curtis Brown, probably encouraged by these signs of renewed literary activity, wrote to him suggesting that he might care to embark on his autobiography. Grahame replied, on 29th April: 'My chief trouble is that I have kept no diaries or memoranda at all [this was not true, though he may have destroyed his diary himself] and since the War my memory seems to have gone all to pot. I doubt much if I could ever get as much as a book together; but I will, as I said, consider if I can get out an article or two on a line of my own, which should be reminiscent in character.' He did, in fact, start making notes about his schooldays, and these have survived; out of them he produced the posthumously published piece, 'Oxford through a Boy's Eyes',[21] and on a combination of the two I have largely based my own account of this period in his life. But that Grahame could be expected to write a full autobiography with any real degree of honesty was clearly out of the question. His memory may well have failed conveniently; at all events, two years went by without his making any attempt to provide Curtis Brown with what he wanted.

In November 1928 Curtis Brown tried again, tempting Grahame with the proposition of a 4–5,000-word article on his experiences at the Bank of England. 'Of course', he added, 'there is deep craft and guile in this scheme, for I figured it out that if you were to do the article you would find it so interesting that you could be tempted to do another later on, and then another, until the first you knew there would be most of that volume of Memoirs I have been yearning for.' But Grahame was not to be drawn. 'Many thanks for your would-be provocative letter,' he replied on the 11th. 'But Nothin' Doin' about B. of E. Much too dull a subject.' Dull? Or unpleasant? It was 1931 before Grahame capitulated, and promised to try and rough out his reminiscences;[22] but by then it was too late.

Grahame was not, however, so out of touch and unworldly that he failed to keep a very sharp eye on his business affairs. He remained the Scots business-man to the end, especially where royalties were concerned. On 21st January 1929 he sent a letter to Curtis Brown about his foreign rights.[23] (Curtis Brown had previously answered his query about the increased commission on foreign translations by explaining 'that if we didn't pay our continental managers their 10 per cent we couldn't expect them to make a real effort. . . . Furthermore . . . our small extra charge on translation transactions was as nothing compared with the 50 per cent commission most publishers then charged on similar transactions.') The letter is highly entertaining, but its waggishness conceals a shrewd insistence on his financial dues:

My dear C.B. Before I received your kind letter of the 18th, I had frankly suspected—& no doubt you suspected that I had suspected—that the account that had so shocked me had been a piece of quite laudable if mistaken departmental over-zeal, which had somehow escaped the eye of the Capitoline Jove. But when I read your classic periods, so firm yet so tender, I wilted, I sagged, I crumpled. I shed bitter tears. I finally collapsed on the floor, a sodden heap of misery. As I lay there, however, I found myself murmuring something, but very soft and low, so that it should not reach your ears. Something like this: 'Alas, yes, how true it is, and how well I knew it, that there are publishers who claim 50% on Foreign rights, and others who ask 100, and many who will demand 150, & then ask for a little bit more for "all their trouble";

but—

but—

(here I became almost inaudible)

since when—(I was now only whispering)—

since when have —— Ltd. based their practice on the tenets of Messrs. B-r-bb-s & Co.?'

Then I shed a few more tears.

Then I rose to my feet & washed and had some light refreshment—the first for days.

So now that is all over, & I will try and be good, and I will try and not do it any more. And I am ever so glad that you couldn't have heard a word of those awful sentiments I murmured to myself as I lay crying on the floor. But . . .

(No, I won't begin again. I have sworn it.) All the same . . .

No; the end of the page is in sight, and I am not going to get on to a new one. At least I *will* turn over a new leaf, of course, for I have said so already. But not a new leaf of this letter. BECAUSE IF I DID—O this unruly typewriter! It all comes of using a Blick. Common little beasts, Blicks. I ought to get something high-class and toney and expensive. 'But how can you if' . . . There he goes again. He must be stopped.

Yours finally and very truly,
KENNETH GRAHAME

Curtis Brown's further reply is not on record; but he may well have reflected to himself that the author of *The Wind in the Willows* was, *au fond*, no different from any other literary man when it came to a question of money.

In October 1929 Roland died. He and Kenneth had not been in communication since their bitter quarrel seventeen years before; and it was Helen, now retired to a house at the Lizard, who sent Kenneth and Elspeth details of his funeral, which of course they had not attended. The Feilings were there, and Anthony Hope Hawkins and his wife, not to mention three elderly representatives from the Bank of England, where Roland, like Kenneth, had spent his working life.[24] Another link was snapped; the children had come a long, bitter, disillusioning journey from that sunlit orchard in Cookham Dene. *Et in Arcadia ego*: Death, too, had come to Arcadia, indifferent to the decree of banishment that Kenneth had pronounced over him. The shadows were lengthening over the lawn, and soon it would be night.

E. H. Shepard, who (with some misgivings) had agreed to illustrate a new edition of *The Wind in the Willows*, visited Grahame at Church Cottage in 1930, and recorded the following details of his interview:[25]

> Not sure about this new illustrator of his book, he listened patiently while I told him what I hoped to do. Then he said 'I love these little people, be kind to them'. Just that; but sitting forward in his chair, resting upon the arms, his fine handsome head turned aside, looking like some ancient Viking, warming, he told me of the river near by, of the meadows where Mole broke ground that spring morning, of the banks where Rat had his house, of the pools where Otter hid, and of Wild Wood way up on the hill above the river. . . . He would like, he said, to go with me to show me the river bank that he knew so well, '. . . but now I cannot walk so far and you must find your way alone'.

He was delighted (as countless children and adults have been) by the drawings Mr. Shepard produced; but it is curious to note that by now the scene of *The Wind in the Willows* had been transferred in his mind to the country and riverside surrounding his new home. So potent, in fact, have the Shepard illustrations been that many people remain convinced to this day not only that Rat and Mole lived near Pangbourne, but that *The Wind in the Willows* was actually written there.

Then, in 1930, came *Toad of Toad Hall*, which introduced the

River-Bankers to a yet wider audience. Curtis Brown had for some years unsuccessfully tried to interest theatrical managers in *The Wind in the Willows*; but they had invariably turned it down on the grounds that it was 'too whimsical, and the characters quite impossible to represent in believable costumes'.[26] It is easy to see their point, which has considerable force; but Grahame was bitterly disappointed. Then it was suggested to A. A. Milne that he might like to try his hand at an adaptation. Milne and Grahame had never met, though they had corresponded sporadically ever since Milne had sent the author of *The Wind in the Willows* a congratulatory letter on the book in February 1918. Milne, delighted, agreed: 'I think it should be a children's play', he wrote, 'with a little incidental music'. He set about it at once, and Harold Fraser Simson composed a delightful score.

Now a good deal of criticism was levelled at Milne, both at the time and later, complaining that he had reduced his original to mere sentimental cosiness. *Punch*[27] declared that he 'perhaps has had his eye too exclusively fixed upon the children and averted from the less important grown-ups. . . . Mr. Milne has jettisoned, perhaps perforce or for policy's sake, all that makes the enchantment of *The Wind in the Willows* for the mature mind.' This is perfectly true; and the result has been that many who came to Grahame's masterpiece by way of *Toad of Toad Hall* were considerably discouraged. Nevertheless, Milne knew exactly what he was about: and if he put his own sentimental stamp on the adaptation, he did it for perfectly intelligible motives.

He saw, more clearly than most people, the difficulty of pinning down these fluid, shifting characters for a stage presentation. 'Once we put Mole and his friends on the boards,' he wrote in his preface,[28] 'we have to be definite about them. What do they look like?' It was an impossible question to answer. 'Of course,' Milne admitted, 'I have left out all the best parts of the book; and for that, if he has any knowledge of the theatre, Mr. Grahame will thank me. With a Rat and a Mole from the Green Room Club, a

Baby Otter from Conti, a Pan from Clarkson's and a wind (off) whispering in the reeds of Harker, we are not going to add any fresh thrill to the thrill which the loveliness of "The Piper at the Gates of Dawn" has already given its readers.' One can only, while agreeing with every word of this, wish that Milne's final version had not been quite so intolerably mawkish: it is hard to shake off its influence when one turns back to the book.

The end was now very near. Dr. Bourdillon, Grahame's medical adviser, cut down both his diet and his long country walks: by the beginning of 1932 he was suffering from high blood pressure, advanced arteriosclerosis, and fatty degeneration of the heart. The walks he could forgo; good food was harder. '*Do* let me have something to eat, Bourdillon!' was his constant cry at every visit, and he still slipped out unrepentantly (eluding Elspeth) to eat ice-creams whenever he could get them. Despite ill-health, he still held himself erect and spoke firmly and clearly, like a man half his age: and on 25th June he went up to London for the Lewis Carroll centenary at Bumpus's bookshop.[29] He still wrote occasional letters in that square, careful handwriting that hardly changed throughout his life.

On Tuesday 5th July 1932 there was no sign of trouble. He did *The Times* crossword in the morning, and complained that it did not last long enough; he spent most of the afternoon by the river. At dinner he performed his traditional ritual of mixing the salad. Constance Smedley described this with some percipience in a letter to Elspeth:[30] 'Beneath the delight in the earth and the fruits thereof, was a great reverence. When he dressed a salad, the oil meant the olive-trees of Italy and France; the herbs— chervil from the sun-baked sand, tarragon from watered soil— were creatures of the elements; the lettuce was the green leaf, wet with dew and strong with rain and sun—the occasion a lovely intimate ceremony.' Now the ceremony, with all its associative meanings, was performed for the last time: an unconscious vale- diction to the things which Kenneth had loved so well. When dinner was over he and Elspeth went for a short stroll, and soon afterwards he retired to bed with Walter Scott's *The Talisman*.

About one in the morning Elspeth heard a noise from his room. She went in immediately to find the light still on and the book lying on the floor. Kenneth was in a deep coma. He had had a cerebral haemorrhage, and died, without regaining consciousness, shortly before 6 a.m.[31]

The funeral took place on Saturday 9th July 1932, at the church of St. James the Less, Pangbourne: and among the other mourners was Annie Grahame. Curtis Brown's secretary, Miss Barnes, has left this description of the scene:[32]

> The church was a marvellous sight—a blaze of glorious colour and sunshine—with masses and masses of flowers, delphiniums and roses (and willows gathered from the river that very morning) and all the things that grow in a cottage garden. And perhaps the most touching thing of all were the flowers sent by children from all over the country, with cards attached in a childish scrawl, saying how much they loved him. The grave was lined with thousands of sweet peas and the scent was unforgettable.

Later Kenneth's body was transferred to a permanent resting-place in Holywell Churchyard, in his beloved Oxford: he had come home at last. Over the grave was carved an inscription composed by Anthony Hope: 'To the beautiful memory of Kenneth Grahame, husband of Elspeth and father of Alastair, who passed the River on the 6th July 1932, leaving childhood and literature through him the more blest for all time'.[33] It would be hard to think of a more just epitaph.

Critics of literature have paid scant attention to the author of *The Wind in the Willows*: he has not even been considered worthy of a place in the *Cambridge Bibliography*. A minor writer? Perhaps. Yet the world he created will be remembered and cherished in years to come by countless readers ignorant of the sources from which it was born. The vision of *The Wind in the Willows* will entrance thousands of children and adults in the future as it has done in the past: how many of them will guess the personal tragedy it represents? And that, after all, is as it should be. A myth has no history; a classic—and by any criterion *The Wind in the Willows* deserves that honourable title—can stand alone. Posterity may well judge that, in the end, Kenneth Grahame found his Golden City without knowing it.

Et in Arcadia ego

CHELSEA—HARLTON
1956–1958

NOTES AND REFERENCES

PP =*Pagan Papers* (3rd ed., 1898); HW = *The Headswoman* (2nd ed., 1921) ; GA = *The Golden Age* (1928 ed.); DD =*Dream Days* (Nelson ed., 1928); WW = *The Wind in the Willows* (31st ed., 1929); Chalmers =Patrick R. Chalmers, *Kenneth Grahame: Life, Letters and Unpublished Work* (1933); Fyrth =D. M. Fyrth, *Étude littéraire: Kenneth Grahame* (Paris, 1937); FW =*First Whisper of 'The Wind in the Willows'*, ed. Elspeth Grahame (1944).

KG =Kenneth Grahame; EG =Elspeth Grahame; AG =Alastair Grahame; CTC =Courtauld-Thomson Collection; NObs =*National Observer*.

There are so many editions of Grahame's main works from which to choose that no one choice will suit every reader; I have, therefore, partly from convenience and partly out of sentiment, used my own copies, which I have possessed since childhood.

INTRODUCTION

1. 'A Dark Star', Chalmers, p. 303.
2. *The Mirror in the Roadway* (1957), p. 241.
3. See Chalmers, pp. xi-xii.
4. *Ibid.* p. xvii.
5. *The Dark Sun* (1957), p. vii.
6. *St. Edward's School Chronicle*, Vol. 12, no. 321.

I. DRAGONS AND PTERODACTYLS, 1859–1867

1. Letter dated 18th April 1933 (CTC).
2. Chalmers, p. 44. James Grahame also composed, *inter alia, Africa Delivered, or The Slave Trade Abolished* (1809); *Thoughts on Trial by Jury in Civil Causes* (1806); *The Siege of Copenhagen* (1808); and *The Birds of Scotland* (1806).
3. Chalmers, pp. 2-3; cf. Helen Grahame's letter of 22nd March 1933 (CTC): 'the failing which he shared with many other clever men increased. . . .'

4. Chalmers, *ibid*. He gives the date of the marriage as 1853, and Bessie Ingles' father's name as John; but these details are corrected by Helen Grahame.

5. See the genealogical table drawn up by Col. John Grahame, and printed by Chalmers opposite p. 2.

6. Chalmers, p. 1.

7. See G. M. Young, *Victorian England*, pp. 196 ff.

8. Chalmers, p. 4.

9. WW 158 ('The Piper at the Gates').

10. 'The Triton's Conch': NObs 16th Dec. 1893.

11. 'The Romance of the Rail': NObs 8th Aug. 1891 = PP 26.

12. 'Loafing': NObs 24th Jan. 1891 = PP 45.

13. 'The Triton's Conch', *passim*.

14. Chalmers, pp. 4-5.

15. Chalmers, p. 7: the letter is dated 2nd Oct. 1863, but the original does not appear to have survived. For this period Chalmers supplies almost the only available evidence.

16. Helen Grahame's letter of 22nd March 1933; Chalmers, pp. 8-9.

17. 'A Dark Star' (1929), reprinted by Chalmers: see p. 292.

18. GA 1: ('Prologue: The Olympians').

19. 'Ideals': *Fortnightly Review*, Dec. 1922; cf. Chalmers, pp. 9, 266, and also 263.

20. Letter of Reginald Ingles to EG, 28th March 1933 (CTC).

21. Letter of Helen Grahame to EG, 5th Oct. 1936 (CTC).

22. Letter of Bessie Luard to EG (CTC): n/d, but probably written after KG's death.

23. See n. 21 above; cf. GA 1.

24. *Crusaders* (1929), p. 150.

25. I am deeply grateful to The Hon. Claude Hope-Morley, the present owner of The Mount, who allowed me (like the young Grahame) to explore there at my leisure.

26. See *Meditations*, 4.3 (tr. Farquharson, p. 51).

27. Chalmers, p. 10.

28. I am only concerned with these two books here in so far as they illuminate KG's own childhood; a fuller analysis will be found in Chapter VIII.

29. Personal information supplied by Dr. Anthony Feiling and Prof. Sir Keith Feiling.

30. KG to Doreen Matthews, 27th Dec. 1931 (CTC); Helen Holmes Spicer (née Dunham) to EG, 18th March 1933 (CTC). The story about the circus was 'The Magic Ring'.

31. GA 11 ('A Holiday').

32. GA 92 ('What they talked about'); DD 63 ff. ('Mutabile Semper') and DD 178 ('A Saga of the Seas').

33. GA 135 ('The Blue Room').

34. GA 147 ('A Falling Out'); DD 36 ('Dies Irae'); cf. *ibid*. pp. 37-8 and DD 95 ('The Magic Ring').

35. See below, Chapter VIII.
36. *Crockford's Clerical Directory*, 1868; letters from Helen Grahame to EG, 18th March 1933 and 5th Oct. 1936; personal information, Miss Marjorie Ingles. Their account substantially corrects that of Chalmers, pp. 7 and 11.
37. GA 4 ('Prologue: The Olympians').
38. Letter of Helen Grahame, 5th Oct. 1936.
39. GA 1.
40. DD 44 ff. ('Dies Irae'); 103-5 ('The Magic Ring'); and especially PP 147 ff. ('Justifiable Homicide').
41. DD 9-10 ('The Twenty-first of October').
42. GA 76 ('A Harvesting').
43. PP 76-9 ('Marginalia').
44. *Twelve Years of a Soldier's Life in India* (1859), by Major Hodson, ed. G. H. Hodson.
45. Cf. Chalmers, p. 11.
46. Letter from Helen Grahame to EG, 22nd March 1933.
47. Chalmers, p. 12; letter from Reginald Ingles to EG, 16th March 1933 (CTC).
48. Personal communication, Mr. Maxfield Parrish.
49. PP 27 ('The Romance of the Rail').
50. *Ibid.* pp. 27-8.

II. THE SPELL OF OXFORD, 1868–1875

1. *Centuries of Meditation* (ed. Dobell, 1908), p. 158.
2. GA 32 ('Alarums and Excursions'); 114 ('The Roman Road'); DD 265 ('A Departure'); GA 100 ('The Argonauts'); DD 22 ('The Twenty-first of October'); GA 165 ('Lusisti Satis').
3. GA 157, 162, 165 ('Lusisti Satis').
4. GA 6 ('Prologue').
5. 'Oxford through a Boy's Eyes' (*Country Life*, 23rd Dec. 1932); Chalmers, p. 18.
6. GA 158 ('Lusisti Satis').
7. The Rev. J. C. Michel in *St. Edward's School Chronicle*, Jubilee Number (Vol. 12, no. 321), p. 264.
8. *Ibid.* p. 270. The founder, Thomas Chamberlain, 'was in close touch and sympathy with the leaders of the Oxford Movement'.
9. PP 158-9 ('The Fairy Wicket').
10. MS notes (CTC).
11. Prize-giving speech: date unknown. Perhaps in Dec. 1906: see *St. Edward's School Chronicle*, Vol. 11, no. 271, p. 92.
12. *Country Life*: see above, n. 5. This passage is omitted by Chalmers. Cf. 'Saturnalia' = Chalmers, pp. 107-8.
13. *St. Edward's School Chronicle*, Vol. 1, p. 209.

14. The Divinity Prize was J. L. Porter-Grant's *Cities of Bashan* (1873); Latin Prose was rewarded with Merivale's *Fall of the Roman Republic*; while for his class prize Grahame received Sanford's *Estimates of the English Kings*. These volumes are at present lying in (of all places) the Runnymede Museum; it would be interesting to know if he chose them, or had them thrust upon him.

15. Vol. 1, pp. 36-7 (1873).

16. PP 79 ('Marginalia'); GA 2 ('Prologue').

17. See especially PP 185 ff. ('Orion').

18. Quoted by F. Sidgwick, *The Complete Marjorie Fleming* (1934), p. vi.

19. *St. Edward's School Chronicle*, Vol. 1, pp. 147-8, 105, 133.

20. Letter to KG from Trant Chambers, 1st Dec. 1908 (CTC).

21. Chalmers, p. 13.

22. *St. Edward's School Chronicle*, Vol. 1, pp. 218, 231.

23. A loose sheet of scribbled MS. notes (CTC), possibly in preparation for 'Oxford through a Boy's Eyes'.

24. 'Oxford through a Boy's Eyes' = Chalmers, p. 20.

25. *Ibid.* = Chalmers, pp. 21-2.

26. *Ibid.* p. 22.

27. MS. in CTC. The second fragment is inked over pencil. After the text as quoted the following is legible in half-erased pencil: 'Here, in these quiet side-ways, the footing was cobble-stones, the house-fronts demure, blanched, and roofing this way or that, & straitened by the needs of a less [word illegible] generation; a generation of oh so prig[gish]. . . .' The rest, about a line and a half, is completely illegible.

28. 'Oxford in the Seventies', in *The Eighteen Seventies* (ed. Harley Granville-Barker, 1929), p. 211.

29. *Ibid.* p. 212.

30. 'Oxford through a Boy's Eyes' = Chalmers, p. 23.

31. Introduction to *Seventy Years a Showman* (1926), by 'Lord' George Sanger, pp. 5-29.

32. T. S. Eliot, 'The Dry Salvages', in *Four Quartets* (1944), p. 25; Chalmers, pp. 26-7. The source of this quotation is unknown; it does not occur among KG's published work or surviving MSS, and probably derives from a letter since lost or destroyed.

33. The tags include such phrases as *lusisti satis, mutabile semper, suave mari magno, hinc illae lacrimae, porta eburnea*. There are also references to Martial and Suetonius, two authors KG almost certainly never read: see PP 106 ('Of Smoking'), and 24 ('The Romance of the Rail'). The references are to Suetonius, *Life of Vespasian*, and Martial, *Epigrams*, 5. 20. For Homeric parodies see pp. 259-61 (Chapter XI); also GA 122 ('The Secret Drawer'); DD 18 ('The Twenty-first of October'), 54 ('Dies Irae'); and perhaps the whole of WW ch. xii ('The Return of Ulysses'), pp. 278 ff. For Marcus Aurelius see GA 114-15 ('The Roman Road'); PP 16 ('The Romance of the Road'), and 125 ('The White Poppy'). KG makes one original citation

in Greek at GA 81: the famous 'love undefeated in battle' tag from the *Antigone* of Sophocles, v. 781. There are also casual references—which do not demand original knowledge—to Aristophanes, Juvenal, Lucretius, Sallust, Tacitus, Livy, Tertullian, and Theocritus.

34. *E.g.* Stevenson, who provided him with the Martial epigram.
35. *The Stones of Venice* (1853), ch. vi.
36. 'An Old Master' = Chalmers, p. 249; cf. 'By a Northern Furrow' = Chalmers, pp. 189 ff.; 'Ideals' = Chalmers, pp. 267-8. See also Graham Hough, *The Last Romantics* (1949), p. vii.
37. T. S. Eliot, *ibid.* (see n. 32).
38. WW 4 ('The River Bank'); 192 ('Wayfarers All').
39. See PP 90-2 ('The Eternal Whither').
40. The holograph MS. (CTC) is in pencil, on a folded sheet of writing-paper. Chalmers transcribes it on pp. 210-11. He claims that KG was 'fond of canoeing', but offers no evidence to support a statement that runs counter to all we know of KG's normal river-habits. He also suggests that the fragment was composed in the Blewbury period (*i.e.* after 1910), though Blewbury is not even on the Thames. In fact (probably at Mrs. Grahame's urging) he, on several occasions, post-dated by twenty years or so work that was, in fact, written much earlier: he places 'By a Northern Furrow' after 1910, when in fact it appeared in 1888; he hints that 'Concerning Ghosts' (1892) belongs to the same period, ascribes the *Yellow Book* poem 'Quis Desiderio?' to the Pangbourne period, after 1924, and describes 'The Barn Door' (1893) as 'one of the infrequent essays of the "Boham" years' (p. 202). There were no essays—apart from 'The Fellow That Goes Alone'—in the Boham years; and that essay, doubtless for private reasons, was not reprinted by Chalmers. Mrs. Grahame may well have been anxious to obscure the fact that, apart from *The Wind in the Willows*, her husband wrote virtually nothing after his marriage in 1899. Conversely, she tended to take as a personal attack any suggestion that what Grahame wrote *before* his marriage was in any way preferable to *The Wind in the Willows* (personal information, Mr. Roger Lancelyn Green). These facts may explain Chalmers' quite deliberate (p. xvi) lack of direct documentation.
41. PP 66 ('The Rural Pan').
42. Holograph MS. fragment (CTC), n/d.
43. Chalmers, pp. 4, 32; letters to EG from Agnes Johnstone (CTC) dated 3rd April 1933; Bessie Luard (CTC), n/d; Helen Grahame, 22nd March 1933 (CTC).
44. Letter to EG from Reginald Ingles, 16th March 1933; Chalmers, pp. 32-3.
45. *Ibid.*; cf. KG's diary for 22nd April 1887 (CTC).

III. A LONDON PRELUDE, 1876-1878

1. Letter from KG to Sir Sydney Cockerell, 19th Feb. 1917 (CTC).
2. Chalmers, pp. 27-8, 31-2; personal communication, Miss Marjorie Ingles.

3. MS recollections sent with a covering letter to EG, 10th March 1933 (CTC). See below, n. 27.
4. Chalmers, p. 28.
5. PP 147 ('Justifiable Homicide').
6. *E.g.* DD 91-2, 97 ('The Magic Ring').
7. Reprinted by Chalmers, pp. 30-31.
8. Letter to EG from Bessie Luard (CTC). Mrs. Luard (David Ingles' daughter) wrote that Dr. Kingdon 'spoke of an uncle of Kenneth's "who did not seem to understand him"—whom I knew must be my father'. Though it is possible that Kenneth resented Uncle David's having got him into the Bank (and they did in fact quarrel in later life, as Miss Marjorie Ingles tells me), it seems much more probable that Dr. Kingdon's anonymous reference was to John Grahame. Uncle David had always been Kenneth's favourite; and in any case Dr. Kingdon would hardly be likely to allude to him in this fashion in Bessie's presence.
9. *The Puritan Tradition in English Life* (1956), pp. 76-7.
10. Entry in the 'ledger-diary' transcribed by Chalmers and reprinted by him, p. 37.
11. 'Plate-smashing and the Conjuror', transcribed from MS notes (CTC). The passage cited does not appear in Chalmers' printed version (pp. 209 ff.).
12. *The Critic*, Vol. 34 (1899), pp. 185-6; cf. Fyrth, pp. 131-2.
13. Holbrook Jackson, *The Eighteen Nineties* (1913), p. 24.
14. *Virginibus Puerisque* (2nd ed., 1887), p. 267 ('Pan's Pipes').
15. E. D. H. Johnson, *The Alien Vision of Victorian Poetry* (1952), p. 149.
16. *A History of the Bank of England*, Vol. 2 (1797-1914), pp. 199-200; cf. pp. 145, 193; 'The Eternal Whither' = PP 91; 'Long Odds' = *Yellow Book* (July 1895), pp. 78-86, cf. Chalmers, p. 82; 'The Eternal Whither' = PP 86, cf. GA 116, 125-6; PP 124-5, 167, and elsewhere.
17. Letter to EG from Annie Grahame, 10th March 1933, and attached 'recollections' (CTC); add Chalmers, p. 31, who, however, has no record of the residence at Draycott Lodge; personal communication, the Rev. J. A. B. Mercier.
18. *The Yellow Book*, Vol. 2 (July 1894), pp. 99-102.
19. G. M. Young, *Victorian England* (1953), p. 166; G. M. Trevelyan, *English Social History* (2nd ed., 1954), Vol. 4, p. 92.
20. Lionel Trilling, *Matthew Arnold* (1939), p. 114.
21. Cf. Kennedy Williamson, *W. E. Henley* (1930), pp. 160-1. The family resemblance between this piece and T. S. Eliot's *The Waste Land* (Section I, vv. 60-8) is unmistakable.
22. Letter to EG from Mrs. Agnes Johnstone, 3rd April 1933 (CTC).
23. David Daiches, *R. L. Stevenson* (1947), p. 156.
24. Letter to EG from Bessie Luard, n/d (CTC).
25. Letter to EG from Annie Grahame (see n. 17). She is very specific about the first date, but attributes the *Uncle Remus* episode to this occasion also.

Uncle Remus, however, was not published in England till 1881. I have assumed, on balance, that Miss Grahame was more likely to have confused two separate holidays than confused the date of the first, which may well have been drawn from a diary.

26. See n. 22 above.

27. Chalmers, p. 102. It is interesting to note that his other attempt to break away was also made in emulation of an author he admired: Matthew Arnold was, as is well known, an Inspector of Schools. See above, p. 51, and n. 3 to this chapter.

28. See Helen Grahame's letter to EG, 22nd March 1933.

29. Chalmers, pp. 34, 41; and daguerreotype opp. p. 40 of his book.

30. Miss Evelyn Lidderdale's reminiscences, as recorded by Chalmers, p. 102.

31. Not in 1886, as Chalmers supposes (p. 43); but this may be merely a misprint for 1876.

32. J. J. Jusserand, in *F. J. Furnivall: A Record* (1911), p. 91.

33. Sir Sidney Lee, *D.N.B.*, 2nd Suppl., Vol. 2 (1912), pp. 61 ff.

34. J. H. Wylie, in *op. cit.* (n. 32 above), pp. 199 ff.

35. *Ibid.* J. C. Castel and C. F. W. Mead, p. 23.

36. *Op. cit.* p. 61, col. 2.

37. *Op. cit.* (n. 32 above), pp. 29 ff.

38. *Transactions* of the New Shakespere Society (1877-9), p. xiii.

39. Sir Sidney Lee, *op. cit.* p. 64, col. 1.

40. Vol. 1, p. 109: 'The Congress is over, and Lord Beaconsfield returns today. His most violent opponents cannot deny that he has achieved a great success, indeed it is very doubtful whether any other statesman that we now have could have so dexterously managed to steer between the two opposite currents of opinion in the country . . .' &c. We may note the political jargon that crops up in *The Golden Age*; cf. GA 23 ('the motion being agreed to without a division, the House went into Committee of Supply'); GA 46, where Charlotte is 'as full of worry and anxiety as a Chancellor on a Budget night'; also 149, 159.

41. Chalmers, p. 35. He prints extracts on pp. xi-xii, 36-9, 101-2, 165-6, 182, and 274. While the loss of this primary evidence is greatly to be regretted, Mr. Roger Lancelyn Green assures me that, to the best of his recollection, the ledger did not in fact contain any diary entries.

42. *E.g.* the dialogue between KG's two selves quoted earlier in this chapter: see above, pp. 53-4, and n. 10.

43. Letter of 2nd May 1957 to the present writer.

44. *E.g.* Chalmers, pp. 38, 182 ('Lizard Lights'); 'As You Like It', NObs, 30th May 1891: partly reproduced by Chalmers, p. 36; 'Quis Desiderio?', NObs, 19th Sept. 1891 = Chalmers, p. 312; 'Love's Reveille', NObs, 27th Feb. 1892: never reprinted till now, see pp. 198-9; 'Cradle Song', NObs, 8th Oct. 1892, never reprinted; 'The Mountain Stream', *Hull Weekly News*,

15th April 1905, never reprinted. The ledger also contained a 'Ballade of Rabelais at Bow Street', the loss of which I find particularly tantalizing.

45. See below, Chapter X. Among possibly relevant titles in the ledger are 'Suzette' and 'The Forsaken Lover'.

46. Robert Herrick, *Hesperides* (1648), ed. L. C. Martin, p. 197: the first line properly reads 'Born *I was* to be old' etc. (To judge by the number of similar misquotations he makes, KG set down such stanzas from memory.) Matthew Arnold, *Poetical Works* (ed. C. B. Tinker and H. F. Lowry, 1949), pp. 248-9. Horace, *Odes*, 1.4.1-2. Cf. Chalmers, pp. 36-9, 274.

47. Letter from KG to 'Miss Joy', 8th Jan. 1909 (CTC).

48. NObs, 5th Nov. 1892; Chalmers, p. 196.

49. 'Ideals', *passim*; 'The Invention of Fairyland', *Academy*, 18th Dec. 1897, p. 542.

50. Chalmers, p. 39; Alan Pryce-Jones in the *London Mercury* (Sept. 1932), p. 446.

51. Chalmers, p. 38.

52. See above, n. 44. The ledger, according to Mr. Lancelyn Green, contained only fourteen poems in all.

53. Chalmers, pp. 43-4.

54. Letter to KG from Trant Chambers, 1st Dec. 1908 (CTC).

55. Chalmers, p. 46.

IV. Ulysses in Threadneedle Street, 1879-1887

1. Chalmers, pp. 28, 31-2, 101.

2. Chalmers, p. 101.

3. Letter from Miss R. M. Bradley to EG, 11th April 1933 (CTC).

4. Mrs. Jane E. Courtney, *Recollected in Tranquillity* (1926), pp. 163-4.

5. Allan Fea, *Recollections of Sixty Years* (1927), pp. 142 ff.

6. *Ibid.* p. 146.

7. *Ibid.* p. 149.

8. Personal information from Mr. A. W. Dascombe, the present Secretary of the Bank.

9. Fea, *op. cit.* pp. 144-5.

10. PP 65 ff.

11. Fea, pp. 143, 146, 197.

12. This was before the construction of new thoroughfares between the Strand and Holborn made it necessary to demolish over four acres of ancient houses and back streets. Cf. Fea, p. 153.

13. *Ibid.* pp. 196-7.

14. See especially 'Loafing', PP 45 ff., and 'The Inner Ear' (*Yellow Book*, April 1895, pp. 73-6 = Chalmers, pp. 70-3) where KG comments on the way in which 'journeymen in this great whirling London mill' become accustomed to the din, in fact cease to notice it; so that 'when we are set down, for a

brief Sunday, far from the central roar, our first sensation is that of a stillness corporeal, positive, aggressive'.

15. Letter from KG to Helen Dunham, 28th July 1896 (CTC).
16. *In a Tuscan Garden* (1902), p. 4. The anonymous author is identified by Annie Grahame as her mother.
17. Louis MacNeice, 'Eclogue for Christmas', in *Collected Poems, 1925–1948* (1949), p. 21.
18. 'Pastels' = Chalmers, pp. 52 ff.
19. Letter from KG to Graham Robertson, 2nd Feb. 1908 (Mr. Kerrison Preston); 'The Invention of Fairyland', *Academy*, 18th Dec. 1897, p. 542; cf. 'The Fabric of the Fairy Tale', *Daily Mail*, 16th Dec. 1899, *ad fin.*
20. 'The Iniquity of Oblivion' = Chalmers, p. 133; 'Cheap Knowledge' = PP 57-8.
21. 'Sanger and his Times', p. 9; 'By a Northern Furrow' = Chalmers, p. 193; 'The Fairy Wicket' = PP 162; Graham Robertson's memoir, reprinted by Chalmers, p. 98; letter to EG from Walter Grahame, 14th Dec. 1932; 'The Romance of the Rail' = PP 25.
22. Undated typewritten MS. (probably *c.* 1925) containing a speech made to the Literary and Dramatic Guild, Pangbourne, at the opening of an exhibition devoted to the work of Eric Kennington (CTC: hitherto unpublished).
23. 'The Iniquity of Oblivion' = Chalmers, p. 133.
24. A period of just over a fortnight (5th-22nd April 1887), for which KG's diary is extant reveals three separate visits: two of these last the whole evening and the other is 'from 3 to 10 p.m.' (CTC).
25. *Op. cit.* p. 74.
26. 'A Departure' = DD 268-9.
27. Letter from Major Reginald Ingles to EG, 16th March 1933, partially reproduced by Chalmers, pp. 34-5.
28. GA 72 ff., especially p. 81.
29. Both these passages are tacitly omitted by Chalmers.
30. 'The Iniquity of Oblivion' = Chalmers, pp. 130-1; letter from KG to Helen Dunham, 28th July 1896 (CTC).
31. Mary E. Richardson, letter to EG, n/d (CTC) = Chalmers, p. 67.
32. Chalmers, p. 69.
33. 'The Secret Drawer', GA 123 ff.
34. *Ibid.* p. 125.
35. PP 86-7 ('The Eternal Whither').
36. Chalmers, pp. 101-2.
37. Published in PP 85-92.
38. 'Ideals' = Chalmers, pp. 271-2; cf. *The Cambridge Book of Poetry for Children* (1916), p. 194.
39. PP 90-1 ('The Eternal Whither').
40. Chalmers, pp. 40-1.

41. Letter to EG, with attached reminiscences, 1st March 1933. The reminiscences were partially reproduced by Chalmers, pp. 110-11, with some of the most interesting passages omitted.

42. Quoted by Chalmers, p. 41.

43. Chalmers, p. 95.

44. Chalmers, pp. 68, 172, 176-82; letter to EG from Mary E. Richardson, n/d (CTC).

45. This is the general impression of witnesses; yet his passport records his height as 5 feet 11 inches. His heavy build, broad shoulders and upright stance may have made him appear taller than he actually was.

46. *In a Tuscan Garden* (1902), p. 13.

47. *Ibid.* pp. 159-60; letter of Annie Grahame to EG, 10th March 1933 (CTC).

48. Entry in the 'ledger-diary' cited by Chalmers, p. 276.

49. 'Ideals' = Chalmers, pp. 265-6.

50. Letter of Annie Grahame as above, n. 47; J. Munro in *F. J. Furnivall: A Volume of Personal Record* (1911), pp. lxxiv-v, Cf. Elsa Forman: 'Beatrice Cenci and Alma Murray', in the *Keats–Shelley Memorial Bulletin* no. 5 (1953), pp. 5-10.

51. All the details of this episode are taken from three torn-out sheets of KG's diary—the sole survivors—which cover the dates Sunday, 27th Feb.–Wednesday, 2nd March, and Wednesday, 6th April–Friday, 22nd April 1887. The pages measure 20 × 12½ cm., and have apparently been torn from a small diary or notebook; they are numbered 5-6, 7-8, 15-16. Presumably they were preserved precisely because they recorded in some detail the occasion of Cunningham Grahame's death and funeral.

52. Grahame adds later that this cemetery 'was chosen by Mr. Currie both because it was altogether more desirable than the great crowded town cemetery, and because the cost of ground for a grave *in perpetuity* was, in the latter, as much as 600 fcs—at Ste Adresse, only 100'.

53. 'Élévation', v. 4: *Les Fleurs du mal* (Éditions Romgaldi, 1950), p. 9.

54. 'By a Northern Furrow' = Chalmers, pp. 189-94.

V. PAGANS AND PHILISTINES, 1888–1893

1. Letter from KG to a Mr. Traill (identity unknown) cited by Chalmers, p. 42. This may be H. D. Traill, author of *The New Lucian*, etc.

2. M. and C. H. B. Quennell, *A History of Everyday Things in England*: part iv (1934), p. 26.

3. Esmé Wingfield-Stratford, *Victorian Sunset* (1932), pp. 26, 86-90.

4. *Hodge and His Masters* (1880), Vol. 2, pp. 254-6.

5. Quoted by Wingfield-Stratford, *op. cit.* p. 249.

6. See R. C. K. Ensor, *England 1870–1914* (1936), p. 334.

7. See R. H. Gretton, *A Modern History of the English People, 1880–1922* (2nd ed., 1930), pp. 342-3.

8. *Op. cit.* p. 66.
9. Gretton, *op. cit.* p. 144.
10. *The Beardsley Period* (1925), p. 97.
11. Wingfield-Stratford, *op. cit.* pp. 138 ff.
12. See in particular Cantos XIII and XVII: *Poems*, ed. F. E. Page (1949) pp. 378-9.
13. *Voces Populi* (1890), pp. 37 ff., 87 ff., and especially 90.
14. This list of Henley's activities is Denis Mackail's.
15. Letter of 18th Sept. 1888, quoted by Chalmers, p. 46. For Greenwood and the *St. James's Gazette* see J. W. Robertson Scott, *The Story of the Pall Mall Gazette* (1950), pp. 251 ff., 422.
16. Vol. 74, pp. 649-67 (June 1933) = Chalmers, pp. 286-310.
17. Letter and attached memoir from Sidney Ward to EG, 1st March 1933 (CTC).
18. Cf. Alan Pryce-Jones in the *London Mercury*, Sept. 1932, p. 446.
19. Kennedy Williamson, *W. E. Henley: a Memoir* (1930), p. 185.
20. J. H. Buckley, *W. E. Henley* (1945), pp. 131-2.
21. Williamson, *op. cit.* p. 195; cf. V. Payen-Payne, *Letters of W. E. Henley*, pp. 7-9.
22. Cf. John Connell, *W. E. Henley* (1949), p. 148.
23. *The Yellow Book*, Vol. 2 (July 1894), p. 283.
24. Letter to Coulson Kernahan, 27th Feb. 1899 (Mr. Charles Feinberg).
25. Quoted by Chalmers, p. 63.
26. *Ibid.* p. 47.
27. *Ibid.* p. 50.
28. Of a lady-novelist he once wrote: 'She is bent on dancing the can-can for a livelihood, and has quite forgotten that she has two wooden legs'.
29. Buckley, *op. cit.* p. 128.
30. *Autobiographies* (1955), pp. 124 ff.
31. C. L. Hinds, *Authors and I* (1921), pp. 103-4.
32. This is untrue: Grahame's hair was dark till it turned, somewhat prematurely, grey.
33. Quoted by Chalmers, p. 51.
34. *Autobiographies*, p. 129.
35. Quoted by Chalmers, p. 48.
36. 'The Romance of the Road' = PP 17-18.
37. 'Of Smoking' = PP 109.
38. *The Yellow Book*, Vol. 3 (Oct. 1894), pp. 146-8. The same issue carries a pastoral fantasy by Ernest Dowson called 'Apple Blossom in Brittany' (pp. 93-109).
39. R. C. Jebb, in his *Life of Bentley* (p. 200), writes: 'He is believed to have liked port, but to have said of claret that "it would be port if it could" '.
40. See Hilaire Belloc's anthology, *The Footpath Way* (1911), which contains contributions on this theme from—besides those quoted in the text—Thoreau, De Quincey, Sydney Smith, Whitman, and John Burroughs.

41. 'The Romance of the Rail' = PP 23.
42. *Virginibus Puerisque*, pp. 107 ff.
43. 'By a Northern Furrow' = Chalmers, p. 194.
44. For open fear, see 'By a Northern Furrow' (Chalmers, pp. 189-94); 'The Barn Door' (Chalmers, pp. 202-4), and preface to *The Cambridge Book of Poetry for Children* (1916), pp. xiii-xv; for gallows'-humour, *The Headswoman* (*passim*); also 'Non Libri Sed Liberi' = PP 35-7; 'The Eternal Whither' = PP 87-90; 'Deus Terminus' = PP 100; 'Justifiable Homicide' = PP 147 ff.; and 'Concerning Ghosts' = Chalmers, p. 197.
45. See *Oxford Dictionary of Quotations* (revised ed., 1949), p. 574b, and authorities there cited. Mlle Fyrth (p. 204) suggests that in Grahame the death-theme is almost totally absent, a theory not borne out by the text.
46. *Scholar-Gipsies* (1896), pp. 12, 17.
47. 'A Bohemian in Exile' = PP 131-43.
48. *Ibid.* pp. 137-8.
49. *Op. cit.* p. 158.
50. 'The Lost Centaur' = PP 180-1.
51. 'Orion', *passim*; PP 185-92.
52. 'Deus Terminus' = PP 100.
53. 'Aboard the Galley' = PP 170-1.
54. 'The White Poppy' = PP 123 ff.
55. 'Cheap Knowledge' = PP 55 ff.
56. 'Deus Terminus' = PP 98.
57. Ensor, *op. cit.* p. 553.
58. Clapham, *op. cit.* Vol. 2, pp. 358-60.
59. Quoted by Chalmers, pp. 109-10.
60. 'The Secret Drawer' = GA 122; 'A Falling Out' = GA 151.
61. Quoted by Chalmers, p. 111.
62. Especially 'The Romance of the Road' = PP 9-18; and 'Loafing' = PP 43-52.
63. PP 10-11.
64. *The Story of My Heart* (2nd ed., 1891), pp. 199, 169-70, 166.
65. *Sat. Rev. of Lit.*, Vol. 8, no. 52 (16th July 1932), p. 837: an editorial obituary notice of KG and his work.
66. 'Loafing' = PP 49-50. It is characteristic of KG that in one short paragraph he should quote—without acknowledgment—both Sir Thomas Browne ('fleshy integument') and D. G. Rossetti ('spins like a fretful midge').
67. Chalmers, p. 275.
68. 'Long Odds' = *The Yellow Book* (July 1895), pp. 78-86; reprinted by Chalmers, pp. 75-83.
69. See Chalmers, p. 81.
70. The first Tube line, the City and South London, was opened in 1890, and St. James's Park Station a year or two later. Therefore if the experience Grahame relates had any basis in fact, it must refer to either 1893 or 1894—

that is, to a time very shortly before 'Long Odds' was written. This increases the likelihood of the episode being based on Grahame's own feelings at the time.

VI. THE RURAL PAN, 1893–1894

1. Letter from KG to John Lane, the Bodley Head, 19th Jan. 1893 (CTC).
2. See Hinds, *loc. cit.*, quoted by Chalmers, p. 50, where 'The Olympians' is described, with notable meiosis, as 'that jolly thing about children'.
3. 'A Whitewashed Uncle', 25th March; 'The Finding of the Princess', 29th April; 'Young Adam Cupid', 20th May; 'The Burglars', 24th June; 'Snowbound', 23rd Sept. They all appeared in the *National Observer*, the first anonymously.
4. They are: 'The Triton's Conch' (23rd Dec. 1893); 'Pastels' (17th Feb. 1894); and 'An Old Master' (24th March 1894), all in the *National Observer*.
5. *The Academy*, no. 1335 (n/s), 4th Dec. 1897, p. 493.
6. Jane E. Courtney, *Recollected in Tranquillity* (1926), pp. 153, 163.
7. This view is attacked by Mr. Lancelyn Green, *Scots Magazine* (July 1945), p. 264. For a fuller discussion of HW see pp. 157-60.
8. Letters from KG to Sidney Lee, 12th March and 14th April 1891: Bodleian MS Eng. misc. d. 177, fols 237^R-240^R.
9. See 'An Old Master' = Chalmers, pp. 249-52.
10. Quoted by Chalmers, p. 55. Cf. *Nicholas Crabbe*, pp. 36 ff.
11. 'Lusisti Satis' = GA 160.
12. Chalmers, p. 56.
13. *Ibid.* pp. 55-8; cf. *Pall Mall Gazette*, 20th March 1894; *Critic*, Vol. 34 (1899), pp. 185-6.
14. Letter from KG to Miss R. M. Bradley, 22nd Dec. 1904 (CTC).
15. *The Nation*, Vol. 75, pp. 206 ff. Cf. J. H. Buckley, *The Victorian Temper* (1952), p. 193.
16. Buckley, *op. cit.* p. 193. Cf. p. 204 for the occultism and 'perverse sexual mysticism' of Laurence Oliphant.
17. *The Pagan Review* (1892), p. 16.
18. Vol. 172, pp. 273-304.
19. See W. Hazlitt, *Complete Works* (Centenary Edition, ed. P. P. Howe, 1930-4), Vol. 4, p. 250; Vol. 6, p. 192; and Vol. 11, p. 33.
20. *Virginibus Puerisque* (2nd ed., 1887), pp. 262 ff.
21. *Memory Hold-the-Door* (1940), pp. 135-6.
22. *The Beardsley Period* (1925), pp. 110-13.
23. *The Dial*, Vol. 3 (1893), p. 18; Vol. 7 (1897), pp. 12, 24.
24. *The Great God Pan* (Caerleon Edition), pp. 13-14; *The Complete Short Stories of 'Saki'* (1930), pp. 187-93.
25. *Dramatic Idylls* (2nd Series, 1880): 'Pan and Luna'. Pan was also supposed to be—and Beardsley certainly knew this—the discoverer of onanism. Cf.

Konrad Wernicke in Roscher's *Lexikon der griechischen und römischen Mythologie*, Vol. 3.1, cols. 1396-7. Cf. also Maurice Hewlett's *Pan and the Young Shepherd*: 'Not heard the song o' the world? Hark then: 'tis couple, and couple, and couple.'

26. Book I, ll. 283-4; cf. ll. 263-8.
27. *Letters*, ed. L. Binyon (1926), p. 84.
28. *Attitudes and Avowals* (1910), pp. 19-20.
29. L. R. Farnell, *Cults of the Greek States* (1909), Vol. 5, pp. 432-4.
30. *Phaedrus*, 279B.
31. Roscher, *op. cit.* col. 1382.
32. 'The Rural Pan' is sub-titled 'An April Essay'; cf. 'A Bohemian in Exile' = PP 140-1.
33. 'The Lost Centaur' = PP 179.
34. 'By a Northern Furrow' = Chalmers, p. 191; 'The Rural Pan' = PP 67.
35. 'The Rural Pan' = PP 67-8.
36. *Ibid.* pp. 69-71.
37. Letter from Mrs. Helen Holmes Spicer to EG, 18th March 1933.
38. *The Times*, 19th July 1932.
39. *The Rising Generation*: cited in *The Modern Child*, ed. Hervey Elwes (1908), pp. 129-30.
40. English translation by M. Gabain (1930): see esp. pp. 91-2, 169-70, 175 ff., 231, 243, 248.
41. *Ibid.* p. 17.

VII. THE GOLDEN YEARS, 1894–1898

1. Netta Syrett, *The Sheltering Tree* (1939), p. 80; Holbrook Jackson, *The Eighteen Nineties* (1913), p. 23.
2. Chalmers, p. 64.
3. 'Reticence in Literature', in *The Yellow Book*, Vol. 1 (April 1894), p. 212.
4. Albert Parry, quoted by Chalmers, p. 65. Cf. *Nicholas Crabbe,* pp. 27 ff.
5. Quoted by Chalmers, p. 68.
6. Letter to EG from Evelyn Sharp (Mrs. H. W. Nevinson), 16th April 1933 (CTC).
7. Netta Syrett, *op. cit.* pp. 77, 97.
8. Quoted by Chalmers, p. 66.
9. *Unfinished Adventure* (1933), pp. 57-8.
10. *Ibid.* p. 64.
11. Syrett, *op. cit.* pp. 97-8; and quoted by Chalmers, p. 66.
12. Sharp, *op. cit.* p. 57.
13. Source as in n. 6.
14. Quoted by Chalmers, p. 55.
15. Cf. William Gaunt, *The Aesthetic Adventure* (Penguin ed., 1957), pp. 151-60.
16. Chalmers, p. 84.

17. Letter to EG, 10th March 1933; Sidney Ward's reminiscences to EG, 1st March 1933 (CTC).
18. See Webster's *Dictionary of Biography* (1943), p. 619, col. 1.
19. See Clapham, *op. cit.* Vol. 2, pp. 360-3.
20. T. T. Greg, *In Varying Mood* (1924), pp. vii-viii. Cf. also *Through a Glass Lightly* (1897), for the essays on wine.
21. Letter to EG from Walter Grahame, 14th Dec. 1932 (CTC).
22. *In Varying Mood*, p. 10.
23. *Ibid.* p. 33.
24. HW, 1-2.
25. *Ibid.* pp. 6-7.
26. Cf. Chalmers, p. 69.
27. 'Reed Talk', in *Scots Magazine* (July 1945), p. 264.
28. HW, 24-5.
29. *E.g.* Mr. Lancelyn Green, *loc. cit.*; and the critic of the *Academy*, no. 1382 (29th Oct. 1898), p. 143.
30. *The Yellow Book*, Vol. 3, pp. 25-47.
31. 'At the next Beltane feast Cathal the Red slept beside Aeaill in the burial-place of the kings at Brugh, and Guthbinn sat in the high seat . . .' &c.
32. See Bibliography.
33. See Chalmers, pp. 86-7.
34. Vol. 67 (1897), pp. 225-7.
35. See Elwes, *op. cit.* pp. 59-60. The following is a typical extract: 'The punishment of the doll is an important element in nursery life. It is apt to be carried out with formal solemnity and often with something of brutal emphasis', &c.
36. *Academy*, no. 1335 (n.s.), 4th Dec. 1897, p. 493.
37. Letter of Miss R. M. Bradley to EG, 11th April 1933 (CTC).
38. Personal information, Mrs. K. R. West.
39. WW 106.
40. WW 204-5; cf. KG's letter to Austin Purves, 24th Aug. 1910: 'the pleasant city of Marseilles—where I once ate a perfectly whacking and stupendous quantity of bouillabaisse'.
41. Clapham, Vol. 2, p. 365.
42. 'The Inner Ear', 'Long Odds', and 'The Iniquity of Oblivion'.
43. Quoted by Holbrook Jackson, *op. cit.* p. 19.
44. *Unfinished Adventure*, p. 57.
45. *Ibid.* pp. 62 ff.
46. Letter to EG from Helen Holmes Spicer, 18th March 1933 (CTC).
47. *The Yellow Book*, Vol. 10 (July 1896), p. 76.
48. Cf. Gretton, *op. cit.* pp. 359, 392, 406-7.
49. *Academy*, no. 1335 (n.s.), p. 493.
50. Personal information, Mr. A. W. Dascombe, the present Secretary.
51. Evelyn Sharp, *op. cit.* pp. 62 ff.

52. Quoted by Chalmers, pp. 112-13.
53. See above, n. 49.
54. *Academy*, 18th Dec. 1897, p. 542.
55. KG to Grace Dunham, 10th March 1898 (CTC).
56. *Bookman*, March 1899, p. 190; *Athenaeum*, 4th Feb. 1899 (no. 3719, p. 142).

VIII. AUNTS, ARTISTS, AND OTHERS

1. F. J. H. Darton, *Children's Books in England* (1932), p. 297.
2. *Edward Lear* (1938), p. 196.
3. Vol. 76 (25th Jan. 1896), p. 140.
4. *London Mercury* (Sept. 1932), p. 448.
5. GA 72-81.
6. GA 116 ; cf. 125-6.
7. DD 206-7.
8. GA 2-5.
9. See 'The Blue Room', *passim*.
10. See Katharine West's *Chapter of Governesses* (1949), esp. pp. 166 f.
11. 'Snowbound' =GA 84.
12. *E.g.* 'Lusisti Satis' and 'A Departure'.
13. 'A Falling Out' =GA 154.
14. *Scholar-Gypsies* (1896), p. 195.
15. GA 81.
16. 'The Twenty-first of October', DD 17; 'Dies Irae', DD 49-51.
17. See pp. 222-44: esp. 240, 228, 233-4.
18. 'Dies Irae' =DD 37-8.
19. 'The Twenty-first of October', *passim*; cf. Fyrth, pp. 91-4.
20. 'The Magic Ring' =DD 100.
21. See Pryce-Jones, *loc. cit.* p. 449; and Fyrth, pp. 98-100.
22. 'Lusisti Satis' =GA 164.
23. *Ibid.*
24. 'The Twenty-first of October' to follow 'A Falling Out'; 'Dies Irae' after 'Mutabile Semper' as a pendant to 'Young Adam Cupid'; 'The Magic Ring' after 'Alarums and Excursions'; 'Its Walls were as of Jasper' between 'The Argonauts' and 'The Roman Road'; 'A Saga of the Seas' to follow 'A Holiday'; 'A Departure' after 'Lusisti Satis'. 'The Reluctant Dragon' is essentially separate from the other stories, and should be so printed.

IX. MR. GRAHAME AND MISS THOMSON, 1899

1. Letter to Lucy Gullett, 20th May 1913; cf. Curtis Brown, *Contacts* (1935), pp. 64-5, Fyrth, pp. 88-9.
2. 'The Fairy Wicket' =PP 160-1.

3. P. 384.
4. NObs, 8th Oct. 1892, p. 535.
5. Chalmers, p. 38.
6. L. A. G. Strong, *Courtauld-Thomson: A Memoir* (1958), pp. 11-12.
7. *Ibid.* p. 15.
8. Sir John Tenniel to EG, 25th Jan. 1898.
9. The Hon. Hugh Fletcher Moulton, *Life of Lord Moulton* (1922), p. 147.
10. Strong, *op. cit.*, p. 14.
11. *D.N.B.* (1912-1921), p. 393.
12. Personal communication, Mr. Dale Purves.
13. Personal communication, Mr. Malcolm Elwin.
14. Personal information, Miss Enid Mitchell.
15. *Daily Mail*, 16th Dec. 1899, p. 4.
16. DD 168-9.
17. 2nd April 1899 (CTC).
18. Personal information, Dr. Anthony Feiling.
19. His informant was Miss R. M. Bradley, who seems to have acted as a discreet confidante throughout the affair.
20. See *D.N.B.* (1912-1921), p. 394, col. 1.
21. The comparison is hardly flattering to Elspeth. Miss Skiffins (*Great Expectations*, ch. 37) 'was of a wooden appearance . . . She might have been some two or three years younger than Wemmick, and I judged her to stand possessed of portable property. The cut of her dress from the waist upward, both before and behind, made her figure very like a boy's kite; and I might have pronounced her gown a little too decidedly orange, and her gloves a little too intensely green.'
22. Personal information, Miss Barbara Euphan Todd.
23. Personal information, Miss Foy Quiller-Couch; F. Brittain, *Arthur Quiller-Couch* (1947), p. 34; Chalmers, pp. 95-6, 182, 185; material in the Courtauld-Thomson Collection.

X. THE WILD WOOD AND THE WIDE WORLD, 1900–1907

1. His income was derived from the family soap and perfume business, which still flourishes under the same name.
2. Personal information, Miss Foy Quiller-Couch, Mr. Lawrence Forbes, Mr. Dale Purves, and Mr. John C. Purves.
3. Letter of 8/9th July 1899 (CTC).
4. Chalmers, p. 84.
5. Emma L. Hardy to EG, 20th Aug. 1899 (CTC).
6. All these verses are taken from EG's MSS in the Courtauld-Thomson Collection.
7. So Chalmers explains his long silence: see p. 120.
8. *Op. cit.* p. 396.

9. Personal communication to the present writer.

10. Grahame, according to A. J. A. Symons, specifically denied having ever met Corvo. Letter to EG, 5th Jan. 1935 (CTC). Cf. *Nicholas Crabbe*, p. 84, and Cecil Woolf's introduction, p. 7.

11. Letter to EG, 11th April 1933 (CTC).

12. Chalmers, p. 96.

13. *Letters*, p. 284.

14. Chalmers, p. 97.

15. *Ibid.*

16. Letter of 20th June 1899 (CTC).

17. Letter of 26th June 1899 (CTC).

18. Letter from KG to Dr. (later Sir William) Collins, the eye-specialist, 18th Nov. 1901 (Mr. Richard G. Hubbard).

19. Not the 4th, as Chalmers supposes.

20. Contemporary newspaper reports in particular *The Times* of Wednesday, 25th Nov., p. 11, and Thursday, 26th Nov., p. 11; Chalmers, pp. 113-17; private letters in the Courtauld-Thomson Collection.

21. In all that follows here I am heavily indebted to the late Mr. L. A. G. Strong's account in *Courtauld-Thomson: A Memoir*, pp. 45-53. Cf. also the brief account by the Hon. Hugh Fletcher Moulton, *Life of Lord Moulton*, pp. 148-9.

22. Letter to Mrs. Ward, 15th May 1904 (Mrs. Ruth Lichtensteiger).

23. Chalmers, p. 121.

24. Pencil draft on the back of Miss Hoveed's letter (CTC).

25. Letter to Mrs. Lane, 6th Dec. 1904 (CTC).

26. This letter is now in the possession of Miss Foy Quiller-Couch.

27. KG to Mrs. S. M. Ward, 14th May 1905 (Mrs. Ruth Lichtensteiger).

28. FW pp. 2-3; KG to Quiller-Couch, 29th Dec. 1905 (Miss Foy Quiller-Couch).

29. FW p. 11.

30. Chalmers, pp. 150-4.

31. KG to Quiller-Couch, 29th Dec. 1905.

32. See Chalmers, p. 28.

XI. THE ROAD TO XANADU, 1907–1908: PART I

1. 'The Eternal Whither' =PP 91-2.

2. Richard Jefferies, *The Open Air* (1885), pp. 113-17; cf. *Nature Near London* (1883), p. 133.

3. Jefferies, *The Life of the Fields* (1884), p. 40.

4. *E.g.* GA 15-16 ('A Holiday').

5. Jefferies, *Nature Near London*, p. 132; *The Life of the Fields*, p. 49; cf. WW 48-9 ('The Wild Wood').

6. *Wood Magic* (1881), p. 108: ' "Sing slower," said Bevis presently, "I want to hear what you are saying." So the Brook sang slower, but then it

was too low, and he could not catch the words.' It it interesting to compare the double theme which preoccupies Grahame in *The Wind in the Willows* —the judgment of Innocence on the World, the deep basic symbolism of the River—with the somewhat different treatment both receive in Mark Twain's *Huckleberry Finn*. Twain's classic had appeared in 1885, and there is little doubt that Grahame knew it well. He certainly gave a copy to his son.

7. Esmé Wingfield-Stratford, *Victorian Aftermath* (1933), pp. 210 ff., 177.
8. Cf. Ensor, *op. cit.* pp. 553-4.
9. Wingfield-Stratford, *ibid.* p. 156.
10. Buckley, *W. E. Henley*, pp. 131-2.
11. 'Cheap Knowledge' = PP 55 ff.; cf. G. D. H. and M. Cole's Introduction to Cobbett's *Rural Rides* (3 Vols., 1930), pp. xxviii-xxix.
12. See above, pp. 59, 103-4.
13. See 'Sanger and his Times': introduction to *Seventy Years a Showman*, by 'Lord' George Sanger, pp. 5-29.
14. Personal information, Mrs. Florence Image.
15. WW 124-5 ('Mr. Toad'); cf. 249-50 ('Like Summer Tempests').
16. WW 52 ('The Wild Wood').
17. WW 255-6 ('Like Summer Tempests').
18. WW 287 ('The Return of Ulysses').
19. Letter to Caroline, Margaret, and Frank Sharpe, 31st Dec. 1908 (CTC).
20. WW 176-7 ('The Further Adventures of Toad').
21. Letter to EG, 13th June 1899 (CTC).
22. See FW pp. 45-6 or Chalmers, p. 159, for the text.
23. WW 182 ('Toad's Adventures').
24. See above, pp. 141 ff.
25. PP 124-5 ('The White Poppy').
26. WW 196-7 ('Wayfarers All').
27. WW 202, cf. 211, 216.
28. Letter to Graham Robertson, 11th Sept. 1908 (Mr. Kerrison Preston).
29. Letter to EG, 10th Oct. 1908 (CTC).
30. See *Punch*, Vol. 135, p. 360 (11th Nov. 1908); *Sat. Rev. of Lit.*, Vol. 106, no. 2772 (12th Dec. 1908), Suppl., p. x; *T.P.'s Weekly*, Vol. 12, no. 318, p. 765 (11th Dec. 1908); *The Nation*, Vol. 4, no. 10, p. 404 (5th Dec. 1908).
31. *Bookman*, Jan. 1909, pp. 190-1.
32. Letter to Philip Sandbach, 28th Sept. 1930 (CTC).
33. *Punch, ibid.*; Chalmers, pp. 127-8; *The New Age*, 24th Oct. 1908 = *Books and Persons* (1917), pp. 57-9.
34. Chalmers, quoting this remark, makes it appear to be Bennett's own opinion. See p. 127 of his book.
35. Grahame quotes Borrow twice: see PP 16, 138. For Morris, see pp. 262-263.

36. GA 122 ('The Secret Drawer'); DD 18 ('Twenty-first of October'), 54 ('Dies Irae'). Cf. GA 106, 130, 165; DD 110 and elsewhere. For Grahame's other classical allusions see above, p. 44, and n. 33 to Chapter II, pp. 354-5.

37. WW 278 ('The Return of Ulysses') and 157-8 ('The Piper at the Gates').

38. Cf. Fyrth, p. 48.

39. KG to R. W. M. Mansel-Carey, 16th Jan. 1925 (CTC), in which he admits the practice, with reference to the carol fragment in 'The Reluctant Dragon'.

40. I have identified quotations from, or allusions to, the following: Matthew Arnold, Daisy Ashford, Blake, Borrow, Miss Braddon, Sir Thomas Browne, Browning, Bunyan, Burton, Samuel Butler, Byron, Lewis Carroll, Caxton, Coleridge, Collins, Crashaw, Defoe, De Quincey, Dickens, Austin Dobson, Doyle, George Eliot, Emerson, Fielding, FitzGerald, Mrs. Gaskell, W. S. Gilbert, Herrick, Ellen C. Howarth, Thomas Hughes, Johnson (L.), Jonson, Keats, Kingsley, Kipling, Lamb, T. E. Lawrence, L'Estrange, Charles Lever, Longfellow, Malory, Marvell, Masefield, Meredith, Milton, Moore (T. S.), More, Morris (W.), Pater, Rogers (S.), Rossetti (D. G.), Ruskin, Scott, Shakespeare, Shelley, Sheridan, Skelton, Sterne, Stevenson, Surtees, Swift, Swinburne, Tennyson, Thackeray, Thoreau, Traherne (?), Tupper, Whitman, Wordsworth, and Charlotte Yonge. Industrious readers will probably find many more that I have missed. For many of these identifications I am greatly indebted to Mr. Lancelyn Green's tireless research on my behalf; I only regret that space forbids my tabulating the exact source of each quotation, with which he kindly supplied me.

41. Graham Hough, The Last Romantics (1949), pp. 25-7. Perhaps I should say here that I only came to read Mr. Hough's brilliantly stimulating book when my own first draft was almost complete. It was comforting to find conclusions at which I had arrived independently confirmed in detail by a scholar of Mr. Hough's standing.

42. See above, pp. 83-4, 96.

43. Op. cit. p. 112.

44. Cf. 'Ideals' = Chalmers, p. 271; private papers (CTC).

45. Prologue to The Earthly Paradise (Nonesuch ed., p. 437).

46. Hough, p. 112; cf. Chalmers, p. 128.

47. Hough, p. 171.

48. FW, p. 31.

XII. THE ROAD TO XANADU, 1907–1908: PART 2

1. Chalmers, p. 122.

2. Eleanor Graham, The Story of 'The Wind in the Willows': How it came to be Written (1950), p. 2.

3. See FW, pp. 64 ff.

4. Ibid. p. 48.

5. There is a Red Lion Hotel at Bourne End just across the river from Cookham; Grahame probably had this in mind.

6. Similarly WW went through successive stages of rough pencil draft, holograph MS, typescript and proofs, with alterations at every point. Fragments of the pencil draft survive among Grahame's papers. For the legend of the uncorrected holograph see Chalmers, p. 123: he must have derived this information from EG.

7. Personal communication, Mr. Edmund R. Purves.

8. *Ibid.* Mr. Purves adds: 'I believe my mother had some evidence that KG actually had the boating trip in mind'.

9. Personal communication, Mr. Dale Purves.

10. See nn. 7-8.

11. Constance Smedley, *Crusaders* (1929), pp. 149-53; Chalmers, p. 125; Thomas Hardy to EG, 31st Aug. 1907 (CTC).

12. Reprinted in FW, pp. 41-7 (with photostat reproduction), and Chalmers, pp. 154-60.

13. *Across the Plains* (1892), pp. 298-300 ('Pulvis et Umbra').

14. Reprinted by Chalmers, p. 138 (10th Oct. 1908).

15. No date; probably Aug.–Sept. 1908 (CTC). See above, p. 258.

16. See *The New Age*, 24th Oct. 1908 = *Books and Persons* (1917), pp. 57-9; and Chalmers, pp. 127-8, where Middleton's *Vanity Fair* notice is reprinted. Cf. above, pp. 258-9.

17. PP 175 ff. Cf. GA 5, where animals are considered nearer reality than the Olympians.

18. FW, pp. 21-2, 33.

19. Letter to EG, 5th Feb. 1933 (CTC).

20. FW, pp. 9-10.

21. WW 92 ('Mr. Badger').

22. See above, p. 58.

23. See above, pp. 63-73, 92, 97-8.

24. *The Road to Xanadu*, p. 430.

25. PP 68 ('The Rural Pan'). Cf. Fyrth, pp. 112-16.

26. *The Happy Prince* (1888), p. 67.

27. *Ibid.* p. 68.

28. Cf. Fyrth, p. 117: 'Rat est rêveur, nonchalant, et un peu bohème; Mole est pratique, positif, et tant soit peu "bourgeois", mais tous les deux savent la valeur des joies essentielles de la vie: les amis et le foyer'.

29. See above, pp. 241-2; and *Amaryllis at the Fair* (ed. E. Garnett, 1904), esp. pp. 31-3.

30. WW 262 ('Like Summer Tempests').

31. Fyrth, pp. 121-2.

32. Gretton, p. 733.

33. See above, pp. 269-70.

34. WW 130 ('Mr. Toad'); cf. 164-6.

35. *Toad of Toad Hall* (1929), p. 31.
36. WW 139; cf. 40 ff., 127-30.
37. See above, p. 166; and cf. WW 31 ff.
38. *The Schoolmistress*, 6th Sept. 1934, p. 579.
39. See WW 226-7 ('The Further Adventures of Toad').
40. Personal information, Mr. Spencer Curtis Brown.
41. *E.g.* those of Paul Bransom (1913); Nancy Barnhart (1922); Wyndham Payne (1927); E. H. Shepard (1931); Arthur Rackham (1940), and Paul Hemming (1947).
42. Letter to the present writer, 3rd April 1957; cf. Chalmers, p. 90.
43. Letter to EG (n.d.) in the Courtauld-Thomson Collection.
44. WW 94 ('Dulce Domum').
45. Cf. Pocock, *ibid.*

XIII. The Vanishing Dream, 1908–1913

1. Chalmers, p. 113; papers in the Courtauld-Thomson Collection.
2. W. M. Acres in *The Old Lady*, Vol. 8, no. 47 (Sept. 1932), p. 206.
3. W. B. Hillkirk, *ibid.* Vol. 26, no. 117 (March 1950), cf. Chalmers, p. 117, and see above, p. 224.
4. FW, p. 46: cf. above, pp. 223-4.
5. See Chalmers, pp. 91-2, 139.
6. *Ibid.* p. 90.
7. Curtis Brown, *Contacts* (1935), p. 60.
8. Fyrth, p. 26, citing a private letter from EG.
9. Smedley, *op. cit.* p. 152.
10. *Ibid.* pp. 180-3.
11. I have quoted these letters direct from photostat copies most generously provided by Mr. Pierre M. Purves. They contain matter silently suppressed by Chalmers, who reprints the series (these omissions apart) between pp. 219-48 of his book.
12. Letter to Austin Purves, 19th Dec. 1908.
13. Letter to KG from Trant Chambers, 23rd Nov. 1908 (CTC).
14. He wrote again on 22nd April 1909, soliciting literary or journalistic work; on 1st Feb. 1910, destitute, starving, and suicidal—on this occasion KG recommended him (unsuccessfully) to a charitable organization; on 17th Oct. 1910, when he was working as a temporary porter at Paddington; and on 31st Oct., when he was resting and recuperating with the Rev. A. B. Simeon, their former master at St. Edward's. After this there is silence till 18th Jan. 1919, when he sent KG a copy of the *School Chronicle*, with the hope that 'you are flourishing in every way you could desire in what is for most of us a rather hard and perplexing world'.
15. Letter to Constance Smedley, 3rd Jan. 1909, reprinted in *Crusaders*, pp. 191-2.
16. p. 274.
17. See above, p. 46 and n. 40, p. 355.

18. Letter to Austin Purves, 27th July 1909.
19. This suggests a congenital defect which Alastair may have inherited on his mother's side: see above, pp. 227-8, 234-5, 312, 318, 322-30.
20. Letters to Quiller-Couch (10th Jan. 1910) and Purves (12th Jan. 1910); cf. Chalmers, p. 188.
21. Letter from Naomi Stott to EG, 15th March 1908 (CTC).
22. Letter to Quiller-Couch, 10th Jan. 1910 (Miss Foy Quiller-Couch).
23. FW, p. 26; Chalmers, p. 194.
24. Letters to Austin Purves (29th May 1910); A. W. Lidderdale (28th May 1910) and Constance Smedley (reprinted by Chalmers, p. 195).
25. Chalmers, p. 211; personal information, Mr. Roger Lancelyn Green.
26. 'Frater Ave Atque Vale': *Bookman*, Vol. 76, pp. 69-74 (Jan. 1933), reprinted FW, pp. 22-32.
27. FW, pp. 26-8. Hamilton writes: 'I cannot, of course, report his words with absolute fidelity; but I can recover at least the gist of his reply'.
28. Personal communication to the present writer, 4th April 1957.
29. FW, p. 24.
30. Letter to A. W. Lidderdale, 3rd Oct. 1910; and to R. E. Moody, 2nd June 1914 (CTC).
31. Personal information, the Rev. K. H. Jocelyn and Mrs. M. Hesketh Williams.
32. Letters of Gordon Home to KG, 27th July and 5th Aug. 1910.
33. Letter from KG to Austin Purves, 15th May 1911 = Chalmers, p. 235.
34. *Id.*, 20th Sept. 1911 = Chalmers, pp. 237-8.
35. *Contacts*, p. 65.
36. Letter to Austin Purves, 8th Feb. 1912 = Chalmers, p. 238.
37. Chalmers, pp. 284-5; FW, pp. 19-20. The Grahames stayed at the celebrated Hotel Julia, which was hardly suggestive of penury—and certainly no cheaper than could be had in Northern Italy. For KG's personal relations with children see also below, p. 311.
38. Letter to Quiller-Couch, 26th Dec. 1911 (Miss Foy Quiller-Couch). The Latin lines (*Epit. Damon.* 48-9) mean: 'But out of doors an evil south wind is whirling everything about, and thundering down on the elms'.
39. Letter to Austin Purves, 4th March 1912; *Contacts*, pp. 58-9.
40. Letter to EG from Sir Sydney Cockerell, 10th Oct. 1932 (CTC).
41. *St. Edward's School Chronicle*, July 1913. See Introduction, pp. 4-6.
42. Personal communication to the present writer, 4th April 1957.
43. *Authors and I* (1921), p. 106.
44. Letter to Graham Robertson, 4th Dec. 1913 (Mr. Kerrison Preston).

XIV. Illusion and Tragedy, 1914–1920

1. Letter from Roger A. Raven to Alastair Grahame, 22nd Oct. 1914 (CTC).
2. 18th Feb. 1915. Chalmers (pp. 246-7) excises the passage. Cf. Rugby School Register (1892-1921), Vol. 4, p. 418.

3. Letter to KG, 27th Nov. 1914 (Miss Foy Quiller-Couch).
4. Chalmers, p. 151.
5. *Ibid.* p. 153.
6. *Ibid.* p. 168.
7. EG to Courtauld Thomson, 29th Dec. 1915 (CTC).
8. KG to Austin Purves, 18th Feb. 1915; EG to Courtauld Thomson, 29th Dec. 1915 (CTC).
9. KG to Mrs. R. P. Boas, 15th Feb. 1916 (CTC).
10. KG to Graham Robertson, 4th Dec. 1913 (Mr. Kerrison Preston); John Masefield to KG, 22nd June 1914 (CTC).
11. 1st June 1916.
12. The *Scotsman*, 20th April 1916; *Morning Post,* 20th April 1916; *Athenaeum*, April 1916; *Aberdeen Daily News*, 17th April 1916.
13. *The Cambridge Book of Poetry for Children* (1916), Vol. 1, pp. xiv-xv.
14. 17th May 1916.
15. EG to Courtauld Thomson, 16th Aug. 1917 (CTC).
16. *Id.*, 30th Dec. 1917.
17. Letter to KG from G. C. Richards, 22nd March 1920.
18. Personal information, Mrs. Beatrice Horton; Chalmers, p. 167.
19. The complete letter is printed by Chalmers, pp. 62-3. It contains many charming details.
20. Chalmers, p. 151.
21. Personal information, the Rev. K. H. Jocelyn.
22. Letter to AG from B. Johnson, Palm Sunday 1920 (CTC).
23. EG to Kenneth Josling, 20th March 1920 (CTC).
24. Ernest Josling to AG, 4th May 1920 (CTC).
25. Chalmers, p. 169; *Oxford Chronicle*, Friday 14th May 1920 (University Pages, iii-iv); personal information, Mrs. M. Hesketh Williams.
26. Personal information, Professor Sir Keith Feiling.
27. Letter to EG, 19th May 1920 (Miss Foy Quiller-Couch).
28. See n. 26.
29. *Oxford Chronicle, ibid.*
30. 'A Funeral': see Chalmers, p. 30. *The Wild Duck* is not the only Ibsen parallel that springs to mind; it seems possible that *Ghosts* is also relevant.

XV. The Reeds by the River, 1920–1932

1. This would appear to be a correct judgment. The only composer Grahame ever mentions by name is Rameau (PP 162). This is suggestive: see below. Elsewhere his attitude seems to resemble that of Wilde in *The Picture of Dorian Gray*, who described Dvořák as having written 'passionate, curiously coloured things'. On the other hand, it is interesting how closely KG's thematic material corresponds to the programmatic titles chosen by a con-

temporary composer such as Debussy. Here are some of them: 'L'Isle joyeuse' (1904); 'Children's Corner' (1906-8); 'Paysage sentimental' (1880); 'Pierrot' (1882); 'La Flûte de Pan' (1897); and 'Hommage à Rameau' (1905). The 'sea and cathedral bells' in the strumming episode of *The Golden Age* (pp. 76 ff.) suggest the as yet unwritten 'Cathédrale engloutie' (1910). Clearly the general atmosphere on which KG drew had permeated all the arts, and was by no means restricted to England.

2. Personal communications to the present writer, Mr. Dale Purves, Mr. Austin Purves, Jr., and Mr. John C. Purves.
3. Letter to the present writer, 26th March 1957.
4. Sale catalogue, Sept. 1920 (CTC).
5. Personal information, Miss Barbara Euphan Todd.
6. Chalmers, p. 276.
7. Letter to EG, 10th April 1933 (CTC).
8. Letter to the present writer, 22nd April 1957.
9. KG to Ernest Josling (who seems to have been negotiating on his behalf), 27th May 1921 (the Rev. K. H. Jocelyn).
10. Chalmers, pp. 257-8.
11. *The Fortnightly Review*, Dec. 1922 = Chalmers, pp. 258-73. See above, pp. 297-8.
12. Personal communication, Miss J. L. G. Crookston, 23rd March 1957.
13. See Chalmers, pp. 145-7.
14. EG to Courtauld Thomson, 10th June 1944. Cf. Chalmers, p. 256.
15. Chalmers, p. 281.
16. Letter to Thomas Woodman, 10th July 1923. I am grateful to Mrs. A. Vere Woodman for supplying me with a photostat of this letter.
17. Anstey Guthrie's MS account (CTC); FW, pp. 34-5; Chalmers, pp. 278 ff.
18. Chalmers, pp. 311-12; personal information, Mrs. Margery Newnham Davis.
19. Personal information, Mrs. Delia Wysard and Lady Rose.
20. Personal communication to the present writer, 9th April 1957.
21. *Country Life*, 3rd Dec. 1932 = Chalmers, pp. 17-26, with minor modifications.
22. KG to Curtis Brown, 17th Jan. 1931 (CTC).
23. See *Contacts*, pp. 63-4.
24. Letter to EG from Helen Grahame, 24th Oct. 1929.
25. 'Illustrating *The Wind in the Willows*', in *The Horn-Book*, April 1954, pp. 83-6.
26. *Contacts*, p. 61.
27. 31st Dec. 1930, p. 746.
28. *Toad of Toad Hall* (1929), pp. viii-x.
29. Chalmers, pp. 313-14.

30. Undated letter to EG, partially destroyed (CTC).
31. Chalmers, pp. 314-15; *Contacts*, pp. 66-7; letter from EG to Quiller-Couch, 11th July 1932 (Miss Foy Quiller-Couch).
32. *Contacts, ibid.* Cf. *The Times*, Monday, 11th July 1932, p. 15.
33. I am indebted to Mrs. Margery Newnham Davis for a copy of this inscription.

BIBLIOGRAPHY I

This bibliography of Kenneth Grahame's writings is based, with minor modifications and additions, on the bibliography published by Mr. Roger Lancelyn Green in *The Times Literary Supplement*, 9th June 1945, and I am deeply indebted to him for permission to use it here. Following his example I have printed the items in chronological order, and placed an asterisk against those originally published anonymously. A citation in brackets after an item— *e.g.* (GA) or (Chalmers)—indicates where the item was subsequently published in book form.

No comprehensive bibliography of Kenneth Grahame exists in the *Cambridge Bibliography of English Literature* or any comparable permanent work of reference. The present check-list is an attempt to fill that gap.

1. 'The Good and Bad Effects of Rivalry', *St. Edward's School Chronicle*, No. 5, Oct. 1873.
2. *'By a Northern Furrow', *St. James's Gazette*, 26th Dec. 1888 (Chalmers, pp. 189-94).
3. *'A Bohemian in Exile', *St. James's Gazette*, 27th Sept. 1890 (PP).
4. *'Of Smoking', *Scots Observer*, 18th Oct. 1890 (PP).
5. *'A Parable (Overheard and Communicated by our own Cat)': *St. James's Gazette*, 19th Nov. 1890 (Reprinted in the present work, pp. 109-110).
6. *'Loafing', *National Observer*, 24th Jan. 1891 (PP).
7. *'The Romance of the Road', *National Observer*, 14th Feb. 1891 (PP).
8. *'Non Libri Sed Liberi', *National Observer*, 28th Feb. 1891 (PP).
9. *'Cheap Knowledge', *National Observer*, 11th April 1891 (PP).
10. *'The Rural Pan', *National Observer*, 25th April 1891 (PP).
11. 'As You Like It' (poem), *National Observer*, 30th May 1891 (Chalmers, p. 36: two stanzas only).
12. *'The Romance of the Rail', *National Observer*, 8th Aug. 1891 (PP).
13. *'The White Poppy', *National Observer*, 5th Sept. 1891 (PP).
14. *'The Olympians', *National Observer*, 19th Sept. 1891 (PP; GA).

377

15. 'Quis Desiderio?' (poem), *National Observer*, 19th Sept. 1891 (Chalmers, p. 312).

16. *'Justifiable Homicide', *National Observer*, 10th Oct. 1891 (PP).

17. *'The Fairy Wicket', *National Observer*, 20th Feb. 1892 (PP).

18. 'Love's Reveille' (poem), *National Observer*, 27th Feb. 1892 (Reprinted in the present work, pp. 198-9).

19. *'Marginalia', *National Observer*, 26th March 1892 (PP).

20. *'The Eternal Whither', *National Observer*, 9th July 1892 (PP).

21. *'Aboard the Galley', *National Observer*, 3rd Sept. 1892 (PP).

22. *'Deus Terminus', *National Observer*, 1st Oct. 1892 (PP).

23. 'Cradle Song', *National Observer*, 8th Oct. 1892.

24. *'Concerning Ghosts', *National Observer*, 5th Nov. 1892 (Chalmers, pp. 196-9).

25. *'Orion', *National Observer*, 12th Nov. 1892 (PP).

26. *'The Lost Centaur', *National Observer*, 26th Nov. 1892 (PP).

27. *'An Autumn Encounter', *National Observer*, 11th Feb. 1893 (PP).

28. *'A Whitewashed Uncle', *National Observer*, 25th March 1893 (PP; GA).

29. 'The Finding of the Princess', *National Observer*, 20th May 1893 (PP; GA).

30. 'Young Adam Cupid', *National Observer*, 20th May 1893 (PP; GA).

31. 'The Burglars', *National Observer*, 24th June 1893 (PP; GA).

32. 'Snowbound', *National Observer*, 23rd Sept. 1893 (PP; GA).

33. *'The Barn Door', *National Observer*, 28th Oct. 1893 (Chalmers, pp. 202-4).

34. *Pagan Papers* (London: Elkin Mathews & John Lane). Published Oct. 1893, but dated 1894 on the fly-leaf.

35. 'What They Talked About', *National Observer*, 16th Dec. 1893 (GA).

36. *'The Triton's Conch', *National Observer*, 23rd Dec. 1893 (Chalmers, pp. 173-6).

37. 'A Harvesting', *National Observer*, 13th Jan. 1894 (GA).

38. 'Alarums and Excursions', *National Observer*, 10th Feb. 1894 (GA).

39. *'Pastels', *National Observer*, 17th Feb. 1894 (Chalmers, pp. 52-4).

40. 'The Argonauts', *National Observer*, 10th March 1894 (GA).

41. *'An Old Master', *National Observer*, 24th March 1894 (Chalmers, pp. 249-52).

42. 'Exit Tyrannus', *National Observer*, 28th April 1894 (GA).

43. 'The Roman Road', *The Yellow Book*, July 1894, pp. 211-26 (GA).

44. 'Sawdust and Sin', *National Observer*, 25th Aug. 1894 (GA).

45. 'The Headswoman', *The Yellow Book*, Oct. 1894, pp. 25-47 (Published in book form 1898).

46. 'The Blue Room', *Phil May's Illustrated Winter Annual*, Dec. 1894 (GA).

47. 'A Falling Out', *The Yellow Book*, Jan. 1895, pp. 195-201 (GA).

48. 'The Secret Drawer', *The Chapbook* (Chicago), 15th Jan. 1895 (GA).

49. 'A Holiday', *New Review*, Vol. 12, no. 70 (March 1895), pp. 225-31 †(GA).

50. 'Lusisti Satis', *New Review*, Vol. 12, no. 70 (March 1895), pp. 231-5 †(GA).

† These two stories were originally published under the common title

'In Arcady'. 'Lusisti Satis' was then called 'Satis Diu Lusisti', and ends at 'rot and humbug, and only fit for kids!', thus lacking the two final paragraphs which appear in *The Golden Age*.

51. *The Golden Age* (London: John Lane). Published Feb./March 1895.

52. 'The Inner Ear', *The Yellow Book*, April 1895, pp. 73-6 (Chalmers, pp. 69-73).

53. 'Long Odds', *The Yellow Book*, July 1895, pp. 78-86 (Chalmers, pp. 75-83).

54. 'The Iniquity of Oblivion', *The Yellow Book*, Oct. 1895, pp. 192-202 (Chalmers, pp. 129-136).

55. 'The Twenty-first of October', *New Review*, Vol. 13, no. 77 (Oct. 1895), pp. 359-66 (DD).

56. 'Dies Irae', *The Yellow Book*, Jan. 1896, pp. 101-14 (DD).

57. 'Saturnia Regna', *New Review*, Vol. 14, no. 82 (March 1896), pp. 248-52 (Chalmers, pp. 103-9).

58. 'Mutabile Semper', *New Review*, Vol. 14, no. 83 (April 1896), pp. 436-444 (DD).

59. 'The Magic Ring', *Scribner's Magazine*, Dec. 1896 (DD).

60. 'To Rollo, Untimely Taken' (poem), *The Yellow Book*, Jan. 1897, pp. 165-6 (Chalmers, p. 45).

61. 'Its Walls were as of Jasper', *Scribner's Magazine*, Aug. 1897 (DD).

62. 'The Invention of Fairyland' (review of Evelyn Sharp's *All the Way to Fairyland*), *Academy*, 18th Dec. 1897, p. 542. (Partly reproduced by Chalmers, pp. 59-61; he conflates it tacitly with part of Item 70: see below.)

63. *The Headswoman* (John Lane), Bodley Booklets, No. 5.

64. 'A Saga of the Seas', *Scribner's Magazine*, Aug. 1898 (DD).

65. Preface to Eugene Field's *Lullaby-Land*, pp. 7-13 (John Lane), 1898.

66. *Dream Days* (London: John Lane, The Bodley Head). Published Dec. 1898. Date on fly-leaf 1899.

67. 'The Reluctant Dragon', first published in DD (66).

68. 'A Departure', first published in DD (66).

69. Introduction to P. J. Billinghurst's *A Hundred Fables of Æsop* (translated by Sir Roger l'Estrange), pp. i-xv (John Lane, 1899).

70. 'The Fabric of the Fairy Tale' (review of children's books), *Daily Mail*, 16th Dec. 1899, p. 4. (Partly reproduced by Chalmers, pp. 59-61.)

71. 'The Mountain Stream' (poem), *Hull Weekly News*, 15th April 1905.

72. *The Wind in the Willows* (London: Methuen & Co.). Published Sept. 1908.

73. 'The Fellow That Goes Alone', *St. Edward's School Chronicle*, Vol. 12, no. 321 (July 1913), pp. 270-1. (Reprinted in the present work, pp. 4-6.)

74. Preface to *The Cambridge Book of Poetry for Children* (1916), pp. xiii-xv (Cambridge U.P.).

75. 'Ideals' (lecture), *The Fortnightly Review*, Dec. 1922 (Chalmers, pp. 258-273).

76. Preface ('Sanger and his Times') to 'Lord' George Sanger's *Seventy Years a Showman* (1926), pp. 5-29 (Dent).

77. 'Oxford through a Boy's Eyes', *Country Life*, 3rd Dec. 1932 (Chalmers, pp. 17-26).
78. 'A Dark Star' (lecture), *The Cornhill*, Vol. 74 (June 1933), pp. 649-67 (Chalmers, pp. 286-310).

UNDATED AND MISCELLANEOUS ITEMS

79. 'A Funeral', set up in proof for the *National Observer*, but never published. Probably *c.* 1890, printed by Chalmers, pp. 28-31.
80. 'Bertie's Escapade', written *c.* April 1907, and first printed by Chalmers, pp. 154-60. Reprinted in FW, pp. 41-7.
81. 'Christmas' (poem), published by Chalmers, pp. 165-6.
82. 'Lizard Lights' (poem), printed by Chalmers, p. 182.
83. 'Plate-Smashing and the Conjuror', published from MS by Chalmers, pp. 209-10. The transcription contains numerous errors and omissions: see above, pp. 54, 356.
84. Letters to his Son: written in 1907, published in FW (1944), pp. 48-89, with photostat.
85. Letters to Austin Purves, 1908-15: published by Chalmers, with omissions, pp. 219-48.

Fragments still in MS and the extracts from the 'ledger-diary' which Chalmers cites, are not included in this Bibliography.

BIBLIOGRAPHY II

The following is a select list of works cited or consulted during the composition of this book. Unless otherwise stated, the place of publication is London.

ACRES, W. M. *The Bank of England from Within, 1694–1900.* 2 vols. 1931.
'Kenneth Grahame: A Memoir', in *The Old Lady*, Vol. 8, no. 47 (Sept. 1932), pp. 206-7.
ANONYMOUS Obituary in *The Times*, 7th July 1932.
Obituary in *The Saturday Review:* Vol. 154, p. 32 (9th July 1932).
Biographical Sketch in *St. Edward's School Chronicle*, July 1932 (reprinted FW, pp. 36-8).
ANSTEY, F. *Vice Versa: A Lesson to Fathers.* 1882.
Voces Populi. 1890.
BARRY, W. F. 'Neo-Paganism', in *Quarterly Review*, Vol. 172 (1891), pp. 273-304.
BENNETT, A. *Books and Persons.* 1917.
BILLINGHURST, P. J. *A Hundred Anecdotes of Animals.* 1901.
A Hundred Fables of Æsop. 1899.
BRITTAIN, F. *Arthur Quiller-Couch: A Biographical Study of Q.* Cambridge, 1947.
BROWN, E. K. *Matthew Arnold: A Study in Conflict.* Chicago, 1948.
BUCHAN, John. *Memory Hold-the-Door.* 1940.
Scholar-Gypsies. 1896.
BUCKLEY, J. H. *The Victorian Temper. A Study in Literary Culture.* 1952.
William Ernest Henley. A Study in the 'Counter-Decadence' of the Nineties. Princeton, 1945.
BURDETT, O. H. *The Beardsley Period.* 1925.
Memory and Imagination. 1935.
CHALMERS, Patrick R. *Kenneth Grahame: Life, Letters and Unpublished Work.* 1933.
CHEATHAM, K. Article in *The Saturday Review of Literature*, Vol. 9, p. 113 (17th Sept. 1932).
CHESTERTON, G. K. *Heretics.* 2nd ed., 1905.
CLAPHAM, Sir John. *The Bank of England. A History.* 2 vols. Cambridge, 1944.
COBBETT, William. *Rural Rides: &c.* Ed. by G. D. H. and Margaret Cole. 3 vols. 1930.

CONNELL, John. *W. E. Henley*. 1949.

COURTNEY, Jane Elizabeth. *Recollected in Tranquillity*. 1926.

CURTIS BROWN, A. *Contacts*. 1935.

DAICHES, David. *Robert Louis Stevenson*. Glasgow, 1947.

DARK, S., and GREY, R. *W. S. Gilbert: His Life and Letters*. 1923.

DARTON, F. J. H. *Children's Books in England: Five Centuries of Social Life*. Cambridge, 1932.

'Children's Books', in *The Cambridge History of English Literature*, Vol. 11, pp. 366-87.

DAVIDSON, John. *Diabolus Amans*. 1885.

Fleet Street Eclogues. 1893.

ELWES, Hervey (ed.). *The Modern Child*. 1908.

ENSOR, Sir Robert C. K. *England, 1870–1914*. Oxford, 1936.

FARJEON, Eleanor. *Pan-Worship*. 1908.

FARQUHARSON, A. S. L. *The Meditations of the Emperor Marcus Aurelius*. Edited, with a translation and commentary, by A. S. L. F. 2 vols. Oxford, 1944.

FYRTH, D. M. *Étude littéraire: Kenneth Grahame. Thèse pour le Doctorat d'Université présentée à la Faculté des Lettres de Paris*. Paris, 1937.

GRAHAM, Eleanor. *The Story of 'The Wind in the Willows': How it came to be written*. 1950.

GRAHAME, Elspeth. *First Whispers of 'The Wind in the Willows'*. Edited, with Introduction, by E. G., 1944.

GRANVILLE-BARKER, H. (ed.). *The Eighteen-Seventies: Essays by Fellows of the Royal Society of Literature*. Cambridge, 1929.

GREEN, R. L. 'Reed Talk: the genius of Kenneth Grahame', in *The Scots Magazine* (July 1945), pp. 262-7.

GREENWOOD, Frederick. *Imagination in Dreams*. 1894.

GREG, T. T. *Through a Glass Lightly*. 1897.

In Varying Mood. 1924.

GRETTON, R. H. *A Modern History of the English People, 1880–1922*. 2nd ed., 1930.

GRIMSDITCH, H. B. Article, 'Kenneth Grahame', in the *Dictionary of National Biography* (1931–40), pp. 257-8.

HAMILTON, C. 'Frater Ave Atque Vale', in *The Bookman*, Vol. 76 (Jan. 1933), pp. 69-74. (Reprinted in FW, pp. 22-32.)

HENLEY, W. E. *Some Letters of W. E. H.* With an Introduction by V. Payen-Payne. 1933.

HEWLETT, M. *Pan and the Young Shepherd: a Pastoral*. 1898.

Letters, ed. L. Binyon. 1926.

HILLKIRK, W. B. 'Kenneth Grahame', in *The Old Lady*, Vol. 26, no. 117 (March 1950), pp. 338-40.

HINDS, C. L. *Authors and I*. 1921.

HOGARTH, Jane. See COURTNEY, Jane Elizabeth.

HOLT, E. 'Kenneth Grahame; an Appreciation', in *The Bookman*, Vol. 82, p. 234 (Aug. 1932).

HOUGH, Graham. *The Last Romantics*. 1949.

JACKSON, Holbrook. *The Eighteen Nineties. A Review of Art and Ideas at the Close of the Nineteenth Century*. 1913.

JEFFERIES, Richard. *After London: or, Wild England*. 1905.

    Amaryllis at the Fair. With an Introduction by Edward Garnett. 1904.

    Bevis. 1891.

    The Life of the Fields. 1884.

    Nature near London. 1883.

    The Open Air. 1885.

    Wild Life in a Southern County. 1879.

    Wood Magic. A Fable. 2 vols. 1881.

    The Story of my Heart. 2nd ed., 1891.

    Hodge and his Masters. 2 vols. 1880.

JENKINSON, A. J. *What do Boys and Girls Read?* 1946.

JOHNSON, E. D. H. *The Alien Vision of Victorian Poetry*. Princeton Studies in English, no. 34. Princeton, 1952.

KENT, Muriel. 'The Man with the Key', in *The Cornhill* (July 1935), pp. 25-33.

    'Modern Magician', in *The Bookman*, Dec. 1932.

LE GALLIENNE, Richard. *Attitudes and Avowals*. 1910.

    The Romantic Nineties. 1925.

    The Worshipper of the Image. 1899.

LOCHHEAD, Marion. *Their First Ten Years*. 1956.

MACHEN, Arthur. *The Anatomy of Tobacco: or, Smoking Methodised, Divided and Considered after a New Fashion*. 1884.

    The Great God Pan. 1894.

MACKAIL, J. W. *The Life of William Morris*. 2 vols. 2nd ed., 1901.

MACY, G. 'Arthur Rackham and *The Wind in the Willows*', in *The Horn Book*, Vol. 16 (3), pp. 152-8 (May 1940).

MARLOWE, John. *The Puritan Tradition in English Life*. 1956.

MILNE, A. A. *Toad of Toad Hall*. 1929.

    Preface to *The Wind in the Willows* (Rackham ed., 1950), pp. v-viii.

MISCELLANEOUS. *Frederick James Furnivall: A Volume of Personal Record*. Oxford, 1911.

MOORE, D. L. *E. Nesbit*. 1933.

MOORE, T. Sturge. *Pan's Prophecy*. 1904.

MOULTON, The Hon. Hugh Fletcher. *The Life of Lord Moulton*. 1922.

MUIR, Percy. *English Children's Books, 1600–1900*. 1954.

National Observer, The; formerly *The Scots Observer*. Ed. W. E. Henley, 1888–1894.

NESBIT, E. *The Story of the Treasure Seekers*. 1899.

    The Wouldbegoods. 1901.

    Five Children and It. 1902.

NEUBURG, Victor B. *The Triumph of Pan*. 1910.

New Review: The; ed. Archibald Grove, 1889–95 (Vols. 1–11); W. E. Henley, 1895–8 (Vols. 12–17).

ONSLOW, Clarence (pseud. of Elspeth Grahame, q.v.). *Amelia Jane's Ambition.* Bristol, 1888.

PATMORE, Coventry. *Poems.* Ed. F. E. Page. Oxford, 1949.

PEARSON, Hesketh. *Gilbert and Sullivan.* 2nd ed., 1950.

PELLING, H. M. *The Origins of the Labour Party, 1880–1900.* 1954.

PIAGET, Jean. *The Child's Conception of Physical Causality.* Trans. M. Gabain. 1930.
   The Child's Construction of Reality. Trans. M. Cook. 1955.
   Play, Dreams, and Imitation in Childhood. Trans. C. Gattegno and F. M. Hodgson. 1951.
   The Child's Conception of the World. Trans. J. and A. Tomlinson. 1929.

POCOCK, Guy. 'The Wind in the Willows', in *The Schoolmistress*, 6th Sept. 1934, p. 579.

PRESTON, Kerrison. *Letters from Graham Robertson.* Ed. by K. P., 1953.

PRYCE-JONES, Alan. 'Kenneth Grahame', in *The London Mercury* (Sept. 1932), pp. 446–9.

Punch. Mr. Punch's Motor Book. 1931.

QUENNELL, Peter. *John Ruskin.* 1949.

QUILLER-COUCH, Sir Arthur. *Memories and Opinions.* Ed. S. C. Roberts. Cambridge, 1944.

ROBERTS, R. Ellis. 'Kenneth Grahame: Escape and Discovery', in the *Observer*, 10th July 1932.

ROBERTSON, W. Graham. *Pinkie and the Fairies.* 1908–9.
   Time Was. 1931.

ROBERTSON SCOTT, J. W. *The Story of the 'Pall Mall Gazette'.* Oxford, 1950.

ROE, F. W. *The Social Philosophy of Carlyle and Ruskin.* 1922.

ROLFE, Frederick ('Baron Corvo'). *Nicholas Crabbe, or The One and the Many.* 1958.

RUSKIN, J. *On the Old Road.* 2 vols. Orpington, 1885.
   The Stones of Venice. 3 vols. 1851–3.

St. Edward's School Chronicle (Oxford, 1875–   ). See also: *New Inn Hall Street, 1863; Summertown, 1873–1933.* Oxford, 1933.
   Annual Report and Year Book (1927–   ).
   The Roll of St. Edward's School, 1863–1939. 5th ed., ed. by R. J. Northcote-Green. Oxford, 1940.

SAINTSBURY, George. *A History of English Prose Rhythm.* 1912.

SHARP, Evelyn (Mrs. H. W. Nevinson). *Unfinished Adventure.* 1933.

SHARP, William. *The Pagan Review.* 1892.

SHEPARD, E. H. 'Illustrating *The Wind in the Willows*', in *The Horn Book*, Vol. 30 (April 1954), pp. 83–6.

SIDGWICK, F. (ed.) *The Complete Marjorie Fleming.* 1934.

SMEDLEY, Constance. *Crusaders.* 1929.

SMITH, Elva S. *The History of Children's Literature.* Chicago, 1937.

STEVENSON, R. L. *A Child's Garden of Verses.* 1885.

Virginibus Puerisque, and other papers. 1881; 2nd ed., 1887.

Essays of Travel. 1905.

Across the Plains. 1892.

Memoirs of Himself. Philadelphia, 1912.

St. James's Gazette, The; An Evening Review and Record of News. Vols. 1-50. 1880-1905.

STRONG, L. A. G. *Courtauld-Thomson: A Memoir.* 1958 (privately printed).

SWINNERTON, Frank. 'Bedside Book', in *Tokefield Papers* (2nd ed., 1949), pp. 175-81.

SYRETT, Netta. *The Sheltering Tree.* 1939.

THOMAS, Rose Haig. *Pan: A Collection of Lyrical Poems.* 1897.

THOMPSON, E. P. *William Morris: Romantic to Revolutionary.* 1955.

TRILLING, Lionel. *Matthew Arnold.* 2nd ed., New York, 1949.

WEBB, Beatrice. *My Apprenticeship.* 2nd ed., 1950.

WERNICKE, Konrad. Article, 'Pan', in W. H. Roscher's *Ausführliches Lexikon der griechischen und römischen Mythologie,* Vol. 3, 1, cols. 1348-1481.

WILDE, Oscar. *The Happy Prince, and Other Tales.* 1888.

WILLIAMSON, Kennedy. *W. E. Henley: A Memoir.* 1930.

WILSON, J. Dover. *Poetry and the Child.* English Association Pamphlet, no. 34 (Feb. 1916).

WILSTACH, J. 'Grahame and the Circus', in *The Saturday Review of Literature,* Vol. 9, p. 34 (6th Aug. 1932).

WINGFIELD-STRATFORD, E. C. *The Victorian Tragedy.* 1930.

The Victorian Sunset. 1932.

The Victorian Aftermath. 1933.

WOOLLCOTT, A. 'Woollcott Presents *The Golden Age*', in *The Saturday Review of Literature,* Vol. 16, p. 13 (23rd Oct. 1937).

YEATS, W. B. *Autobiographies.* 1955.

Yellow Book, The; An Illustrated Quarterly. 13 vols. 1894-7.

YOUNG, G. M. *Victorian England: Portrait of an Age.* 2nd ed., Oxford, 1953.

INDEX

Characters in Kenneth Grahame's books as well as the titles of books are given in italics

387

ABOUT THE AUTHOR

Peter Green, born in London in 1924, attended Charterhouse School and Trinity College, Cambridge; in 1954 he obtained his Ph.D. from Cambridge with a thesis on Roman Magic. He was Director of Studies in Classics and Craven Research Student at Cambridge before turning in 1953 to free-lance writing. A regular contributor of reviews and articles, especially on the classics and ancient history, to such periodicals as the *Times Literary Supplement*, the *Observer*, and *History Today*, Mr. Green is also novel-critic to the London *Daily Telegraph* and a well-known translator. He is the author of four previous books, the most recent of which was *The Sword of Pleasure*, a fictional autobiography of the Roman dictator Sulla, published by The World Publishing Company in 1958, and for which he received the Heinemann Foundation Award for Literature in England. His venture into modern biography is not so surprising as it might seem; he has wanted to write about Kenneth Grahame ever since he was six, and regards the present book as fulfilling one of his lifelong ambitions. Mr. Green served with the Royal Air Force in Burma during World War II, and has traveled widely in Europe since. He is married to the novelist Lalage Pulvertaft; they live in a seventeenth-century cottage near Cambridge with their two sons.